LEWIS & CLARK

LEXICON

DISCOVERY

Alan H. Hartley

Washington State University Press
Pullman, Washington

Washington State University Press
PO Box 645910
Pullman, Washington 99164-5910
Phone: 800-354-7360
Fax: 509-335-8568
E-mail: wsupress@wsu.edu
Web site: wsupress.wsu.edu

Library of Congress Cataloging-in-Publication Data

Hartley, Alan H., 1946-
    Lewis and Clark lexicon of discovery / Alan H. Hartley.
        p. cm.
    Includes bibliographical references and index.
    ISBN 0-87422-278-8 (pbk. : alk. paper) — ISBN 0-87422-279-6 (Spiral-bound : alk. paper)
    1. Americanisms—West (U.S.)—Dictionaries. 2. Lewis and Clark Expedition (1804-1806)—Dictionaries. 3. English language—West (U.S.)—Glossaries, vocabularies, etc. 4. English language—Dialects—West (U.S.)—Glossaries, vocabularies, etc. 5. English language—19th century—Glossaries, vocabularies, etc. 6. Lewis, Meriwether, 1774-1809—Language—Glossaries, etc. 7. Clark, William, 1770-1838—Language—Glossaries, etc. 8. West (U.S.)—Dictionaries. I. Title.

PE2970.W4H37 2004   427'.978'09034--dc22

Fine Quality Books from the Pacific Northwest

Table of Contents

Acknowledgments

I am grateful to Glen Lindeman of Washington State University Press for his encouragement and careful editing, and for helping me through the publication process. The University of Nebraska Press published the superb new edition of the Lewis and Clark journals on which my work mainly depends. Gary Moulton of the University of Nebraska (the editor of the journals), and Gary Lentz, of Discovery Presentations, read the manuscript with a constructively critical eye, caught many errors, and suggested additions. My reading of the journals for this project proceeded simultaneously with my work on them for the *Oxford English Dictionary* (Oxford University Press), under the direction of Jesse Sheidlower, Principal Editor (North America).

Bill Labov helped me place the English of the journals in the context of American dialects, and Michael Montgomery shared his experience with the language of historical American texts; both made many helpful suggestions. Leonard Zwilling assisted with questions pertaining to the *Dictionary of American Regional English*.

In the field of native languages I received help from many people, among them Bill Bright (American Indian names for people and places); David Costa, Ives Goddard, and Michael McCafferty (Algonquian); Doug Parks (Arikara); Dell Hymes, Henry Zenk, and Michael Silverstein (Chinookan); Wally Chafe, Marianne Mithun, and Blair Rudes (Iroquoian); Haruo Aoki and Gene Hunn (Sahaptian); Drusilla Gould and Chris Loether (Shoshone); Randy Graczyk, Wesley Jones, John Koontz, and Bob Rankin (Siouan); and many subscribers to the Chinook and Siouan listservs.

Duane Esarey, Michael McCafferty, and Lawrence Sommer shared their knowledge of the early history of the north-central United States. Carol Baskin, Jerry Baskin, and James Reveal advised me on some botanical questions. My brother, Guilford Hartley, helped with several medical questions, and my cousin, Susan Hartley, with equine veterinary medical terminology. The librarians at the University of Minnesota Duluth have been cordially helpful. The staff of the Adler Planetarium confirmed the identification of Venus as the morning star in August 1804.

My daughter Kate Hartley proofread the quotations, and my wife, Susan Rice Hartley, advised me on astronomical matters and encouraged me to persevere in what became a lengthy project. Besides these personal communications, I have relied heavily on the sources listed in the References. None of these generous correspondents or published sources bears any responsibility for the errors that will be found in the *Lexicon*.

My mother, Ann Haselton Hartley, nurtured my interest in language for many years, and I regret that she will not see this small reflection of her love of English. To her, and to my father, Alfred Hartley, who passed away the day the galley-proofs arrived at my door, I dedicate this book.

Alan H. Hartley
Duluth, Minnesota

The Language of the Corps of Discovery

Two centuries have passed since the men of the Lewis & Clark expedition and their compatriots in the young American republic spoke the words in this *Lexicon*. Though a short period in the 1,500-year history of the English language, it is has been long enough—and cultural changes have been profound enough—to give the language of the journals an archaic character, causing the modern reader to pause over many of the words used by the explorers. Yet the reader's effort is handsomely repaid. William Clark's masterful cartography and Meriwether Lewis's drawings of flora and fauna are a vital graphic record of the journey to the Pacific Ocean, but it is principally through the captains' *words*—and those of Charles Floyd, Patrick Gass, John Ordway, and Joseph Whitehouse—that we see what they saw and feel what they felt. It is the aim of this *Lexicon* both to explain the difficult and interesting words in the Corps of Discovery journals and to give the reader a feeling for American English in the first years of the 19th century.

How were words selected from the journals for inclusion in the *Lewis and Clark Lexicon of Discovery*? Some are here because they illustrate archaic or dialectical pronunciations (e.g., HOLLOW, KETTLE), while others shed light on important aspects of the expedition experience (e.g., HARD[2], TRADE). Others are modern terms pertaining to the discussion of words in the journals (e.g., the names of American Indian language families, such as SAHAPTIAN). Most words, however, are included here because they are in some way obscure or otherwise interesting in themselves to modern readers. The reasons for their obscurity range from the obvious (as when a word's form or that which it designates, its *referent*, is wholly unfamiliar today), to the subtle (as when we must work our way back in time through slight shifts in a word's meaning—from a meaning we know, to an earlier one inferred from historical and textual contexts).

The *Lexicon* makes no pretense to exhaustive coverage of the Corps of Discovery vocabulary. Space does not allow the inclusion of every biographical, geographical, scientific, and historical term, or all the names of the smaller native groups encountered by the explorers (especially in the Pacific Northwest). Included here are those meanings that will be of special interest to readers of the journals. The entries in the *Lexicon* can be classified as follows by the reasons they are unfamiliar to us today.

Obsolete words: e.g., BRICKLE, CHITTEDIDDLE, DISEMBOGUE, HIGGLER, HIPPED, MERIDIAN, SLAKY, SOLUS, THAWY.

Obsolete in general use, but still in restricted dialect use today: e.g., A, LIKELY, NEAR, STOUT, SIGHT[1], SAWYER[2,3].

Obsolete referents: e.g., (BURNING) GLASS, (PORTABLE) SOUP, TANNER'S OOZE.

slash (swamp)

Obsolete sense of familiar words (analogous to the *false friends* that sometimes plague present-day foreign-language learners): e.g., BAIT (feed a horse), BUTCH (to butcher), CARBONATED (carbonized), CONSIDERATE (important), (OF) COURSE (as a result), INFORMATION (shaping), JOCKEY (cheater), LAX & RELAX (diarrhea), MRS. (misters), NOON (as a verb), OFFICIOUS (eager to be of service), PUKE (an emetic), SLASH (swamp).

Unfamiliar forms and referents: e.g., BASILICON, CABRIE, CLYSTER, CORVUS, ESPONTOON, FRIZZEN, FUSIL, HYSSOP, PETTIAUGER, SPANCEL.

Identities obscured by alternate spellings (particularly evident in Clark's erratic writing): e.g., BAR[1,2], BAYOU (many variants), BILE & BOIL, CAULK, EAT, HOLLOW, QUEUE.

Extended sense of familiar words: e.g., DOG is often used in the sense of 'dog meat,' a distinctly unmodern meaning. Names of old-world creatures were applied to new-world animals; ANCHOVY (eulachon), ANTELOPE (pronghorn), ARGALI & IBEX (bighorn sheep).

Canadian French: e.g., BOIS ROULÉ, BRAROW, CAJEU, ENGAGÉ, FEMME, GROS VENTRE, LOUP[1,2], PATROON, PEKAN, ROCHE JAUNE RIVER.

Indian terms and names (plentiful in the journals; usually referring to things new to the explorers): e.g., CAMAS & PASHECO, EULACHON, SALAL, SEWELLEL, WAPATO, YAMPA.

Native people (numerous): e.g., BIG BELLY, CHOPUNNISH, DOG INDIAN, FLATHEAD, SALISH, TILLAMOOK, WETESOON.

Words having special meaning in the context of Indian relations: e.g., DOUBLE-SPOKEN, MAKE[2], MEDAL, MILK, NATION, PAROLE, PIPESTONE. In modern use SQUAW often has a pejorative sense, but in the journals it usually appears to mean just 'Indian woman, or wife.'

Outmoded and obscure technical terms—

Flora and Fauna: CALUMET-BIRD, (WHITE) CEDAR, Carolina PARAKEET (now extinct), passenger PIGEON (now extinct), (BLACKTAILED) DEER, (COMMON) DEER, (FALLOW) DEER, (MULE) DEER. The captains' nomenclature for DEER in general is confusing to the modern reader.

Guns: CUT OUT, PAN, PLATOON, SNAP, WIPER.

Medical: BILIOUS, HYSTERICAL, RISING, SIMPLE. Medical advances have made many terms and meanings obsolete.

Measures: BRACE[1], LEAGUE, LINE, PERCH, POLE, SLEEP.

Topography: BOIL[2], (BLOWING) CAVERN, CUT-OFF, DRAIN, GORGE, PUMICE, SIDELING, SPANISH, SUCK.

Trade: (SQUAW-)AX, (FIRST) COST, HAIR-PIPE.

Travel. Terms for horse management (HOBBLE, NEAR), navigational astronomy (NONIUS, (MERIDIAN) ALTITUDE), boat handling (DOUBLE-MAN, (IRON) BOAT), surveying (TRAVERSE, VARIATION), wilderness know-how (BRAINS, CACHE, FIRE-STEEL, (POUNDED) FISH).

(See Appendix 1 for an additional classification of Corps of Discovery words.)

Speech Communities

Each speaker's dialect and experiences helped shape the daily language of the Corps of Discovery. The words as we read them in the journals, however, are not always precisely what was spoken—they have been filtered through the process of writing. In Lewis & Clark's era, spelling was not standardized, and most writers had only a minimal grammar school education, a fact evident in the journal entries. Sometimes, too, they purposely adopted a more formal style in writing. We see this clearly occurring whenever Clark copied Lewis's journal entries; he retained Lewis's more formal written language. Joseph Whitehouse, too, edited his first-draft vernacular entries into more literate second-draft versions.

There are great differences between the "backwoods" character of Clark's original writing, and Lewis's more literate style. Lewis used words—such as PERSPICUITY, RIGHT OF SOIL, and (*imps of*) SATURN—that were accessible only to a well-educated person. Consequently, Lewis's more careful and standardized spelling largely hides the Virginia accent that we would so much like to hear from him. Clark, on the other hand, often spelled words as he heard them. His writing is closer to the spoken word, as in BEAR, DRAIN, and KETTLE, and his misspellings are an invaluable gift, providing hints of his actual speech. Though their setting down of words on paper partly disguises the explorers' daily spoken English, a careful reading of the journals—assisted by the active participation of our "mind's ear," and the insight of later phonetic studies—can bring much of their speech back to us.

The voices of the expedition were many—Virginia drawl, Ohio River backcountry lingo, New Hampshire twang, lilting French Canadian, and American Indian. All contributed to the common speech of the expedition—a kind of microcosm of the way that American English was evolving in the early 19th century. The predominant dialects, however, were those of Virginia and the coastal South, and, to a lesser extent, the Midland of south Pennsylvania and the western Appalachians.

Of the approximately two-score capable English-speakers in the Corps of Discovery in 1803-4, a little less than one-half were born in Virginia or Kentucky, or had moved to Kentucky in youth—a slight majority of these men were civilians before joining the Corps. Of the others, one-fifth were born in Pennsylvania and another one-fifth were from New England—these men largely had come to the Ohio-Mississippi country as U.S. soldiers. Of the journalists, Meriwether Lewis, William Clark, and Joseph Whitehouse were born in Virginia; Charles Floyd in Kentucky; Patrick Gass in Pennsylvania; and John Ordway in New Hampshire.

The Upper South

The history of language in KENTUCKY contributes to our understanding of the expedition's English. Kentucky's occupation by native groups before white contact is poorly known, but it did include the Cherokee and Iroquois (mostly Seneca), as well as the SHAWNEE (whose language was literally George DROUILLARD's mother tongue). Despite intermittent tribal resistance, Kentucky became the first trans-Appalachian region to be settled (1775) by English-speaking immigrants, mostly stemming from Virginia and Pennsylvania.

A look back at Pennsylvania's history is helpful here. More than a half century earlier, thousands of people of English, Scottish, and Irish ancestry had immigrated to Pennsylvania, replacing an earlier, and much smaller, Swedish and Dutch occupation. (The *Scotch-Irish* of this immigration were so named for their Scottish forebears, who had been the main Protestant group occupying the northern part of Ireland under British rule.) Joining Pennsylvania's Anglophone immigrants were significant numbers of German settlers, known in the vernacular of the time as DUTCH. (They included the ancestors of privates Peter M. Weiser and William Werner; and Private John Potts, who himself was born in Germany.) In 1759, the German language was so prevalent at Bedford in south-central Pennsylvania that the British Army found it necessary to advertise in German for wagoners (Stevens *et al.*, series 21652, p. 224). Attracted in part by cheap land to the southwest, Pennsylvanians soon migrated in significant numbers to the western parts of Virginia (including today's West Virginia) and North Carolina.

When the permanent settlement of Kentucky began in the late 1770s, however, Virginia English immediately predominated, being brought by settlers coming directly west from the large and influential colony of Virginia, as well as from adjoining North Carolina. Meanwhile, emigrants coming down the Ohio River were introducing the Midland dialect of Pennsylvania. Additional Pennsylvanian influence also came indirectly with the descendants of the Pennsylvanians who earlier had settled in the western Appalachians.

In two decades, the Indian threat in the Ohio-Kentucky country was largely removed (1795), and immigration accelerated, with Virginia and Midland influences continuing further west. Emigrants reached the MISSISSIPPI and settled near French-speakers in the ILLINOIS country, BOONE'S SETTLEMENT, and at St. Louis. Consequently, when the captains began assembling the Corps of Discovery in 1803, Virginia English and the Midland dialect dominated in the scattered American settlements from the Appalachian Mountains to the Mississippi River.

North American French

Knowledge of FRENCH (and Indian) speechways was extended by the arrival of American immigrants in the Ohio-Mississippi country and by their interaction with the region's French traders and settlers. In the late-17th century, French fur seekers from eastern Canada had spread south via the Great Lakes into the Mississippi-Ohio country. From small, widely dispersed outposts and settlements, they controlled the Indian trade throughout most of the 18th century, even though France's imperial claims were extinguished following its defeat in the French and Indian War (1754–63). In 1762, the SPANISH acquired Upper Louisiana (i.e., the lands west of the Mississippi) by diplomacy, while the British (1763) and then the new American republic (1783) gained control of the Ohio country and the east side of the Mississippi. French Canadian traders and rivermen, however, who often married Indians, continued to play a prominent role in the fur trade.

Five FRENCH and French-Indian frontiersmen joined the Lewis & Clark expedition's permanent party, including Toussaint CHARBONNEAU, Pierre CRUZATTE, George DROUILLARD, François Labiche, and Jean Baptiste Lepage.

In 1804, an additional 11 or so French ENGAGÉS helped man the Corps of Discovery flotilla up the Missouri River to the Mandan villages—a few paddled back down to St. Louis in late 1804, others remained in the Upper Missouri area through the winter of 1804–5, and some returned with Corporal Warfington's keelboat detachment to St. Louis in the spring of 1805. These men, as well as translators temporarily hired by the captains on the Upper Missouri (e.g., Pierre Dorion Sr., Joseph Gravelines, and René Jusseaume), and other French traders and trappers met on the river, were, of course, fluent in their native tongue. The expedition's journalists borrowed and recorded a number of French words, including native terms adopted by the French during a century of interaction with tribal people.

American Indian

When explorers in North America traveled into strange lands, they needed new names for the unfamiliar things they encountered. Lewis & Clark drew largely from two sources. (1) They made innovative use of English words by coining descriptive terms like (MULE) DEER, or giving existing English names to similar types of things, such as SAGE[2] for *Artemisia* (sagebrush), or GOAT for PRONGHORN. And (2), they borrowed words from the native occupants of these new places. In this manner, the expedition continued the process underway since the 16th century by which English was enriched through contact with native languages. Just as English colonists had previously

spruce-pine *(spruce* originally meant a species of fir from *Prussia)*

adopted Indian words to distinguish native footwear (MOCCASIN) from their own, and native women (SQUAW) from white or black women, the journalists adopted native names for new places (NEMAHA RIVER) and peoples (KALAPUYA), for unfamiliar plants (UPPAH) and animals (QUINNAT), and for cultural objects (POGAMOGGAN) and food made by Indians (SAPOLIL).

For Lewis & Clark, language also was the most important criterion in differentiating among the new native groups they met; the captains defined a NATION primarily by the language the people spoke. Tribal names in America arose in various ways. A designation for a particular people might be borrowed from a neighboring group, with all the possibilities for misrepresentation that can accompany such exchanges. The French Canadians, for example, borrowed an Ojibway name for the DAKOTA— *Nadouessioux*, shortened to SIOUX, probably with the pejorative meaning 'rattlesnake.' The captains' use of DOG INDIAN for CHEYENNE perpetuated a French misinterpretation of a Siouan name, *chien* 'dog.' On the lower Columbia, Clark apparently mistook a Chinookan expression meaning 'look at him' as a tribal name, SKILLOOT.

Some of the names appearing in the journals are, however, a people's self-designation (e.g., DAKOTA, meaning 'friendly, allied'), or were at least bestowed by closely related neighbors (e.g., CATHLAMET and CLATSOP, divisions of the same cultural group on the lower Columbia). Sometimes the tribe names recorded in the journals were simply Indian identifications of places (e.g., WATLALA, 'small lake (place),' and WALLA WALLA, 'little rivers'), or the inhabitants of a location, (such as the *Clahclellahs* of Watlala on the Columbia River, and the REPUBLICAN Pawnee of the Plains, who resided on the Republican River, which was named for them.)

Many tribes were identified by several names, as might be expected given the large number of native groups and their mobility. Confusion arose when the same (or a similar sounding) name was applied to different peoples. The most striking example is that of the ATSINA and HIDATSA, who were linguistically and geographically unrelated (ALGONQUIAN and SIOUAN, respectively, and residing in Montana/Alberta and North Dakota). Perhaps because of sign-language misunderstandings, both tribes were called BIG BELLY, GROS VENTRE, and MINITARI. To avoid ambiguity, it was sometimes necessary to add the qualifiers *of the Missouri* (for the Hidatsa) and *of the Prairies* (for the Atsina) to their names.

Numerous Indian languages were spoken by people connected with the Lewis & Clark expedition, particularly the FRENCH contingent that included Jean Baptiste Lepage, François Labiche (a speaker of several native tongues, as well as English), Toussaint CHARBONNEAU (HIDATSA), Pierre CRUZATTE (OMAHA), and George DROUILLARD (SHAWNEE). SACAGAWEA spoke SHOSHONE and HIDATSA (but not French or English). Other people temporarily involved with the expedition had a familiarity with SIOUAN and other Plains languages—including the ENGAGÉS, René Jusseaume, Old Dorion, Joseph Gravelines, and other French Canadian and British traders encountered on the Missouri. Some expedition members, such as Drouillard and Cruzatte, were experts in SIGN[2] language.

These language skills were essential wherever the Corps met with tribal groups. While in the Rockies in early September 1805, for example, the captains counciled with the FLATHEAD through a translation chain of five languages—i.e., by the use of SALISH, Shoshone, Hidatsa, French, and English, spoken by a half-dozen people in succession from a Flathead tribal leader, to a Shoshone boy, to Sacagawea, to Charbonneau, to Labiche, to the captains, and then the reverse. (Charbonneau's skill in English appears to have been poor.) Similar arrangements involving Sacagawea, Charbonneau, Drouillard, Labiche, and other French expedition members proved useful with the Shoshone, Walla Walla, Nez Perce, and various Plains tribes. François Labiche later continued as Lewis's interpreter (along with René Jusseaume) as part of an Indian delegation to Washington, D.C., in late 1806.

CORPS OF DISCOVERY ROSTER

Antecedents of the permanent party (1803–6), return party/FRENCH engagés (1803–5), and temporary interpreters/pilots (1804-5, 1806). The exact number of ENGAGÉS attached to the expedition in 1804-5 is unknown, but probably included about 11 boatmen. The expedition's known journalists are indicated in **bold** type. This information is drawn largely from Moulton *Journals,* with additions from other sources.

Born in or lived in the South (especially Virginia, KENTUCKY)

William E. Bratton (Private/permanent party)—Born in Virginia (1778), migrated to KENTUCKY at about age 12, inducted into the Corps at the Falls of the Ohio River (10/20/1803).

William Clark (2nd Lieutenant ["Captain"]/permanent party)—Born in Virginia (1770), migrated to KENTUCKY at age 14, U.S. Army officer in the Old Northwest (1792–96), joined the Corps at the Falls of the Ohio River (10/1803).

John Collins (Private/permanent party)—Born in Maryland, inducted into the Corps in ILLINOIS (1/1/1804).

John Colter (Private/permanent party)—Born in Virginia (c. 1775), migrated to KENTUCKY, inducted into the Corps at the Falls of the Ohio River (10/15/1803).

Joseph Field (Private/permanent party)—Born in Virginia (c. 1772), migrated to KENTUCKY in youth, inducted into the Corps at the Falls of the Ohio River (8/1/1803).

Reubin Field (Private/permanent party)—Born in Virginia (c. 1771), migrated to KENTUCKY in youth, inducted into the Corps at the Falls of the Ohio River (8/1/1803).

Charles Floyd (Sergeant/permanent party)—Born in KENTUCKY (1782), inducted into the Corps at the Falls of the Ohio River (10/1803), died near present-day Sioux City, Iowa (8/20/1804).

Robert Frazer (Private/permanent party)—Probably born in Virginia, inducted into the Corps from the return party (10/8/1804), **kept a journal (now lost)**.

Meriwether Lewis (Captain/permanent party)—Born in Virginia (1774), joined U.S. Army (1794) and served in OHIO and the Old Northwest, President Jefferson's private secretary (1801–3).

Nathaniel Hale Pryor (Sergeant/permanent party)—Born in Virginia (1772), migrated to KENTUCKY at about age 11, inducted into the Corps at the Falls of the Ohio River (10/20/1803).

John SHIELDS (Private/permanent party)—Born in Virginia (1769), migrated to Tennessee at about age 15, inducted into the Corps at the Falls of the Ohio River (10/19/1803).

Richard Warfington (Corporal/return party, spring 1805)—Born in North Carolina (1777), enlisted U.S. Army (1799) and served in Tennessee, joined the Corps in ILLINOIS (winter 1803–4).

William Werner (Private/permanent party)—Born in KENTUCKY(?), inducted into the Corps in ILLINOIS (1803–4).

Joseph Whitehouse (Private/permanent party)—Born (c. 1775) probably in Virginia, migrated to KENTUCKY at about age 9, enlisted U.S. Army and served in ILLINOIS, inducted into the Corps in ILLINOIS (1/1/1804).

York (William Clark's black servant/permanent party)—Probably born in Virginia (c. 1770), joined the Corps at the Falls of the Ohio River (10/1803)

Born in Pennsylvania

John Boley (Private/return party, spring 1805?)—Probably born in Pennsylvania, resided in ILLINOIS, enlisted U.S. Army (1803) and served in ILLINOIS, joined the Corps in ILLINOIS (winter 1803–4).

Patrick Gass (Private & Sergeant/permanent party)—Born in Pennsylvania of Irish ancestry (1771), enlisted U.S. Army (1799) and served in ILLINOIS, inducted into the Corps in ILLINOIS (1/1/1804).

George Gibson (Private/permanent party)—Born in Pennsylvania, resided in KENTUCKY, inducted into the Corps at Falls of the Ohio River (10/1803).

Hugh McNeal (Private/permanent party)—Born and reared in Pennsylvania, inducted into the Corps in ILLINOIS (winter 1803–4).

John Newman (Private/return party, spring 1805)—Born in Pennsylvania (c. 1785), enlisted U.S. Army and served in ILLINOIS, joined the Corps in ILLINOIS (winter 1803–4).

George Shannon (Private/permanent party)—Born in Pennsylvania (1785), migrated to OHIO at about age 15, inducted into the Corps at the Falls of the Ohio River (10/19/1803).

Peter M. Weiser (Private/permanent party)—Born (1781) and probably raised in Pennsylvania, apparently enlisted U.S. Army and served in ILLINOIS, inducted into the Corps in ILLINOIS (winter 1803–4).

Born in New England

John Dame (Private/return party, spring 1805)—Born in New Hampshire (1784), enlisted U.S. Army (1801) and served in ILLINOIS, joined the Corps in ILLINOIS (winter 1803–4).

Silas Goodrich (Private/permanent party)—Born in Massachusetts, inducted into the Corps in ILLINOIS (1/1/1804).

Hugh Hall (Private/permanent party)—Born in Massachusetts (c. 1772), enlisted U.S. Army (1798) and served in Tennessee, inducted into the Corps in ILLINOIS (winter 1803–4).

Thomas Proctor Howard (Private/permanent party)—Born (1779) and reared in Massachusetts, enlisted U.S. Army (1801) and served in Tennessee, inducted into the Corps in ILLINOIS (1/1/1804).

John Ordway (Sergeant/permanent party)—Born (c. 1775) and probably reared in New Hampshire, enlisted U.S. Army and served in ILLINOIS, inducted into the Corps in ILLINOIS (1/1/1804).

John Robertson (Private/detached 1804?)—Born (c. 1780) probably in New Hampshire, enlisted U.S. Army and served in ILLINOIS, joined the Corps in ILLINOIS (winter 1803–4).

Ebenezer Tuttle (Private/return party, spring 1805?)—Born in Connecticut (1773), enlisted U.S. Army (1803) and served in ILLINOIS, joined the Corps in ILLINOIS (winter 1803–4).

Isaac White (Private/return party, spring 1805?)—Born in Massachusetts (c. 1774), enlisted U.S. Army (1801) and served in ILLINOIS, joined the Corps in ILLINOIS (winter 1803–4).

Alexander Hamilton Willard (Private/permanent party)—Born in New Hampshire (1778), resided in KENTUCKY, enlisted U.S. Army (1800) and served in ILLINOIS, inducted into the Corps in ILLINOIS (winter 1803–4).

Others

John Potts (Private/permanent party)—Born in Germany (1776), enlisted U.S. Army (1800) and served in Tennessee, inducted into the Corps in ILLINOIS (11/1803).

Moses B. Reed, (Private/return party, spring 1805)—Antecedents unknown, joined the Corps in ILLINOIS (winter 1803–4).

John B. Thompson, (Private/permanent party)—Antecedents unknown, resided in Indiana(?), inducted into the Corps in ILLINOIS (winter 1803–4).

Richard Windsor (Private/permanent party)—Antecedents unknown, served in U.S. Army in ILLINOIS, inducted into the Corps in ILLINOIS (1/1/1804).

FRENCH *from the* MISSISSIPPI *and* MISSOURI *valleys*

E. Cann (ENGAGÉ/return party, spring 1805?)—Born in MISSISSIPPI?

Charles Caugee (ENGAGÉ/return party, spring 1805?)—Antecedents unknown.

Toussaint CHARBONNEAU (INTERPRETER/permanent party 1805–6)—CANADIAN, probably had resided in MISSOURI, living among the HIDATSA for 5 years, appointed to the Corps at Ft. Mandan (11/4/1804).

Joseph Collin (ENGAGÉ/discharged at Ft. Mandan, fall 1804?)—CANADIAN?

Jean Baptiste Deschamps (PATROON/return party, spring 1805?)—Resided in MISSOURI?

Pierre Dorion, Sr., or "Old Dorion" (INTERPRETER, Upper Missouri, 1804)—Born in Canada before 1750, long residence among the YANKTON.

Joseph Gravelines (INTERPRETER & pilot/Upper Missouri, 1804, & return party, spring 1805)—Trader residing among the ARIKARA.

Charles Hebert (ENGAGÉ/discharged at Ft. Mandan, fall 1804?)—CANADIAN, resided in MISSOURI.

René Jusseaume (INTERPRETER, Upper Missouri, 1804, 1806)—Trader at the MANDAN villages.

Jean Baptiste La Jeunesse (ENGAGÉ/discharged at Ft. Mandan, fall 1804)—Probably CANADIAN, resided in MISSOURI.

La Liberté (ENGAGÉ/deserted summer 1804)—Antecedents unknown.

Jean Baptiste Lepage (Private/permanent party)—CANADIAN fur trader, inducted into the Corps at Ft. Mandan (11/3/1804).

Etienne Malboeuf (ENGAGÉ/return party, spring 1805?)—Born in Canada (c. 1775), resided in MISSOURI and ILLINOIS.

Paul Primeau (ENGAGÉ/discharged at Ft. Mandan, fall 1804)—CANADIAN, resided in MISSOURI.

François Rivet (ENGAGÉ/remained on Upper Missouri, 1805?)—Born in Canada (c. 1757), resided in MISSISSIPPI Valley.

Peter Roi (ENGAGÉ/remained on Upper Missouri, 1805?)—Antecedents uncertain.

Of "known" FRENCH *and Indian extraction*

Jean Baptiste Charbonneau (infant/permanent party)—SHOSHONE-FRENCH, born in North Dakota (2/11/1805).

Pierre CRUZATTE (Private/permanent party)—OMAHA-FRENCH, inducted into the Corps in MISSOURI (5/16/1804).

George DROUILLARD (INTERPRETER/permanent party)—SHAWNEE-FRENCH, probably born in Canada, migrated in youth to MISSOURI, appointed to the Corps in ILLINOIS (1/1/1804).

François Labiche (Private/permanent party)—OMAHA-FRENCH, MULATTO, inducted into the Corps in MISSOURI (5/16/1804).

Peter Pinaut (ENGAGÉ/return party, spring 1805?)—MISSOURI-FRENCH, born (c. 1776) and resided in MISSOURI.

Of Indian extraction

SACAGAWEA ("Interpretress"/permanent party)—A Lemhi SHOSHONE of the ROCKY MOUNTAINS, captured by the HIDATSA at about age 12 and residing in North Dakota during the winter of 1804-5.

THE SOUNDS OF VIRGINIA PLANTATION ENGLISH

The erratic spelling of the journalists has sometimes been derided by modern commentators, for whom a standardized orthography (and formal education) wields far more influence today than it did in the early 19th century. The journalists' nonstandard spellings, however, have unintentionally given us a valuable insight into the sounds of the expedition's voices. Their accents are revealed by their phonetic spellings.

The journalists struggled between phonetic truth and orthographic standardization in their writing. Standardization generally triumphed, but the writers did use enough nonstandard spellings to provide us with a surprisingly good idea of how they spoke. The salient features of their pronunciation, insofar as they can be deduced from the journals, are summarized here with the hope that the reader will be able to recite a passage from the journals with some assurance that it would sound familiar to its writer. (See Appendix 4 for a more extensive analysis of the journalists' vocabulary and pronunciation.)

The men of the Corps of Discovery spoke various dialects of American English, but the dominant accents represented in the journals are those of the plantations of eastern and central Virginia. I began my phonetic inquiries into the Lewis & Clark journals with the assumption that I would find clear indications of what is now called Midland English (of southern Pennsylvania, Kentucky, and the Appalachians). After all, Lewis & Clark had both served in the U.S. Army in the Old Northwest, and Clark had moved with his family to Kentucky when a teenager. But the journals show no substantial evidence of Midland English in the captains' speech; they apparently kept the Virginia accents they grew up with.

R-*lessness*

The most striking feature of the spelling in the journals is the deletion and addition of the written letter *r*. Though the addition of *r*'s often disguises the fact, the spoken English of the journalists was that of an *r*-dropping (*nonrhotic*) dialect of the kind still heard in parts of New England and the South. *R*'s following same-syllable vowels and preceding a consonant, or occurring at the end of a word (*postvocalic r's*), were not pronounced, though initial *r*'s and those between vowels at syllable boundaries and those following consonants were retained (e.g., *advosary* for *adversary*, *had* for *hard*, *resoce* for *resource*, *figue* for *figure*, *rive* for *river*). Appendix 4 lists many more examples of *r*-dropping.

The dropping of *r*'s after vowels is characteristic of Virginian English and distinguishes it from the *rhotic* English of the South Midland (though in many other respects the two dialects are similar). South Midland, as we know it today, not only pronounces those *r*'s missing from the Virginian dialect, but also characteristically adds *r*'s (e.g., in words like *holler, winder,* and *musquetor*) where neither plantation Virginian nor standard English would pronounce them. The captains, too, added these final *r*'s when writing in their journals, but whether they actually pronounced them is uncertain.

(There is, at first glance, one situation other than postvocalic in which *r* is sometimes dropped, and that is for the prefix *pre-*; see below, under *Reduction of consonant clusters*. These are, however, actually postvocalic *r*'s; the *pre-* or *pro-* having changed to *per-* or *por-* before the *r* was dropped.)

Though the written words in the journals are essentially non-rhotic, we can be sure that some of the men did *not* drop their *r*'s. The journals of John Brown (Newsome, 1934) and Jacob Fowler (Coues, 1898) give an idea of what the speech and writing (if literate) of the Pennsylvanians in the Lewis & Clark expedition might have been like. Brown, from Lewistown, Pennsylvania, was an agent for a group of land-investors, on whose behalf he made a horseback journey from Pennsylvania to North Carolina in 1794–95. Fowler was born in New Jersey (or New York) in about 1765 and moved to Kentucky as a youth, later serving with William Clark's brother, General George Rogers Clark, against the SHAWNEE. In 1821–22, Fowler led an expedition to the Spanish Southwest, which he recorded in his journal. The nonstandard spelling of these two journalists probably represents the Midland type of English that was spoken by Sergeant Patrick Gass, Private George Shannon, and several other of the men born in Pennsylvania.

Though Brown's and Fowler's spellings show many of the same characteristics as those of the captains', they differ essentially in the treatment of postvocalic *r*'s. There are very few examples of a dropped *r* (*suppe* for *supper*, *pasten* for *pastern*) and of reverse spellings with added *r* (*mogerson* for *moccasin*). However, they do contain idiosyncratically spelled words that would be expected to show a dropped *r* if the speaker were non-rhotic (*coarthouse, firtil, hoarses, forsed, mager* for *major, aughter* for *otter*), and several words that might have been written with "phantom" *r*'s by non-rhotic speakers (*gon* rather that *gorn* for *gone, Hollow* rather that *holler* for *hallo*).

In summary, we can surmise that the pronunciations of most members of the Lewis & Clark expedition had much in common, except for their treatment of postvocalic *r*—the Virginians and New Englanders dropping theirs, and the Midlanders keeping theirs.

Phantom r*'s*

The journals' disappearing *r*'s are clear evidence of a nonrhotic pronunciation, but what are we to make of the many cases in which the journalists *add* a written *r* where none would be expected, as in *Nemarhar* for NEMAHA, *gorn* for *gone, Shark* for *Jacques, parth* for *path, cultervation* for *cultivation*, and *idear* for *idea*? In almost all such cases, with the possible exception of the *holler*-type words discussed above, the added *r* was not pronounced, but was introduced in a reversal of the process of *r*-dropping—a sort of *reverse spelling* in which the writer assumed that the broad *a* sound in *Nemaha* should be spelled with a following *r*, like the *a* in *embark*, for example. Knowing that he tended to drop his *r*'s in certain cases, the writer tried to correct himself by adding *r*'s after similar vowels in words that never contained *r*'s. An added *r* can thus be thought of as an orthographic way of specifying the quality of the preceding vowel—in *Nemarhar*, the *ar*'s signify broad *a*'s; while in *idear*, the *ar* is to be pronounced like the *r*-less final vowel in *rive(r)*. Another common case of reverse spelling is that of *gone* as *gorn*, which is a reversal of the *r*-dropping in words like *born*.

There are two arguments for the silence of these phantom *r*'s. First, Clark comes close to stating this principle explicitly when, in the pronunciation key preceding his catalog of Indian tribes of the Missouri [3.389], he writes, "^ over *a*, denotes that it sounds as in dart, part [and] *a*, without notation has its primitive sound as in ray, hay…except only when it is followed by *r* or *w*, in which case it sounds as *â*." For Clark, the phonetic spellings *ar* and *aw* apparently rendered the same sound, a broad *a*.

The second argument is exemplified by Indian words like *Multnomah* and SACAGAWEA, which the journalists had never seen in writing, with or without *r*'s. The Chinookan and Hidatsa originals of those names contain no *r*-sound whatsoever, so it seems clear that whether the journalists write the name with *ar* or with *ah*, the sound they intend to represent is an *r*-less broad *a*. (Clark's variant spellings of *exhaust* exhibit the same spelling technique—*exorst* and *exost*. So also *Jacke* and *Jarcke* for the French name *Jacques*.)

Desarters, entarpreters, and pertisons

R's also sometimes affect the way in which the sound of a preceding vowel in the journals differs from the standard pronunciation—the modern *ur*-sound of *deserter* and *curtain*, for instance, was *æ* in *Desarter* and *Cartin*. The modern *ahr* of *partisan* and *starve* is probably an *æ* in *pertison* and *sterve*.

The standard sound *eh* in *bear* (the mammal) becomes *æ* (as in *cat*) and so becomes an icon of southern pronunciation—Daniel Boone (North Carolina, Kentucky) writes *baar skines* in 1790. (The *ahr*-sound in popular portrayals of southern speech, as in Davy Crockett's *bar*, is actually rare.)

Loss of distinction between short e and short i

After the dropping and adding of *r*'s, the most obvious idiosyncrasy of the journalists' spelling is the substitution of short *i* for short *e* (*chimical* and *Mackinzie*) and vice versa (*Enfluenzey* and *Seckamore*), primarily before *m* and *n*. At least two words show both substitutions at once, *emince* for *immense* and *errigular* for *irregular*, and there is the revealing pair *Meadle* for *middle* and *midal* for *medal*. (A caveat—the journalists often wrote under difficult field conditions, a fact reflected in their handwriting. At times it is difficult to distinguish a small *e* from a small *i*, the former sometimes being written without an open loop, and the latter without the dot. Clark, for example, failed to dot almost half his *i*'s.) It is unclear from the texts whether the pronunciation of the two vowels converged consistently on some sound intermediate between *eh* and *ih*, or alternated in some way between *eh* and *ih*, though the examples like *errigular* suggest convergence. (It is unlikely that the latter spelling actually represents the pronunciation eh-RIH-gu-ler.)

We can at least say that the journalists did not distinguish between the two vowels in the way that speakers of standard English do today. The pronunciation of short *e* as short *i*, especially before *m* and *n*, is a hallmark of present-day Southern American English, but it was also common throughout the East in the 17th to mid-19th centuries.

(Ben Franklin, from Boston and Philadelphia, wrote *frind* and *git*, and Revolutionary War soldiers from Massachusetts and Rhode Island wrote *rigiment, yit, git, yisterday, frinds.*)

No evidence for the modern Southern pronunciation of long i *as* ah, *for extensive diphthongization, or for the Virginian pronunciation of* garden

A most striking finding from the journals is the fact that there is no phonetic evidence for the pronunciation of the diphthong *ī* , (as in *high* pronounced *hah-ih*), as the monophthong *ah* (pronounced *hah*), a feature that William Labov (*Atlas of North American English*) considered so characteristic of modern Southern pronunciation that he used it to define the limits of the Southern dialect region. (Throughout the East Coast in the 18th and early-19th centuries, *ī* had several diphthongal pronunciations, including that of *oi* as noted below, but never that of a monophthong.) This feature is accompanied by a series of further changes (such as *ay* to *ī* in *rise* for *raise*) in the modern pronunciation of Southern vowels, known as the Southern Shift, evidence for which is also lacking in the Lewis & Clark journals. The journals thus apparently were written before the onset of these changes in Southern speech.

Another characteristic of Southern English is the pronunciation of what in standard English are usually monophthongal vowels (like the *eh*-sound in *bed*) as diphthongs instead (*beh-ed*). Though such sounds are difficult for even creative spellers to write down, the general lack of evidence for them in the journals suggests that the captains' vowels were less diphthongal than in modern Southern English.

Also missing from the journals is any evidence for a pronunciation that formerly was characteristic for parts of Virginia and the Carolinas in which a *y*-sound is inserted between the initial consonant and the *a*-sound in *garden* {GYAH-d'n} and *car* {kyah} and some other similar words. Clark spelled *garden* phonetically in ways that indicate a pronunciation beginning with {gah-} (*gardain* [2.233], *Gardin* [3.233, 3.454]), and he also spells *gartering* as *guartering* [2.441] and *Gart[erin]g.* [2.439], neither of which implies a *gy-* sound (for which we would expect a spelling like *geardin* or *giardin*). Given that {GYAH-d'n} was widespread in Virginia and the Carolinas and, in Lewis & Clark's era, even more widespread in the East, its absence from the journals is puzzling. (A British pronouncing dictionary of 1791 even recommends {GYAH-d'n} as the preferred pronunciation.)

Other variations in vowels

In American English, the vowels generally prove to be the most useful markers for distinguishing among dialects, and the journals provide a variety of examples. A few highlights are mentioned here; see Appendix 4 for a more complete tabulation. *Oi* is sometimes written in the journals as though pronounced *ī*, as in BOIL[1] (spelled *bile*) and *point* (spelled *pint*), and conversely, long *ī* is written as *oi*, as in BILE (*boil*) and *pint* (*point*). In modern Northern and Western American English, the diphthongs *ī* and *oi* are given distinct pronunciations, *ah-ih* (as in *buy*) and *oh-ih* (as in *boy*) respectively, but in the early 1800s they probably converged on an intermediate diphthong like *uh-ih*, as seems to have been the case all along the East Coast for the preceding 150 years. (Canadian French *oi* is often pronounced *weh* or *way*: see Illinois.) Also characteristic of the journals are *eh* for standard *æ* (*gether* for *gather*, *shellow* for *shallow*), *æ* for *eh* (*brackfast, yallow*), *ee* for *ə* (*Athabaskey* in Athabasca, *peninsoley*), *ə* added (*casterate, Sundery*) and *ə* dropped (*Buflow, differnt*), *ə* or *ee* for *yoo* (*figer, Siteated*), *o* for *oo* (*pore* for *poor*, *more* for *moor*), and *yoo* for *oo* (*diew, niew*).

Consonants other than r

The journals provide a curious variety of phonetically spelled consonantal sounds. In some cases, voiced and voiceless variants are interchanged—*b~p* (*prarrow* for BRAROW, *bitch* for *pitch*), *d~t* (*tirty* for *dirty, trate* for *trade, gred* for *great, Latidude*), and *f~v* (*disvigored* for *disfigued, Sefere* for *severe*). In other cases, the consonants are produced in a different part of the mouth—*n* for *m* (*becon, Custon, Sometines*), *n for ng* (*anythin, lenth, nothin*), and sometimes *n* is overcorrected to *ng* (*mounting* for *mountain, suddingly*); and *s~sh* (*shumate* in SUMAC, *cutlash*; *fisery* for *fishery, Srimp, Srub*).

Besides the usual variation with *v*, *f* is involved in a particularly interesting set of equivalencies—for *Warfington* we find *Warvington* and *Worbington*, and for *Woolford* there is *Wolpard*. Even more interesting, though, is *Worthington* for *Warfington*—we find the inverse equivalent, *f* for *th*, in Clark's spelling of *warmth* as *womph* (with the expected dropping of postvocalic *r*). *F* for *th* is a characteristic feature of some southern dialects and of Black English.

N and *t* are sometimes added to words in which they "genetically" have no place— *breanth, climent, mockinson* (for *breadth, climate, moccasin*); *Mahometant, Chrismast, trought* (for *Mohammedan, Chistmas, trough*).

Metathesis, in which sounds change places in a word

This occurs most often with the prefixes *per*, *pur*, *pre*, and *pro*—*prespiration, prosue, pervale, percure*. Note also *apern* for APRON, *circlier* for *circular*, and *industerous* for *industrious*.

Reduction (simplification) of consonant clusters

It is common in the South and South Midland dialects, though not unique to them, for clusters of more than one consonant to be simplified by dropping one of the consonant sounds, as—

> *d* in *dth, ld, nd, rd*: *breth, weth* (for *breadth, width*), *househole, armban, dasterly*. In what are perhaps reverse spellings in the journals, *d* is sometimes added superfluously to *l*, *n*, and *r*: *bold, Mandand, dollard* (for *bowl*, MANDAN, *dollar*).

> *r* in *thr*: *thee* for *three, thow* for *throw, though* for *through*

> *r* in *pr*, probably after metathesis in the prefixes *pre-* and *pro-*: *pepare, pesume, povide, Suppised*. Lewis outdoes himself in his botanical write-up of SACKACOMMIS

THE PERMANENT PARTY

Fort Mandan to the Pacific Ocean (1805-6)—The 33 members of the Permanent Party included 2 officers, 2 interpreters, 26 enlisted men, York, Sacagawea, and Jean Baptiste (infant).

"Nine Young Men from Kentucky"; civilians inducted at the Falls of the Ohio River—
Pvt. William Bratton
Pvt. John Colter
Pvt. Joseph & Pvt. Reubin Field (brothers)
Pvt. George Gibson
Sgt. Nathaniel Pryor (cousin Sgt. Charles Floyd died 8/20/1804)
Pvt. George Shannon
Pvt. John Shields

Men with known prior U.S. Army service—
"Capt." William Clark
Pvt./Sgt. Patrick Gass
Pvt. Hugh Hall
Pvt. Thomas Howard
Capt. Meriwether Lewis
Sgt. John Ordway
Pvt. John Potts
Pvt. Joseph Whitehouse
Pvt. Alexander Willard
Pvt. Richard Windsor

Prior U.S. Army service uncertain, but probable for most of these men—
Pvt. John Collins
Pvt. Robert Frazer
Pvt. Silas Goodrich
Pvt. Hugh McNeal
Pvt. John Thompson
Pvt. Peter Weiser
Pvt. William Werner

French Canadian/Indian civilians inducted —
Pvt. Pierre Cruzatte
Pvt. François Labiche
Pvt. Baptiste Lepage

Interpreters—
Toussaint Charbonneau
George Drouillard

Civilians—
Jean Baptiste ("Little Pomp")
Sacagawea
York

(the bearberry plant), whose branches he describes as "more *poperly pocumbent* than creeping," that is, "properly procumbent."

t in *ct, ft, nt, pt, st*: *chatarac, sexton, kep, mois* (for *cataract, after, sextant, kept, moist*)

A Cautionary Note Regarding Dialect Evolution

Modern dialect labels, such as *South, South Midland*, and *New England*, are convenient, but sometimes might be misleading in the study of the American English spoken and written two centuries ago. America's dialect boundaries and their phonetic and lexical characteristics—*as we now understand them*—were by and large established and documented in the 20th century in such large compilations as the *Dictionary of American Regional English*, the Linguistic Atlas of the United States and Canada, and the *Atlas of North American English*. Present day dialects are descended from those of the early 1800s, but their character and distribution have continued to evolve in complex ways.

For example, the distinction in pronunciation that exists today between the New England and Southern dialects was less marked two centuries ago. Two characteristic features of modern Southern speech, discussed earlier, would not at that time have distinguished a speaker as being Southern—(1) the falling together of short *i* and short *e* (as in *pin* and *pen*) was common in New England and Long Island public records from the 17th to 19th centuries (Krapp, *The English Language in America*); and, (2) the pronunciation of long *i* as *ah* (as in *ahm* for *I'm*) did not develop until after Lewis & Clark's time.

Also, the *r*-dropping so characteristic of the coastal South today was likewise a prominent feature of coastal New England and New York speech as early as the 17th century. Philadelphia, in fact, is the only major East Coast city with a population that does not generally drop *r*'s. It was the original rhotic Philadelphians and their descendants, of course, who spread the Midland dialect down the Appalachians and to the west.

Bold-face labels in the *Lexicon*, (e.g., **South, South Midland, New England**) refer to modern dialects, but keep in mind that a particular L&C word or pronunciation may have been used more widely in early 19th century American English than it is today.

Guide to the *Lexicon* Entries

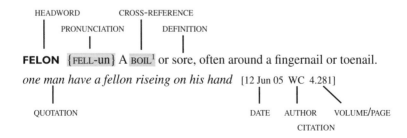

The form of the HEADWORD is chosen to help the reader find a word or expression most easily. The standard English spelling is used wherever possible. A compound word will be alphabetized under its more salient part (e.g., MARROW-BONE, but MEAL, PARCH-). This is a subjective process, so if a compound word cannot be located under one of its parts, please try the other. A headword marked with an **asterisk** (e.g., SAHAPTIN*) indicates a modern term that is not found in the journals, but which provides pertinent background information. (See Appendix 1 for a subject index, and Appendix 2 for spelling variants.)

PRONUNCIATION (usually as reconstructed for the expedition's Virginians) is given in a respelled form, with stressed syllables printed in small capitals when a word has more than one syllable. The pronunciation for a word is omitted when it is obvious to the reader, or where there is insufficient evidence. Despite the caveats in Appendix 4, a pronunciation for a word for which there is no direct evidence has sometimes been inferred from another word that we are quite sure of. In such cases, this lexicographer can only plead good intentions based on considerable experience with nonstandard spellings; please do not accept these suggestions uncritically. In regard to vowels— those marked with a tilde (as $\tilde{a}$) are nasalized like certain French vowels; $\bar{\iota}$ is in modern standard American pronunciation like the *i* in *kite*, but in the journals probably as *uh-ih*; *O* like the vowel in the British pronunciation of *bought*; *ə* like the *a* in *sofa*; *æ* like the *a* in *bat*; and *ü* like an *ee*-sound pronounced with rounded lips. Characters from the International Phonetic Alphabet are used in some pronunciations in the main body of the *Lexicon* (see Appendix 4 for a key to phonetic values).

A DEFINITION follows the headword. Geographic labels in boldface (e.g., **South, Midland**) identify words characteristic of the various modern dialects of eastern American English (with particular reliance on the *Dictionary of American Regional English* and Kurath's *A Word Geography of the Eastern United States*). An analysis of a meaning or word-origin considered to be more than usually speculative is bracketed by diamond symbols ♦♦. Prices are given in the currency of the time—the dollar's buying-power in the early 1800s was, *very* roughly, 10 to 15 times greater than today.

A CROSS-REFERENCE to another entry is printed in SMALL CAPS, directing the reader to an additional example, or a further discussion of the word under consideration.

QUOTATIONS are taken verbatim from the journals, without change in spelling or punctuation. Editorially omitted material is indicated by a triple-dot ellipsis (e.g. *we have plenty of Elk beef...and a little salt*), and brief comments or additions are enclosed in [square brackets]. Text deleted by a journalist is printed as ~~stricken through~~. (Note: Appendix 3 explains the abbreviations and symbols used by the journalists.)

The CITATION within square brackets following each quotation begins with the DATE (e.g., 12 Jun 05). The AUTHOR is identified by his initials—WC (William Clark), CF (Charles Floyd), PG (Patrick Gass), ML (Meriwether Lewis), JO (John Ordway), JW

(Joseph Whitehouse), and NB (Nicholas Biddle). (Biddle, the original editor of the captains' journals, wrote notes in their manuscripts in 1810 based on his interviews with Clark and George Shannon; Biddle also consulted the Ordway and Gass journals). The VOLUME/PAGE reference indicates either Gary E. Moulton's *The Journals of the Lewis and Clark Expedition*, 13 volumes (e.g., 4.281), or Donald Jackson's *Letters of the Lewis and Clark Expedition,* 2 Volumes (e.g., Jackson *Letters* (ed. 2) 1.071). A few references cite James J. Holmberg's *Dear Brother: Letters of William Clark to Jonathan Clark* (for William Clark only; e.g., WC *Letters* 168).

The venerable *Oxford English Dictionary* is referenced as *OED.*

A

A A meaningless prefix used with present participles. It originated as a variant of the preposition *on*, often used with verbal nouns ending in *-ing*. (**South, South Midland**)

Rain came on as we was a goeing to start [20 Jun 04 JW 11.027]

Capt. Clark and 10 of his men and my Self went to the Mahas Creek a fishen and Caut 300 and 17 fish of Difernt Coindes [15 Aug 04 CF 9.395]

The river a riseing a little. [31 Aug 04 WC 3.033]

the Buffelow was Close to us a Comeing in [2 Dec 04 JW 11.110]

Capt. Lewis and the Greater part of the party went up to the 2nd village of the mandans a frolicking [2 Jan 05 JO 9.107]

they met 3 Squaws on the Side of the mountain a digging roots [17 Aug 05 JW 11.272]

John Colter…asks leave of our officers to go back with Mr. Dixon a trapping [17 Aug 06 JO 9.351]

Also can mean 'on, in,' as in the modern expressions *aboard, afoot, ajar, alive.*

came across three Indians a horseback [10 Sep 05 JW 11.308]

ABACK, TAKE (Of the wind) to strike a sail suddenly on the forward side, endangering the mast and boat. The phrase now also means 'to take (someone) by surprise,' usually in an unpleasant manner.

the Wind shifting suddenly…took the Pettyauger aback [14 May 05 JW 11.157]

ACCOUTREMENTS {ə-KOO-tə-mənts} Accessories; military equipment other than weapons and uniforms.

the Assinniboins…are a vicious illy disposed nation…accordingly we inspected the arms and accoutrements [of] *the party and found them all in good order.* [10 May 05 ML 4.136]

the Indians had stolen their arms and accoutrements [15 Nov 05 PG 10.171]

ADDITIVE (Of an error in an observation with an instrument) high. When calibrating a thermometer, Lewis called the error additive because it gave a reading further below the freezing point than the actual temperature. *See* SUBTRACTIVE.

By two experiments made with Ferenheit's Thermometer…I asscertained it's error to be 11° too low or additive…I tested it with water and snow mixed for the friezing point, and boiling water for—the point marked boiling water. [Jan 04 ML 2.169]

Error of Octant 2° additive. [3 Dec 03 ML 2.121]

the errour of the instrument is 1° 20' 00" + ad + [18 Dec 03 WC 2.135]

ADZE {ædz} An ax-like tool with a curved blade at right angles to the handle, used by carpenters and coopers in rough-dressing wood. A *foot adze* was long-handled and swung down between a worker's feet.

2 Foot Adzes [Jun 03 ML in Jackson Letters (ed. 2) 1.071]

one man Shannon Cut his foot with the ads in working at a perogue [6 Mar 05 WC 3.309]

the ten men...had ground and prepared their axes and adds this evening [9 Jul 05 ML 4.370]

AFFECTION Disorder, disease.

the latter complained of a lax and rheumatic effections. [18 May 06 ML 7.269]

AFTER PART {ÆF-tə PAHT} Afternoon and evening.

in the after part of the day killed two gees [11 Apr 05 WC 4.023]

AGAIN {uh-GIN, with hard *g*} Against.

the towing line...broke in the pitch of the rapid and the canoe was near turning over nocking again the rocks. [1 Aug 05 JO 9.193]

AGREEABLE TO In accordance with.

I punished Hall agreeable to his Sentence [17 May 04 WC 2.235]

the female at this age [puberty] *is surrendered to her sovereign lord and husband agreeably to contract* [19 Aug 05 ML 5.120]

AGUE {modern AY-gyoo, in the journals perhaps AY-guh} An intermittent chill alternating with fever; often symptoms of malaria, a mosquito-borne disease formerly widespread in the United States. The word originally was applied to the fever stage, but came to usually mean the associated shivering and chill. In some cases in the journals, ague probably refers simply to COLDS or INFLUENZA. It is an Old French word meaning 'acute.' *See* BILIOUS, FIT.

The fever and ague and bilious fevers here [on the upper Ohio River] *commence their banefull oppression* [14 Sep 03 ML 2.081]

I was siezed with a violent ague which continued about four hours and as is usual was succeeded by a feever which...abated in some measure by sunrise the next morning [13 Nov 03 ML 2.086]

he was...at the time with a chill of the agu on him [3 Sep 06 WC 8.346]

AHWAHAWAY Subdivision of the HIDATSA people, also known as the *Amahami*, from a Hidatsa word for 'mountain.' (In the Hidatsa language, *w*, which occurs in normal, rapid speech, is replaced in careful pronunciation by an *m* after a pause; *see* SACAGAWEA.) *See* MAHAHA, SHOE, WETESOON.

the Knife river falls in [to the Missouri] *near the Village of the Ahwahharways on the S. side—a little above the Mandans.* [winter 04–05 ML 3.362]

Lewis recorded a form with *w* in one place, and *m* in another. (The *r*'s in *Arwerharmays* are silent.)

it is a custom when a person of either sex becomes so old and infurm that they are unable to travel on foot...for the children or near relations...to leave them without compunction...this custom prevails even among the Minetares Arwerharmays and Recares [6 Jan 06 ML 6.169]

AIR-GUN   A .31-caliber repeating rifle powered by compressed air, probably manufactured by Isaiah Lukens in Philadelphia and used mostly by the captains to impress tribal people and settlers. (*See* MEDICINE.) At Lewis's first stop on the Ohio River after setting out from Pittsburgh, an accidental firing of the weapon creased a woman bystander's temple—a curious gentlemen had carelessly shot it through her hat. Lewis initially feared she was dead, but "in a minute she revived to our enespressable satisfaction."

Cap Lewis Shot his air gun a few times which astonished the nativs [3 Aug 04 WC 2.439]

ALDEBARAN   {æl-DEB-ə-rən} The red alpha star of the constellation Taurus, high in the winter night sky, sighted by Lewis & Clark for lunar OBSERVATIONS.

must for the longitude depend on the observation...made with Aldeberan and Regulus [3 Dec 03 ML 2.120]

ALGONQUIAN*   {æl-GONG-kee-ən} A widespread language family of Canada and the northeast United States, comprising the ATSINA, BLACKFOOT, CHEYENNE, CHIPPEWA, CREE, KICKAPOO, MIAMI-ILLINOIS, POTAWATOMI, SAUK, SHAWNEE, and other languages.

ALLOW   To believe, declare.

the party informed us, that the South fork, was most probably the Course that we should take, and Captain Clarke allow'd it would be the case. [6 Jun 05 JW 11.188]

ALTITUDE, MERIDIAN   Altitude of the sun at local noon time (i.e., its angular height above the horizon when due south), measured with an OCTANT or SEXTANT to determine LATITUDE. Knowing due south, the captains marked the moment that the sun reached the meridian and accordingly set their timepieces to noon.

Took equal altitudes, and the Meridian altituade of the Suns L[ower] L[imb] [27 Jun 04 WC 2.325]

we delayed at 12 oClock for the Captains to take the Meridian altidude & Set their watches [16 Jul 04 JO 9.026]

ALTITUDES, EQUAL   A method by which the observer calibrated a chronometer to local noon by taking the midpoint between the times in mid-morning and mid-afternoon when the sun was at exactly the same altitude. (The chronometer had to be accurately calibrated for the calculations necessary for determining the party's position.) Such observations required open views to the southeast and southwest—sometimes necessitating the felling of trees—and the weather had to be clear, both morning and afternoon.

I have made several attempts to obtain Equal altitudes...but have been uniformly defeated untill now by the flying clouds and storms in the evening. [30 Jun 05 ML 4.345]

ALTOGETHER {ɔll-tə-GÆ-thə} Completely, exclusively, entirely.

their yells were not hea[r]d by the party in the perogue, a mistake altogether [10 Jul 04 WC 2.364]

the [river-]bed seems to be composed of mud altogether. [22 Apr 05 ML 4.060]

our toe rope which we are obliged to make use of altogether broke [31 May 05 WC 4.228]

I caused her to drink the mineral water altogether. [16 Jun 05 ML 4.300]

we use the seting poles today almost altogether. [8 Aug 05 ML 5.059]

they [Shoshone] *fight on horseback altogether.* [14 Aug 05 ML 5.092]

ALUM Aluminum potassium phosphate, an astringent (puckering) salt.

we pasd. an allum Stone clift [22 Aug 04 JW 11.059]

this water partakes of the taste of glauber salts and slightly of allumn. [14 Apr 05 ML 4.036]

AMAZING Amazingly. (**South**)

the River Small & amazeing crooked [10 Aug 05 JO 9.200]

rained a mazeing hard…and all the men thursty drunk harty out of the puddles. [first version; 24 Jun 05 JW 11.210]

Whitehouse's second version of his June 24, 1805, entry standardized the above wording to *rained amazingly hard* and *they drank heartily.*

AMERICAN BOTTOM The swath of populated, rich bottomland extending along the Mississippi's east shore from Cahokia on the north to the Kaskaskia River at the south. The name served to distinguish this locality from bottomlands on the Spanish, or western, bank of the river. The American Bottom was first settled by the French at the end of the 17th century, and passed to British control by terms of the 1763 Treaty of Paris. In 1778 during the American Revolution, George Rogers Clark, the eldest brother of William Clark, led an expedition forcefully wresting the area from British control. *See* Bottom, Illinois.

Leave Caho. 8 O'C Thursday mor[n]ing—and arive at Kas. by way of the American bottom 6 O'C Friday evening [c. Apr 04 (unknown writer) 2.197]

AMMUNITION, FIXED = Cartridges.

Capt. C. also scelected the articles to be deposited in the cash…2 blunderbushes, ½ a keg of fixed ammunition [et al.] [26 Jun 05 ML 4.334]

AMORITE {ÆM-ə-rite} Lover, from Latin *amor* 'love.' Lewis probably confused the English word *amorist* with the Semitic name for an Old Testament tribe, the *Amorites.* *See* Battery, for example.

ANCHOVY {ÆN-choh-vee} = Eulachon.

the Anchovey is so delicate that they soon become tainted unless pickled or smoked. [4 Mar 06 ML 6.378]

Gave us Some wapa toes & anchoves to eat. [27 Mar 06 JO 9.282]

ANSWER {ÆN-sə} To serve the purpose. *See* BLEED.

the habits of those people [Mandan] *has ancered to bare more Cold than I thought it possible for man to indure.* [10 Jan 05 WC 3.271]

those [elk skins] *we had prepared at Fort Mandan being injured in such manner that they would not answer.* [6 Jun 05 ML 4.261]

we found it difficult to obtain as much wood as answered our purposes. [26 Mar 06 ML 7.016]

ANTARES {æn-TEHR-eez} The red-giant alpha star of the constellation Scorpius. The Greek name means *anti-Ares,* the *rival* (or *equal*) *of Ares,* or Mars, with which Antares was compared in color and brightness.

Observed time and distance of ☽ *and Antares* ★ *West, with Sextant.* [22 Jul 04 ML 2.410]

ANTELOPE = PRONGHORN.

passed a hunting Camp of Minetarees...waiting the return of the Antilope [9 Apr 05 WC 4.017]

the Antelopes...are extremely fleet and dureable. [29 Apr 05 ML 4.085]

APARTMENT {ə-PAHT-mənt} A portion of a structure set *apart* for a particular purpose. Here, a section of a Mandan earth-lodge occupied by horses, in order to secure the animals from theft.

they Seldom...Clean the horse appartment [winter 04–05 WC 3.489]

APPEARANCE Visible evidence of something, as, for example, mineral salts in the soil. Often refers to animal SIGN[1].

great appearance of beaver on this river [8 May 05 ML 4.125]

at this encampment he Saw great appearanc of horses [12 Aug 06 WC 8.291]

APPLE, WHITE Indian breadroot, *Pediomelum esculentum,* of the pea family. Lewis [4.125] described the edible root as "a fine white substance, somewhat porus, spungy and moist, and reather tough before it is dressed." The name is a translation of Canadian French *pomme blanche* (**Plains**). *See* POTATO.

the Indian woman...gathered a considerable quantity of the white apples of which she eat so heartily in their raw state [19 Jun 05 ML 4.309]

the men dug great parcel of the root which the Nativs call Hankee and the engagees the white apple which they boiled and made use of with their meat. This is a large insipid root...the nativs use this root after it is dry and pounded in their Seup. [10 Aug 06 WC 8.288]

APPREHEND To fear, to be apprehensive.

the indians [Nez Perce]*...apprehend that the Minnetares of fort de Prarie have distroyed them* [Flathead] [30 Jun 06 ML 8.066]

The morning was somewhat cloudy I therefore apprehended rain [10 Aug 06 ML 8.153]

APPROPRIATE To set aside or designate.

one half of those houses is apropriated for the Storeing away Dried & pounded fish which is the principal food [24 Oct 05 WC 5.335]

APRON {AY-pə(r)n, a typical southern pronunciation} In accurate nautical terms, a wood piece reinforcing the afterside of the stem (the wooden post at a vessel's bow).

their canoes are calculated to ride the highest waves, they are built of white cedar or Pine verry light wide in the middle and tapers at each end, with aperns, and heads of animals carved on the bow [28 Oct 05 WC 5.348]

AQUILA {ÆCK-will-ə} Altair, the alpha or brightest star of the constellation Aquila, sighted in lunar OBSERVATIONS. The pale yellow star also is one of three bright stars forming the prominent summer triangle, the others being Vega and Deneb. *Aquilae* is the possessive form of the Latin word *aquila,* 'eagle.'

the clouds this morning prevented my observing the moon with α *Aquilae* [26 Apr 05 ML 4.072]

ARBORVITÆ {ah-bə-VY-tee} = (WHITE) CEDAR. Latin for 'tree of life.'

considerable of Strait handsome timber on these ridges, which...is called Arbervity. [20 Sep 05 JW 11.324]

the Arborvita increases in quantity and size. I saw several sticks today large enough to form eligant perogues of at least 45 feet in length. [21 Sep 05 ML 5.226]

ARGALI {AH-gə-lee} Name of an Asian mountain sheep, which Lewis applied to the BIGHORN.

great abundance of the Argalia or Bighorned animals in the high country [29 May 05 ML 4.215]

ARGIL {AH-jihl} Pottery clay.

I am confident that this earth Contains argill [7 Jan 06 WC 6.178]

bighorn (3½ ft. high
at the shoulder)

Hence *argillaceous* {ah-jih-LAY-shus}, composed of clay.

the earth of which this mud is composed...appears to be argillacious. [9 Aug ML 5.062]

ARIKARA {ə-RICK-ə-rə, RICK-ə-ree, etc.} A people originally residing along the Missouri River in north-central South Dakota. They spoke a Caddoan language closely related to that of the Skiri PAWNEE, from whom they separated in late prehistoric times. The journalists hardly ever spelt the name the same way twice. *See* REE, RIC.

we Should not land any more untill we got to the Rick Rea Nation...We passed an old village on S.S. where the Rick Rias lived [29 Sep 04 JO 9.072]

2 french men were at the house with good[s] to trade with the Seauex which he expected down from the rickerries every day [1 Oct 04 WC 3.135] *we halted at a Camp of 10 Lodges of Ricaras...& were friendly recved by all* [15 Oct 04 WC 3.174]

ARSENIC {ÆS-nee} A poisonous metallic element. Sergeant Ordway's identification is doubtful.

we found also a burning bank.... it had a Sulpheras Smell, we found in it a great quantity of asney & a great quantity of different kinds of mineral Substance [24 Aug 04 JO 9.043]

ARSESMART {ÆSS-smaht} Smartweed, a plant of the genus *Polygonum* secreting a caustic juice. A 1617 book (cited in *OED*) explained the name: "Arsmart...because if it touch the taile or other bare skinne, it maketh it smart, as often it doth, being laid into the bed greene to kill fleas." A modern source (*Dictionary of American Regional English*) suggests the name arose from the painful results of the plant's use in wiping one's backside.

The Black Bear is found in abundance as high as the little Sioux river...The Ass smart is also found in the Same neighbourhood. [undated WC 8.416]

ARTICHOKE {AH-tə-choke} A plant, *Helianthus tuberosus*, of the sunflower family, having edible tubers—the Jerusalem artichoke, not the Old World artichoke, *Cynara scolymus*.

the squaw busied herself in serching for the wild artichokes which the mice collect and deposit in large hoards. [9 Apr 05 ML 4.015]

ASSIMILATE To liken.

I cannot conceive how the engages ever assimilated this animal [eastern short-horned lizard] *with the buffaloe* [29 May 06 ML 7.303] *See* (PRAIRIE) BUFFALO.

ASSINIBOINE {ə-SIN-ə-boyn} A nomadic people who separated from the SIOUX in recent prehistory, moving northwest to southern Manitoba and Saskatchewan and northern Montana and North Dakota, where they subsisted primarily on buffalo and engaged in almost constant conflict with the Dakota Sioux. They spoke a Sioux dialect, but their name in English is borrowed from the Chippewa, literally meaning 'rock-Sioux,' perhaps with reference to their residing toward the Rockies. (The Rocky Mountains also were so named in Chippewa and Cree).

They [Sioux] *fell in with the Ossiniboin who killed them and took the horses* [25 Oct 04 WC 3.197]

one of our Intrepters & a frenchman returned who had been up the river...to a nation of Indians called the osnaboins after fur [13 Jan 05 JW 11.119]

we do not wish to see those gentlemen just now as we presume they would...be the Assinniboins and might be troublesome to us. [8 May 05 ML 4.126]

ATHABASCA COUNTRY {æth-ə-BASS-kə, -kee} The fur-rich region of north-central Canada named for Lake Athabasca. A Cree name meaning 'reedy or grassy place.'

it [Porcupine River] *would afford a very favorable communication to the Athebaskay country, from whence the British N. W. Company derive so large a portion of their valuable furs.* [3 May 05 ML 4.103]

ATONEMENT A sense of equality or harmony. The modern meaning refers to the restoration of such feeling between two people. The word originated in the phrase *at onement*, the state in which two people are *at one* with one another.

the Officer Commanding Gave Each...Some Small presents which made them all on an Eaqual Satisfactory Atonement for their Visit. [3 Aug 04 JW 11.050]

ATSINA* {æt-SEE-nə} An Algonquian-speaking plains people of Alberta, Saskatchewan, and Montana, who at times joined a confederation headed by the BLACKFOOT. Their language is closely related to that of their relatives, the Arapaho, of the central Great Plains. They also were known as the GROS VENTRES *of the Prairies*, and the MINITARIS and BIG BELLIES *of Fort de Prairie*. It is a Blackfoot name, perhaps borrowed from Plains Cree *ahtsiyiniw*, 'stranger, enemy; Atsina.'

AWL, MOCCASIN- A pointed hand-tool used to punch holes in leather when making and repairing moccasins and other items. Awls were useful to the party, and a valuable trade-good.

Indian Presents...4 Groce Mockerson awls assorted [Jun 03 ML in Jackson Letters (ed. 2) 1.072]

Saddlers seat awls...answer for mockasin awls [Jun 03 ML in Jackson Letters (ed. 2) 1.074]

they [Chopunnish]*...seem anxious always to obtain articles of utility, such as knives, axes, tommahawks, kettles blankets and mockerson alls.* [13 May 06 ML 7.253]

AWNING {ɔ-ning} A piece of canvas stretched like a tent, as over the open part of a BOAT or PIROGUE, for protection from sun and rain.

we assembled the Cheifs & Warriors under an Orning and delivered a Speech [19 Aug 04 WC 2.490]

having no shelter on land I betook myself to the orning of the perogue which I had, formed of Elkskin [6 Aug 06 ML 8.149]

Whitehouse likewise used a spelling with *-r-* in his first draft, but corrected it to *awning* in his second version.

the wind shifted in N. W. and took the Sail of a Sudden and had it not been for the eairning and mast She would have turned up Side down. [14 May 05 JW 11.156]

AX, BATTLE- Also **war-ax**. A trade-ax with a diamond-shaped blade about 8 inches long, extending at right angles from the end of a handle.

The blacksmith makes war-axes, and other axes to cut wood [26 Jan 05 PG 10.071]

they are pecuarly attatched to a battle ax formed in a very inconvenient manner in my opinion. [5 Feb 05 ML 3.286]

AX, FALLING- Large ax for felling trees.

the articles to be deposited...consisted of 2 best falling axes [10 Jun 05 ML 4.275]

AX, SQUAW- A smaller trade-ax, of the sort preferred by Indian women for wood-gathering.

as we Got the Blacksmiths Shop fixed they Brought their Squaw axes & kittle to fix [29 Dec 04 JO 9.106]

AXLETREE {ÆX-(t)'l-tree} Fixed beam of wood, or axle, on the ends of which the wheels of the expedition's portage wagons were mounted. Ordway's spelling suggests a pronunciation analogous to the common dialect pronunciation of *ax* {æxt}. *See* TRUCKLE.

we have made two axeltrees of the mast of the white peroge [17 Jun 05 ML 4.303]

4 men Set at makeing axtletrees and repair the carriages [30 Jun 05 JO 9.177]

AZIMUTH {ÆZ-ə-məth} The angular distance of an observed object from some reference point. A magnetic azimuth is measured from magnetic north, which differs from true north by the amount of VARIATION.

by means of this instrument [circumferentor] *adjusted with the sperit level, I have taken the magnetic azimuth of the sun and pole Star.* [22 Jul 04 ML 2.413]

> Azimuths were usually given within 90-degree quadrants of the compass. *S 88° W. 2 miles* [2.283], for instance, means 88 degrees clockwise from due south, or almost due west. Occasionally, older nautical terminology was used in which the compass circle is divided into 32 equal *points*, each of 11¼ degrees. In the following example, the bearing is to be read "southeast by south," signifying a direction 11¼ degrees clockwise toward the south from due southeast (in other words, half way between southeast and south-southeast):
>
> *Set out at 7 oClock, under a Jentle Braise from the S, E by S* [6 Jun 04 WC 2.281] *See* COURSE.

B

BACK[1] Inland from a river.

The district of Commandant Lorimiere [Cape Girardeau, Missouri] *estends from the grand bend of the Mississippi to Apple River without limitation back* [23 Nov 03 ML 2.108]

The wood land...is...of a good quallity as far as our hunters was back [26–29 Jun 04 WC 2.332]

back the plains become leavel and extencive. [27 Jul 06 WC 8.238]

the Mahars...had fields of corn growing at the back part of the bottom [4 Sep 06 JO 9.358]

Also, to lie inland from.

a fine preare...Baks the Mussiry [21 Jul 04 JW 11.043]

BACK[2] The sloping portion of a fireplace above and behind the hearth, requiring more heat-resistant materials than the sticks and clay walls of the rest of the chimney.

1 of the pearogues Sent a Short distance down the River for Stone for the Back of our chimneys[.] 4 backs made [21 Nov 04 JO 9.097]

we found that our huts Smoaked by the high winds…we built backs and enside chimneys in our huts which made them much more comfortable than before. [26–27 Dec 05 JO 9.262]

BACKLOAD A load carried on the back by one person.

we all harnised up our back loads of the baggage to make an eairly Steart in the morning. [25 Jun 05 JW 11.211]

I then returned with a back load of white roots [cous] to the Encampment. [22 May 06 JO 9.313]

BACKTRACK The route by which one has arrived, when followed in the reverse direction. Also *back route.*

we pursued the back tarck of these Indians [Shoshone] [13 Aug 05 ML 5.077]

it was…possible that they may have taken our back rout [7 Jul 06 WC 8.169]

BACKWATER {BACK-wah-tə} Water of a river inundating a tributary's lower reaches.

I…found the Creek only Contained back water for 1 mile up [19 Jun 05 WC 4.310]

BAIT To feed (an animal).

halted to baite our horses. [24 Jul 06 JO 9.340]

BALD Bare of timber. (*Bald-pated* means 'bald-headed.')

This Prarie I call Ball pated Prarie, from a range of Ball Hills parrelel to the river [16 Jul 04 WC 2.384]

bottoms wider, hills on the right is bald [7 Sep 05 WC 5.194]

over a steep high balld toped hill for 2 M. [6 Jul 06 ML 8.094]

BALL A lead bullet loaded singly into a gun, often contrasted with SHOT. *See* LEAD, MUSKET, POT-METAL, POWDER, RIFLE, SWIVEL.

Capt. [Clark] Shot Several times at one [elk] but his rifle carried a Small Ball [8 Aug 04 JO 9.036]

most of those nations have Guns but find it much Cheaper to kill their game with arrows than with Ball [winter 04–05 WC 3.484]

the hail was as large as musket balls [6 Jul 05 ML 4.364]

a smal onion about the size of a musquit ball [22 Jul 05 ML 4.416]

shot at a mark with the indians, struck the mark with 2 balls. dist. 220 yds. [12 May 06 ML 7.249]

A *ball screw* was used to extract a bullet lodged in the gun-barrel.

Arms & Accoutrements...15 Ball Screws [Jun 03 ML in Jackson Letters (ed. 2) 1.070]

BALLAST Added weight placed low in a boat's hull to help keep the vessel upright and stable.

the white pearogue could hardly Sail for want of Ballass, we put in Several kegs of pork &.C. [21 Aug 04 JO 9.042]

To load ballast aboard a boat.

We were employed in putting Stones in our Canoes to ballast them. [12 Nov 05 JW 11.392]

BALLOT {French bæ-LO} A bale of trade-goods or furs, weighing approximately 100 pounds, two of which normally were backpacked by each man on a PORTAGE. French for 'small bale,' from *balle* 'bale.'

The rout which I should propose to carry on this trade...is from St Louis by the Missouri...in Balluax of [blank] Weight [c. Sep 06 WC 8.412]

BALSAM[1] {BɔL-səm} Colloquial designation for various true fir species (genus *Abies*) or Douglas fir (*Pseudotsuga menziesii*), so named for exuding clear, fragrant pitch. Pitch was applied to CAULK and PAY expedition boats.

the pine cedar and balsum fir grow on the mountains in irregular assemleages [19 Jul 05 ML 4.402]

a narrow bottom of alder & Small balsam between the Ponds and the Mountn. [18 Nov 05 WC 6.065]

balsam

we Continue to put up the Streight butifull balsom pine on our houses [13 Dec 05 WC 6.124]

BALSAM[2] Various medicines and aromatic ointments generically termed in druggist's Latin, *balsamum.*

Balsam copaiba, a stimulant and diuretic, is a resin exuded by a South American tree.

¼ [lb.] Bals. Copaiboe [$].37 [26 May 03 in Jackson Letters (ed. 2) 1.081]

I...anointed her a little with balsom Capivia. [6 May 06 WC 7.217]

Turlington's Balsam of Life was a popular cure-all of the time, an 1744 patent having been granted in London. *Turlington's* became available in the American colonies in the 1760s and was sold under that name until 1907, when it was reformulated and marketed as *tincture of benzoin.*

Medicine...4 oz Turlingtons Balsam [June 03 ML in Jackson Letters (ed. 2) 1.073]

Tincture of benzoin also was called *balsamum traumaticum* or 'wound ointment.'

¼ [lb. Bals.] Traumat. [26 May 03 in Jackson Letters (ed. 2) 1.081]

BANDEAU {BAN-doh} Head-band.

the [Shoshone] *men frequently wear the skin of a fox or a broad strip of that of the otter around the forehead and head in form of a bando.* [21 Aug 05 ML 5.135]

A bando of some kind usually surrounds the head [13 May 06 ML 7.253]

BANDITTI Gang of outlaws, Italian for 'those who are banned or banished.'

Our officers proceeded on...not wishing to have any further connection with such a banditti of Villains. [28 Sep 04 JW 11.091]

BAR[1] {bah} A deposit of mud, sand, or gravel obstructing a waterway. *See* SAND.

Past another bear or ripple with more dificulty [30 Aug 03 ML 2.065]

if I can reach, and get over the George-town barr...I can get on [3 Sep 03 ML 2.070]

Saw Gravelly bars which was the first we Saw on this [Missouri] *River.* [9 Apr 05 JO 9.128]

passed Som bad Sand bares [4 Aug 04 CF 9.392]

BAR[2] Also **bier**, **beare** {BEE-ə} Mosquito-net, a light-weight fabric suspended over a sleeping person as a barrier to insects while allowing air to pass. Biddle [4.412] noted that the biers were *made of duck or gauze.* The word is first recorded in English as *baire* in 1775, a borrowing of the North American French term *baire* (or *ber*), meaning 'barrier; mosquito-net.' *See* INDURABLE.

the Musquetoes are extreemly troublesome this evening and I...left my bier, of course suffered considerably, and promised in my wrath that I will never be guil[t]*y of a similar peice of negligence while on this voyage.* [16 Jul 05 ML 4.387]

the men are all fortunately supplyed with musquetoe biers [21 Jul 05 ML 4.412]

those tormenting insects found their way into My beare and tormented me the whole night. [3 Aug 06 WC 8.275]

the bier in which the woman [Sacagawea] *carrys her child and all it's cloaths wer swept away as they lay at her feet* [29 Jun 05 ML 4.341]

> Sacagawea probably carried her infant son Jean Baptiste on her back, perhaps slung in a mosquito-bar, though materials used for this purpose usually would have been heavier, such as blanket cloth or an animal hide. ◆The word *bier/bear* might refer instead to a cradleboard, a rigid framed carrier used by an Indian woman to haul a baby on her back. In this context, the word may have had a different origin, derived from the expedition's ENGAGÉS use of the archaic French word *ber* (also *bers, biers*), 'cradle.' By the 18th century, *ber* was replaced by *berceau* in standard French, but *ber* still is applied in the sense of 'cradle' in rural Quebec and the francophone areas of western Canada.◆ Near the Great Falls of the Missouri, Sacagawea's *bier/bear* was lost in a flash-flood that nearly swept away Charbonneau, William Clark, and her.

the woman lost her Childs Bear & Clothes [29 Jun 05 WC 4.343]

BARGE {bahdj} = BOAT. Generally, a vessel considerably broader than a keelboat. Here, however, referring to the Corps of Discovery's keelboat.

The Big Barge corked & Got ready to descend the Missouri. [30 Mar 05 JO 9.124]

Fort Mandan...we dismissed the barge and crew with orders to return...to S. Louis [7 Apr 05 ML 4.007]

BARKS {bahks} The quinine in the *Peruvian bark* of the South American cinchona tree kills the malarial parasites in the blood of malaria victims, thus relieving fever, which is the disease's main symptom. Barks also were used to treat other disorders, including non-malarial fevers, against which it was ineffective.

I found that two dozes of barks and opium...had produced an alteration in her pulse for the better [16 Jun 05 ML 4.300]

Lewis applied barks in dressing a wound in his backside (suffered in an accidental shooting by Cruzatte, who mistook him for an elk in the willows). *See* RIFLE.

I had last evening applyed a poltice of peruvian barks...wrighting in my present situation is extreemly painfull [12 Aug 06 ML 8.158]

Lewis purchased a stock of barks (and most of the expedition's other medicines) from Gillaspy and Strong, a Philadelphia pharmacy. *Pulvis corticis Peruviani* is druggist's Latin for 'powder of Peruvian bark.'

15 lbs. best powder'd Bark [Jun 03 ML in Jackson Letters (ed. 2) 1.073]

15 lb. Pulv. Cort. Peru $30.00 [26 May 03 ML in Jackson Letters (ed. 2) 1.080]

BARK-STONE = CASTOR. *See* STONE.

BARREL A container of fitted, elongate pieces of wood (*staves*) tightly bound by iron straps, and closed at the ends with round wood pieces (called *heads*) secured in grooves cut into the stave ends. Barrels in the following example held about 19 gallons each. *See* BILGE, COOPER, FLAG, FROE, HOWEL, KEG.

Articles in readiness for the Voyage...7 Barrels of Salt of 2 bus: each...750 W [May 04 WC 2.217]

BASE Also **prisoner's base**. Originally called (*prison*) *bars*, this chasing-game was played by two teams, each with a home base, the object being to tag opposing players and imprison them. *See* QUOITS.

our party exercised themselves running and playing games called base [8 Jun 06 JO 9.320]

Several foot races were run by the men of our party and the Indians; after which our party divided and played at prisoners base untill night. [8 June 06 WC 7.347]

Prisoner's base usually was a children's game, but adults have long played it as well. An English law enacted in 1332 during Edward III's reign, and quoted in the original French in *OED,* decreed that "no child or other person shall play at bars or other games in the vicinity of Westminster Palace [in London] when

Parliament is in session." (French had been the language of the English government and elite since the Norman conquest in AD 1066.) The confusion of the forms *bars* and *base* probably arose from the earlier pronunciation of both as {bahz or bæz}. ◆It recently has been suggested that *base*, a running game with bases, may be one of the antecedents of *baseball* <http://www.sabruk.org/examiner/05/sportinglife.html> (2004). Perhaps the men of the Corps of Discovery played an ancestral form of the national game.◆

BASILICON {bə-SILL-ə-kahn} An ointment compounded of pine resin, bee's wax, and lard. From the Greek word meaning 'royal,' with reference to the medication's supposed SOVEREIGN virtues, particularly in treating skin disorders.

Medicine...2 lbs. Yellow Basilicum [Jun 03 ML in Jackson Letters (ed. 2) 1.073]

In the following example, solid bear oil perhaps answered for lard.

the inflamation has subsided intirely, we discontinued the poltice, and applyed a plaster of basilicon [5 Jun 06 ML 7.334]

BAT A bird, the nighthawk, *Chordeiles minor.*

There are a number of large bat or goatsucker here [30 Jun 05 ML 4.344]

Also, the small nocturnal flying mammal.

saw the first leather winged bat. [16 Apr 05 ML or WC 4.094]

BATEAU {modern standard bæ-TOH or BÆ-toh; BÆ-too in the journals?} A boat of typical French-Canadian design, flat-bottomed with tapering ends, smaller than a KEELBOAT and larger than a canoe. (Lewis & Clark use the French plural form as singular.)

◆Reasoning backwards, Clark's spelling *Batteau* for *Batture* (*see* BATTURE) implies a pronunciation of *bateau* different from the standard bæ-TOH or BÆ-toh, perhaps something like BÆ-tə. The pronunciation BÆ-too is recorded from New York and Pennsylvania (Stevens *et al.*, series 21645, p. 264), and BÆ-tee occurs at least occasionally in modern dialects, including those of Newfoundland, New Jersey, and Louisiana. ◆ Twenty bateaux built by the British army on the Ohio in 1763 were 32 feet long and 6 feet 4 inches broad at the top, tapering to 3 feet 4 inches at the bottom (Stevens *et al.*, series 21654, p. 111).

Those boats are from Canada in the batteaux form...their length about 30 feet and the width 8 feet & pointed bow & Stern, flat bottom and rowing Six ores [20 Sep 06 WC 8.367]

the yellowstone...possesses suficient debth of water for battauxs even to the mountains [3 Aug 06 WC 8.278]

Here, referring to the expedition's BOAT.

The expedition was embarked on board a batteau and two periogues. [14 May 04 PG 10.001]

when the Batteaux is under way, one Sergt. shall be stationed at the helm [26 May 04 ML 2.256]

A niew mast made for the Batteaux to day. [15 Aug 04 JO 9.040]

BATTERY {BÆ-tree} An object designed to be struck by something else, to be *battered*. Here, it applies to a game played with sticks and pottery rings.

they had a Battery fixed for the rings to Stop against. [15 Dec 04 JO 9.104]

Also, that which *does* the battering, such as an artillery emplacement (though in Whitehouse's following example, it describes the appearance of natural features).

Nature had formed some batterys and Redoubts [7 Jul 04 JW 11.036]

Lewis referred to the female genitalia as the *Battery of Venus* after the Roman goddess of love. *See* AMORITE, VENEREAL.

when she stoops...this battery of Venus is not altogether impervious to the inquisitive and penetrating eye of the amorite. [19 Mar 06 ML 6.435]

♦The latter quotation might be a metaphorical reference to protected cannon emplacements just barely visible to a penetrating eye, or perhaps is a play on the word *battery*, as a synonym of FRIZZEN. In firing a flintlock weapon, the COCK, holding the flint, strikes the *battery* (*see* FRIZZEN) in a way perhaps thought reminiscent of copulation.♦

BATTURE {BÆTCH-er, BÆTCH-ə in modern English, ba-TÜR in French, and probably BÆ-too or BÆ-tə in the journals} A French term for SHOAL, specifically a sand or mud bank formed on the inside of a river-bend or rocky reef.

passed a Batteau [batture] *or Sand roleing where the Boat was nearly turning over* [13 Jun 04 WC 2.296]

Also, a wide beach along a river; a BOTTOM. In modern English and lower Mississippi Cajun French, it means the land lying between a river and a levee.

un batteur La benne [Benoit?] *River* [25 Jun 04 WC 9.383]

Here, with French *a deux charmes* meaning 'with two hornbeam trees.'

a pt. S. Sd. called Batue a De charm [4 Jul 04 WC 2.275]

BAYOU {BY-yoh, BY-you, BAY-you, and probably other pronunciations, including some with the stress on the second syllable; *cf.* the Spanish spelling *bayú*} A small, usually slow-flowing watercourse either connecting with or isolated from a larger body of water, especially along the lower Mississippi. (**South, Midland**)

Bayou originated in the Choctaw word *bayuk* and was adopted into English from French. Lewis & Clark first applied the term shortly after reaching the Mississippi, where they encountered French Canadians familiar with lower Louisiana's local topographic terminology. The explorers continued using *bayou* throughout their waterborne travels for any smaller river channel, spelling it with incredible variety.

the Island is formed by a byo which makes out nearly in the...observed course of the river [18 Nov 03 ML 2.093]

passed the mouth of a Beyeu leading from a Lake [4 Jul 04 CF 9.385]

saw a vast number of beaver in many large dams which they had maid in various bayoes of the [Jefferson] *river which are distributed to the distance of three or four miles on this side of the river over an extensive bottom* [30 July 05 ML 5.014]

BEADS Glass beads were among the most valued of all trade goods. *See* KAMOSUK, PENNYWEIGHT, WAMPUM.

we now sold our canoes for a few strands of beads [24 Apr 06 ML 7.163]

[The Nez Perce] *do not appear to be so much devoted to baubles as most of the nations... blue beads however may form an exception...this article among all the nations of this country may be justly compared to goald or silver among civilized nations.* [13 May 06 ML 7.253]

BEAM The main trunk of an antler.

with the mule deer the horns consist of two beams which at the distance of 4 or 6 inches from the head divide themselves each into two equal branches [10 May 05 ML 4.137]

BEAR (the animal) {BÆə was a common southern pronunciation}

he Saw three Bar on the other Side of the Prarie [27 Dec 04 WC 2.142]

by the time we butchered thes two elk and bar it was nearly dark [10 Jul 06 ML 8.099]

BEAR, BROWN or WHITE or YELLOW = (GRIZZLY) BEAR.

we saw also many tracks of the white bear of enormous size [13 Apr 05 ML 4.031]

Ordway shows that he pronounced *bear* and BAR[1] the same way.

killed a verry large bair which the natives and the french tradors call white [5 May 05 JO 9.143]

[Bratton] *had shot a brown bear which...turned on him and pursued him a considerable distance but he had wounded it so badly that it could not overtake him* [11 May 05 ML 4.141]

I am induced to believe that the Brown, the white and the Grizly bear of this country are the same species [13 Jun 05 ML 4.286]

while I was gazing...on the poor anamal [a buffalo just shot] *discharging blood in streams from his mouth and nostrils, expecting him to fall every instant, and having entirely forgotton to reload my rifle, a large white, or reather brown bear, had perceived and crept on me within 20 steps before I discovered him* [14 Jun 05 ML 4.292]

grizzly bear

BEAR, GRIZZLY Large brown bear of the North American West (*Ursus horribilis*), distinguished from the smaller, less

aggressive, black bear. The journalists heretofore generally wrote *white bear. Grizzly* originally meant 'gray.'

in the evening we Saw a Brown or Grisley beare on a Sand beech [5 May 05 WC 4.114]

BEARD {BE-əd} Barb of a fish-GIG or thorn.

a bone from 4 to 6 inches long, one end Sharp the other with a whole to fasten on the end of the pole with a beard to the large end [21 Aug 05 WC 5.139]

prickly pear

Hence **bearded**.

Prickly peare...with Strong Thorns which is So birded as to draw the Pear from the Cluster after penetrateing our feet. [8 Sep 05 WC 5.191]

BEAR-GRASS A variety of plants with narrow, sword-like leaves growing in a basal cluster around a tall flower-stalk. Bear-grass currently is classified in what is thought to be an overly-inclusive lily family. (**South, South Midland**). For other fiber-producing materials, *see* (WHITE) CEDAR, SILK-GRASS, WATAP.

> Various species of yucca are widespread in the United States. A member of the agave family, it is a favorite food of black bears. *Bear-grass* is a frontier-English synonym for Adam's needle, *Yucca filamentosa*, which since the early 17th century was called *silk-grass* in the more settled parts of the Southeast. The *OED* first records *bear-grass* in 1750 from Thomas Walker's diary of an exploratory journey from Virginia through eastern Kentucky. (Physician and surveyor Walker was a close friend of Peter Jefferson, the father of Thomas Jefferson.) ◆When Walker wrote "Beargrass" on April 12, he probably meant Adam's needle or the closely related *Y. flaccida:*◆ "[R]ode four miles to Bear grass River [later called the Powell, near Cumberland Gap]. Small Ceder Trees are very plenty on the flat ground nigh the River and some Barberry Trees on the East Side of the River. on the Banks is some Beargrass." This suggests a sunny, probably sandy, habitat favorable to yucca. On the Ohio River at what would become Louisville, Kentucky, *Beargrass Creek* was a main landing for Pennsylvania riverboats as early as the 1770s.

In southern South Dakota, Clark's *bear grass* is probably soapweed, *Yucca glauca*, common in the Plains states. ◆By *Rhue*, Clark probably means a species of the SUMAC genus *Rhus.*◆

I observe Bear grass & Rhue in the Sides of the hills [2 Sep 04 WC 3.040]

Lewis & Clark extended the name *beargrass* to *Xerophyllum tenax* in the bunchflower family, which has long, rough-edged leaves and grows in drier locations in western Montana, north Idaho, and the western parts of Washington, Oregon, and northern California. Its tough, fibrous leaves were used in basket-making, hence bear-grass was a prominent item in intertribal TRADE. (Another species, *X. asphodeloides*, is found in New Jersey and western Virginia and North Carolina.)

7 Squars Came over the portage loaded with Dried fish & Beargrass [2 Nov 05 WC 6.007] *their baskets are formed of cedar bark and beargrass so closely interwoven...that they are watertight without the aid of gum or rosin* [17 Jan 06 ML 6.215]

Bargrass...grows only on their mountains near the Snowey region; the blade is about 3/8 of an inch wide and 2 feet long Smothe plient & Strong; the young blades which are white...are those which are most Commonly employ'd, particularly in their neatest work. [17 Jan 06 WC 6.217]

BEAT UP ONE'S QUARTERS {KWɔ-təz} To pay someone an unexpected visit. In 1708, Thomas Nairne (A. Moore, 53) noted, "the Chactaws often beat up the quarters and kill Travellers in this path."

the bear were about our camp all last night, we have therefore determined to beat up their quarters tomorrow, and kill them or drive them from their haunts [1 Jul 05 ML 4.350]

BEAVER {BEE-və} *Castor canadensis,* whose fur was the preeminent economic asset of the early northwest frontier.

It gives us [Arikara] *pain that we do not Know how to work the Beaver* [11 Oct 04 WC 3.159]

Beaver activity is a major factor in shaping stream environments. *See* BAYOU.

the river in many places among the clusters of islands is constantly changing the direction of such sluices as the beaver are capable of stoping or of 20 yds. in width. this anamal...I beleive to be very instrumental in adding to the number of islands with which we find the river crouded. [24 Jul 05 ML 4.423]

Beaver could be defensive.

Drewyer killed two beaver and shot [a] *third which bit his knee very badly and escaped* [7 Jul 06 ML 8.096]

one of the party wounded a beaver, and my dog as usual swam in to catch it; the beaver bit him through the hind leg and cut the artery; it was with great difficulty that I could stop the blood [19 May 05 ML 4.166]

BEAVERHEAD ROCK A prominent limestone outcrop in southwestern Montana. Clark's spelling of the Indian name represents Shoshone HAH-*nay-ham* 'of the beaver' and *pahp* 'head,' ◆plus a diminutive suffix◆. Note that in this Shoshone dialect, the word for 'head' has no *m; see* POMP, YAMPA.

proceeded...into that butifull and extensive Vally open and fertile which we Call the beaver head Vally which is the Indian name in their language Har na Hap pap Chah. from the No. of those animals in it & a pt. of land resembling the head of one [10 Jul 06 WC 8.175]

a high point of land...which the Shoshones call the beavers head. [11 Jul 06 WC 8.177]

BEEF Edible meat, not necessarily of domestic cattle.

we suped this evening as we had dined[,] on horse-beef. [7 May 06 ML 7.221] *they killed eleven buffaloe...the bulls are now generally much fatter than the cows and are fine beef.* [11 Jul 06 ML 8.106]

we have plenty of Elk beef...and a little salt [16 Jan 06 ML 6.211]

BELLOWS A device for producing a strong blast of air in operating a forge.

The black Smiths fixed up the bellowses & made a main Spring to Capt [Lewis's] air Gun [10 Jun 05 JW 11.192]

BIG BELLY A translation of the French GROS VENTRE, referring to either of two native peoples.

= HIDATSA:

the Sioux has latterly taken horses from the Big Bellies or Minitaries [25 Oct 04 WC 3.196]

we gave the Swivvel to the Big Belleys or Grousevauntaus. [15 Aug 06 JO 9.350]

Chabonoe our big belly interpeter [18 Dec 04 WC 3.259]

= ATSINA:

the Big bellies of Fort de Prarie Killed great numbers of the Shoshons [23 Jun 06 WC 8.048]

BIG BEND A large loop in the Missouri River in central South Dakota, 30 miles around by water, and only a little over a mile by land across the neck. *See* DETOUR, GORGE.

Detchd. 3 men across the Big bend...to stay and hunt & jurk provisions [20 Sep 04 WC 3.092]

BIGHORN A wild sheep (*Ovis canadensis*) of the Rocky Mountains, with thick, curved horns. *See* ARGALI, IBEX.

Capt. C. killed a big horn on these clifts which himself and party dined on. [1 Aug 05 ML 5.027]

BILE One of the humors, the imbalance of which in the body was thought to cause illness. Variant spellings are largely a result of the similarity in pronouncing *bile* and *boil*. *See* BILIOUS, RUSH'S PILLS.

Gibson's fever still continues obstenate...I gave him a doze of Dr. Rush's which...I have found extreemly efficatious in fevers which are in any measure caused by the presence of boil. [16 Feb 06 ML 6.318]

BILGE A bulge in the side of something, as of a BARREL, or island.

N 51° W to a Belge of an Isd [6 Jun 04 WC 2.282]

Today, as here, the word refers to the lowest portion of a vessel's hull, where *bilgewater* accumulates.

the Lockers which is covered with Tarpoling...Threw of the water & prevented any quantity Getting into Bilge of the Boat [14 Jul 04 WC 2.378]

BILIOUS {BILL-ee-yəs} Affected or caused by excessive BILE in the body. **Bilious fever** was malaria. *See* AGUE.

The fever and ague and bilious fevers here [on the Ohio River] *commence their banefull oppression* [14 Sep 03 ML 2.081]

Capt. C. thought himself somewhat bilious and had not had a passage for several days; I prevailed on him to take a doze of Rushes pills [27 Jul 05 ML 4.436]

Lewis obtained the Corps' basic medical supplies in Philadelphia. *See* RUSH'S PILLS.

50. doz. Bilious Pills to Order of B. Rush...[$]5.00 [26 May 03 ML in Jackson Letters (ed. 2) 1.080]

Floyd's fatal ailment probably was an acute abdominal infection.

Serjeant Floyd is taken verry bad all at onc with a Beliose Chorlick [19 Aug 04 WC 2.493]

we named this Hill Serjeant Floyds bluff. The disease which occasion'd his death, was a Bilious cholic, which baffled all medical aid [20 Aug 04 JW 11.058]

BISCUIT A hard-baked bread in flat cakes, which kept well unless exposed to moisture. An Old French word meaning 'twice baked.'

my bisquit was much injurd I had it picked and put up in these [oil-skin] *baggs* [17 Sep 03 ML 2.084]

half a bisquit each and some jirk of Elk [17 Sep 04 ML 3.081]

every thing in the perogue was wet damiged a keg of powder a bag of buiscuit and... other articles [8 Apr 05 JO 9.127]

BITUMINOUS {bye-TOO-mə-nəs} (Of geological substances) tarry, impregnated with inflammable organic matter.

we procieve Several Stratums of bituminious Substance which resembles Coal [11 Apr 05 WC 4.023]

BLACK HILLS The captains applied the name broadly to several mountain ranges east of the Rockies proper, including today's Black Hills of western South Dakota. The name is a translation of CÔTE NOIRE, or of native names meaning the same.

The White Turkey of the black hills [of which L&C editor Elliott Coues remarked in a note between lines, *rara avis!*, a rare bird!] [17 Sep 04 ML 3.085]

The high Country in which we are at present...I take to be a continuation of what the Indians as well as the French Engages call the Black hills. [26 May 05 WC 4.204]

the Coat Nor or Black Mountains [26 Jul 06 WC 8.232]

BLACKFOOT An Algonquian-speaking people of the Montana and Alberta prairies.

Those people [Nez Perce] *are much affraid of the black foot indians, and the Big Bellies of Fort deprarie establishment.* [12 May 06 WC 7.250]

BLACKGUARD {BLAG-əd} Villainous.

two French Perogues pass up the river to day, and peregoue with black guard Americans, passed down the river [24 Dec 03 WC 2.140]

Hence, to abuse verbally.

one of the [Upper Chinookan] *Indians could...Speak Some words English Such as curseing and blackguard* [4 Nov 05 JO 9.250]

7 of them [Teton] *halted on the top of the hill and blackguarded us, told us to come across and they would kill us all* [30 Aug 06 WC 8.331]

BLACKSMITH One who worked iron with forge, hammer, and anvil, and also often a farrier (shoer of horses) or horse-doctor.

The blacksmith was employed shoeing the horses [13 Feb 05 JW 11.125]

Hannerberry [probably Patrick Heneberry], *the blacksmith has traveled far to the north, & Visited the Mandols [Mandans]* [1 Jan 04 WC 2.144]

Heneberry probably was warmly welcomed by the Mandan—early in their relations with whites, Indians across the frontier recognized the value of craftsmen who repaired firearms, patched kettles, and manufactured axes and other tools. (*See* SHIELDS.) In treaty negotiations, natives often requested a blacksmith to reside with them. In 1695, an Iroquois spokesman requested that the British "Let our Indians have powder & lead instead of rum Let the Blacksmith repair our armes for nothing" (*DCHNY* 4.123); in 1762, a Sauk chief asked the English "to send a Smith...to mend our Guns and Tomhawks &c. as we are greatly Straitned...to support our families Occasioned by our Guns being out of Repair" (Stevens *et al.*, series 21655, p. 170).

BLANK Point-blank; that is, at so short a range that any falling of the projectile in flight need not be taken into account when aiming and firing a weapon. From French *blanc* 'white,' referring to the center area of a target.

the Indians were pointing their arrows blank [25 Sep 04 WC 3.112]

BLAZE To remove, as with a hatchet, a patch of bark from a tree as a marker, or signal. The word is distantly related to BRAROW.

one man Sent back...to Blase a tree...to notify the party on Shore of our passing [9 Jul 04 WC 2.362]

To mark a route, as here on the return through north Idaho's Bitterroot Range.

follow the Indians...and get them to halt if possible, till the party should come up; but if not...follow them on and blaze the way [23 Jun 06 PG 10.243]

BLEAT UP {blate} In deer hunting, to imitate a fawn's call.

The does now haveing their young the hunters can blait them up, and...kill them with more facillity [23 Jun 06 WC 8.047]

BLEED To remove blood from a patient by opening a vein, usually with a lancet, in order to treat disease.

the Indian woman verry Sick, I blead her which appeared to be of great Service to her [11 Jun 05 WC 4.279]

Whitehouse…much heated and fortiegued on his arrivall dank a very heavy draught of water and was taken almost instanly extreemly ill. his pulse were very full and I therefore bled him plentifully from which he felt great relief. I had no other instrument with which to perform this opperation but my pen knife, however it answered very well. [26 June 05 ML 4.334]

Drewyer was taken last night with a violent pain in his Side. I bled him. [17 Mar 06 WC 6.430]

BLIND (Of a trail or path) indistinct, difficult to follow.

the road became so blind that it could not be that which we had followed [10 Aug 05 ML 5.064]

BLOW, IN In bloom.

the river bottoms form one emence garden of roses, now in full bloe. [4 Jun 05 ML 4.256]

BLUBBER {BLUH-bə} To bubble. (**South, South Midland**)

this Spring…actually blubbers with heat for 20 paces below where it rises. [7 Jul 06 WC 8.170]

BLUNDERBUSS {BLUN-də-bus} A short-barreled, smooth-bored gun with a flared muzzle that made loading easier. From Dutch *donderbus*, literally 'thunder-gun.' *See* PRIMING, SWIVEL.

the buffalo…had also broken the spindle, pivit, and shattered the stock of one of the bluntderbushes on board [29 May 05 ML 4.215]

we Saluted the Village by three rounds from our blunderbuts [21 Sep 06 WC 8.369]

BOAT The usual term for the expedition's KEELBOAT, which was about 55 feet long, 8 feet wide, and rode 4 feet deep in the water when loaded; *see* DRAW. Patterned after Spanish river-galleys of the 1790s, it was designed to carry about 8 tons, had one MAST (on the Ohio) or two (on the Missouri), and was equipped with about 20 oars. The upbound crew on the Missouri included about 25 men, while downstream in the spring of 1805, the complement was 9. Sailing downriver required less manpower. *See* BATEAU.

after Loading the Boat maned her with 20 oares & went the middle of the river & up the Mississippi a fiew miles [8 May 04 WC 2.213]

Capt. Clark went with Some men from the Big Boat to their assistance. [28 Aug 04 JO 9.046]

BOAT, IRON Lewis's specially fabricated boat built in the East, consisting of an iron frame (36 feet long and 26 inches deep) to be assembled in the wilderness and covered with animal skins attached with willow bark. The expedition hauled the packed metal frame up the Missouri, where the boat eventually was assembled and launched above the Great Falls for its intended purpose as transport up shallow streams over the Rockies and then for descending the Columbia. The vessel leaked like a sieve (for lack of pitch), and soon was dismantled and cached at the Great Falls, never to be used. Also called the *experiment,* and the *leather boat; see* also YAWL

had the frame of my Iron boat clensed of rust and well greased. [19 Jun 05 ML 4.309]

BOIL¹ {bīl, a common dialect pronunciation} A swollen, inflamed, and puss-filled infection under the skin, usually caused by staphylococcus bacteria. *See* BILE, RISING, TUMOR.

Ordway, Gibson & my Servent Sick Several with Biles on them & bruses [22 Dec 05 WC 6.135]

The tumors…were biles that broke out under the arms on the legs & generally in the parts most exposed to action. [c. Apr 10 NB in Jackson Letters (ed. 2) 2.512]

BOIL² A place in a river where the water is so turbulent that it appears to boil. *See* SUCK.

passed through the little narrows…bad whorly boils & Sucks. [24 Oct 05 WC 5.377]

BOIS BRULÉ {bah-BROO-lee; modern bah-BROOL} The French name—pronounced bwah-broo-LAY and literally meaning 'burnt woods'—of a band of the TETON (Lakota) or Yankton Sioux. It is not used in the journals in the common sense of a person with mixed native and Euro-American ancestry. *See* BURNT WOODS.

The Tetons Bois brûlé killed and took about 60 of them [Omaha] *last summer.* [winter 04–05 WC 3.399]

Ordway's spelling reveals the prevailing pronunciation.

we-u-che—head chief, of the Bob Brulee tribe [31 Aug 04 JO 9.048]

he had two Batteaux and 18 hands and are on their way to the babruleys and yanktons [3 Sep 06 JO 9.358]

BOIS ROUGE French for REDWOOD.

the only timber in this part of the Countrey is willow, a fiew Cotton trees…Boxalders and red wood. (Bois roche arrow wood) [3 Jul 05 WC 4.358]

BOIS ROULÉ {French bwah-roo-LAY} A French-Canadian name (literally 'rolled wood') for various dried plant materials smoked in pipes, often including the inner bark of willow or red-osier dogwood. *See* SMOKABLE.

polecats Skins, for to hold ther Bais roly for Smokeing [26 Sep 04 WC 3.117]

BOLD (Of a topographic feature) steep, prominent.

we came too…under a boald welltimbered bank which sheltered us from the wind [18 Apr 05 ML 4.051]

a bold Snow mountain…bears East [15 Jul 06 WC 8.187]

(Of a stream) fast, having a strong current. *See* HARD², STOUT, STRONG.

it is a beatifull bold runing stream [3 May 05 ML 4.103]

The little Missouri...sets in with a bould current [12 Apr 05 ML 4.026]

BOONE'S SETTLEMENT An American community on the north side of the Missouri near the mouth of the FEMME Osage River.

the Osage woman's river...waters a fertile well timbered country inhabited by about fifty American families. this part of the country is generally called Boon's settlement [winter 04–05 ML 3.338]

> Boone's settlement was founded in 1799 by Daniel Boone, on land granted by the Spanish government after he had left KENTUCKY (which he had explored and settled a quarter century earlier). Born in Pennsylvania of English Quaker parents and migrating with them to North Carolina, Boone is representative of the other main current of English-speaking settlers in the Mid-West, which met the Virginian speakers typified by Lewis & Clark.

BOOT, TO (Something additional) into the bargain. In modern use, it has come to mean simply *in addition*, without reference to trade.

we Swapped 7 horses which were lame...Gave Some Small articles to boot. [5 Sep 05 JW 11.301]

BOOTED (Of birds) having feathered legs.

This frenchman gives an account of a white booted turkey an inhabitant of the Cout Noie [1 Oct 04 WC 3.135]

BOTTOM¹ The flood-plain of a river, on which periodic floods deposit fertile alluvial soils. (**South, South Midland**). *See* AMERICAN BOTTOM.

this bottom...is certainly the richest land from it's being liable some times to be overflowed [2 Sep 03 ML 2.069]

the Snow Drifting from one bottom to another [28 Dec 04 WC 3.263]

This bottom we...Call fannys bottom [26 Mar 06 WC 7.017]

Also, as *second* or *third* or *high bottom*, an elevated river terrace; the remnant of an old flood-plain.

a Second bottom...rises to about 20 feet higher [than] *the first & is 1 m. wide* [15 Jul 06 WC 8.187]

BOTTOM² Endurance; the use of *bottom* in the sense of something that underlies and supports. *See* DURABLE.

if they [pronghorn] *happen accedentaly in the woodlands and are allarmed they run immediately to the plains, seeming to plaise a just confidence in their superior fleetness and bottom.* [25 Jul 05 ML 4.426]

BOW The forward end of a boat. *See* STERN.

Persons accustomed to the navigation of the Missouri and the Mississippi...take the precaution to load their vessels heavyest in the bow when they ascend the stream in order to avoid the danger incident to runing foul of the concealed timber [15 May 04 ML 2.230]

[a lower Columbia] Canoe... large, and ornimented with Images on the bow & Stern. That in the bow...Bear, and in Stern the picture of a man [5 Nov 05 WC 6.023]

BOWER {BOW-ə} A shelter.

we cleared away the willows & pitched our Tents and built boweries [22 Jul 04 JO 9.029]

Capt. Clark Sick. we built a bower for his comfort. [28 Jul 05 JO 9.191]

we saw som resent [Shoshone] bowers or small conic lodges formed with willow brush. [12 Aug 05 ML 5.073]

BOW-MAN Also **bowsman**. The member of a boat-crew stationed at the bow with a pole. *See* STERN-MAN.

our bow man Peter Crousat a half Mahar Indian [21 Jun 04 WC 2.312]

Sent George Drougher and ouer...Bowsman wo is aquainted with the nations [23 Jul 04 CF 9.389]

BOWLING-GREEN A smooth, level grassy area for lawn bowling.

the shortness and virdue of grass gave the plain the appearance...of beatifull bowlinggreen in fine order. [17 Sep 04 ML 3.080]

BRACE[1] As a measure of cloth or strung beads, approximately a FATHOM (six feet) in length. The word is labeled obsolete in *OED* (last recorded in 1710), and in the journals probably shows the influence of French *brasse* in the same sense. *See* LEAGUE, SCARLET.

our menetarre interpeter had received a present from Mr. Chaboilleiz of the N. W. Comapny of...3 Brace of Cloath 1 Brace of Scarlet [7 Mar 05 WC 3.310]

we gave to each woman of the lodge a brace of Ribon of which they were much pleased. [29 Oct 05 WC 5.351]

BRACE[2] A rope extending from either end of the yard of a (SQUARE) SAIL down to the deck. Used to control the angle of sail across the boat.

See LUFF for an example.

BRACKISH A salinity intermediate between seawater and fresh water, and sometimes having a laxative effect similar to GLAUBER'S SALTS.

all the Streems...So brackish that the water Can't be Drank without effecting the person making use of it as Globesalts [19 Oct 04 WC 3.184]

The Porpus is common on this coast and as far up the river as the water is brackish. [13 Mar 06 ML 6.410]

BRAINS   Animal brains, cooked into a mush containing emulsified oils for preparing leather. *See* GRAIN².

the 2 men...had killed 6 buffalow, and Saved only the tongues, & brains for to dress Skins. [3 Jul 05 JO 9.179]

The men...are still busily employed in dressing Elk's skins for cloathing, they find great difficulty for the want of branes [23 Jan 06 ML 6.230]

BRAN   The coarse outer parts of cereal grains, a byproduct when meal is produced during milling.

the horses appeared much fatieged I directed some meal brands given them moisened with a little water [12 Feb 05 ML 3.292]

BRANCH   A small stream, especially a tributary to a creek or other stream. *See* CREEK. (**South, South Midland**)

we Encamped at this Branch in a thickly timbered bottom which was Scercely large enough for us to lie leavil [16 Sep 05 WC 5.209]

Several hunters went on up the branch a hunting. [2 May 06 JO 9.303]

we followed the creek downwards...passing a stout branch at 1 m. [13 May 06 ML 7.252]

BRAROW   {BREH-roh, -rə} Badger (*Taxidea taxus*), a burrowing carnivore. From the standard French *blaireau*, originally meaning the white mark, or *badge*, on a badger's head, and related to the word BLAZE.

badger

one of the men killed a Shee Brarrow [7 Oct 04 WC 3.149]

Shabono was thrown from his horse to day in pursute of a Buffaloe, the hose unfortunately Steping into a Braroe hole and threw him over his head. [18 Jul 06 WC 8.200]

BRAVE   A warrior, a CONSIDERATE man. Lewis & Clark applied the word specifically in the American Indian sense twenty years before it was so recorded in the *OED*. The journals' first editor, Nicholas Biddle, glosses Clark's *Brave man* as 'Conside[rate] man' [3.122].

The name of this [Arikara] *Chief of War is...Raven brave.* [7 Apr 05 WC 4.011]

we caused all the old and brave men to set arround and smoke with us. [23 Apr 06 ML 7.160]

BREAK UP   (Of river ice) to break into pieces during thawing and float downstream. *See* DRIFT ICE.

the river brake up in places [2 Mar 05 WC 3.308]

we found a number of carcases of the Buffaloe lying along shore, which had been drowned...and lodged on shore by the high water when the river broke up [13 Apr 05 ML 4.031]

BREAKFAST {BRACK-fəst} While traveling by boat, the expedition's routine was to set out at LIGHT (before dawn) and stop for breakfast at a convenient place, by "8 A. M. our usual time of halting" [5.061]. *See* DINNER.

after Brackfast we were Visited by the Old Chief of the Big Bellies [29 Oct 04 WC 3.208]

Clark's spelling of the noun reveals a common dialect pronunciation. He uses the same form for the past tense of the verb, in place of *breakfasted*.

Killed a Buffalow on which we Brackfast [16 Jul 05 WC 4.387]

BREECH {britch} **Breeches** (or **britches**) are pants (**South, South Midland**). The word came to refer to a person's posterior intended to be covered by pants, and to the back end of a gun barrel.

I gave the Chief Comowooll a pare of sattin breechies with which he appeared much pleased. [3 Jan 06 ML 6.163]

[McNeal] *had not time to Shoote but drew his gun and Struck the bear across the head and broke off the brich of his gun and Stonded the bear So that he had time to climb a Sapling. the bear kept him on the tree about 3 hours.* [19 Jul 06 JO 9.338]

the ball had lodged in my breeches which I knew to be the ball of the short rifles such as that he [Cruzatte] *had* [11 Aug 06 ML 8.156]

BRICKBAT A piece of brick. Brickbats made handy weapons in street fights, with the meaning later extended to mean 'uncomplimentary criticism,' as in the expression *to hurl brickbats (at someone).*

the soil...has now become as firm as a brickbat [20 Jul 06 ML 8.118]

BRICKLE Brittle. Of Scottish or northern English origin. (**South, Midland**)

this timber [cottonwood] *is tall and heavy...Brickle & Soft* [9 Nov 04 WC 3.232]

BRIG A sailing ship with two masts carrying (SQUARE) SAILS. *See* SCHOONER, SHIP, SLOOP.

Davidson Visits this part of the Coast and river in a Brig for the purpose of Hunting the Elk [1 Jan 06 WC 6.156]

BRINDLE (Of an animal) marked with darker spots or streaks.

black white brown and brindle are the most usual colours [of Indian dogs]. [16 Feb 06 ML 6.318]

The large Black and Brindle Wolf is found as high up as the Mahars Village [undated WC 8.416]

BRISKET The ribs and breast-meat of an animal.

an excellent supper...of a marrowbone, a piece of brisket of boiled Elk that had the appearance of a little fat on it. [7 Feb 06 WC 6.285]

there is no wooll on a small part of the [mountain goat] *body behind the sholders on each side of the brisquit* [22 Feb 06 ML 6.337]

BROKEN   (Of land) rough, much dissected with rugged, steep ravines, gulches, and valleys.

The little Missouri...takes it's rise in a broken country West of the Black hills [12 Apr 05 ML 4.026]

(Of medicine) administered in several doses.

we gave him [Gibson] *broken dozes of diluted nitre and made him drink plentifully of sage tea, had his feet bathed in warm water and...gave him 35 drops of laudanum.* [15 Feb 06 ML 6.312]

(Of an activity) interrupted.

The flees so bad last night that, I made but a broken nights rest [12 Dec 05 WC 6.122]

Charbono an LaPage returned, having made a broken voyage. [1 June 06 ML 7.322]

(Of a horse, as **broke**) tamed, trained to be ridden. *See* UNBROKEN.

the Sorrel...is a Strong active well broke horse [6 May 06 WC 7.217]

BROOK   A small stream. The word now is considered to be restricted mainly to northeastern speech. In the expedition's time, however, its use was more widely distributed across the East (**New England**). *See* CREEK.

The Shore on each Side is lined with hard rough Gulley Stones of different Sises, which has roled from the hills & out of Small brooks [21 Sep 04 WC 3.098]

[burrowing squirrels] *never visit the brooks or river for water* [23 May 05 ML 4.184].

we...moved our camp around a point to a Small wet bottom at the mouth of a Brook [12 Nov 05 WC 6.043]

BROWN, SPANISH   An earthy material colored reddish-brown by iron oxide, used as a pigment in a similar manner to whitewashing.

Some of these hills are red Earth resembling Spanish brown [29 Apr 05 JO 9.140]

BUBBY   A woman's breast, probably the source, through *booby*, of the modern word *boob*. (**South, Midland**)

aged women in many of whom I have seen the bubby reach as low as the waist. [19 Mar 06 ML 6.435]

BUCKSHOT   Heavy lead SHOT ($\frac{1}{4}$ to $\frac{1}{3}$ inch in diameter), originally for hunting deer.

I...order every man to have 100 Balls for ther Rifles & 2 lb. of Buck Shot for those with mussquets &. F[usees] [10 May 04 WC 2.213]

the 2 other Swivels loaded well with Buck Shot [25 Sep 04 JO 9.068]

the fruit [of the pin cherry] is a globular berry about the size of a buck-shot [12 Aug 06 ML 8.158]

BUFFALO The journals' first mention of buffalo (*Bison bison*) occurs only after the expedition had proceeded half way across Missouri, an indication of the widespread destruction of the herds occurring in the Mississippi River country by 1804.

Some buffalow Sign to day. [6 Jun 04 WC 2.282]

The central and western plains were dominated by vast herds of buffalo at the time of the expedition. In the East, buffalo had never been as abundant, but they were not rare either. In 1708 in Mississippi, Thomas Nairne (A. Moore, 52) noted that Indian hunters "go to the Clay pitts and shoot Buffeloes...and the paths leading to these holes ar as many and as well Trod, as these to the greatest Cowpens in Carolina." A year later, John Lawson (*New Voyage*, 115) counted the "Buffelo, or wild Beef" among the "Beasts of Carolina" and reported their presence on the headwaters of the Cape Fear River, which flows into the Atlantic in southern North Carolina. Thomas Walker and his companions, in the first well-documented Virginian expedition into Kentucky (1749–50), killed thirteen during their journey (Walker, 13 Jul 1750). The first North American record of the word *"buffalo"* in *OED* is from Maryland, ca. 1635, almost a century and a half before *"bison"* was first recorded in America. Given its significantly later appearance on the scene, it is fruitless to maintain, as do some dictionaries, that *bison* is "correct" and *buffalo* a misnomer. Their argument is that the latter word referred originally and properly to an Eurasian animal such as the water buffalo and should not be transferred to the American bovid, but the word *bison* itself originally meant a wild Eurasian ox and so is an equally alien term. Should we refuse to call the red-breasted thrush of North America a *robin* simply because the name was earlier used for a European bird?

BUFFALO, PRAIRIE The eastern short-horned lizard, *Phrynosoma douglassi brevirostre*. The name probably is a translation of the Canadian French *boeuf de prairie*. (Lewis was the first to apply the name *horned lizard*.) *See* ASSIMILATE.

A speceis of Lizzard called by the French engages prarie buffaloe are native of these plains as well as those of the Missouri. I have called them the horned Lizzard. [29 May 06 ML 7.302]

BUFFALO-GREASE = GRAISSE DE BUFFLE.

the red berry or Buffalow Grees bushes [27 Jul 06 WC 8.238]

BURNT HILLS Hills of the upper Missouri with smoldering beds of lignite (low-grade coal). Their rusty color is due to the clinker formed from adjacent materials by the burning coal. *See* PUMICE.

I have observed but five burnt hills, about the little Missouri, and I have not Seen any pumey stone above that River [14 Apr 05 WC 4.039]

Coal birnt hills and pumicestone, these appearances seem to be coextensive. [7 Aug 06 ML 8.150]

BURNT WOODS = BOIS BRULÉ.

they had been robed by the indians and the former wounded last winter by the Tetons of the birnt woods [12 Aug 06 ML 8.157]

BURR[1] {bə} Pine-cone. Pine-cones and birch-wood were welcome evidence to the explorers that the Missouri rose in high country, across which lay the Columbia River and Pacific Ocean.

they Saw...Pine burs & Sticks of Birch in the Drift wood [16 Sep 04 WC 3.078]

I Saw to day Bird of the wood pecker kind which fed on Pine burs [22 Aug 05 WC 5.146]

BURR[2] A hard, silica-rich rock suitable for making mill-stones.

I believe it to be calcarious and an imperfect species of the French burr [20 Sep 04 ML 3.095]

BURR[3] A peculiarity in speech, here referring to a number of consonantal sounds in the Salishan language of the FLATHEAD that seemed very foreign to English or French speakers. *See* CLUCKING.

they appear to us to have an Empeddiment in their Speech or a brogue or bur on their tongue [5 Sep 05 JW 11.301]

BUSHEL A measure of volume, still much used in the grain business, equal to about 1.24 cubic feet. *See* (PARCH-)MEAL. A bushel of salt weighs approximately 160 pounds, so the brine described below (in 1810) was about 8% salt by weight, a reasonable concentration for a salt spring. By contrast, normal seawater is about 2% salt. *See* LICK, SALINE, SALT-WORKS.

a large lick & salt spring—220 gallons make a bushel of salt [c. Apr 10 NB in Jackson Letters (ed. 2) 2.509]

As a liquid measure equal to approximately 10 gallons, *bushel* is recorded in the *OED* only in one quotation (marked as questionable) from the year 1483. Seven pounds of salt per bushel of water works out to the same concentration as a bushel of salt per 220 gallons.

a large Salt Lick & Spring...one bushel of water will make 7 lb. of good Salt [6 Jun 04 WC 2.282]

BUTCH To butcher.

they then took him [a bear] *on shore and butched him when they found eight balls had passed through him* [14 May 05 ML 4.151]

had the buffalow butched and brought in and divided. [27 Aug 06 WC 8.325]

BUTT {BUTT (*not* BYOOT)} A prominent bluff. (**South Midland**)

we Came to a hi CLift or Buut [bluff at Council Bluffs, Iowa] [28 Jul 04 JW 11.046]

the butt [a sandstone bluff where the Cannonball River joins the Missouri] *is principally composed of this sand* [ML? 3.473]

In the western United States, the word *butte* denotes a flat-topped hill rising abruptly from its surrounding area. Both *butt* and *butte* stem from an Old French term for a mound of earth serving as a backstop behind an archery target. The form *butte* is North American French, while *butt* came with immigrants from England.

BUTTON   A game where a button is secretly transferred from one child's hands to another's among children sitting in a circle. Players then attempt to guess who holds the button. (**North, North Midland**)

[The Shoshone] *have a game…most like playing butten only they kick singing and do all by motions* [27 Aug 05 JO 9.212]

BUZZARD   {BUZZ-əd}

Here, the California condor of the lower Columbia, now extinct. *See* VULTURE.

the bald Eagle and the beatifull Buzzard of the columbia still continue with us. [3 Jan 06 ML 6.162]

Here, the turkey vulture.

the Turkey buzzard appears. [5 Jun 05 ML or WC 4.347]

C

CABLE   A large-diameter rope (usually hemp), made of three strands (CORDS) twisted together and used as a vessel's anchor-rope. (Not today's wire *cable*.) *See* SOLDIER.

the exerssions of all our Men…aded to a Strong Cable and Anchor was Scrcely Sufficent to Keep the boat from being thrown up on the Sand Island, and dashed to peices [14 Jul 04 WC 2.377]

CABRIE   {kab-ree} = PRONGHORN. French *cabri*, a young goat.

Several men with Tamborens highly Decorated with Der & Cabra Hoofs to make them rattle, assembled and began to Sing & Beat [26 Sep 04 WC 3.116]

Saw large flocks of Cabberrie or antilope which is a Specie of the Goat kind, on the Sides of the hills [28 Apr 05 JO 9.139]

CACHE   {kæsh or kahsh} A storage place, often a pit dug in dry ground, filled with baggage and carefully covered so as to conceal it from people and animals. French for 'hidden.' *See* DEPOSIT.

we set some hands to diging a hole or cellar for the reception of our stores. these holes in the ground or deposits are called by the engages cashes [9 Jun 05 ML 4.269]

4 men Sent to dig a carsh [21 Aug 05 JW 11.279]

Hence, to secure in a cache.

we carried our baggage we conclude to carsh to the place of cashing [21 Aug 05 JW 11.279]

CADDOAN* {KÆD-oh-wən} A Great Plains language family including, among others, the ARIKARA and PAWNEE languages.

CAHOKIA {kə-HO-kee-yə} A trading post and fort located across the Mississippi from St. Louis at the upper (north) end of AMERICAN BOTTOM in ILLINOIS. The French name is borrowed from *caoukia* of the Illinois language; the Cahokia were a subdivision of the ILLINOIS people.

Capt Lewis, who is [in] Kohokia on business of importance to the enterprise [2 Jan 04 WC 2.145]

I sent Newman with Letters to Koho. [24 Mar 04 WC 2.180]

CAJEU {kah-ZHO, kah-SEE, kay-SEE} A small raft consisting of logs or planks (or two canoes catamaran-style) lashed together. Canadian French *cajeu* (plural *cajeux*) was used in Quebec at least by 1742.

This day we met 3 men on a Cajaux from the River of the Soux above the Mahar nation [8 Jun 04 WC 2.287]

> ♦Perhaps this is a variant of the standard French *cageot* 'crate' (the diminutive form of *cage* 'cage, box'), referring to construction of wooden parts lashed together, and probably carrying a pejorative connotation—compare with English slang *crate* 'broken-down vehicle.' *Cageot* is pronounced {kah-ZHO}, as might be the journalists' *cajaux*.♦ Other forms in the journals include *caissie, caissee, casiex, causee* (in PAWNEE), *caussea.*

CALCAREOUS {kal-KEH-ree-əss} (Of rock or soil) containing calcium carbonate, the principal constituent of limestone.

every species of stone...partook so much of the calcarious genus that they burst into small particles on being exposed to the heat [3 Feb 05 ML 3.285]

CALCULATE ON {KAL-kə-late} Count on, figure on. (Note that all three expressions have the same basic sense.)

The horses are handsom...we cannot Calculate on their carrying large loads & feed on the Grass which we may Calculate on finding in the Mountain [29 Aug 05 WC 5.178]

we Calculate on three bushels [of salt] *lasting us from hiere to our deposit...on the Missouri.* [3 Feb 06 WC 6.276]

CALCULATED Suited to, designed for.

we proceeded on and found a Small Canoe...calculated to Carry 3 men [6 Jan 05 WC 6.171]

the largest...Lodge is Calculated for 2 fires only [9 May 06 WC 7.235]

CALUMET {KAL-ə-met} A tobacco-pipe, often smoked ceremonially as a symbol of peace in tribal assemblies. A calumet's bowl often consisted of PIPESTONE. The pipe-stem originally was a reed, for which the French word is *calumet*. Peace-pipes were centrally important in diplomacy among Siouan and other peoples. *See* WAMPUM.

I walked on Shore to See this great Pass of the Sioux and Calumet ground [19 Sep 04 WC 3.089]

CALUMET-BIRD   The golden eagle (*Aquila chrysaetos*), so named (by way of the French Canadian *engagés*) for the use of its feathers in decorating a CALUMET. Also called *calumet eagle, war eagle. See* PAINT.

the Indian Chief Say that the Callemet Bird live in the hollows of those hills [19 Oct 04 WC 3.184]

Among the Mandan in the 1830s, a war-eagle tail purchased a *tolerable good horse* (Catlin 1.114). Decorating calumets with eagle feathers was widespread. In April 1708, Thomas Nairne in northern Mississippi wrote, "Pacifie them by carrying them the Eagle pipe to smoak out of" (A. Moore, 40).

CAMAS   {KAHM-us; KWAH-mash} *Camassia quamash*, an edible plant resembling a hyacinth, which grows in meadows that are moist in spring and dry in summer and fall. In early summer, camas meadows covered by the plant's blue blossoms seemed to Lewis [8.022] like "lakes of fine clear water." (Botanists generally have listed camas in the lily family, but recent taxonomic advances suggests it should be classified in the agave family, or in a new, as yet unnamed family; *see* BEAR-GRASS.) Starchy camas bulbs, dug in summer after the flower stalk withers, were a native staple throughout the Pacific Northwest, and figured widely in intertribal trade. *See* PASHECO, SWEAT[2]. (**Northwest**)

camas

Thought originally to be Nootkan in origin because of its adoption into CHINOOK Jargon, *camas* clearly is derived from the plant's Nez Perce name. The Chinook Jargon borrowed the name from French Canadians—rather than directly from the Nez Perce—as is shown by the common Jargon spelling *lakamass*, which incorporates the French definite article *la-*.

considerable quantities of the quâ-mash in the bottoms through which we passed this evening now in blume. [2 May 06 ML 7.200]

the place at which we met with the Chopunnish last fall, called by them the quawmash grounds [18 May 06 ML 7.269]

Camas sometimes referred to the cakes made from its roots.

these natives have a large quantity of this root bread which they call Commass. [22 Sep 05 JO 9.228]

they gave us a Small piece of Buffalow meat, Some dried Salmon beries & roots in different States, Some round and much like an onion which they call quamash the Bread or Cake is called Pas-she-co...of this they make bread & Supe [20 Sep 05 WC 5.222]

CAMEAHWAIT   {KAY-mee-AH-wite} A chief of the Shoshone (the first tribal people encountered by the expedition when crossing the continental divide) and brother of

SACAGAWEA. Meaning literally 'he doesn't walk,' the name reflects the high status conferred on a man by horse ownership. In describing Shoshone horsemen, Lewis noted [5.121] that a "man considers himself degraded if he is compelled to walk any distance." The chief also was known by a war-name, *Too-et-te-con-e* or Black Gun, literally 'black gun owner' [5.159].

this added Cameahwait, with his ferce eyes and lank jaws grown meager for the want of food, would not be the case if we had guns, we could then live in the country of buffaloe and eat as our enimies do and not be compelled to hide ourselves in these mountains and live on roots and berries as the bear do. [14 Aug 05 ML 5.091]

CAMPMENT Encampment, from French *campement.*

Saw the remains of their Campt on the 2d river [19 Sep 04 WC 3.089]

formed a Campment on Drift logs [10 Nov 05 WC 6.039]

this Campment is formed of two Lodges built...of mats and Straw. [9 May 06 WC 7.235]

CANADIAN French Canadian (the term did not apply to those of English extraction). *See* ENGAGÉ, FRENCH.

this man [French commandant at Cape Girardeau] *agreeably to the custom of many of the Canadian Traders has taken to himself a wife from among the aborigines of the country...a Shawnee woman* [23 Nov 03 ML 2.107]

number [of Cree] *has been reduced, by the small pox, since they were first known to the Canadians.* [winter 04–05 WC 3.433]

the plant Called by the Canadian Engages of the N. W. Sac a commis produces this berry [25 Jan 06 WC 6.236]

CANE The giant cane or switch cane, *Arundinaria gigantea*, a tall, dark-green bamboo grass growing in wetlands throughout southeast America, and much sought in earlier times as horse and cattle feed. Cane typically grows in thickets called *canebrakes*. For similar fodder plants, *see* REED, (SAND-)RUSH. (**South, South Midland**)

I have seen but little cain since we left the Ohio [22 Nov 03 ML 2.102]

Lewis here compares a grass of the Nez Perce country to **maiden cane**, genus *Amphicarpum*, another tall southeastern grass, now endangered in many areas.

among the grasses of this country I observe a large speceis... It has much the appearance of the maden cain as it is called in the state of Ge[o]rgia [5 Jun 06 ML 7.335]

CANISTER, POWDER- {KAN-is-tə} A waterproof lead container for gunpowder. Each of the expedition's canisters held sufficient powder for shooting the bullets made by melting down the canister. [5.053]. *See* POWDER.

I...waxed the stoppers of my powder canesters anew. [19 Jun 05 ML 4.309]

Sealed by the manufacturer, **canister powder** was of a more consistent quality and less subject to damage during transport than powder shipped in kegs.

123 lbs. English Cannister Powder at 90 cts pr. lb. [28 May 03 in Jackson Letters (ed. 2) 1.087]

I Deliver out 12 flints and Some Canstr. Power to hunters. [28 Jan 04 WC 2.166]

CANTON To quarter (troops).

losses he sustained on his farm by the troops which were cantoned on it [undated ML 2.138]

300 of the american Troops had been Contuned on the Missouri a fiew miles above it's mouth [3 Sep 06 WC 8.346]

CANTONMENT A military post.

he determined to leave our winter cantainment at the mouth of River Dubois the next day [20 May 04 ML 2.242]

we...proceeded on down to the Contonemt. at Coldwater Creek [22 Sep 06 WC 8.370]

CAP-A-PIE From head to foot. (Of Old French origin.)

these men had come out armed cap a pe for action [13 Aug 05 ML 5.080]

CAPARISON {kə-PAIR-ə-sun} Outfit, equipment. *See* (BOAT-)HOOK.

The usual caparison of the Shoshone horse is a halter and saddle. [24 Aug 05 ML 5.160]

Also, to outfit, clothe.

one of the...young men is sclected and disguised in a robe of buffaloe skin, having also the skin of the buffaloe's head with the years and horns fastened on his head in form of a cap, thus caparisoned he places himself at a convenient distance between a herd of buffaloe and a precipice [29 May 05 ML 4.216]

CAPOT {KAP-oh} A long, heavy coat, or cloak with hood. *See* (BLANKET-)COAT.

while [I was] Serching for the Tomahawk one of those Scoundals Stole a Cappoe of one of our interpreters [4 Nov 05 WC 6.018]

one of those men I took to be a freinch man from his...blanket Capoe & a handkerchief around his head. [30 Aug 06 WC 8.329]

CARBONATED {KAH-bə-nay-təd} Carbonized; converted into lignite (a low-grade coal) by the action of heat.

great quantities of Coal or carbonated wood is to be seen in every Bluff [31 Jul 06 WC 8.259]

CARCAJOU {KAH-kə-zhoo} Wolverine (*Gulo gulo*), especially as a fur-bearer. The name comes through Canadian French from Montagnais, an ALGONQUIAN language of eastern Canada related to Cree. (**North**)

wolverine

Carkajous wolverine or Beaver eaters [winter 04–05 ML 3.438]

CAREEN {kə-REEN} To tilt (a boat) to one side. *See* KEEL[2].

the Boat was Creaned on the Side from the Wind [14 Jul 04 WC 2.377]

Lewis uses the botanical term *carinated* 'having a longitudinal ridge,' which comes from the Latin *carina* 'keel,' the ultimate source also of *careen.*

the leafets...are also veined, glossy, carinated and wrinkled [12 Feb 06 ML 6.299]

CARROT A thick plug of twisted or rolled tobacco-leaf, often wrapped in jute and larger than a TWIST. (In the Canadian fur-trade and probably here also, weighing about 3 pounds and around 18 inches long.)

we gave those boys two Carrots of Tobacco to Carry to their Chiefs [23 Sep 04 WC 3.106]

[The Arikara form tobacco leaves] *into carrots of the thickness of a mans arm role them closely with willow bark and hang them in the smoke of their lodges to dry.* [winter 04–05 ML 3.461]

one of the men bought a Sea otter Skin...for a peace of Tobacco not the half of a carrit. [13 Feb 06 JO 9.271]

CARRYING PLACE A place where it was necessary to PORTAGE cargo and, sometimes, boats. Here, around the GREAT FALLS[1] of the Missouri.

We now lay at Camp, at the commencement of the carrying place [20 Jun 05 JW 11.205]

CARTRIDGE {KAHT(-ə)-rij} A paper cylinder containing powder for a single shot. The user tore open the paper, poured the powder into the muzzle, and rammed home the BALL. Cartridges were difficult to keep dry and apparently not commonly used on the expedition, the powder more often being transported in kegs, lead CANISTERS, and powder HORNS. Also called (FIXED) AMMUNITION. *Cartridge* is descended from French *cartouche* of the same meaning.

15 Cartouch Box Belts [18 May 03 in Jackson Letters (ed. 2) 1.098]

men...with Powder Cartragies and 100 Balls each [13 May 04 WC 2.214]

I assort our articles for to be left at this place buried...2 blunderbuts, Caterrages [26 Jun 05 WC 4.335]

CASE[1] Physical condition. *See* ORDER.

These horses appeared in good case. [14 Apr 06 PG 10.210]

CASE[2] To remove the skin of an animal.

the deerskins which we have had cased for the purpose of containing our dryed meat are not themselves sufficiently dryed for that purpose [5 Apr 06 ML 7.075]

the skin of the head of the sheep with the horns remaining was cased in such a manner as to fit the head of a man [10 Apr 06 ML 7.101]

CASTOR {KASS-tə} Castoreum, a strongly scented, creamy substance from the dried anal glands of the male BEAVER, earlier used as medicine, and later for making perfume and beaver-trapping bait. Also called BARK-STONE, presumably from a similarity to TANNER'S OOZE.

beaver

The male beaver has six stones, two of which contain a substance much like finely pulvarized bark of a pale yellow colour and not unlike tanner's ooz in smell, these are called the bark stones or castors [7 Jan 06 ML 6.175]

catfish

CAT Catfish.

Mr. Ducett made me a present of rivr Catts & Some Herbs [18 May 04 WC 2.237]

those Cat are So plenty that they may be Cought in any part of this river [29 Jul 04 WC 2.426]

CAT, TIGER- A wild-cat, probably here the Oregon bobcat, *Lynx rufus fasciatus.*

Had a large coat completed out of the skins of the Tiger Cat [15 Jan 06 ML 6.206]

The tyger Cat is found on the borders of the plains and in the woody country lying along the Pacific Ocean. [21 Feb 06 ML 6.333]

CATAPLASM {KAT-ə-plaz-əm} = POULTICE.

[Sacagawea] *complains principally of the lower region of the abdomen, I therefore continued the cataplasms of barks and laudnumn* [16 Jun 05 ML 4.301]

CATHLAMET A Chinookan people on the Oregon side of the lower Columbia River, just upstream from the Clatsop.

they Call them Selves Cat-tar-bets [26 Nov 05 WC 6.087]

The Chinnooks Cath lâh mâh & others in this neighbourhood bury their dead in their Canoes. [30 Nov 05 WC 6.097]

The Cath lâ mâhs left us this evening on their way to the Clatsops, to whome they perpose bartering their wappato for the blubber & Oil of the whale, which the latter purchased for Beeds &c. from the Kilámox [11 Jan 06 WC 6.199]

> The prefix *cathla-* 'people of [a place]' is found commonly in tribal names along the lower Columbia (e.g., Cathlapoutle, Cathlaminimin, Cathlasco, Cathleyacheyach). *Cathla-* is the English rendition of CHINOOKAN *gaLa-* where the *L* represents a breathy sort of *l* not found in English, but like the Welsh *-ll-*; the *-thl-* in *athlete* is a rough approximation. The name CLACKAMAS contains the related prefix *giLa-*.

CAULK {kɔk} To seal seams or cracks in a boat. Though the captains' spelling and Lewis's simile suggest otherwise, cork was not used in caulking.

had all the Canoes, the Perogus corked pitchd & lined oover the Cotton Wood, which is win Shaken [27 Mar 05 WC 3.320]

The Canoe Calked, the Baggage aranged [10 Jun 05 JO 9.165]

we corked the canoes and put them in the water and also launched the boat, she lay like a perfect cork on the water. [9 Jul 05 ML 4.368]

Hence **caulking**, the material so used.

in Lousening the boat from the ice Some of the Corking drew out which Caused her to Leake for a few minits [24 Feb 05 WC 3.302]

CAVERN, BLOWING {KÆ-vən} A cave producing sounds by the flow of air through its openings, hypothesized by the captains to be the source of the booming and rumbling heard in the Great Falls vicinity. The *engagés* thought the sounds came from rich silver mines bursting in the nearby mountains [4.375].

I...heard a nois...as loud and resembling precisely the discharge of a piece of ordinance of 6 pounds at the distance of 5 or six miles...it might be caused by running water in Some of the caverns of those emence mountains, on the principal of the blowing caverns [20 Jun 05 WC 4.320]

CEDAR, RED {SEE-də} The juniper tree (*Juniperus virginiana*) of the eastern Plains, often scattered across grassy landscapes. Here Clark records its presence along the Missouri River in the Iowa/Nebraska area.

this Bluff has...a fiew Red Ceeder on the tope [12 Aug 04 WC 2.471]

A year later in western Montana, Lewis remarked on the similar Rocky Mountain juniper or red cedar (*J. scopulorum*, literally 'juniper of the rocks') growing along with the shrubby common juniper (*J. communis*).

on the river about the mountains wich Capt. C. passed today he saw some large cedar trees and some juniper also [1 Aug 05 ML 5.028]

CEDAR, WHITE The western red cedar (*Thuja plicata*), often growing to an enormous size, is native to northern Idaho and western Washington and Oregon; *see* ARBOR VITÆ. The journalists learned the name in the East, where it refers to the eastern white cedar (*Thuja occidentalis*).

the country... is covered with a very heavy growth of several species of pine & furr, also the arbor vita or white cedar and a small proportion of the black Alder [10 Jan 06 ML 6.194]

Cedar was of great use to the lower Columbia Indians. *See* APRON, SILK-GRASS.

The women wear a Short peticoat of the iner bark of the white Ceder [21 Nov 05 WC 6.074]

Their bows...are very flat and thin, formed of the heart of the arbor vita or white cedar, the back of the bow being thickly covered with the sinews of the Elk laid on with a gleue which they make from the sturgeon; the string is made of the sinues of the Elk also. [15 Jan 06 ML 6.206]

the most esteemed and valuable of these robes are made of strips of the skins of the Sea Otter net together with the bark of the white cedar or silk-grass. [19 Mar 06 ML 6.434]

CHANCE   A quantity (of something). Ordway is the first person known to have used the word in English with this meaning. (**South, South Midland**)

the men returned with a fine chance of Elk meat. [8 Dec 05 JO 9.259]

CHANGE   To exchange.

I…Changed for his horse which was fresh & proced on…this horse threw me 3 times which hurt me Some. [22 Sep 05 WC 5.229]

CHAPTER OF ACCIDENTS   {CHAP-tə} The unknown future. This bookish expression, of a sort more likely to be found in Lewis's journal than Clark's, probably was borrowed into English from the French expression *chapitre des accidents,* which appeared in the 17th century.

there seems to be a sertain fatality attatched to the neighbourhood of these [Great] *falls, for there is always a chapter of accedents prepared for us during our residence at them.* [15 Jul 06 ML 8.110]

not finding Capt. Clark I…determined to proceed as tho' he was not before me and leave the rest to the chapter of accedents. [8 Aug 06 ML 8.152]

CHAR   Sockeye salmon, *Oncorhynchus nerka.* (In modern use, the name refers to a fish of the genus *Salvelinus*, related to trout and salmon.)

five [lower Columbia] *Indians Came down in a Canoe loaded with fish of Salmon Spes. Called Red Charr* [11 Nov 05 WC 6.040]

the common net is…employed in taking the samon, Carr and trout [16 Jan 06 ML 6.211]

CHARBONNEAU   {SHAH-bə-noh} Toussaint Charbonneau led a long and checkered career as a fur-trader and INTERPRETER on the upper Missouri, mainly among the MINITARI and MANDAN. In winter 1804–5 at Fort Mandan, Lewis & Clark engaged Charbonneau (middle-aged at the time) and his teenage Shoshone wife, SACAGAWEA, for the western expedition. (Charbonneau was hired after several days of contentious contract negotiations; *see* MIFF.) On February 11, 1805, Sacagawea bore a son, Jean Baptiste, whom his parents took along on the journey. After the exploration, Charbonneau lived on to be 80 or so, surviving several close calls, including a stabbing with a canoe-awl by a SAULTEAUX woman when supposedly raping her daughter, and taking two bullets through his hat in a confrontation with the Sioux (Abel, *Chardon's Journal* 271, 386). The surname *Charbonneau* is one of the oldest and most common in French Canada.

a french man by Name Chabonah, who Speaks the Big Belley language visit us, he wished to hire & informed us his 2 Squars were Snake Indians, we engau him to go with us and take one of his wives to interpet the Snake language [4 Nov 04 WC 3.228]

Charbono struck his indian Woman for which Capt. C. gave him a severe reprmand. [14 Aug 05 ML 5.093]

CHARGE   {chahj} To load a boat, gun, or horse.

Charged the Boat and Perogue after a Small Shower of rain [27 Jul 04 WC 2.421]

I...determined never again to suffer my peice to be longer empty than the time she... required to charge her. [14 June 05 ML 4.293]

we charged our packhorses and set out. [9 May 06 ML 7.233]

CHECK[1] To reprimand. From the game of chess, meaning to threaten the King.

I checked our interpreter for Strikeing his woman at their Dinner. [14 Aug 05 WC 5.093]

CHECK[2] Fabric printed with a checked pattern resembling a chess or checker board.

we purchased about 1½ bushels of those roots for which we gave Some fiew red beeds Small peaces of brass wire & old Check [29 Dec 05 WC 6.144]

CHEHALIS {chə-HAY-ləss} A Salishan people occupying the Pacific coast and adjacent areas north of the Chinook. Originally the Chehalis name of a principal village, meaning 'sand.'

Several Indians Visit us to day...Some of the Chiltz Nation who reside on the Sea Coast near Point Lewis [21 Nov 05 WC 6.075]

CHEYENNE {shee-AHN, modern shy-ANN, -EN} A people of eastern Wyoming and western South Dakota (with a southern division in Colorado), speaking an Algonquian tongue not closely related to any other in the ALGONQUIAN language family. Their name was borrowed into French from the Sioux name for the Cheyenne, meaning literally 'little Cree.' Also called DOG INDIAN, SHARHA.

The Cheaun, Mandin & Grovanter...The Mandans Cheeons, & Grovanters [3 Aug 04 WC 2.438]

The Chyenne Nation has about 300 Lodges hunt the Buffalow, Steel horses from the Spanish Settlements [1 Oct 04 WC 3.133]

passed an old Shian fort...where the Chian nation of Indians lived Some years ago. [16 Oct 04 JO 9.085]

CHILLY (Of the air) chilling, tending to cause shivering, aching, or numbness. Though now practically synonymous with *cold*, Whitehouse and Ordway's use of *cold* and *chilly* in the same phrase implies a distinction in meaning between *cold* (having a low temperature) and *chilly* (producing characteristic human reactions to cold). *See* COLD.

cloudy and verry chilley and cold. [8 Sep 05 JW 11.305]

the air on the mountains verry chilley & cold. our fingers aked with the cold [4 Sep 05 JO 9.218]

CHINK To pack crevices in log walls with such materials as moss or pieces of old tarpaulin in order to make a structure weather-tight. *See* DAUB.

all hands at work about the huts Chinking them [17 Dec 05 WC 6.127]

CHINOOK {chih-NOOK, shih-NOOK} One of several tribal groups of the lower Columbia River speaking languages of the Chinookan family. The "Chinook" proper, renowned as canoe-builders and traders, resided in wooden houses on the Columbia

River estuary's north side, subsisting mainly on fish and other marine resources. The neighboring CHEHALIS originally applied the name *Chinook* to a village on Baker Bay, located adjacent to the Columbia's mouth. This Salishan name was adopted by the Chinook themselves and was included in the Chinook Jargon (see below). (The 1792 log-book of the American ship *Columbia Rediviva* identifies the village as *Chinouk*.)

the name of the nation is...Chin-nook and is noumerous live principally on fish roots a fiew Elk and fowls. they are armed with good Fusees. [17 Nov 05 WC 6.060]

Based on CHINOOK proper, **Chinook Jargon** is a trading language (or pidgin) with a simplified grammar incorporating vocabulary from several other native languages, especially NOOTKA of western Vancouver Island. In its later form, English and French words also were added. (*See* KAMOSUK, SALAL, SAPOLIL, TUM, TYEE.) It is clear that the Jargon existed by 1805, but exactly when and how it originated is uncertain, in part because early writers often did not distinguish between the main Chinook language and Chinook Jargon. At its peak in the mid-19th century, the Jargon perhaps comprised about 1,500 words. There are still a few speakers of the Jargon, and it has an active presence on the Internet.

CHINOOKAN* A family of languages (Lower Chinook or Chinook proper, CATHLAMET, and Upper Chinook) on the lower Columbia River. Chinookan words form a significant part of CHINOOK Jargon. *See* CLACKAMAS, CLATSOP, CLUCKING, WAKIACUM, WATLALA.

CHIP Thin strips of wood utilized in fashioning hats and baskets.

These [Clatsop cedar bark and bear-grass] *hats...are nearly water proof, light, and... much more dureable than either Chip or Straw* [19 Jan 06 WC 6.222]

CHIPPEWA {CHIP-ə-way, modern CHIP-ə-wah} An ALGONQUIAN people, also called *Ojibway*, inhabiting a large area of central and eastern Canada and the north-central United States. From the 17th century onward, they were bitter enemies of the SIOUX, whose lands west of Lake Superior they progressively occupied. *See* SAULTEAUX.

Mr. Cameron of St peters [on Minnesota River] *has put arms into the hands of the Souis to revenge the death of 3 of his men Killed by the Chipaways latterly* [28 Feb 05 WC 3.305]

CHITTEDIDDLE Katydid. *See* KASKASKIA, SAWYER[3].

The green insect known in the U' States by the name of the sawyer or chittediddle, was first heard to cry on the 27th of July [8 Aug 04 ML 2.462]

CHOICE OF, BE To value (something) highly, and thus be unwilling to part with it. (**New England**)

they [Flathead] *have buffaloe robes but are verry choice of them.* [23 Sep 05 JW 11.329]

CHOKE (Of a horse) to suffer an obstruction of the esophagus, usually from eating too fast or without adequate chewing, though in this case perhaps from the ingestion of noxious plants. *See* DISTEMPER.

Several of the horses chokd. by eating Some kind of a weed in this bottom, but they got over it [30 Apr 06 JO 9.301]

> Sharp points developing on a horse's molars can cause choke, resulting in an insufficient grinding of feed before it is swallowed. Though choke can prevent a horse from eating, it usually does not obstruct breathing as choking does in humans, unless the impaction becomes severe enough to compress a horse's windpipe.

CHOP To change direction suddenly.

wind from the S. E. wind choped around to the N W. [15 Jan 05 WC 3.274]

CHOPUNNISH {CHAH-pə-nish, or SHAH-pə-nish} = NEZ PERCE.

The Cho-pun-nish or Pierced nose Indians are Stout likeley men, handsom women, and verry dressey in their way [10 Oct 05 WC 5.258]

the head chief of the Chopenish tribe Camped with us [4 May 06 JO 9.304]

Some Chopuniesh are flatheads [c. Apr 10 NB in Jackson Letters (ed. 2) 2.500]

> ♦Haruo Aoki, a Nez Perce language expert, presents the most widely accepted etymology of the name. Aoki believes the source is Nez Perce *tsoopnit* 'piercing (with a pointed object),' with reference to nose-piercing for the wearing of a dentalium shell (*see* NEZ PERCE). It would be unusual, though, for a native people to designate themselves in such a way. It seems possible that Lewis & Clark learned the name from a neighboring tribe, probably the Salish speaking FLATHEAD, through whose lands the expedition passed when approaching the Nez Perce. Clark states [5.222], "they call themselves *Cho pun-nish* or *Pierced Noses*," but he often lumped together all peoples west of the Shoshone as "Flatheads," and thus may actually have learned the name from a Salishan rather than a Nez Perce speaker. Furthermore, the Plateau practice of wearing a dentalium shell in the nasal septum was not widespread, and in fact declining, among the Nez Perce in the early 1800s. Several interior Salishan languages had names for the Nez Perce similar to the modern Flathead *saHahptnee*, often with the suffix *-sh* 'inhabitant' (*H* represents a deep, guttural *h*-sound). These Salishan names are the source of SAHAPTIN and SAHAPTIAN and may have given rise to *Chopunnish* as well. Future research may allow us to choose more surely between the Nez Perce and the Salishan etymologies.♦

CHORD A straight line joining two points of a curve.

this course and distance forms the cord line to a general circular bend of the river [22 Jul 05 ML 4.418]

CHRONOMETER {krə-NAHM-ə-tə} An accurate and expensive special watch used for navigational and mapping purposes. A mahogany case housed Lewis's chronometer. *See* LONGITUDE, RATE OF GOING, (MEAN) TIME.

1 Gold Chronometer $250. [19 May 03 in Jackson Letters (ed. 2) 1.088]

To a new Box of Mohoconey Wood...[$]2 25 [10 June 03 in Jackson *Letters* (ed. 2) 1.091]

A Chronometer; her ballance-wheel and scapement were on the most improved construction. she rested on her back, in a small case prepared for her, suspended by an universal joint. she was carefully wound up every day at twelve oclock. [22 Jul 04 ML 2.412]

the rains of the last night unfortunately wet the Crenomuter in the fob of Capt. L. breaches. [17 May 06 WC 7.268]

chronometer

CIRCUMFERENTOR {sə-KUM-fren-tə} A surveyor's compass equipped with sighting vanes for measuring AZIMUTHS, presumably so named for its use in laying out the boundary or *circumference* of a parcel of surveyed land.

Capt Clark...asscertained by the Circumferenter and projection that the width of the Ohio from the point was—1274 Yards [15 Nov 03 ML 2.087]

A Circumferentor, circle 6 Inches diameter...by means of this instrument adjusted with the sperit level, I have taken the magnetic azimuth of the sun and pole Star. It has also been employed in taking the traverse of the river [22 Jul 04 ML 2.413]

CLACKAMAS An Upper CHINOOKAN people living on the Clackamas and lower Willamette rivers of Oregon. The Chinookan name consists of *giLa-* 'those of' prefixed to the stem *-q'imash* 'Clackamas River.' *See* CATHLAMET, WELSH INDIANS.

the Clarkamos nation...live principally on fish of which those Streams abound and also on roots [7 Apr 06 WC 7.093]

CLATSOP {KLAT-sop} A Chinookan people closely related to the CHINOOK and occupying the south side of the Columbia River estuary. The expedition erected Fort Clatsop on Clatsop lands for winter quarters, 1805–6. The name means 'pounded salmon' in the Lower Chinookan language. *See* (POUNDED) FISH.

in the evening Seven indians of the Clot Sop Nation Came over in a Canoe, they brought with them 2 Sea otter Skins for which they asked blue beads [23 Nov 05 WC 6.081]

CLEVER {KLEH-və} Good-natured(-ly). (**New England, South, South Midland**)

most of them [Walla Walla] went away peaceable & behaved verry clever and honest with us [28 Apr 06 JO 9.299]

CLEVERLY Skillfully, dexterously.

we then made an attempt at the Barge but our Rope which was made of elk Skin broke Several times. we mended it Got hir cleverly Started. [25 Feb 05 JO 9.118]

CLIFF {klift} Starting in the 16th century, *cleft* (with its variant *clift*) 'fissure, crevice,' and *cliff* were almost completely confused.

the high lands juts to the river and form a most tremendious Clift [4 Dec 03 WC 2.123]

a Cleft above [7 Jul 04 WC 2.355]

CLIMATE   Region, especially in the sense of a particular latitudinal zone with a characteristic climate.

the brown Curloo has left the plains...and retired to some other climate and country. [29 Jul 06 ML 8.140]

A *bird of clime* is migratory, breeding in one climate and wintering in another.

[Pelicans] are a bird of clime remain on the coast of Floriday and the border of the Gulph of mexico...during the winter and in the Spring...visit this country...for the purpose of raising their young [8 Aug 04 ML 2.460]

CLOVER, IN   {KLOH-və} High off the hog.

we once more live in clover; Anchovies fresh Sturgeon and Wappetoe. [11 Mar 06 ML 6.402]

CLUCKING   (Of a language) characterized by consonants formed in the throat and back of the mouth—sounds that often seem extremely foreign to the Euro-American ear.

those tribes of flat heads we have passed...all have the Clucking tone anexed which is predomint. [27 Oct 05 WC 5.345]

The clucking extends all below the falls—a sound difficult to describe—but more like a hen or duck guttural & disagreeable [c. Apr 10 NB in Jackson Letters (ed. 2) 2.501]

Most Indian languages of the Pacific Northwest, such as the CHINOOKAN ones mentioned here and the SALISH and SAHAPTIAN languages, have intricate consonantal systems. The *clucking* that so struck the captains' ears may have led them to lump speakers of these otherwise unrelated northwestern languages together as FLATHEADS. *See* BURR[3], GUGGLE.

CLYSTER   {KLY-stə} An enema, administered with a syringe.

1. Clyster Syringe [$]2.75 [26 May 03 in Jackson Letters (ed. 2) 1.080]

we gave [Sacagawea's son]...a doze of creem of tartar which did not operate, we therefore gave it a clyster in the evening. [25 May 06 ML 7.286]

clyster syringe

COAL   Charcoal, as opposed to (PIT-)COAL. *See* (COAL-)KILN, (TAR-)KILN.

we are now burning a large Coal pit, to mend the indians hatchets [28 Jan 05 ML 3.281]

men building perogus, makeing Ropes, Burning Coal, Hanging up meat & makeing battle axes for Corn [1 Mar 05 WC 3.308]

the men generally employed at cutting and Splitting coal wood & Setting up the pit [25 Jan 05 JO 9.111]

COAL, PIT   Mined coal, as opposed to charcoal. Here, probably lignite, a low-grade coal.

there are many fine mines of pitt Coal on this stream [25 Nov 03 ML 2.112]

COAL, STONE = (PIT-)COAL.

passed a Coal-mine, or Bank of Stone Coal [25 Jun 04 WC 2.321]

COARSE {kohs} (Of clothing) roughly made, inexpensive.

Several of the party exchanged leather for linen Shirts and beaver for Corse hats. [6 Sep 06 WC 8.351]

> In November 1803, Corporal Warfington was issued, in addition to finer clothing, *coarse shirts* and *overalls* (Moore & Haynes, 78). Runaway slaves often were described in newspaper announcements as wearing *coarse shirts* or *coats* (made of TOW-linen) when they disappeared. *Coarse hats* consisted of woolen material. Though of lower quality than *fine hats*, they were valued highly enough to be mentioned in Virginia newspaper and probate inventories of the eighteenth and nineteenth centuries. They cost fifty cents apiece, more or less.

COAST To follow the shoreline in a boat, rather than cutting across an expanse of open water exposed to the wind. *See* DOUBLE.

we had passed Meriwethers bay and commenced coasting the difficult shore [23 Mar 06 ML 7.007]

COAT, ARTILLERY- An artilleryman's uniform coat. In circa December 1803, several enlisted men from a KASKASKIA artillery company were detailed to Lewis's command.

our Captains made a chief & Gave him a meddel and an artillery coat a Shirt knife &.C. [22 Mar 05 JO 9.123]

COAT, BLANKET- A heavy coat (often hand-made during the upper Missouri fur-trade era), consisting of woolen blanket material. *See* CAPOT.

This morning was cloudy and so could that I was obleged to have recourse to a blanket coat [5 Jun 05 ML 4.257]

COCK Part of the mechanism for discharging a firearm, consisting of a lever that is raised, and then released by a trigger.

one of those Indians...has a gun with a brass barrel & Cock of which he prises highly [3 Nov 05 WC 6.013]

> In a flint-LOCK, a cock is a spring-loaded lever for holding a FLINT, which strikes against the FRIZZEN, sending sparks into the priming powder in the PAN. The cock was so called for its resemblance to a pecking rooster. (Both the English word and its German equivalent *Hahn* mean 'rooster,' 'gun-cock,' and 'penis,' the latter sense perhaps lending itself to a pun regarding BATTERY). A gun had to be fully cocked before firing. When reloading, it was *half-cocked*, with the cock drawn part way back to a locked position, which was far enough to allow the PAN cover to remain closed and protect the priming powder. Half-cock was the

"safety" position in which a gun could be safely loaded, but a firearm might *go off half-cocked* during loading if the cocking mechanism was worn or defective. *See* LOCK, MISFIRE, SNAP.

A *cock screw* held together the upper and lower jaws of the cock vise that clamped the flint in position.

The guns of Drewyer and Sergt. Pryor were both out of order... the second had the cock screw broken [20 Mar 06 ML 6.441]

COLD Any illness attributed to exposure to the cold, including but not limited to the viral respiratory infections so called today.

one other with the Tooth ake has taken cold in the Jaw [12 Jun 05 WC 4.281]

her [Sacagawea's] *disorder originated...from an obstruction of the mensis in consequence of taking could.* [16 Jun 05 ML 4.301]

COLIC {Kɔ-lick} Acute abdominal pain coming in waves. *See* BILIOUS.

Sgt. Floyd taken very Sudenly Ill this morning with a collick. [19 Aug 04 JO 9.041]

I found Wiser very ill with a fit of the cholic. I sent Sergt. Ordway...for some water and gave him a doze of the essence of Peppermint and laudinum [24 Aug 05 ML 5.158]

Men & women for cholic balancing themselves on sharp stick—Mandans. [c. Apr 1810 NB in Jackson Letters (ed. 2) 2.506]

COLLATION {kə-LAY-shən} A light meal, snack.

we...regailed ourselves with a could collation which we had taken the precaution to bring with us from St. Louis. [20 May 04 ML 2.241]

COLLIER {KɔL-yə} Charcoal-maker.

you cut and split a sufficient parsel of wood which is set on end as the coliers commence the base of their coal pitts [spring 04 ML 2.224]

COLT A last-ditch food resource in the game-poor western Rockies, or Bitterroot Range. *See* BEEF.

we could find no water deturmd to Camp...and make use of Snow for to boil our Coalt meat & make Supe. [15 Sep 05 WC 5.206]

COLUMBIAN Pertaining to the Columbia River, its valley, and tributaries.

the wapatoes they geather in the ponds but all other grow spontaineously in every part of the Columbian valley [5 Apr 06 JO 9.287]

COME TO (In traveling by water) to stop, specifically to go ashore. *See* LAY BY, LIE BY, TAKE UP.

came too about a mile below the riffle...pretty early in the evening [4 Sep 03 ML 2.071]

COMFORTABLE {KUM-f(ə)-tub'l} Sustaining, nourishing.

we made a comfortable meal of the Elk [1 Aug 05 ML 5.025]

COMMISSARY = CONTRACTOR. *See* PUBLIC[1].

hauled Logs to day with the Comosaries Teem [20 Dec 03 WC 2.139]

Comy Kiled a Beef [3 Jan 04 WC 2.145]

Maj Rumsey the Comsy arrived with Some provisions in a waggon of Mr. Todd [15 Jan 04 WC 2.156]

COMPLAIN To express physical suffering or pain, rather than dissatisfaction or discontent as in modern use.

one frenchman...has got an abscess on his they [thigh]*, he complains verry much   we are makeing every exertion to reiev him* [21 Sep 04 WC 3.099]

CONCEIT To imagine, consider.

he Conceited himself a little better than he was [healthwise] [24 May 06 WC 7.285]

CONFIDENTIAL Enjoying or deserving one's confidence.

to take old Durioun back as fur as the Soux nation with a view to get some of their Chiefs to Visit the Presdt. of the United S. (This man being a verry Confidential friend of those people...) [12 Jun 04 WC 2.294]

CONNECT To lay down the positions of geographic features on a map, especially rivers, thus establishing their relationships to each another.

I engage my self in Connecting the Countrey from information. [19 Dec 04 WC 3.260]

Hence **connection**, a map.

I imploy my Self drawing a Connection of the Countrey [5 Jan 05 WC 3.268]

CONSIDERABLE A fair amount or number.

considerable of cotton timber along the River bottoms [31 Jul 05 JO 9.192]

Also, considerably.

the water in that place is considerable above blood heat. [13 Sep 05 JW 11.313]

CONSIDERATE Important; of some social stature, or worthy of consideration. Peter Pond, a late 18th century Connecticut trader, was accompanied to Mackinaw by "Eleve[n] Chefe...Beside A Number of Considerd Men" (*Narr.* 48). In this sense, the word comes perhaps from French *considéré* 'principal man (of an Indian tribe).' The Spaniards on the Mississippi applied the analogous term *considerado*. *See* BRAVE.

the Cheifs and considerate men came in a body to where we were seated [12 May 06 ML 7.247]

CONTRACTOR {KƆN-trak-tə} A person or company contracting with the U.S. Army to provide goods and services. *See* COMMISSARY.

No whiskey shall...be delivered from the Contractor's store except for the legal ration [20 Feb 04 ML 2.175] *the Contractors Boat return to St. Louis* [5 Apr 04 WC 2.192]

CONTRIBUTE To attribute. *See* DYSENTERY.

Several men Complain of a looseness and gripeing which I contribute to the diet, pounded fish mixed with Salt water [30 Nov 05 WC 6.097]

CONVENIENT Morally proper.

The dress of these people [Shoshone] *is quite as desent and convenient as that of any nation of Indians I ever saw.* [21 Aug 05 ML 5.135]

COOPER {KOO-pə} A BARREL-maker, an occupation requiring much skill and some specialized tools to produce tight containers. *See* FLAG.

we now scelected the articles to be deposited in this cash...some chissels, a cooper's Howel, some tin cups [et al.] [10 Jun 05 ML 4.275]

COPPERAS {KƆ-pə-rəs} Iron sulfate (or green VITRIOL), for dyeing brown and for tanning.

pasd...a run of allum & copperass water. [13 Sep 04 JO 9.059]

COPSE {kɔps} A thicket of small trees or brush.

The Prarie...is...Covered with Grass from 5 to 8 feet high intersperced with Copse of Hazel, Plumbs [et al.] [1 Aug 04 WC 2.434]

Drewyer discovered a brown bear enter a small cops of bushes [31 Jul 05 ML 5.018]

CORD {kɔd} = (TOW-)ROPE.

the banks were firm and shore boald which favoured the uce of the cord. I find this method of asscending the river, when the shore is such as will permit it, the safest and most expeditious mode of traveling, except with sails in a steady and favourable breze. [17 May 05 ML 4.158]

the chord is our only dependence for the courant is too rappid to be resisted with the oar and the river too deep in most places for the pole. [30 May 05 ML 4.222]

Also, one of the strands in a CABLE.

Set Some men to make a Toe Rope out of the Cords of a Cable which had been provided by Capt Lewis...for the Cable of the boat [17 Jun 04 WC 2.306]

CORN, LYED {līd kɔn} Mature HULLED corn soaked in a diluted lye solution to create HOMINY. Lye was made by steeping wood-ash in water. *See* GREEN (CORN).

lyed corn and grece will be issued to the party [26 May 04 ML 2.258]

CORVUS {KƆ-vəs} Any bird of the crow family (Corvidæ). *Corvus* is Latin for 'crow.'

Here, the PARTICOLORED magpie.

magpie

The Corvos or Magpye is verry Common in this quarter [Arikara territory] [6 Oct 04 WC 3.147]

Here, meaning the Steller's jay of western forests.

The blue crested Corvus bird has already begun to build it's nest. [31 Jan 06 ML 6.261]

COST, FIRST The purchase cost of trade goods, exclusive of additional expenses such as for transportation. Had the latter been figured in, the actual cost of these items to the expedition would have been considerably greater.

most of those [horses] *he has bought as yet was for about 3 or 4 dollars worth of marchandize at the first cost* [27 Aug 05 JO 9.212]

CÔTE NOIRE {French koht-NWAHR} = BLACK HILLS. French 'black hill,' probably a translation of Lakota (TETON) *paha-sapa. See* BOOTED.

the Coat Nur or Black m[ountain] *is high and Some parts retain Snow all Summer, Covered with timber principally pine, Great number of goats and a kind of anamal with verry large horns* [1 Oct 04 WC 3.133]

it was a young french man who lived with Mr. Valley a trader from little Coat. [1 Oct 04 JO 9.074]

I Saw Some of the Chien or Dog Indians, also a man of a nation under the Court new [12 Oct 04 WC 3.163]

Goats...prosceed on their journey to the Court Noir [18 Oct 04 WC 3.182]

COTTON(-WOOD) Any of several tree species of the genus *Populus*, growing along water courses (*see* WILLOW) and having cottony seeds (*see* PARACHUTE). The branches provided feed for horses (common in the West where grass, CANE, or REED often were lacking). The wood, though of poor quality (*see* WINDSHAKEN), served the expedition for constructing dugout canoes and a replacement boat-mast. (Two dugout cottonwood canoes, for example, built above the GREAT FALLS were about three feet across, and 25 and 33 feet long, respectively.)

cottonwood

the banks are falling in takeing with them large trees of Cotton woods which is the Common groth in the Bottoms Subject to the flud [10 Jun 04 WC 2.291]

We made a Mast of Cotton wood [2 Jul 04 WC 2.341]

we Camped...in a Small grove of Cotton trees [26 May 05 WC 4.205]

COUNTER-CURRENT {KOWN-tə KUH-rənt} An upstream current, caused by an obstruction along a bank or in midstream, and forming an eddy that could be hazardous to boatmen.

the counter courent driving with great force against the E. side of the rock would instandly dash them to attoms and the whirlpool would as quickly take them to the botom. [26 Nov 03 ML 2.115]

the river appears to be Confd. in a verry narrow Channel, and the Current Still more So by Couenter Current or Whirl on one Side & high bank on the other [26 June 04 WC 2.324]

COUNTRY The surrounding region, the countryside.

I derect a Slay to be built to haul things from the Countrey [26 Jan 04 WC 2.165]

Also, neighboring. *See* FOLKS.

Several of the Countrey people In Camp Shooting with the party [6 May 04 WC 2.212]

COUPLING = (COUPLING-)TONGUE.

COURSE One of several directional legs—each labeled with a compass bearing, mileage, and termination point—into which a day's route was divided. Using special compass and sighting techniques, the captains meticulously wrote down TRAVERSE notes for every day that the Corps was on the move (mainly in Clark's journal and to a lesser extent in Lewis's). By plotting the *course and distance* of the sequential legs end to end, a day's progress was laid down. *See* POINT[1].

Course distance &c. 20th of April 1805...
N.45°W. 1½ mile to a tree in a Glade in a bend to the Starboard Side a Sand pt. opsd.
S. 45°W. 2 miles to a point of low willows on the Sd. Side... [etc.]
[20 Apr 05 ML 4.056]

S27°W 1¼ m[il]es on the S. point.
West 1¼ m[il]es. to the lower point of a Bluff on the L. S...
N. 18 W. 2½ m[il]es to a pt. of high wood on the L, S. passed. a Creek...[etc.]
[22 Aug 04 WC 2.501]

Good visibility was desirable for taking bearings.

I am obliged to make the next Corses Short on ackount of the flying Sands which rasies like a Cloud of Smoke from the Bars [23 Aug 04 WC 2.502]

Numbering in the thousands, these *course* readings depict the expedition's entire 7,000 mile route to the Pacific Ocean and back. Recently, Martin Plamondon II has converted these *traverses* onto 530 finely crafted maps in *Lewis and Clark Trail Maps: A Cartographic Reconstruction, Volumes I, II, & III*, WSU Press, 2000, 2001, 2004.

COURSE, OF {kɔ(ə)s} Thus, as a result. Also **in course**. (Today, its meaning continues in the expression *as a matter of course*.) The transition to the modern sense 'certainly' was gradual and probably imperceptible.

The women...being viewed as property & in course Slaves to the men have not much leisure time [winter 04-05 WC 3.488]

we caught two Antelopes at our encampment in attempting to swim the river; these anamals are but lean as yet and of course not very pleasant food. [16 May 05 ML 4.157]

we are a little South of the Mandans but have had cold weather as yet. it must of course be a healthy country. [22 Jun 05 JO 9.172]

[The Moon] *having passed into her third quarter and of course her Western limb somewhat imperfect.* [9 Sep 05 WC 5.193]

it was fortunate for us that this storm was from the S. W. and of course on our backs. [3 May 06 ML 7.203]

COUS {kowss} A western plant (*Lomatium cous*) of the carrot family (*see* YAMPA), the tubers of which were an important native food and an expedition staple west of the Rockies. The roots were dug from early spring until early summer, when the plant declined, and maturing CAMAS became a more important resource. *See* SAPOLIL, UPPAH. **(Northwest)**

a great portion of the Chopunnish...are now distributed in small vilages through this plain collecting the quawmash and cows; the salmon not yet having arrived to call them to the river. [4 May 06 ML 7.205]

these plains are Smooth Soil rich & filled with commass wild onions and white roots calld. halse [9 May 06 JO 9.308]

We also got bread made of roots, which the natives call Co-was, and sweet roots which they call Com-mas. [12 May 06 PG 10.225]

> The word *cous* is of Sahaptian origin, from Nez Perce *qaws* or Sahaptin *Xawsh*, where *q* represents a *k*-sound made deep in the throat, and *X* a rough *h*-sound, which probably explains Ordway's spelling it with an initial *h*-. Cous also came to be known as *biscuit root*. Cous was dried in the sun, pounded into meal, and eaten as a sort of bread, or as soup or mush.

the noise of their women pounding roots reminds me of a nail factory. The indians seem well pleased...not more so than our men who have their s[t]omachs once more well filled with horsebeef and mush of the bread of cows. [10 May 06 ML 7.239] (Lewis probably was acquainted with Thomas Jefferson's nail factory.)

this morning we eat the last of our birds and cows [25 Jul 06 ML 8.126]

Cous also was applied as a POULTICE.

Pott's legg is inflamed and very painfull to him. we apply a poltice of the roots of Cows. [22 Jun 06 ML 8.046]

COVE A piece of land largely surrounded by higher ground; a HOLLOW. **(South Midland)**

towards evening we descended the mountain down in a lonesome cove [16 Sep 05 JW 11.318]

I dispatched two hunters this evening into the cove to hunt [23 Aug 05 ML 5.149]

COVENTRY {KUH-vən-tree} The usual meaning of being driven *into Coventry* is that of being ostracized for objectionable behavior. The phrase probably originated in the mid-1600s during the English Civil War, when adherents of Parliament captured representatives of King Charles I and sent them to imprisonment in the city of Coventry.

The Mandans punish Capatal Crimes with Death, Smaller Crimes by reason[,] Contempt & Conventrey. [winter 04–05 WC 3.485]

In the following example, the word refers to a woman segregated during a menstrual period. *See* SICK, SITUATION.

there was an appendage of the soletary lodge, the retreat of the tawny damsels when nature causes them to be driven into coventry [9 May 06 ML 7.233]

COVERT {KUH-vət} Cover for game animals.

timber...appears to be handsome Coverts for the Deer [25 Oct 05 WC 5.339]

Also (of a bird), small feathers that cover the bases of larger feathers on parts of the body.

the head neck, the whole of the body including the coverts of the wings...are of a fine gossey bright indigo blue Colour [undated ML 6.132]

CRAWFISH The crayfish, a freshwater crustacean resembling a very small lobster. The word has a long history in Virginian English; Captain John Smith refers to *great craw-fishes* in 1624. (**South, Midland**)

I killd a prarie woolf which together with the ballance of our horse beef and some crawfish which we obtained in the creek enabled us to make one more hearty meal [21 Sep 05 ML 5.226]

CREE* *Christano* {KRISS-tə-no} is an old name for the Cree. These Algonquian people were widespread across Canada and sometimes ranged south into North Dakota and Montana, often in company with the ASSINIBOINE. *Cree* is an abbreviation of *Christano*.

The principal inducement with the British fur companies, for continuing their establishments on the Assinniboin river, is the Buffaloe meat and grease they procure from the Assinniboins, and Christanoes [14 Apr 05 ML 4.035]

CREEK {kreek, modern **South**; krick, modern **North Midland**} In its original use in England and the Atlantic colonies, a creek was an ocean inlet. In the journals, however, it usually identifies a small tributary to a river. (For another word that underwent a similar extension of meaning, *see* FRESH.)

the timber appeared to be confined to the River Creeks & Small branches [19 Jul 04 WC 2.394]

2¼ miles to the mouth of Miry Creek; passd. a...Small run S. S. [9 Apr 05 WC 4.017]

all the Creeks which fall into the Missouri on the Std. Side Since entering the Mountains have extencive Valies of open Plain...the Creeks & runs have timber on them generally [21 Jul 05 WC 4.414]

This Creek appears to be nothing more than the conveyance of Several Small dreans from the high hills and the ponds on each Side near its mouth. [18 Nov 05 WC 6.065]

the water was quite sweet. therefore concluded that it must be supplyed from a large crick. [30 Nov 05 ML 6.096]

When traveling on the Missouri River, the journalists called the largest watercourses *rivers*, while usually identifying tributaries —large or small—as *creeks* (and less commonly *runs*). In other circumstances, *creek*, BRANCH, BROOK, DRAIN, and RUN[1] appear to be used interchangeably, though *creek* connotes a larger size and *drain*, smaller. The term FORK is usually applied to those various streams smaller than a large river. In a random sample taken by this lexicographer comprising 123 cases, the journalists used *creek* 46% of the time, *drain* 25%, *fork* 19%, and *run* and *branch* each about 5%, while *brook* occurred only once. By comparison, Filson's 1784 map of Kentucky—which, granted, is drawn on too small a scale to show *drains*—indicates *creek* 80% of the time, *fork* 15%, and *run* 5%. Leaving *drains* aside, *creek* and *fork* are respectively the first and second most frequent stream-terms both in the journals and on the Kentucky map.

There were two ways that the explorers encountered streams when traveling:

1. While proceeding along another stream—in which case the relation of one stream to another is obvious, and it was logical to call a tributary a *creek* (if one is already on a river) or a *branch* or *fork* (if already on a creek). On July 19, 1804, Clark apparently laid out his hydrological hierarchy, with creeks being tributary to rivers, and branches to creeks.

2. While traveling cross-country—in which case the relation of a stream to others in an area often was unknown. In the Lemhi Pass region on August 15, 1805, for example, the captains recorded *creek*, *branch*, and *run* (as well as *stream*) without apparent distinction.

Benjamin Hawkins, an experienced North Carolina woodsman and a superintendent of Indian affairs, used a similar dual classification in Georgia in 1796–97:

1. When he knew the relationship of one stream to another, Hawkins clearly made *branches* tributary to *creeks* ("cane on the creek and reed on the branches," [*Letters*, 61]; "this is a branch of the creek I crossed at Tunpanejies," [87].) During a journey through eastern Kentucky half a century earlier, Thomas Walker neatly summed up a similar scheme, stating, "We went down the Branch to Hunting Creek & kept it to Milleys River" [22 May 1750].

2. While traveling cross-country and lacking a hydrological frame of reference, however, Hawkins equated *creek* and *branch*, "[crossing] 3 small creeks or branches," [33], though *branch* does seem, in such situations, to connote a smaller stream than *creek*. (Hawkins and Walker seldom recorded *run*.)

CROUP {kroop} The rump (of an animal).

the oldfield lark with a yellow brest and a black spot on the croop [22 Jun 05 ML 4.325]

CROW A Siouan people occupying south central Montana. The journalists also refer to them as *Absaroka* (the Crow name, traditionally said to be derived from a word for some sort of bird), as *Corbeau* (French for 'crow'), as RAVEN INDIANS, as ROCKY

MOUNTAIN INDIANS, and—with reference to a quarrel with the HIDATSA over a buffalo-stomach—as the PAUNCH. The Crow language is closely related to Hidatsa.

this Smoke must be raisd. by the Crow Indians...as a signal for us, or other bands. [18 Jul 06 WC 8.201]

CROWD SAIL   To carry all possible sail on a vessel to make maximum speed.

We Crouded Sail and Saild 16 miles [15 Jun 04 JW 11.024]

CRUZATTE, PIERRE {kru-ZAHT or kru-ZĂT} Half OMAHA and half FRENCH Canadian, Cruzatte served as an interpreter and was the most skilled boat-handler and principal violinist of the expedition. During the tense encounter with the TETON in September 1804, Cruzatte gained crucial information from the Tetons' Omaha prisoners, which he translated to Lewis & Clark. Cruzatte had the use of only one eye [8.290], which may help explain his accidental shooting of Lewis while hunting on August 11, 1806. *See* also BOW-MAN, MENDING HAND, SNAG², VIOLIN.

Peter Crusat who Spoke Mahar came in the night and informed me that the mahar Prisoners told him that the Tetons intended to Stop us [27 Sep 04 WC 3.121]

I dispatched Peter Crusat (our principal waterman) back to follow the river and examine the practibility of the Canoes passing [31 Oct 05 WC 5.361]

CRY   (Of an animal) to make its characteristic sound. *See* CHITTEDIDDLE.

I heard the frogs crying for the first time this season [15 Apr 05 ML 4.041]

the small species of Goatsucker or whiperwill begin to cry [17 May 05 ML 4.236]

CULWHAMO   The Chinookan word for LICORICE. (**Pacific Northwest**)

a Liquorice root Cul-wha-mo [undated WC 6.495]

two Clotsops Came with a mat and Some fiew roots of Cut wha mo, for which they asked a file [1 Jan 06 WC 6.153]

CUR-DOG   Any of several short-haired breeds of working and hunting dogs; not derogatory as in the present-day sense of *cur*. Also called *mountain cur* and *bear-dog*.

[The prairie-wolf] Bark so much resembles or Sounds to me like our Common Small Cur dogs that I have frequently mistaken them for that Speces of dog [11 Sep 06 WC 8.357]

CUT   To castrate (a horse). *See* GELD.

we had this horse imedeately Cut with 2 others which we had not before thought proper to Castrate. [19 May 06 WC 7.273]

CUT OUT   To regroove a worn RIFLE barrel.

John Shields Cut out my Small rifle & brought hir to Shoot very well. [8 Apr 06 WC 7.095]

CUT-OFF   A place where a river has cut a new, shorter channel, as across the neck of a bend, leaving the old channel cut off from the river. (**South**)

we Set out early at the great Cut off [6 Sep 06 WC 8.351]

D

DAKOTA = SIOUX. A self-designation meaning 'friendly, allied'; the TETON equivalent is *Lakota*.

This nation call themselves—Dar co tar. [31 Aug 04 WC 3.027]

DAM, FISH- = WEIR.

2 fish dams or weares across the North fork to catch Salmon [30 Sep 05 WC 5.238]

DANGER OF {DANE-jə} Risk to.

continue the barks with Bratton, and commenced them with Gibson...I think therefore that there is no further danger of his recovery. [17 Feb 06 ML 6.321]

DAUB {dɔb} To seal log walls with mud. *See* CHINK.

men imployed untill late in dobing their huts [16 Nov 04 WC 3.237]

DEADFALL A trap consisting of a heavy log, which when triggered falls on an animal.

the nativs take a fiew of them [raccoon] *in Snars, and deadfalls* [24 Feb 06 WC 6.344]

DEADLY Terrible, awful.

we proceeded up the river passing a Sucession of rapids & Cascades to the Falls, which we had herd for Several miles makeing a dedly Sound [17 Jun 05 WC 4.304]

DEER, BLACK-TAIL(ED) {DEE-ə} = (MULE) DEER.

Capt. Clark did not get a Goat or a black taile deer the objects of his pursuite. [9 Sep 04 JW 3.058]

the tail...terminates in a tissue of black hair of about 3 Inches long. from this black hair of the tail they have obtained among the French engages the appelation of the black taled deer [10 May 05 ML 4.138]

DEER, COMMON = (WHITETAILED) DEER, the only species known to Lewis & Clark before they encountered the large-eared *mule deer* in South Dakota. *See* DEER (MULE).

Colter Killed...a curious kind of deer of a Dark gray Colr...the ears large & long...8 fallow Deer 5 Common & 3 buffalow killed to day [17 Sep 04 WC 3.083]

> The captains apparently made a distinction between varieties of whitetail deer (perhaps the eastern and western subspecies), calling some *common* and others *fallow*. Differences among whitetail subspecies are subtle and gradational, while those between mule and whitetail deer are clearer and consistently indicated in the journals. The whitetail probably originally was called *common* (or *fallow*) to distinguish it from other members of the deer family (the Cervidæ), such as moose (*moose-deer* [8.095]) and elk.

DEER, FALLOW Usually = (COMMON) DEER. *Fallow* refers to the color of the deer's coat, variably described as brownish, yellowish, or reddish. The original *fallow deer* is a European species.

they killed two Mule deer, one common fallow or longtailed deer [et al.] [10 May 05 ML 4.136]

The ricara Indians inform us that they find no black tail Deer as high up as this place, those we find are of the fallow Deer Kind [18 Oct 04 WC 3.183]

Occasionally, though, Lewis uses it for (BLACK-TAIL) DEER.

The Black tailed fallow deer are peculiar to this [Pacific] *coast* [19 Feb 06 ML 6.328]

DEER, MULE A deer (*Odocoileus hemionus*) of western North America, with "peculiarly large" [4.137] ears, whence the name bestowed by Lewis & Clark.

from the appearance of the Mule deer and the bighorned anamals we beleive ourselves fast approaching a...mountainous country [10 May 05 ML 4.136]

DEER, RED = (WHITETAILED) DEER.

we have killed no mule deer since we lay here [at the Missouri forks], *they are all of the longtailed red deer* [29 Jul 05 ML 5.010]

DEER, WHITETAILED The Virginia deer, *Odocoileus virginianus*. Clark's use of the term here is the earliest known. Lewis & Clark usually called them *common* or *fallow*.

I Saw great numbers of Elk & white tale deer [5 Jun 05 WC 4.259]

DELAWARE {DELL-ə-weh-ə, DILL-, DELL-ə-way} An ALGONQUIAN-speaking people, widely dispersed by 1800 from their original 17th century home along the Delaware River on the eastern seaboard, to New York, Ontario, Ohio, Wisconsin, and the Mississippi prairies, including the Cape Girardeau area, where they were associated with the SHAWNEE. Southeast Missouri's Delaware population in 1815 numbered about 500 (*ASPIA* II. 76).

we found here som Shawnees and Delawars incamped [16 Nov 03 ML 2.089]

Som Delaways pass down to St. Louis [27 Nov 03 WC 2.182]

a sufficient scope of country for the Shawnees, Dillewars, Miames, and Kickapoos. [winter 04–05 WC 3.391]

DEPARTURE, POINT OF {də-PAHT-chə} A starting-point for navigational computations. Ideally there would have been but one for the exploration, but the occasional stopping of the chronometer necessitated several.

The mouth of the River Dubois is to be considered as the point of departure. [c. 14 May 04 ML 2.228]

DEPOSIT Place where something is deposited; a depot or CACHE.

he could not overtake the Souis war party, (who had in their way distroyd all the meat at one Deposit which I had made & Burnt the Lodges) [21 Feb 05 WC 3.299]

Here, of canoes submerged for safe-keeping until the expedition's return to east of the Rockies.

about noon we arived at the canoe deposite [9 Jul 06 JO 9.333]

DERNIER RESORT {French dern-YAY reh-ZOR} Last resort.

we now determined as the dernier resort to prepare a parsel of Iron spikes and attach them to the end of small poles...and endeavour by means of them to free the vessels from the ice. [3 Feb 05 ML 3.285]

DESK Though only a lap-desk, nonetheless a surprising item to portage over the Rockies. *See* also VIOLIN.

Several horses Sliped and roled down Steep hills which hurt them verry much The one which Carried my desk & Small trunk Turned over & roled down a mountian for 40 yards & lodged against a tree, broke the Desk the horse escaped and appeared but little hurt [15 Sep 05 WC 5.207]

DETAIN To delay (one's own departure).

we detained 2 hours [14 Jun 04 WC 2.300]

DETOUR The cause of going out of one's way. For French boatmen, meaning a large bend in a river, which entailed traveling a far greater distance by water than walking across the GORGE. *See* BIG BEND.

Soues or Darcota rove on both Sides of the Missourie about the Grand de tour...or big bend [winter 04–05 WC 3.415]

DINNER {DIH-nə} A midday (not evening) meal. The usual routine when traveling by water was to set out at LIGHT (before dawn) and then stop at convenient places for breakfast around 8 a.m. [5.061], dinner around noontime (which also allowed the captains to make noon OBSERVATIONS), and at day's end make supper and camp. *See* BREAKFAST, NOON IT.

we halted at 12 oC. took dinner at the Mouth of a River [8 Oct 04 JO 9.078]

Hence **dine**. (*See* also BEEF.)

we landed at 12 o.C. to dine at a large bottom prarie [4 Sep 04 JO 9.053]

DIRK {dək} A dagger. *See* EXPOSE.

I have my Sword, Durk &c. fixed [20 Apr 04 WC 2.205]

DISAGREEABLE (Of weather) unpleasant.

Cloudy & Disagreeable and Som hard Showers [14 Sep 04 WC 3.070]

(Of people) uncomfortable.

The day proved Cloudy with rain...we are all wet cold and disagreeable [5 Nov 05 WC 6.024]

DISEMBOGUE {dis-əm-BOHG} (Of a stream) to discharge into another body of water.

The little Missouri disembogues on the S. side of the Missouri 1693 miles from the confluence of the latter with the Mississippi. [12 Apr 05 ML 4.026]

DISORDERED {dis-OH-dəd} Suffering from a medical disorder.

they brought Several disordered persons to us for whome they requested Some Medical aid. [28 Apr 06 WC 7.180]

DISTANCE *See* COURSE.

DISTEMPER {dis-TEM-pə} A disease of young horses, now usually called *strangles.*

one of Thompson's horses is either choked...or has the distemper very badly [21 Jun 06 ML 8.043]

> Strangles is a contagious bacterial (streptococcal) infection of the lymph glands of the head and neck. Swelling and an excessive production of pus and mucus cause choking, breathing difficulties, and a loss of appetite. Strangles also may cause feed to be coughed out of the nose, producing nasal discharges that might be confused with those of CHOKE.

DIVIDING Separating one river-drainage from another; compare with the modern expression *continental divide.*

they have now come over the dividing ridge to trade their horses [22 Aug 05 JW 11.280]

Capt. Lewis Settled & paid off the Indian women who helped us over the divideing mountain, then began to trade with the natives for horses. [27 Aug 05 JW 9.212]

DOCTOR {DOCK-tə} To practice medicine, at which the captains must have excelled (or enjoyed good fortune), as only one expedition member died. (Sergeant Charles Floyd succumbed to a ruptured appendix or peritonitis; even Dr. Benjamin Rush of Philadelphia probably could not have cured him.) *See* GLAUBER'S SALTS and NITER for typical courses of treatment. (**South Midland**)

Jos: Fields got bit by a Snake, which was quickly doctered with Bark by Cap Lewis. [4 Jul 04 WC 2.347]

his feet was froze verry bad. they got him to our fort. Capt. Lewis doctered him. [9 Jan 05 JW 11.118]

he [a Walla Walla] *brought a fine horse and gave Capt. Clark for doctering hir* [30 Apr 06 JO 9.300]

DOG An animal important to the expedition, as well as many native peoples of the Great Plains, as a source of meat.

They [Sioux] *had a fat dog Cooked as a feest* [29 Aug 04 WC 3.022]

Lewis preferred it.

the dog now constitutes a considerable part of our subsistence...certain I am that it is a healthy strong diet...I prefer it to lean venison or Elk, and is very far superior to the horse in any state. [13 Apr 06 ML 7.115]

Clark never acquired a taste for it.

all the Party have greatly the advantage of me, in as much as they all relish the flesh of the dogs [10 Oct 05 WC 5.256]

Nor did the Nez Perce.

while at dinner an indian fellow verry impertinently threw a poor half starved puppy nearly into my plait by way of derision for our eating dogs...I was so provoked...that I caught the puppy and threw it with great violence at him...and shewed him if he repeated his insolence I would tommahawk him, the fellow withdrew...and I continued my repast on dog without further molestation. [5 May 06 ML 7.210]

DOG, SPANIARD'S Spaniel. The word *spaniel* comes from Old French *espaignol* 'Spaniard.'

the men plunged into the water like Spaniards Dogs after those fowls [10 Dec 05 WC 6.120]

DOG, TURNSPIT A small dog on a treadmill that turned a spit. "A certaine dogge... when any meate is to bee roasted they go into a wheele...turning rounde about with the waight of their bodies" (1576, *OED*).

The [brarrow's] *forelegs remarkably large and muscular and are formed like the ternspit dog.* [26 Feb 06 ML 6.352]

DOG INDIAN Applied to the CHEYENNE through confusion with the French word *chien* 'dog.'

a number of the Shian or dog Indians came from the village to visit us. [2 Dec 04 JO 9.100]

DOLLAR, SPANISH MILLED {Dɔ-lə} A SPANISH or Spanish-American silver coin worth 8 *reales* or *bits* (a *piece of eight*), the edge of which during coining was marked by the milling process.

Frazer got 2 Spanish mill dollars from a squaw for an old razer we expect they got them from the Snake Indians who live near the Spanish country to the South. [29 May 06 JO 9.316]

DOMINICKER {DAH-mə-nick-ə} An American breed of chicken (*Gallus gallus domesticus*) with barred plumage, rose combs, and yellow legs. (**South Midland**)

that kind of dunghill fowl, which the henwives of our Countrey Call dommanicker. [2 Mar 06 WC 6.373]

Here, Lewis means the spruce grouse, *Falcipennis canadensis*.

we killed...a female of the large dommanicker or speckled pheasant [26 Jun 06 ML 8.052]

DOSE OF SALTS A dose of PHYSIC, believed to purge the body of poisons, such as the arsenic Lewis imagined he had inhaled while grinding a rock specimen for study. *Like a dose of salts* came to mean 'very rapidly.' Thirty years later, Davy Crockett claimed he would *go through the Mexicans like a dose of salts*. See GLAUBER'S SALTS.

Capt Lewis took a Dost of Salts to work off the effects of the Arsenic [22 Aug 04 WC 2.501]

DOTED (Of wood) rotten, punky.

we find the trunks of many large pine trees s[t]anding erect...they are much doated and none of them vegetating [14 Apr 06 ML 7.118]

DOUBLE To follow the coastline around a point of land. *See* COAST.

at ½ after five we doubled point William [23 Mar 06 ML 7.007]

DOUBLE-MAN To double up crews to pass boats through difficult stretches of river.

they were obliged to double man the canoes and drag them over the stone and gravel. [3 Aug 05 ML 5.037]

we had to Man our Crafts doubly in order to get them over Safe. [27 May 05 JW 11.175]

the rocks Show themselves across the River and appear Shallow all the way across. we double manned and got up Safe. [25 Jul 05 JW 11.240]

DOUBLE-SPOKEN (Of Indians) dishonest.

the 2d Chief...was a Double Spoken man [28 Sep 04 WC 3.125]

DOUSE To lower (a sail).

a violent gust of wind...took the Sail and before they had time to douse it it turned the perogue down on one Side So that she filled with water [14 May 05 JO 9.148]

DRAFT¹ = RAVINE.

Captain Clarke and his party returned, having found a tolerable good road except where some draughts crossed it. [20 Jun 05 PG 10.104]

the snow was not so deep in the drafts between [the mountains] [26 Jun 06 PG 10.244]

DRAFT² The maximum amount that a scale is capable of measuring at one time. A grain elevator, for example, with a 2,000 bushel scale, needs five drafts to weigh 10,000 bushels of grain.

obliged to weigh it in small draughts not having any method of weighing entire [16 Nov 03 ML 2.090]

DRAG An improvised drag-net made of brush. *See* SEINE, TRAIL.

with a Brush Drag caught 308 fish [15 Aug 04 WC 2.483]

we...made a fish drag of willows and caught 520 fine pan fish. [22 Aug 05 JO 9.208]

DRAIN {dreen, drane} A small stream. *See* CREEK. (**South, South Midland**) *passing Several Small Dreens, falling into the river* [24 Aug 04 WC 2.504]

dined in the mouth of a little drane [5 Jul 06 ML 8.090]

passed a drean N. W. side [16 Jul 06 WC 8.189]

Also, a tear-duct.

on the inner corner of each eye there is a drane or large recepicle [10 May 05 ML 4.138]

DRAM A small drink of spirits. The word comes ultimately from the Greek *drachma*, which is the name of the unit of currency in modern Greece. *See* GILL. (**South Midland**)

the party drank a Drachm of whisky [15 Jun 04 JW 11.024]

we then gave them a Dram & broke up the Council [19 Aug 04 WC 2.493]

to add in some measure to the general pleasure which seemed to pervade our little community, we ordered a dram to be issued to each person; this soon produced the fiddle [26 Apr 05 ML 4.070]

DRAW (Of a boat) to require a certain amount of water to float.

the Boat Drew too much water to cross the quick Sands...She draws 4 foot water [5 Jun 04 WC 2.278]

DRIFT Driftwood. French voyageurs called drift laced into an impenetrable tangle an *embarass*; *see* EMBARRASSMENT.

camped at 6 oClock (after expirencing great dificuselty in passing Some Drifts) [23 May 04 WC 2.246]

We Saw this day 4 otter on a drift. [21 Apr 05 JO 9.135]

a hard wind...Loosened the Drift trees which is verry thick on the Shores, and tossed them about in Such a manner, as to endanger our Canoes very much [9 Nov 05 WC 6.037]

DRIFT ICE Loose ice running downstream during the fall freeze-up or spring break-up. Drift ice could be difficult or impossible to cross and occasionally formed ice jams, causing rapid upstream flooding. *See* BREAK UP.

much drift ice running in the river [27 Nov 04 ML 3.249]

DROUILLARD, GEORGE {DREW-yə} Half French and half Shawnee, a sign language expert, and perhaps the expedition's most skilled rifleman.

The means I had of communicating with these people [Shoshone] *was by way of Drewyer who understood perfectly the common language of jesticulation or signs which seems to be universally understood by all the Nations we have yet seen.* [14 Aug 05 ML 5.088]

This morning sent out Drewyer and one man to hunt, they returned in the evening, Drewyer having killed seven Elk; I scarcely know how we should subsist were it not for the exertions of this excellet hunter. [12 Jan 06 ML 6.199]

DRUM (Of a gamebird) making a booming sound by beating the wings.

the indians informed us that neither of these [grouse] *speceis drumed* [26 Jun 06 ML 8.053]

DRY GOODS Textile fabrics and related merchandise.

overtook two keels from Louisville bound to Kaskaskias loaded with dry goods and whiskey [22 Nov 03 ML 2.101]

DUB = DRUM.

The [sharptailed grouse] *male also dubbs something like the pheasant, but by no means as loud.* [15 Apr 05 ML 4.042]

DUCKANMALLARD {DUCK-ən-MAL-əd} A dialect name for the mallard duck, *Anas platyrhynchos.*

Killed...4 Duck in Malade [20 Oct 05 WC 5.309]

the duckinmallard which bread in this neighbourhood, is now laying it's eggs [12 Apr 06 ML 7.193]

DUNGHILL-FOWL {DUNG-'l foul} A common barnyard chicken, not pure-bred. *See* DOMINICKER.

[Heath cocks] *are much larger than the common dunghill fowls* [12 Aug 05 ML 5.074]

I killed a Pheasent at the Indian Camp larger than a dungal fowl [20 Aug 05 WC 5.131]

DURABLE Having great endurance. *See* BOTTOM[2].

they [antelope] *are extremely fleet and dureable.* [29 Apr 05 ML 4.085]

DUTCH German, a sense continuing today in *Pennsylvania Dutch.*

West from Cape Jeredeau about 16 miles is a large settlement of duch descendants who have emigrated from the Atlantic States [23 Nov 03 ML 2.108]

DYSENTERY {DISS-ən-ter-ee} Inflammation of the lower intestine caused by various infections transmitted under poor sanitary conditions. Characterized by abdominal pain and diarrhea, dysentery is a debilitating and dangerous disease, sometimes referred to as the *bloody flux.*

Several have the Decissentary, which I contribute to the water [14 Jun 04 WC 2.306]

Joseph Fields was very sick today with the disentary had a high fever [4 May 05 ML 4.109]

E

EAR, ROASTING {ROHS-tən [Y]EE-ə} Corn harvested when "green" or "in the milk" and suitable for roasting. (**South, South Midland**) *this nation have returned to get Some Green Corn or rosting Ears* [23 Jul 04 WC 2.416]

EAR-BOB {[Y]EE-ə bob} Jewelry hung from an ear-lobe. (**South, South Midland**)

the natives [Shoshone] *gave Capt. Lewis ear bobs to put in ears and an ornament to Spread over his Shoulders* [17 Aug 05 JO 9.206]

I gave his Son a par of ear bobs and a pece of ribon [27 Dec 05 WC 6.139]

EAT {ETT} Past tense of eat, here used intransitively, meaning 'to have a certain taste or consistency.'

they Gave us the tails and Some of the [beaver] *meat which eat verry Good* [10 Apr 05 JO 9.129]

Here applied transitively.

we cooked and eat a haisty meal [10 Aug 05 ML 5.063]

killed and eat a colt [14 Sep 05 WC 5.242]

For other examples, *see* (WHITE) APPLE, COUS, HUMP, PEMMICAN.

ELECTRICITY A recently developed therapy—as here for paralysis—not yet available in the wilderness.

we informed the indians that we knew of no releif for him...I am confident that this would be an excellent subject for electricity and much regret that I have it not in my power to supply it. [25 May 06 ML 7.286]

ELK A large deer species (*Cervus canadensis*) with long, branching antlers. Elk meat was an important food during the winter spent at FORT CLATSOP, though much of it spoiled in the mild temperatures of the Pacific Northwest winter.

a fiew Wap-e-to roots, which I eate in a little Elk Supe [3 Dec 05 WC 6.106]

I prosue'd this gang of Elk through bogs which the wate of a man would Shake for ½ an Acre [8 Dec 05 WC 6.117]

EMBARRASSMENT Obstacle. The French voyageur word for a stream obstruction, such as a tangle of DRIFT, was *embarrass*, meaning in standard French 'trouble, awkward position, embarrassment.'

in addition to the imbarrasments of the rappid courant, riffles, & rockey point...the banks and sides of the bluff were more steep than usual [30 May 05 ML 4.222]

Also, encumbrance.

to releive our horses from the embarasment of their loads...we should continue our march to the first water [8 May 06 ML 7.228]

ENGAGÉ {French ahng-gə-ZHAY} Generally, a fur-trade company employee; in the journals, French-Canadian boatmen hired by the expedition. French for *engaged man*, 'one who is engaged (to work).' *See* HIRELING.

all other soldiers and engaged men of whatever discription must perform their regular tour of guad duty. [26 May 04 ML 2.258]

The names of the french Ingishees, or Hirelens [4 Jul 04 WC 2.347]

these men had assended the missouri with us the last year as engages. [7 Apr 05 ML 4.007]

the white apple as called by the angegies [8 May 05 WC 4.128]

deep purple berry...the engagees Call it the Indian Current. [9 Aug 06 WC 8.286]

ENTRAILS {IN-tə-rəls, EN-trəls, typical southern pronunciations} Internal organs.

[The badger's] *Interals like the interals of a Hog* [30 Jul 04 WC 2.430]

they had killed 6 Elk...which they left lying, haveing taken out their interals [3 Dec 05 WC 6.107]

we gave this cheif...some venison, horsebeef, the entrels of the four deer, and four fawns [8 May 06 ML 7.227]

we...roasted a quarter of it [deer] *and the Intrals which we eat* [9 Jul 06 JO 9.333]

EQUIPAGE {EH-kwə-pəj} Equipment, ACCOUTREMENTS.

examine the mens arms and equapage [28 May 04 WC 2.261]

ESCULENT {ESS-kə-lənt} Edible.

nature...has distributed a great variety of esculent plants over the face of the Country [28 May 06 WC 7.300]

ESPONTOON {ess-PAHN-toon} A half-pike and spear pointed weapon about six feet long, carried by infantry officers. The word comes through French from Italian *spuntone* 'large pointed object.' *See* HELVE.

I...met with 2 porcupines...I approached so near one of them before it percieved me that I touched it with my espontoon. [3 May 05 ML 4.104]

we saw a great many wolves in the neighbourhood of these mangled [buffalo] *carcases they were fat and extreemly gentle, Capt. C....killed one of them with his espontoon.* [29 May 05 ML 4.217]

In passing along the face of one of these bluffs...I sliped...and but for a quick and fortunate recovery by means of my espontoon I should been precipitated into the river [7 Jun 05 ML 4.262]

my gun is true and I had a steady rest by means of my espontoon [14 Jun 05 ML 4.294]

ESSENTIALLY Seriously.

One of the canoes overset and was very near injuring 2 men essencially. [17 Jun 05 ML 4.303]

Inherently, referring to the essence (of something).

in the act of liteing this bird [long-billed curlew] *lets itself down by an extention of it's wings without motion holding their points very much together above it's back, in this rispect differing ascentially from any bird I ever observed.* [4 Jun 05 ML 4.254]

EULACHON {modern YOO-lə-kahn} The Chinookan name for candlefish (*Thaleich-thys pacificus*), a small, oily fish related to smelt, which runs up Pacific Northwest rivers in springtime. When dried, a eulachon could burn like a candle. Roasted in the Chinookan fashion (on a spit, without scaling or gutting), eulachon was Lewis's favorite food at Fort Clatsop. *See* ANCHOVY. (**Pacific Northwest**)

The Natives came to the Fort & brought some dried fish, which the Indians called All-Can [21 Mar 06 JW 11.430]

No single English spelling adequately renders the pronunciation of the Chinook *uLXan*, where *L* represents a breathy sort of *l* not found in English, but like the Welsh -*ll*-, and *X* is a rough *h*-sound.

the small fish, which they call Ulken. [9 Mar 06 PG 10.197]

here some Clatsops came to us in a canoe loaded with dryed anchovies, which they call Olthen' [25 Mar 06 ML 7.012]

EVENING The period from noon till dark. (**South, South Midland**)

it was one in the evening before he returned [24 Apr 06 ML 7.163]

EXPECT To suppose, imagine, believe.

I expect that those Indians are on their way to war against the Osages nation [5 Jun 04 WC 2.279]

La Liberty has not returned. it is expected that he has deserted. [18 Aug 04 JW 11.057]

EXPOSE To lay out (trade goods) for inspection by a buyer; to put up for sale.

we exposed a few old clothes my dirk and Capt. C's swoard to barter for horses [25 Apr 06 ML 7.165]

EXPRESS A messenger.

Express returned from Koho [29 Jan 04 WC 2.167]

Sent Sjt. Ordway with a perogue to St Louis after Colter arrived express [7 May 04 WC 2.212]

EYE-DAG A dagger with a hole or eye in the handle for attaching a lanyard.

they wanted an instrumet which the Northwest traders call an eye-dag which we had not. [15 Apr 06 ML 7.123]

the others were armed with bows and arrows and eyedaggs. [27 Jul 06 ML 8.135]

EYE-WATER {WƆ-tə} A therapeutic eye-wash, typically containing zinc sulfate and lead acetate. Zinc has some limited antibiotic activity, but lead acetate can actually damage the cornea. *See* SATURN, SORE-EYES, VITRIOL.

sore eyes is a universal complaint with all the natives we have seen on the west side of the Rocky mountains. Capt. C. was busily engaged for several hours this morning in administering eye-water to a croud of applicants. [6 May 06 ML 7.215]

F

FAGGOT-BONE One of many small, Y-shaped bones (also called *y-bones* and *feather-bones*) characteristic of the flesh of suckers and some other fish species.

it has the faggot bones, from which I have supposed it to be of the mullet kind. [19 Aug 05 ML 5.119]

FALL AWAY To deteriorate, waste away.

Our horses...have fallen away very much, since we came into the Mountains. [19 Sep 05 JW 11.323]

FALL DOWN To descend (a river).

we Set out and fell down to the lower Village [1 Nov 04 WC 3.224]

FALLING (Of weather) raining or promising rain. Probably so called from the decrease in barometric pressure preceding wet weather. (**Midland**)

The weather has been warm, and no falling weather [27 Mar 04 WC 2.185]

FARE {FEH-yə} To be (well or poorly) provided with food.

the beaver was large and fat we have therefore fared sumptuously today [7 Jan 06 ML 6.174]

Also, the food itself.

every one appears content with his situation and his fare. [16 Jan 06 ML 6.211]

FAT A desirable characteristic of meat, especially in winter when a high calorie-intake meant survival. *See* HUMP, MARROW-BONE, SUET.

a number of the Savvages came to our Garrison. Some of them brought Some fat meat and Gave to our officers. [9 Dec 04 JO 9.102]

FATHOM A measure of length, six feet (approximately the span of a man's outstretched arms). *See* BRACE[1].

The Common Current taken with a Log runs 50 fathen in 40" [seconds] [17 Jul 04 WC 2.389]

I purchased a canoe from an Indian today for which I gave him six fathoms of wampum beads [1 Apr 06 ML 7.050]

FATIGUE Tiring or troublesome labor.

rested today after a hard fatigue [22 Feb 05 JO 9.117]

Also, a military detachment.

a fatiegue of 6 men employed in jerking the Elk beaf. [14 Jan 06 ML 6.203]

FELON {FELL-ən} A BOIL[1] or sore, often around a fingernail or toenail. *See* TUMOR, WHITLOW.

one man have a fellon riseing on his hand [12 Jun 05 WC 4.281]

FEMME {fahm} French word for woman, wife. The reference in the first quotation is to the Femme Osage River (literally, 'the river of the Osage's wife') in Missouri.

passed the wife or faim of the Hoozaw River [23 May 04 JO 9.007]

If you...will bring down your Son your famn Janey [Sacagawea] *had best come along with you to take care of the boy* [20 Aug 06 WC in Jackson Letters (ed. 2) 1.315]

FENNEL = YAMPA.

Shabonos Squar gatherd a quantity of fenel roots which we find...nurishing food. [16 May 06 WC 7.265]

FERRIAGE {FER-ee-əj} The price for being ferried across a stream.

I was asked for ferrage and paid a pin [8 Jan 06 WC 6.181]

FILBERT {FILL-bət} Hazelnut, genus *Corylus*.

they gave us Philburts, and berries to eate [22 Oct 05 WC 5.323]

purchased five dogs some roots, shappalell, filberds and dryed burries [14 Apr 06 ML 7.119]

FILLET A narrow band or strip of cloth or similar material.

we gave a fellet of Sheep Skin (which we brought for Spunging) to 3 Chiefs [24 Dec 04 WC 3.261]

Also, a narrow cut of tender meat from the LOINS.

See (WHITE) PUDDING for an example.

FIRE[1] {FĪ-ə} The campfire of one Indian family, as a census unit.

This nation (Missouries) once the most noumerous nation in this part of the Continent now reduced to about 80 f[ir]*es.* [13 Jun 04 WC 2.296]

FIRE[2] To set on fire, especially as a signal.

one Perogue...answered us by firing a prarie near them. [25 Aug 04 WC 3.008]

FIRE-STEEL A piece of steel used with FLINT to strike sparks for starting a fire. *See* STEEL.

we gave him a fire steel by way of compensation [to a Nez Perce returning two powder canisters]. [7 May ML 7.220]

FISH, POUNDED Among the Columbia River tribes, dried fish, mostly salmon, was pounded to a fine consistency and stored in baskets (made of grass and rushes, lined with salmon skins, and holding about 100 pounds) for use in winter (**Pacific Northwest**). Large quantities of salmon obtained through trade helped sustain the expedition through the winter at FORT CLATSOP. *See* APPROPRIATE, CLATSOP.

nothing to eate but Pounded fish [10 Nov 05 WC 6.039]

FISH, SCALE- Fish with scales, as contrasted with scaleless species, such as catfish.

goodrich has caught a considerable number quantity of Small fish. Some of them Skale fish   the most part are...Smallish sized cat fish. [5 Jun 05 JW 11.187]

we caught considerable quantity of Small flat Scale fish [16 Jun 05 JO 9.168]

FISH-HOOK An important trade item.

I employd Those Indians to take up one of our Canoes...for which Service I gave them each a fishing hook of a large Size [20 Nov 05 WC 6.072]

FIST (FEIST) A sort of small dog with a pugnacious behavior, giving rise to the word *feisty. Fist* originally meant 'fart' and probably was applied to dogs as a term of contempt. (**South, South Midland**)

This Prarie Wolf barked like a large fest and is not much larger [12 Aug 04 WC 2.471]

FIT A sudden attack of mental or bodily illness.

one of their women was taken with the crazey fit by our fire...She...took a Sharp flint from hir husband and cut hir arms in Sundry places So that the blood gushed out. [9 Oct 05 JW 11.344]

Yesterday evening I had a fit of the ague, and have been very unwell to day; so much so that I am unable to steer my canoe. [10 Oct 05 PG 10.152]

FIX To prepare (for something).

a Cloudy morning fixing for a Start [14 May 04 WC 2.215]

FLACK To splash.

I also had Buffalow Skin tacked on So as to prevent the waters flacking in between the Two canoes. [24 July 06 WC 8.217]

(Of beaver) to slap the water with the flat of the tail.

the beaver was flacking in the river about us all the last night. [12 Jul 06 WC 8.177]

FLAG The cattail, *Typha latifolia*, with long, flat leaves.

They had a number of lodges made out of Flags & Cedar bark [22 Oct 05 JW 11.366]

cattail

Cooper's flag was used to caulk between BARREL staves.

The Indians...eat the root of the Cattail or Cooper's flag. [1 Mar 06 ML 6.366]

FLAG, RED The standard, internationally recognized signal for battle, opposed to the white flag showing peaceful intentions. The protocol of civilized warfare had apparently preceded Lewis & Clark into Sioux lands. *See* TALK.

we hoisted a white flag, and a red flag for peace or war, and was determined to fight our way [28 Sep 04 JW 11.090]

the Indians assembled on S. Shore hoisted a white flag. we then took down our red flag. directly after they hoisted another. We then took them to be our friends. [30 Sep 04 JO 9.073]

FLANK = FLANKING PARTY.

The flank came in & informed they heard two Guns [28 Jul 04 WC 2.424]

FLANKER {FLANK-ə} A member of a FLANKING PARTY.

Saw a fire on the S. S. Supposedly the four flankers, to be theire [9 Jul 04 WC 2.362]

FLANKING PARTY {FLANK'n PAH-tee} A detachment of men proceeding in a direction parallel with a main force, usually in order to protect it.

Saw a fire on the N. Side thougt it was ouer flanken partey [9 Jul 04 CF 9.386]

the flanking party who were with the horses did not join us this night [15 Jul 04 JO 9.026]

FLANNEL A soft cloth of wool, or wool and cotton. *See* LINIMENT. (**South, South Midland** variant)

the weather being warm I had left my leather over shirt and had woarn only a yellow flannin one. [14 Jun 05 ML 4.294]

FLATHEAD In modern use, as possibly in this quotation from Clark as well, the name refers to a specific SALISH-speaking people of western Montana. There is no evidence that they practiced head-flattening.

we Crossd. Glade Creek...at a place the Tushepaws or Flat head Indians have made 2 wears across to Catch Sammon [14 Sep 05 WC 5.205]

There is no evidence either that this name, as applied to interior Northwest peoples, originated with the Lower Columbia Chinookans, who indeed did practice head-flattening. "Flathead" was a literal translation of the French term *Tête Plate* that Lewis & Clark learned from Canadian traders on the upper Missouri. The French designation was borrowed from a native tongue, probably Crow or Hidatsa, as speakers of those languages were in frequent contact with the "Flathead" and their neighbors, the Shoshones. It has been suggested that a Shoshone name for the Flathead meant 'people with shaved heads' (*see* TUSHAPAW). Possibly that designation was transferred by translation to neighboring languages. (Supporting a Shoshone origin is the fact that the Shoshones are the only tribe in the area not referred to by the journalists as *Flatheads*.) The explorers no doubt were struck by the radical difference between the relatively simple inventory of consonant sounds in the Siouan languages of the Plains, and those of the Pacific Northwest's Salishan, Sahaptian, and Chinookan languages, which are rich in consonants difficult for Euro-Americans to distinguish or pronounce (*see* CLUCKING). (So struck by this difference were the journalists, in fact, that some thought the Flathead must be the rumored WELSH INDIANS.) The complexity of these speech-sounds perhaps was the reason the captains lumped all peoples west of the Siouans (except the Shoshone) as "Flatheads," while underrating the significant differences among northwest languages. They did, however, distinguish between "dialects" of the Tushapaw and the Chopunnish, whom, nevertheless, Clark considered "origneally the Same people" [5.222]). They did recognize the distinction between the Sahaptian and Chinookan languages of the lower Columbia. The name *Flatheads* was applied in the journals to the Salish, the NEZ PERCE and some other Sahaptins, and the Chinookans.

our officers took down Some of the language from these [Chinookan] *Savages and Compared with all other we have passd. and find them to be all of a flat head nation but different tribes. we think the flat head nation to be more than ten thousand Strong.* [26 Oct 05 JO 9.245]

the first flat heads or Cho-pun-nish Nation [21 Oct 05 WC 5.319]

it is from this peculiar form of the head that the nations East of the Rocky mountains, call all the nations on this side, except the...snake Indians, by the generic name of Flat heads. [19 Mar 06 ML 6.433]

the Flatheads...live on the west side of the Rocky Mountains, and extend some distance down the Columbia [21 Mar 06 PG 10.200]

The following references are to one of the groups that *did* flatten their infants' foreheads, probably the Chinookan Wasco-Wishram people just east of the Cascade Range.

We suppose them to be a band of the Flathead nation, as all their heads are compressed into the same form [27 Oct 05 PG 10.162]

Came too...at 3 Houses of flatheads and Encamped on the Stard. Side [29 Oct 05 WC 5.350]

FLAWY {FLƆ-ee} (Of wind) gusty. (**Atlantic coast**)

The wind...became violent & flowey accompanied with thunder and a little rain. [12 Apr 05 WC 4.028]

we Sailed Some with a Southerly flawey wind. [16 Apr 05 JO 9.132]

FLEA A pest often encountered by the Corps during stops at Indian lodges, especially along the lower Columbia, and a constant companion in the Fort Clatsop huts. Fleas seem to have been a long standing problem; in 1865, Julia Gilliss, the wife of an Army officer stationed on the Columbia, wrote "the plague of my life are the fleas. Oh! there are shoals of them" (Knuth, 87).

flea

The Flees which the party got on them at the upper and great falls, are very troublesom and dificuelt to get rid of, perticularly as the me[n] have not a Change of Clothes to put on, they Strip off their Clothes and kill the flees, dureing which time they remain neckid. [26 Oct 05 WC 5.343]

[Villages] *both of which are abandened by all their inhabitents except Two Small dogs nearly Starved, and an unreasonable portion of flees* [6 Nov 05 WC 6.027]

Also, to rid something of fleas.

we dry our wet articles and have our blankets fleed [26 Dec 05 WC 6.138]

FLEECE A piece of fatty meat on either side of the backbone.

This being my birth day I order'd a Saddle of fat Vennison, an Elk fleece & a Bevertail to be cooked and a Desert of Cheries, Plumbs, Raspberries Currents and grapes [1 Aug 04 WC 2.433]

they gave us some of the fleese of the seal which I found a great improvement to the poor Elk. [25 Mar 06 ML 7.012]

Also, to cut meat off a carcass and into thin strips for drying or for rendering oil.

we fleece all the meat and hang it up over a Small Smoke [17 Dec 05 WC 6.127]

it [bear] *was a female in fine order, we fleesed it and extracted several gallons of oil.* [1 Aug 06 ML 8.145]

FLESH-SIDE The inside of an animal hide. *See* GRAIN[2].

those People are all naked, Covered only with Breech Clouts Blankits or Buffalow Roabes, the flesh Side Painted of Differant Colours & figures. [19 Aug 04 WC 2.492]

FLINT A hard, fine-grained, silica-rich rock.

Invoice...500 Rifle flints [18 May 03 in Jackson Letters (ed. 2) 1.098]

a Skil lute brought a gun which he requested me to have repared...I put a flint into his gun [31 Dec 05 WC 6.147]

A piece of flint, held in a small vise on the COCK of a flintlock gun, produced sparks when striking the FRIZZEN, igniting the primer powder in the PAN and the main charge in the barrel. If a flint came loose in the vise, a firearm might MISFIRE or SNAP. To ensure a secure grip, a flint was partially wrapped in a bit of leather when inserted in the vise. A gunflint lasted for only a few dozen firings before becoming too worn and small to work properly. A flint periodically was *picked* or chipped to sharpen and freshen its surface to ensure good spark production. Approximately one or two flints were used per pound of lead. Gunflints cost about a penny apiece.

Flints also were used with FIRE-STEELS.

100 Flints [*for striking or making fire*] [Jun 03 ML in Jackson Letters (ed. 2) 1.071]

FLITCH A thin strip of meat, dried quickly over a slow fire or in the sun.

the ballance of the party were employed in cuting the meat we had killed yesterday into thin fletches and drying it [21 Jun 05 ML 4.323] *those* [blubber] *flickes they usially expose to the fire on a wooden Spit* [8 Jan 06 WC 6.183]

the blubber, from which the oil was only partially extracted...was laid in their lodges in large fliches [10 Jan 06 ML 6.193]

FLOAT, ON Afloat.

the trees we camped on was all on flote for about 2 hours [11 Nov 05 WC 6.040]

FLOG To defeat, an extension of the original sense 'to whip, beat.' (Modern-day English uses the latter two words in the same sense.)

they [Clax-ter nation] *latterly floged the Chinnooks, and are a Dasterly set* [winter 05–06 WC 6.155]

FLOOD = (flood) TIDE.

The Tides at every flud come in with great Swells [13 Nov 05 WC 6.044]

FLY, BLOWING- Any fly (now called a blow-fly) laying eggs in meat or in open sores or wounds. Such flesh is said to be fly-blown.

the green or blowing flies are still in swarms. [7 Aug 05 ML 5.056]

FLYING (Of clouds) wind-driven, a vivid expression unfortunately no longer current. (The *Flying Cloud* was a famous clipper-ship of the 1850s.)

Som fiew drops of rain in the morning and also in the evening, flying Clouds all day [1 Jun 05 WC 4.240]

FOB A small pants-pocket for a watch or other valuables. Only later in the 19th century was the word applied to a chain or small ornament attached to a watch.

it seemed a little extraordinary that every part of my breechies which were under my head, should have escaped the moisture except the fob where the time peice was. [17 May 06 ML 7.266]

FODDER-HOUSE {FAH-də} An A-frame structure for winter storage of corn tops and leaves (*blades*) for animal feed, consisting of posts supporting a long ridge-pole, against which other poles were laid on each side tent-style. The sloping sides often were thatched with corn tops, with the blades stored inside. (**Virginia**)

This [Nez Perce] *lodge is built much after the form of the Virginia fodder houses; is about fifty yards long, and contains twenty families.* [5 May 06 PG 10.222]

FOG To be foggy.

Cloudy and fogging all day [7 Nov 04 WC 3.231]

FOLKS Neighbors, people of the COUNTRY.

I send Shields with Mr. Griffeth to purchase me some butter on the other Side of the river...[from] the folks [24 Dec 03 WC 2.140]

FONDLY Willingly, gladly.

they did not think it safe to venture over to the Plains of the Missouri, where they would fondly go provided those nations would not kill them. [12 May 06 ML 7.248]

FOR TO   In order to. *See* BOIS ROULÉ, BRAINS, CARTRIDGE, COAL, COLT, HAW, LUMBERSOME, OBLIGE.

at this place, the french had a tradeing house, for to trade with the Kanzes [3 Jul 04 WC 2.344]

FORE-PART {FƆ-paht} Early portion.

the fore part of the day fair [3 Jun 04 WC 2.272]

We had in the forepart of last night, Showers of Rain, & high wind [16 Jun 05 JW 11.200]

FORELOCK, TAKE TIME BY THE   Grasp an opportunity when it presents itself. Edmund Spenser wrote in 1595 (*Amoretti and Epithalamion*, sonnet LXX) "tell her the ioyous time wil not be staid vnlesse she doe him by the forelock take." A *forelock* is the hair growing from the forehead, the FORETOP.

this reminded us of the necessity of taking time by the forelock, and keep out several parties [hunting] *while we have yet a little meat beforehand.* [3 Jan 06 ML 6.163]

FORETOP   The front portion of the top of the head, or the hair growing there.

others tigh a Small bundle of the docked foretop in front of the fore head. [29 Apr 06 WC 7.185]

FORK {fɔk} In the original sense, two or more streams of roughly equal size meeting to form a larger water course; in the extended sense, any stream smaller than a large river. *See* CREEK. (**South, South Midland**)

G. Drewyer...informed us that we had got the wrong fork & that their was 3 forks [6 Aug 05 JW 11.257]

great numbers of Indians reside on all those foks as well as the main river [22 Sep 05 WC 5.230]

As **forks**, the place where two or more streams (or roads) join.

[Sacagawea] *was taken prisoner at the forks of the three rivers* [30 Jul 05 JW 11.247]

FOUL   (Of a vessel or marine mammal) afoul, hung up, entangled, or in collision with.

the barge run foul...on logs [15 May 04 ML 2.229]

The Whale is...frequently killed by runing fowl on the rocks of the coast [12 Mar 06 ML 6.407]

FOUNTAIN   A spring.

I have not seen a bould fountain of pure water except one since I left the Mandans [20 May 05 ML 4.171]

FOWLER {FOW-lə} A bird hunter.

our hunters and fowlers killd 2 Deer 1 Crane & 2 ducks [16 Nov 05 WC 6.053]

FREESTONE A fine-grained sandstone, or less commonly limestone, that can easily be cut. *Free* has the archaic sense of 'free-born, noble, of excellent quality.'

observed a very fine quarry of white freestone [22 Nov 03 ML 2.103]

Freestone water contains little dissolved mineral. Lewis's is the earliest recorded use of the term (**South Midland**). *See* STRONG.

we passed a number of fine bold springs... they wer very cold and freestone water. [25 Jul 05 ML 4.426]

FRENCH French Canadian HIRELINGS or ENGAGÉS were an important contingent of the expedition. A number were engaged as boatmen. *See* CANADIAN.

4 or five french water-men...will be esscential [28 Sep 03 ML in Jackson Letters (ed. 2) 1.125]

the French Hands who have families maybe allowed to Stay with their families [4 May 04 JO 2.212]

450 Inhabetents principally frinch [16 May 04 WC 2.232]

FRESH A flood.

if the present fresh continus a fiew days, the water...will Wash off all that immence quantity of mud [7 Feb 04 WC 2.174]

> A *fresh* was originally a freshwater stream flowing into tidewater. As early settlers were confined to coastal areas, their point of view was necessarily maritime, and the large volume of water delivered by a flood to the sea came to be named for its salient characteristic, the lack of salt. For a similar development in meaning, *see* CREEK.

FRIZZEN {FRIZZ-ən} The roughened steel piece against which the FLINT of a flintlock firearm strikes to produce sparks; also called *frizzle* or BATTERY. *See* LOCK.

> The *frizzen* and the pan-cover are parts of the same piece. A spring holds the combined pan-cover/frizzen in place over the PAN (or *in battery*), until the flint strikes the frizzen, knocking it forward (*out of battery*), allowing sparks to drop into the priming charge in the pan.

See SNAP for an example.

FROE {FROH} An L-shaped tool with a wedge-shaped blade at right angles to its wooden handle, used for splitting wood into shingles, BARREL-staves, etc. The blade, purposely made dull so as not to cut across the wood fibers, is driven into the piece of wood with a *mallet*.

Frow malet Beeds Bells [7 Dec 05 WC 6.113]

FROSTED Frost-bitten. No part of the body was immune from the effects of subzero temperatures.

my Servents feet also frosted & his P—s a little [8 Dec 04 WC 3.255]

FURL To gather in a sail and lash it to a yard or mast.

See SPRIT for an example.

FUSIL {FYOO-zee} A relatively short and lightweight flint-LOCK gun, either smooth-bored or rifled. The word survives in modern English as *fusillade*. *See* BUCKSHOT, MUSKET.

The arms of the nations on the Missouri is fusees & Bows & Arrows [winter 04–05 WC 3.484]

the Indians may well fear this anamal [grizzly bear] *equiped as they generally are with their bows and arrows or indifferent fuzees* [29 Apr 05 ML 4.085]

I lost at the river in the torrent the large Compas, an eligant fusee, Tomahawk Humbrallo [et al.] [29 June 05 WC 4.343]

G

GALLED (Of land) bare, stripped of soil. (**South, South Midland, esp. Virginia**)

the upland is extreemly broken, chonsisting of high gaulded nobs [14 Apr 05 ML 4.035]

GANG A herd (of buffalo, elk), a flock (of geese, turkeys, ducks). The word originally meant simply 'going' (as in the word *gangway*), and then 'those who go about in a group.' (**South Midland**)

I Saw a white brant in a gangue on the Sand bar [5 Oct 04 WC 3.144]

I counted in view at one time 52 gangues of Buffalow & 3 of Elk, besides Deer & goats [19 Oct 04 WC 3.184]

GATE Speed, pace; the original spelling of *gait*. The word was borrowed into English from Old Norse *gata* 'path, road' during the Viking occupation of parts of Britain late in the first millennium AD.

we...hoisted both the sails in the White Perogue...which carried her at a pretty good gate [13 Apr 05 ML 4.029]

the feet of the men...So Stuck with Prickley pear & cut with the Stones that they were Scerseley able to march at a Slow gate [20 Jul 05 WC 4.410]

we Shall go on our own gate [24 Nov 08 WC Letters 168]

GEAR {GEE-ə, with hard *g*} Harness for a draft animal.

strike Medicine river and hunt down it to it's mouth in order to procure the necessary skins to make geer [8 Jul 06 ML 8.097]

they have geers fixed for the horses. [19 Jul 06 JO 9.338]

Hence **gear up** = TACKLE.

we geered up the 4 horses and Set out [23 Jul 06 JO 9.339]

GELD {with hard *g*} = CUT.

several of the horses which were gelded yesterday are much swolen particularly those cut by Drewyer [15 May 06 ML 7.261]

Hence **gelding**, a castrated horse. *See* (STONE-)HORSE.

we made Several attempts to exchange our Stalions for Geldings or mar[e]s without success [14 May 06 WC 7.258]

GENTLE {JIN-t'l} (Of animals) tame. *See* SHY. Lewis's standardized spelling disguises the pronunciation revealed by Clark's rendition.

these anamals [beaver] *in consequence of not being hunted are extreemly gentle* [2 May 05 ML 4.100]

we observe...Buffalow, Elk, Antelopes & Mule deer inumerable and So jintle that we could approach near them with great ease [11 May 05 WC 4.143]

GENTLEMAN   Here, an ironic or humorous term of respect. *See* ASSINIBOINE, YELLOW.

these [grizzly] *bear being so hard to die reather intimedates us all; I must confess that I do not like the gentlemen and had reather fight two Indians than one bear* [11 May 05 ML 4.141]

GET {git, with hard *g*} To become. (**South Midland**)

it is now gitting a Small Stream [10 Aug 05 JO 9.200]

GIG {gig, with hard *g*} To fish with a spear. (**South**)

we fixed some spears after the indian method but have had too much to attend to of more importance than gigging fish [4 Sep 03 ML 2.071]

one of the guard at the river guiged a Salmon Trout, which we had fried in a little Bears Oil [26 Oct 05 WC 5.343]

> *Gig* is an abbreviation of *fishgig* or *fizgig*, derived from Spanish *fisga* 'harpoon.' *Fisga* is distantly related to English *fix*.

Also, *gig* is the barbed spearhead so used.

40 fish Giggs such as the Indians use with a single barbed point [Jun 03 ML in Jackson Letters (ed. 2) 1.073]

the forks of this river is famous as a gig fishery and is much resorted to by the natives. [21 Aug 05 ML 5.138]

They [Shoshone] *kill but fiew Deer but catch considerable quantity of fresh water Salmon with poles with a Sharpened bone fixed on a pole for a gig.* [27 Aug 05 JO 9.212]

Hence **gigger** {GIG-ə, with hard *g*}, one who fishes with a gig.

our guiggers also turned out with 2 guigs [20 June 06 WC 8.041]

GILL {jill} (Of spirits) a quarter pint. *See* DRAM.

our officers Gave out one Gill of ardent Spirits per man. So we made merry fidled and danced [26 Apr 05 JO 9.137]

GIVE BACK To retreat.

Those who become members of this [Sioux] *Society must be brave active young men who take a Vow never to give back let the danger be what it may* [30 Aug 04 WC 3.025]

GLADE An opening in a forested area; a PRAIRIE, whether well drained or wet. Glades are an "edge" habitat between differing environments, hosting a variety of plants and attracting wildlife.

In those Small Praries or glades I saw wild Timothey, lambs-quarter, Cuckle burs; & rich weed. on the edges Grows Sumr. Grapes, Plum's, & Gooseberries. [14 Jul 04 WC 2.378]

The Country as usial except the Glades which is open & boggey, water Clare and Sandey. [13 Sep 05 WC 5.202]

at dark we Camped at a Small glade where was pleanty of feed for our horses [15 Jun 06 JO 9.323]

Hence **glady**.

7 miles over a mountain & on a dividing ridge of flat gladey land [13 Sep 05 WC 5.237]

GLASS, BURNING- or SUN- A magnifying lens for starting fires, valued by the Indians in trade.

the main Chief Brack fast with us naked; & beged for a Sun glass. [19 Aug 04 WC 2.490]

he hired one of the Cashhooks, for a birning glass, to pilot him to the entrance of the Multnomah river [2 Apr 06 ML 7.054]

GLAUBER'S SALTS {GLɔ-bə-salts} Sodium sulfate, a strong PHYSIC, named after a 17th century German chemist. (*Sal* is druggist's Latin for 'salt.')

6 lb. Sal Glauber...[$].60 [26 May 03 in Jackson Letters (ed. 2) 1.080]

the water Can't be Drank without effecting the person...as Globesalts [19 Oct 04 WC 3.184]

Joseph Fields was very sick today with the disentary had a high fever I gave him a doze of Glauber salts, which operated very well, in the evening his fever abated and I gave him 30 drops of laudnum. [4 May 05 ML 4.109]

Lewis also applied the term *Glauber Salts* in reference to mineral deposits later called *alkali. See* BRACKISH.

saw some wild goats or antelopes on the hill above the Glauber Salts Springs [5 Sep 04 ML 3.050]

the earth is strongly impregnated with glauber salts, alum, copperas and sulphur [winter 04–05 WC 3.418]

the appearance of the glauber salts and Carbonated wood still continue. [12 Apr 05 ML 4.027]

GNAT, EYE- Tiny biting flies that assault the eyes.

our trio of pests still invade and obstruct us on all occasions, these are the Musquetoes eye knats and prickley pears, equal to any three curses that ever poor Egypt laiboured under, except the Mahometant yoke. [24 Jul 05 ML 4.423]

the eye knats have disappeared. [7 Aug 05 ML 5.056]

GOAT = PRONGHORN.

we Saw a flock of Goats Swimming the River [5 Oct 04 JO 9.076]

GOATSUCKER = BAT (in the first sense).

GONORRHEA {gɔ-nə-REE-ə} A sexually transmitted bacterial disease affecting primarily the mucous membranes of the urogenital tract and characterized by painful urination and discharge of puss. There was no effective treatment, despite the inclusion of penis syringes in the expedition's medical kit. *See* LUES VENEREA, PEWTER.

the same decoctions [lobelia and sumac] *are used in cases of the gonnaerea and are effecatious and sovereign…in my whole rout down this* [Columbia] *river I did not see more than two or three with the gonnaerea and about double that number with the pox.* [27 Jan 06 ML 6.240]

GORGE {gɔdj} The French word for 'neck, throat.' A neck of land, such as that leading to an area enclosed by the BIG BEND of the Missouri. *Gouge* is an *r*-dropper's spelling of *gorge*.

the gorge of the [Missouri's] Bend is 1 mile & quarter (from river to river or) across, from this high land which is only in the Gouge, the bend is a Butifull Plain [20 Sep 04 WC 3.093]

we…Encampd. on the gouge of the lookout bend of 20 miles around and ¾ through [24 Aug 06 WC 8.321]

In describing a "fortification" on the Missouri, Clark applied the word in a military sense as the 'neck of a bastion.'

a thick wall…passing from the Rivers edge at the gouge of the work perfectly Strieght to the bend of the River [c. 1 Sep 06 WC 8.343]

GORGET {Gɔ-jit} A neck ornament.

found the Manitarree Chief about Setting out on his return to his village, having recieved of Captain M. Lewis a medel Gorget armbans, a Flag [9 Mar 05 WC 3.311]

I gave…one a wampom Shell gorget [5 Oct 05 WC 5.246]

GRAIN[1] A very small weight (now standardized at about 0.0023 ounces) for medicinal formulations. Abbreviated *gr.* See PENNYWEIGHT, VITRIOL.

it's weight—1 oz 17 Grains Troy [16 Oct 04 ML 3.178]

to this [castor] *you will add half a nutmeg, a douzen or 15 grains of cloves and thirty grains of cinimon finely pulverized* [7 Jan 06 ML 6.174]

GRAIN[2] To scrape the FLESH SIDE of an animal hide. (Lewis appears to use the term loosely.) The basic steps in dressing a hide were to SHAVE, grain, BRAIN, and smoke it. Whitehouse was the expedition's professional skin-dresser.

Captain Lewis gave them a grained deer skin to stretch over a half keg for a drum. [30 Aug 04 PG 10.033]

we saw where an Indian had recently grained, or taken the hair off of a goat-skin [8 May 05 ML 4.126]

Several men employed in Shaveing & Graneing Elk hides for the Iron boat [21 Jun 05 WC 4.324]

GRAISSE DE BUFFLE or DE BOEUF This French name for RABBIT-BERRY means 'buffalo fat'; the plant also has been called BUFFALO-GREASE and *beef-suet tree* in English. The Arikara and Mandan names literally mean 'buffalo berry' and '(buffalo) bull berry' respectively, names that are also used in English for 'rabbit berry.' *See* GREASE. (**Plains**)

the bush...bears a red berry, called by the engages greas de buff [11 Apr 05 ML 4.094]

we found a large quantity of Graze the Buff. or Rabit Berryes of which we eat freely off. they are a Small red berry, Sower & Good to the taste. [23 Oct 05 JO 9.089]

GRASS, SHORT Any of several species of short-bladed grasses characteristic of semi-arid Plains. (**Plains**)

they passed through high plains, where nothing groes but Short grass & prickley pears. [6 Jun 05 JW 11.188]

GRATEFUL Pleasing.

Those roots & berres, are greatfull to our Stomcks as we have nothing to eate but Pore Elk meet, nearly Spoiled [27 Dec 05 WC 6.139]

GREASE Animal fat, usually of buffalo or bear. *See* GRAISSE DE BUFFLE, PEMMICAN.

I have purchased from Mr Louiselle's Pattroon three hundred pounds of voyager's grease [12 Jun 04 ML 2.294]

GREAT FALLS[1] (Of the Missouri) four or five high PITCHES and several smaller ones constituting a spectacular obstacle to the expedition's progress; often just *the falls*. *See* TRUCKLE.

I did not...loose my direction to this point which soon began to make a roaring too tremendious to be mistaken for any cause short of the great falls of the Missouri. [13 Jun 05 ML 4.283]

GREAT FALLS[2] (Of the Columbia) later known as Celilo Falls.

encamped near five Lodges of nativs, drying fish those are the relations of those at the Great falls [21 Oct 05 WC 5.318]

GREEN (Of fish) fresh, as opposed to dried or smoked.

We purchased Some green fish, & wap pa to for which we gave Imoderate pricie's. [26 Nov 05 WC 6.089]

(Of corn) immature, sweet and tender. Green corn did not require the extensive processing that mature corn needed. *See* (LYED) CORN, (ROASTING) EAR, HOMINY.

the Nation have returned to get green Corn [23 Jul 04 WC 2.415]

(Of animal skins) uncured. *See* SIGHT[1].

a boy half white was Saved un hurt in the midst of the flaim...The Cause of his being Saved was a Green buffalow Skin was thrown over him by his mother [29 Oct 04 WC 3.211]

we put the Iron boat which we covered with green hides in to the water. [9 Jul 05 JO 9.181]

GREENSWARD {GREEN-swɔd} Lewis's use of it here in the sense of 'lawn-grass' also is found in the 1778 memorandum-book of Thomas Jefferson, Lewis's instructor in natural history: *35 pints greensword seed.* (The usual modern meaning of the word is 'lawn.')

it...is covered with a fine terf of greenswoard. [27 Jul 05 ML 4.434]

near the coast on the tops of some of the untimbered hills there is a finer and softer species which resembles much the green swoard. [13 Feb 06 ML 6.304]

I do not find the greenswoard here which we met with on the lower part of the Columbia. [5 Jun 06 ML 7.335]

GREENWICH {GREN-idj} A London borough located on the Thames River and site of the Royal Observatory, chosen in 1884 as the internationally recognized zero-point (or *prime meridian*) for reckoning mean TIME and LONGITUDE.

Longtd. by Chrotr. W. from Grent. [18 May 04 ML 2.238]

Estimated Greenwich time of the Observation [23 Feb 05 ML 3.301]

GRIDDLE A grill, grillwork.

Several Curious pieces of wood bent in Circleler form with sticks across them in form of a Griddle [24 Jul 06 WC 8.218]

GRIPING Abdominal cramps, often accompanied by the *looseness* or LAX of diarrhea.

Several men Complain of a looseness and gripeing which I contribute to the diet, pounded fish mixed with Salt water [30 Nov 05 WC 6.097]

GRIST-MILL A mill for grinding grain, usually water-powered.

the Creek...has a considerable number of inhabitants on it, and as many as three gristmills. [27 Nov 03 ML 2.116]

GROG Rum or other spirits diluted with water, first issued to sailors of the British Royal Navy in 1740.

they refreshed themselves at the Spring with a drink of good grog. [6 Jun 05 JW 11.188]

GROS VENTRE {gro-VAHN-tər, now GRO-vahn}

= HIDATSA. French for 'big belly.' The Hidatsa sometimes were called *Gros Ventres of the Missouri* to distinguish them from the *Gros Ventres of the Prairie*, or ATSINA; see below. *See* BIG BELLY.

we Sent the Cheifs of the Gross Vantres to Smoke a pipe with the Grand Chef of the Mandins in his Village [28 Oct 04 WC 3.208]

many buffaloe have visited the Grosventers [15 Dec 04 ML 3.265]

the war axes these [Nez Perce] *Indians have they got from the Grousevauntares on the Missourie & they got them from us at the Mandans.* [6 May 06 JO 9.306]

= ATSINA. In this sense, *Gros Ventre* sometimes included the affiliated BLACKFOOT Indians.

they had a skirmish with a party of the Prairie Grossventres, or Bigbellied Indians [28 Jul 06 PG 10.259]

GUGGLE To make a sound like liquid poured from a narrow-necked bottle; to gurgle. *See* CLUCKING.

we assembled the [Flathead] *Chiefs & warriers and Spoke to them (with much dificuely as what we Said had to pass through Several languajes before it got in to theirs, which is a gugling kind of languaje Spoken much thro the Throught)* [5 Sep 05 WC 5.188]

GULLEY = RAVINE. From French *goulet* 'gullet, throat.' *See* BROOK, DRAFT, HOLLOW.

gullies...make down from the hills [11 May 05 ML 4.140]

As the Missouri landscape became more rugged, gullies caused increasing difficulties in navigation. Flash floods had deposited rocky debris some distance out from gully mouths, forming obstructions to vessels being towed or poled along the shore.

the river becomes more rappid and is intercepted by shoals and a greater number of rocky points at the mouths of the little gulies [27 May 05 ML 4.207]

Land dissected by gullies also made cross-country travel difficult.

my Self and party much fatigued haveing walked Constantly as hard as we Could march over a Dry hard plain, dcending & assending the Steep river hills & gullies [6 Jun 05 WC 4.261]

GUN A shot from a gun—in this case, the keelboat's SWIVEL-GUN—fired in honor of persons, as part of festivities, or as a signal.

after the talk was inded...three Guns was fired from our Bow peace. [10 Oct 04 JO 9.079]

GUNWALE {GUN-'l} The reinforced upper edge of a boat's side; originally, the horizontal timber (*wale*) along a vessel's side, supporting swivel-mounted guns.

a fifth has streigned his back by sliping and falling backwards on the gunwall of the canoe. [31 Jul 05 ML 5.018]

a larger Canoe is now reversed...resting with its gunnals on the Cross bars [30 Nov 05 WC 6.097]

GUST A squall or storm, not simply a burst of wind as in modern use. (**central Atlantic coast**)

the gusts of Snow and hail continue untill 12 oClock [18 Dec 05 WC 6.130]

we...had a gust of rain, hail, thunder and lightening, which lasted an hour [18 Jun 06 PG 10.241]

GUT A narrow channel. (**New England, South Atlantic**)

passed the mouth of a Gut from a pond [9 Jul 04 WC 2.362]

Capt Lewis and my Self walked down to See the place the Indians pointed out as the worst place in passing through the gut [The Dalles of the Columbia] [25 Oct 05 WC 5.338]

GUTS Intestines, here as eaten for breakfast. *See* PAUNCH, PLUCK.

I ate of the small guts of the buffaloe cooked over a blazing fire in the Indian stile without any preparation of washing or other clensing and found them very good. [16 Jul 05 ML 4.386]

GUTTER {GUH-tə} To dress wood with an ADZE, leaving typical scalloped, gutter-like marks, probably as a step following HEWing.

commenced hughing & Guttering the punchien for the purpose of covering the huts. [10 Nov 04 JO 9.095]

H

HACKLE A tool with steel-wire teeth for combing out flax or hemp fibers.

the men...have not only their own wight to bear in treading on those hacklelike points [of hard, dried earth] [23 Jun 05 ML 4.328]

HACKMATACK {HACK-mə-tack} Western larch. Originally, an Eastern ALGONQUIAN word for eastern larch, meaning literally 'snowshoe-conifer' with reference to its use in making snowshoe frames. *See* TAMARACK. The species referred to in the following quotation is uncertain. (**New England**)

Covered thickly with Spruce pine arbor vita Hackmatack as called [6 Nov 05 WC 6.026]

HAIR-PIPE {HEH-ə} A sort of tubular hair ornament, valued in trade. In 1818 on the upper Mississippi, hair-pipes sold for 33½ cents apiece (*ASPIA* II. 332).

Baling Invoice of Sundries for Indian Presents...1 Hairpipe [winter 04–05 3.493]

I can't find Hair Pipes purchased of Mr. Chouteau. Mr. Hays says they are necessary. [Apr 04 WC in Jackson Letters (ed. 2) 1.175]

HALF-BREED The offspring of white and nonwhite (Indian or black) parents. *See* MULATTO.

they have ben up three years with the Indianes 2 of them is half preades of the poncas. [14 Jun 04 CF 9.380]

HALF-LEG DEEP A measure of 18 inches, more or less; knee-high. *See* MIDDLE-DEEP, MIDRIB-DEEP. (**South, South Midland**)

the canoe...went of[f] of a sudden & left myself and three more Standing on the rock half leg deep in the rapid water [14 Oct 05 JO 9.238]

HARANGUE {hə-RANG} To make a formal public speech.

We halted...to Smoke with the Indians...harranged them [16 Oct 05 WC 5.278]

[Walla Walla chief] *Yellept haranged his village in our favour* [27 Apr 06 ML 7.174]

Also, the speech itself.

during the time of this loud and animated harangue of the Cheif the women cryed wrung their hands, toar their hair and appeared to be in the utmost distress. [12 May 06 ML 7.247]

HARD[1] {hahd} (Of wind) strong.

wind so hard we were unable to proceed [27 May 05 ML 4.237]

HARD[2] (Of a river) difficult to navigate. *See* BOLD, STOUT, STRONG.

Hard water & logs, Bank falling in [25 Jun 04 WC 2.321]

> The expedition's punishingly *hard* labor of pulling and pushing a boat up the Missouri by cord and pole was routine: "The obstructions of rocky points and riffles still continue...at those places the men are compelled to be in the water even to their armpits, and the water is yet very could...the banks and bluffs along which they are obliged to pass are so slippery and the mud so tenacious that they are unable to wear their mockersons, and in that situation draging the heavy burthen of a canoe and walking ocasionally for several hundred yards over the sharp fragments of rocks...their labour is incredibly painfull and great, yet those faithfull fellows bear it without a murmur." [31 May 05 ML 4.224]

HARD-SCRABBLE A term describing a place or situation where it is difficult to get along, where one must *scrabble* to make progress. *OED* credits Whitehouse as the first writer to use this phrase, though the word *scrabble* occurs as early as 1794 in the United States in the sense of 'scramble; a confused struggle, a free-for-all.'

Got on our way at hard Scrable Perarie [25 Jun 04 JW 11.030]

HAT, COCKED A man's hat with a wide, stiff brim turned up on two or three sides forming, respectively, two or three points (*bicorne* or *tricorne*). Manufactured hats routinely were shipped up the Missouri, and were among the trade-goods carried by the expedition; *see* KENTUCKY.

our officers...Gave the head chiefs a Suit of cloaths and a quantity of Small Goods for their nations, cocked hats & feathers &.C. [29 Oct 04 JO 9.092]

to give them further confidence I put my cocked hat with feather on the chief [16 Aug 05 ML 5.104]

HATCHET, BURY THE To make peace. A figure of speech in Indian-white diplomacy as early as the 1680s (*DCHNY* 3.395). See MOCCASIN, (WAR-)STRIPES.

I will berry my hatchet and be at peace with all [31 Aug 04 WC 3.030]

HAW The small, apple-like fruit of the hawthorn (genus *Cratægus*); the thornapple.

Deer frequent this Lake dureing Summer Season, and feed on the hows &c. [19 Jun 04 WC 2.309]

we purchased 10 fat dogs, a Quantity of Salmon & some dried haws, for to eat. [11 Oct 05 JW 11.348]

HE Male. *See* SHE.

one of the men...was attcd by an old hea bear [6 Jun 05 JW 11.188]

Collins returned...with the two bears which he had killed...one of them an old hee was in fine order, the other a female with Cubs was Meagure. [14 May 06 WC 7.259]

HEAD (Of a cross-country traveler) to go around the head of a stream or valley, usually in order to avoid crossing it.

passed through an open roleing Prarie, So as to head the two reveins [17 Jun 05 WC 4.304]

(Of a stream) to rise, originate.

this Creek...Heds near the River platt [11 Jul 04 CF 9.387]

HEAD-RIGHT A right to land. Granted (in this case by the Spanish government) to the head of an immigrant family, or to a person paying for the transport of a number of other family heads. (In colonial Virginia, such a person himself was called a *headright*.)

they are allowed a bounty in lands proportioned to the number of their respective familys which are called head rights [23 Nov 03 ML 2.107]

HEAVE IN SIGHT To appear. Originally a nautical expression.

to our great joy those men hove in Sight at 6 P. M. [30 Aug 06 WC 8.331]

HELVE A wooden handle for a tool or weapon. See HILT.

it [battle-ax] is somewhat in the form of the blade of an Espantoon but is attachd to a helve of the dementions before discribed [5 Feb 05 ML 3.287]

Also, to install such a handle.

we went about helving our axes and git in readiness to begin the Canoes. [26 Sep 05 JW 11.334]

HEW To shape wood with an ax. *See* GUTTER.

this Tradeing house is built all of ceeder high and covered with hughn guttered ceeder [22 Sep 04 JO 9.064]

Jo Fields finish for Capt Lewis and my Self each a wide Slab hued to write on [24 Dec 05 WC 6.136]

HIDATSA* {hih-DAHT-sə} A farming people residing in earth-lodges along the Knife River, a western tributary to the upper Missouri in North Dakota. They spoke a Siouan language closely related to CROW. *See* AHWAHAWAY, GROS VENTRE, MINITARI, SACAGAWEA.

HIGGLER {HIG-lə} A hard bargainer, one who haggles. *See* STICKLE, TIGHT.

these like the natives below are great higglers in dealing. [30 Mar 06 ML 7.032]

HILT {HILTH} A wooden handle for a tool or weapon. *See* HELVE.

we Substitute the Cherry in place of Hickory for ax hilthes ram rods, &c. [10 Jul 05 WC 4.374]

HIPPED (Earlier *hypped*.) Hypochondriacal—in the older sense of 'depressed'—of which *hipped* is an abbreviation.

two of the women I gave a carthartic, one whose Spirets were very low and much hiped [19 May 06 WC 7.273]

> *Hypochondria* was a disorder believed to be seated *below the cartilage* of the breastbone and ribs, that is, in the upper abdomen immediately beneath the rib cage. At the time of the expedition, the modern sense of hypochondria as a morbid preoccupation with one's own health began to supplant the older sense of depression. For another disordered state of mind imputed to the lower abdomen, *see* HYSTERICAL.

HIRELING {HĪə-lin} A hired hand. The word here lacked the pejorative sense that it usually has today. *See* ENGAGÉ.

the French higherlins Complain for the want of Provisions, Saying they are accustomed to eat 5 & 6 times a day [17 Jun 04 WC 2.306]

HOBBLE To fasten together the legs—usually the forelegs—of a horse to prevent straying; also, the rope or hide thong so used. When the legs were tied together on one side, a horse was said to be *side-hobbled* (or *side-lined*). This is the earliest record of the form *hubble*, though *hopple* is recorded from the 16th century.

we had all our horses side hubbled and turned out to graize [23 Apr 06 ML 7.160]

one of the hunters horses broke his hobbles and got away. [3 May 06 JO 9.303] *we…had him as we thought securely hubbled both before and at the side, but he broke the strings in the course of the night and absconded.* [2 May 06 ML 7.199]

The verb *hobble* has been generalized to mean 'to inhibit one's freedom of action,' hence 'to walk painfully, with a limp.'

Capt Lewis hobled up on the bank [1 Sep 06 WC 8.337]

HOIST {hīst, a common dialectical pronunciation brought from England in the 17th century} To raise. Here, in regard to a flag (*colors*).

Histed ouer Collars in the morning for the Reseptions of Indians [24 Jul 04 CF 9.390]

HOLE The hold of a vessel; here the vertical dimension of the (IRON) BOAT.

the iron frame of my boat is…26 Inches in the hole. [24 Jun 05 ML 4.330]

HOLE, GAUGE A small hole in the bottom of a boat, fitted with a plug for draining water when a boat was on shore. Probably so named from the similarity to a hole bored in a cask to allow the gauging of its contents.

I employed all hands in drawing the perogue on shore…drove out the plugs of the gage holes of her bottom and covered her with bushes and driftwood [18 Jun 05 ML 4.305]

HOLLOW {HAH-lə} A small valley between hills. Expedition writers are the first on record as having spelled this typical Appalachian word with *-er. See* COVE, DRAFT, GULLEY, RAVINE. (**South, South Midland**)

I crossed a Deep holler [26 May 05 WC 4.204]

the Indian road…lead us over steep hills and deep hollows [12 Aug 05 ML 5.075]

Saw a buffaloe feeding in a holler [14 Apr 05 JO 9.131]

the fog rose up thick from the hollars [29 Jun 06 JO 9.328]

HOMINY {HAHM-nee} Dried and HULLED corn boiled whole or ground into grits. Clark applied the term to similar foods produced from roots. *See* (LYED) CORN.

Capt Lewis & my Self much indisposed—I think from the Homney w[e] *Substitute in place of bread* [28 Aug 04 WC 3.019]

I saw & eat…Grou[n]*d potatoe made into a Kind of homney* [26 Sep 04 WC 3.119]

HOOK, BOAT A long pole with a steel hook on one end, for fending off objects or dragging them in.

1 Boat and her caparison, including spiked poles, boat hooks & toe line to be furnished at Pittsburgh [18 May 03 in Jackson Letters (ed. 2) 1.099]

this morning to hunt for the anker. Searched Some time with the Boat hook & poles, could not find it. [28 Sep 04 JO 9.071]

HOPPUS {HAH-pəs} A burden-strap, or tump-line, crossing the upper chest or forehead in order to carry a load on one's back. Also, the tump-line and backpack considered as a unit, since they were used together.

Materials for making up the Various Articles into portable Packs 30 Sheep skins... dress'd only with lime to free them from the wool; or otherwise about the same quantity of Oil Cloth bags well painted[.] *Raw Hide for pack strings*[.] *Dress'd letter* [leather] *for Hoppus-Straps* [Jun 03 ML in Jackson Letters (ed. 2) 1.074]

Happerst, a spelling of *hoppused*, means 'rigged up with or as a hoppus.'

I had now my sack and blanket happerst in readiness to swing on my back, which is the first time in my life that I have ever prepared a burthen of this kind [3 Jun 05 ML 4.250]

> *Hoppus* comes from the Delaware Indian word (Unami dialect) *hápiis* (Ives Goddard, personal communication, 2004). John Knight's 1782 captivity narrative provides a Virginian connection for the word's adoption. Knight was a Virginian physician serving with American volunteers during the Revolutionary War near Fort Pitt (present-day Pittsburgh) on the Ohio River. After being captured by a Delaware band, Knight later was able to drive off his Delaware guard, noting, "I took his blanket, a pair of new moccasins, his hoppes, powder horn, bullet bag, (together with the gun) and marched off." Knight previously was acquainted with the Delaware people and may have adopted the term from them. The word also appears in 1791 in treaty negotiations with the Iroquois in western New York (*ASPIA* I. 151): "You are just now rising from your seats, with your backs bent, bearing your loaded hoppas." The term continued in use on the frontier into the 1820s.

HORIZON, ARTIFICIAL A flat, reflective surface used by Lewis & Clark in their astronomical observations in place of the uninterrupted natural horizon available to navigators at sea. For night observations, the captains utilized mirrors made precisely horizontal with spirit-levels.

Observed Meridian altitude of ⊙ *U. L. with Sextant and glass artifical Horizon.* [13 Jan 05 ML 3.273]

The artifil. Horizon...in which water forms the reflecting surface, is used in all observations which requirs the uce of an Artificial horizon, except where expressly mentioned to the contrary. [12 Apr 05 ML 4.025]

HORN, POWDER {hɔn} A cow or buffalo horn containing gunpowder. The large end was plugged with a carefully fitted piece of wood or other hard material, while the small end held a tight-fitting removable plug.

powder horn

the fire caught in the Woods, and burned up his shot pouch, powder horn and stock of his Rifle [23 May 05 JW 11.166]

The powder in maney of the mens horns are wet from their being so long exposed to the rain [26 Dec 05 WC 6.138]

HORN, SOUNDING A horn (here probably a bugle) for music or signaling, as distinguished from a powder-horn.

15 of the party went up to the 1st village of Mandans to dance...carried with us a fiddle & a Tambereen & a Sounden horn. [1 Jan 05 JO 9.107] *on hearing the Sound of the horn, the left Wing, would join the right* [16 Feb 05 JW 11.127]

HORSE {hɔss} Horse-meat. *See* BEEF.

they gave us Several fresh Salmon & Som horse dried [16 Oct 05 WC 5.277]

HORSE, STONE- A stallion, or uncastrated male horse. Testicles and other glands were called *stones*; *see* BARK-STONE, QUIETING, STONE, STUD.

we have found our stone horses so troublesome that we indeavoured to exchange them with the Chopunnish for mears or gelings [14 May 06 ML 7.257]

HOT-HOUSE An Indian sweat-lodge, often partly below ground. *See* SWEAT[1].

Dined at the forks, passed a Hot hous covd with Earth [12 Sep 05 WC 5.201]

HOUGH {huff} The *hock*, or lower joint of a quadruped's leg, corresponding to the human ankle.

they [bighorn] *have great resemblance of the deer kind, especially the leggs, but the head & huffs resemble a Sheep.* [25 May 05 JO 9.155]

HOUNDS Horizontal wooden bars reinforcing the running-gear of a wagon. Originally a nautical term referring to wooden projections from a vessel's mast. Lewis's use with reference to a wagon is the earliest on record. *See* TRUCKLE.

we were obliged...to renew both axeltrees and the tongues and howns of one set of wheels [22 Jun 05 ML 4.325]

HOWEL {how'l} A plane with a convex surface, used to smooth the insides of barrel staves.

See COOPER for an example.

HUDSON'S BAY COMPANY Incorporated in 1670, the HBC monopolized the Canadian fur trade until its competitors formed the NORTH WEST COMPANY in the late 18th century.

5 men of the N W Company & Several of the hudsons Bay Company had arrived with goods to trade with the indians [19 Nov 04 WC 3.238]

HUG, NATIONAL The customary greeting of the Shoshone.

we wer all carresed and besmeared with their grease and paint till I was heartily tired of the national hug. [13 Aug 05 ML 5.079]

they take us round the neck and S[q]*weze us in token of friendship...in Stead of Shakeing hands* [17 Aug 05 JO 9.206]

HULLED Of corn prepared for human consumption, with the kernals separated from the indigestible hulls and fibrous skin. A BUSHEL of hulled corn weighed 10½ pounds less than the modern standard 56-pound bushel of corn. The light weight of the expedition's maize products probably was due to processing in lye. *See* (LYED) CORN.

Articles in readiness for the Voyage...11 Bags of Corn Hulled of 2 bus: each about 1000 W [May 04 WC 2.217]

HUMP The highly prized fatty portion of meat from a buffalo's back.

we killed a fat Bull and took out the hump and...broiled the hump and eat a hearty meal of it. [27 Jun 05 JO 9.175]

HYSSOP {HISS-əp, ISS-əp} Also **hisop**. = SAGE². From *Hyssopus officinalis*, a small, bushy, aromatic herb of southern Europe. Lewis & Clark adopted the name for the newly-discovered sagebrush.

next to the hills Great quantity of wild Isoop. [14 Apr 05 WC 4.039]

we...proceeded on through the level Sandy plain or desert covred with nothing but wild hysop & golden rod, and prickley pears. [25 Aug 05 JO 9.210]

hyssop

HYSTERICAL (Of a woman) afflicted with hysteria, a disorder of the mind originally thought to have its cause in the uterus (Greek *hystera*). *See* HIPPED.

to a third who appeared much dejected and who from their account of her disease we supposed it to be histerical, we gave 30 drops of Laudanum. [19 May 06 ML 7.272]

I

IBEX {EYE-bəks} = BIGHORN.

I killed a Ibix on which the whole party Dined [1 Aug 05 WC 5.029]

ILLINOIS Also **Illinois country**. A region, originally mostly prairie land, bounded by the Mississippi River to the southwest, and extending northeast between the Illinois River on the northwest and the Wabash River to the east in what is now the state of Illinois.

Illinois usually referred in a restricted sense to its more densely settled southwest section (also known as AMERICAN BOTTOM) between the towns of Cahokia at the north and Kaskaskia to the south, and including Fort de Chartres, a French military headquarters until the British takeover. In English, the region was known as *the Illinois* as early as 1708 (A. Moore, 49), named for the Illinois Indians, a loose confederation of Algonquian-speaking peoples (*see* MIAMI). However, by the late 18th century most of the native inhabitants had moved west of the Mississippi. Illinois' political development was as follows: in 1778, a Virginia county; in 1787 incorporated into Northwest Territory; in 1800 included in Indiana Territory; in 1809 became Illinois Territory; and in 1818 gained statehood.

our Bacon which was given us...we examined and found Sound and good Some of that purchased in the Illinois Spoiled [30 Jun 04 WC 2.333]

we met two trappers...they were from the Ellynoise country [12 Aug 06 JO 9.348]

I...was somewhat gratified by being ordered (shortly after I joined the Service) to Kaskaskias Village, in the Illinois Country. [c. 1806 JW 11.005]

By 1670, the name was borrowed into French as *Ilinois* from an old Ojibway word, in turn borrowed from the Illinois, meaning 'speaks in the ordinary way.' The Canadian French pronunciation accurately represented the Ojibway pronunciation, ill-ih-NWEH or -NWAY, which has prevailed since the 17th century. It can be assumed that French and at least some English-speaking members of the Lewis & Clark expedition used the Canadian pronunciation (perhaps with the first syllable suppressed). A 1759 list of tribal names includes the *"Lenways* a Nation living on the Mississippi, consisting of about One Thousand fighting men" (Stevens *et al.*, series 21655, p. 87). In circa 1773, Peter Pond (*Narr.* 38) noted, "this frenchman was a Solder in the troops that ware stasond at the *Elenoas.*" (At the end of a word, Pond's *a* usually represents an *ay* sound.) Fur-traders recorded *Irroque* for *Iroquois* in 1802 (*Saskatchewan Jrnls.*, HBC Record Soc. *Publ.* 26.14), and the same pronunciation of *oi* is shown by the English spelling *de Tret* for *Detroit* in 1701 (*DCHNY* 4.908). For English speakers familiar with the standard spelling *Illinois*, there probably always was a tendency to use the spelling pronunciation, ill-ih-NOY(Z), so it cannot be determined with certainty how the journalists pronounced the name.

ILLY Poorly, badly.

Those [Walla Walla] *Indians are cruel horse masters; they ride hard and their Saddles illey constructed.* [30 Apr 06 WC 7.190]

we directed one of the largest of our colts to be killed. we found the flesh of this animal fat tender and by no means illy flavoured. [22 May 06 ML 7.277]

IMPOSTUME {im-POSS-tyoom} An abscess.

Charbono's son is much better today, tho' the swelling on the side of his neck I beleive will terminate in an ugly imposthume a little below the ear. [27 May 06 ML 7.291]

INDURABLE Intolerable, unendurable. The word is not recorded in the *OED* after 1607.

Musquetors excessively troublesom...they are almost indureable perticelarly by the party with me who have no Bears [i.e., BARS[2]] *to keep them off at night* [4 Aug 06 WC 8.280]

INFLUENZA An Italian word in the sense of 'epidemic'—probably because such outbreaks of disease were ascribed to the "influence" of the stars and planets—and later applied to the specific viral disease we now call influenza. The word also referred loosely to any illness producing fever and respiratory symptoms.

the general complaint seams to be bad colds and fevers, something I beleive of the influenza. [22 Feb 06 ML 6.336]

I think that I..have the Enfluenzey. [23 Feb 06 JO 9.273]

INFORMATION {in-fə-MAY-shən} Shaping, molding, giving form to.

I had as yet done but little...to advance the information of the succeeding generation. [18 Aug 05 ML 5.118]

INSOMUCH To such an extent.

the river...was very rapid and rocky insomuch that it was impossible for us to pass [13 Aug 05 ML 5.081]

the bottoms are perfectly covered with frost insomuch that they appear to be covered with snow. [21 Aug 05 ML 5.133]

INSTANT Of the current calendar-month. *See* ULTIMO.

Chronometer too slow as deduced from observation on 16th inst. [21 Nov 03 ML 2.097]

Alexander Willard was...Charged with "Lying down and Sleeping on his post whilst a Sentinal, on the night of the 11th. Instant" [12 Jul 04 WC 2.371]

INTERPRETER {in-TUH-pə-tə} Interpreters, particularly Labiche, CRUZATTE, SACAGAWEA, DROUILLARD, and CHARBONNEAU, played a vital role in the expedition's success. Also **interpretress**.

passed the place the Squar interpretress was taken [30 Jul 05 WC 5.016]

At the Mandans Toussaint Sharbono and his Indian woman & child joined as Interpreters and Interpretess to the Snake Indians. [22 Mar 06 JO 9.279]

Translating often required intermediate language links, as here between English and Nez Perce.

by the assistance of the snake boy and our interpretters were enabled to make ourselves understood...altho' it had to pass through the French, Minnetare, Shoshone and Chopunnish languages. the interpretation being tedious it ocupyed nearly half the day before we had communicated to them what we wished. [11 May 06 ML 7.242]

we found a Shoshone woman, prisoner among these people by means of whome and Sahcahgarweah we found the means of conversing with the Wollah-wollahs. [28 Apr 06 ML 7.178]

INTERSTICE A narrow opening or intervening space, a crevice.

several fine springs burst out at the waters edge from the interstices of the rocks. [19 Jul 05 ML 4.403]

INWARD {IN-wəd} (Of fever and other medical conditions) internal, felt by a patient to be deep-seated, rather than peripheral or superficial.

Several applyed to me to day for medical aides, one a broken arm another inward fever and Several with pains across their loins, and Sore eyes. [29 Apr 06 WC 7.186]

IOWAY {EYE-ə-way} A people originally inhabiting much of present-day Iowa and speaking a SIOUAN Chiwere dialect closely related to OTOE and MISSOURI.

wrote the Speaches to the...Ioways [5 Apr 04 WC 2.192]

below this High Land...the Aiawuay Indians formerly lived [28 Jul 04 WC 2.424]

ISINGLASS {EYE-zən-glass} Mica, a class of silicate minerals occurring in thin, shiny plates in many types of rock.

the Stone...appears to be a Sement of Isin glass [and] *black earth* [31 May 05 WC 4.229]

J

JADED (Of a horse) worn out. (**South Atlantic, Gulf**)

our horses are weak and much jaded. [21 Sep 05 PG 10.146]

JALAP {JAL-əp} A strong laxative and purgative, produced from the root of the Mexican morning-glory vine (*Ipomoea purga*). It was a major component of RUSH'S PILLS, and was also purchased separately as a powder (Latin *pulvis*).

jalap

½ [lb. Pulv.] Jalap [$].67 [26 May 03 in Jackson Letters (ed. 2) 1.080]

Several men taken Sick on the way down, I administered Salts Pils Galip, Tarter emetic &c. [26 Sep 05 WC 5.234]

JAPANNED {jə-PAN'd} Coated with a hard, black varnish, in a style originating in Japan.

they [Chinook] *keep their powder in small japaned tin* [15 Jan 06 ML 6.206]

JERK {jək} To dry meat in thin strips over a slow fire or in the sun for preservation, especially for travel rations. *Jerky* was a staple of the expedition. The word comes into English through Spanish *charqui* from Quechua, the official language of the Inca Empire. *See* FLEECE.

Jurked the Vennison Killed yesterday [5 Jun 04 WC 2.277]

they had camped & were Jurking an Elk & 5 Deer [25 Aug 04 WC 3.008]

we Stopd to Girk our meat on account of the weather being warm [24 Jun 04 JW 11.029]

Also, the jerky itself. *See* PEMMICAN.

I have been living for two days past on poor dryed Elk, or jurk as the hunters term it. [9 Jan 06 ML 6.186]

JIBE {jīb} (Of a fore-and-aft sail) to swing rapidly, usually unexpectedly, and often dangerously from one side of a vessel to the other.

in this state of alarm he threw the perogue with her side to the wind, when the spritsail gibing was as near oversetting the perogue as it was possible to have missed. [13 Apr 05 ML 4.029]

JOCKEY One who cheats, especially in horse-trading.

Those people are great jokies and deciptfull in trade. [20 Apr 06 WC 7.149]

JUGGLER {JUG-lə} A magician or MEDICINE-man. In this sense, the English word is perhaps from Canadian French *jongleur.*

many of them beleive...that a ball cannot penitrate their sheilds, in consequence of certain supernaural powers with which they have been inspired by their jugglers. [23 Aug 05 ML 5.151]

The Juggler (of the Wallowallah) told his nation when we returned that he had predicted it...that he had got it from the moon. [c. Apr 10 NB in Jackson Letters (ed. 2) 2.532]

JURY Temporary. A nautical term that has come ashore, as when saying something is *jury-rigged.*

we Set up a jury mast & Sailed [5 Sep 04 WC 3.048]

K

KALAPUYA {kal-ə-POO-yə} A native people residing south of the Columbia River in the Willamette and Umpqua river drainages. The Kalapuya spoke languages unrelated to the CHINOOKAN, SAHAPTIAN, and SALISHAN ones more familiar to Lewis & Clark. Their name in English is, however, borrowed from Chinookan.

the multnomah [i.e., Willamette R.] *above the falls was Crouded with rapids and thickly inhabited by indians of the Cal-lah-po-é-wah Nation.* [7 Apr 06 WC 7.093]

KAMOSUK A Chinookan word for the glass BEADS that served widely on the Northwest Coast as a form of currency. The word became part of the CHINOOK Jargon term *tyee kamosuk,* applied to the most highly prized large blue beads (*see* TYEE). **(Pacific Northwest)**

these coarse blue beads are their f[av]orite merchandiz, and are called by them tia Commáshuck´ or Chiefs beads. [17 Jan 06 ML 6.214]

KANSA A people, also called KAW, residing on the Kansas River and speaking a Dhegiha language of the SIOUAN family. The name comes either from the Kansa clan-name and self-designation *kãze,* or from the name in one of the other Dhegihan languages, and is found in French, as *Kansa,* on Marquette's 1673 map.

the Kansas Nation hunted on the Missourie last Winter and are now persueing the Buffalow in the Plains [5 Jun 04 WC 2.277]

an old Trading house built by a French merchant from St. Louis to Trade with the kansars Indians. [3 Jul 04 JO 9.020]

The Osage & Kansies are the Same language [3 Aug 04 WC 2.438]

KASKASKIA {kass-KASS-kee-ə} A trading post and fort at the lower end of AMERICAN BOTTOM near the junction of the Kaskaskia and Mississippi rivers in ILLINOIS. It was located at an Illinois Indian village site visited by Father Marquette in 1673. The name in the Illinois language originally was for a subdivision of the Illinois people, meaning 'katydid'—literally 'it rasps.' In 1803, the United States recognized the Kaskaskias as the legal successor to the entire Illinois confederation, and Governor William Henry Harrison of Indiana Territory concluded a treaty with them. *See* CHITTEDIDDLE, DRY GOODS, SAWYER[3].

leave Kaskaskias at 6 A. M. on Monday and arrive on Tuesday 5 Oclock P. M. at Cahokia [c. Apr 04 ML 2.197]

KAW = from the French *Kans* {kã}, an abbreviation of KANSA.

encamped at an Old deserted Indian settlement...formerly belonging to the Caw Nation [15 Jun 04 JW 11.025]

The Kansas River took its French name from that of the tribe.

halted at the river de Caugh [28 Jun 04 JW 11.032]

KEEL[1] = KEELBOAT.

See BOAT.

KEEL[2] (Of a vessel resting on its keel) to roll to one side or the other. *See* CAREEN.

the Barge Struck a Sandbar She Keeld On her labord the Sand Being Quick Vanquishd Suddently from Under her [13 Jun 04 JW 11.023]

KEELBOAT Also **keeled boat**. A sharp-prowed river boat, propelled by oars, (SETTING-)POLE, (TOW-)ROPE, and SAILS, and to be distinguished from the other classic vessel of the Mississippi and its tributaries, the boxy *flat boat*. The *keel* was a longitudinal timber along the centerline of a boat's bottom that served as protection of the hull in passing over shoals. The keel also helped keep a vessel on course. A loaded keelboat sat approximately three feet deep in the water. (In American use, the name probably was borrowed from the Dutch *kielboot*.) The expedition's keelboat was usually referred to as the BOAT, and sometimes BARGE or BATEAU.

1 Keeled Boat light strong at least 60 feet in length her burthen equal to 8 Tons [Jun 03 ML in Jackson Letters (ed. 2) 1.073]

met two Keeled boats loaded with...[furs] for New-Orleans [22 Nov 03 ML 2.102]

this keel Boat was well loaded down with Marchandizes and is going up to the Mahars and yanktons to winter [12 Sep 06 JO 9.361]

The party on Starting from Wood river had one large Keel boat of about 55 Keel decked 10 feet in stern &ten feet in bow—drew three feet water—with one square sail—rowing 22 oars [c. Apr 1810 NB in Jackson Letters (ed. 2) 2.534]

KEEP To remain.

The day keeps cloudy, and the mosquitoes are very troublesome. [24 June 06 PG 10.244]

Also, to follow (a particular route or topographic feature).

passed a branch...to our right Keeping a dividing ridge [18 Sep 05 WC 5.239]

KEG {kig, keg, probably also kag} A small wooden barrel (with approximately a five to ten gallon capacity) for transporting provisions, gunpowder, etc. An average keg of pork held 70–75 pounds. Five gallons of spirits in a keg was approximately 35 pounds. When empty a keg weighed about sixteen pounds.

6 Kegs of 5 Gallons each...of rectified spirits such as is used for the Indian trade...6 Kegs bound with iron Hoops [Jun 03 ML in Jackson Letters (ed. 2) 1.072]

Articles in readiness for the Voyage...50 Kegs of Pork (gross 4500)...3705 W [May 04 WC 2.217]

we now scelected the articles to be deposited in this cash...1 Keg of flour, 2 Kegs of parched meal, 2 Kegs of Pork, 1 Keg of salt [et al.] [10 Jun 05 ML 4.275]

KENTUCKY {colloquially CAIN-tuck, cain-TUH-kee} Originally the lower Kentucky River area and the adjacent bluegrass prairies, bounded by the KNOBS and the Ohio River.

Two Keel Boats arrive from Kentucky to day loaded with whiskey Hats &c. &.[18 May 04 WC 2.237]

> The name *Kentucky* is of Iroquois origin. During the 18th century, the Iroquois, especially the Seneca, expanded southwest from New York and Pennsylvania along the OHIO River. The Senecas named the open, fertile lands along the Kentucky River kë-TAH-geh, 'place of meadows or prairies.' (Similar Seneca geographical names were recorded in New York in the 1670s.) The Iroquois arrival on the Ohio led to continuing warfare with the Cherokee, resulting in relatively sparse Indian settlement of Kentucky. For that reason, and its agricultural promise, the region gained a reputation as a sort of Eden for white emigrants, especially from North Carolina and Virginia. North Carolinian Daniel Boone explored Kentucky in the late 1760s, and successfully established a permanent white settlement there in 1775; *see* also BOONE'S SETTLEMENT. The name appears in the usual early dialect form *Caintuck* in William Calk's 1775 journal of a trip from Virginia to Kentucky (Speed *Wilderness Road* 37).

KETTLE {KIT-'l, a typical pronunciation of the **South Midland** and **Northeast**} MESS kettles were issued to each of the Corps' squads. Kettles also were important as trade-goods.

Nests of camp kettles: brass is much preferr'd to Iron, tho both are very useful to the Indians[.] *size from 1 to 4 gallons.* [Jun 03 ML in Jackson Letters (ed. 2) 1.075]

the ice that was on the Kittle left near the fire last night was ¼ of an inch thick. [3 May 05 WC 4.105]

we have now only one Small kittle to a mess of 8 men. [19 Apr 06 WC 7.144]

KICKAPOO {KICK-ə-poo} A historically wandering people of the ALGONQUIAN language family, found at various times in locations from Michigan to northern Mexico. In the early 1800s, American expansion was displacing them from central Illinois, and they were known to hunt occasionally on the Missouri River.

Heard the 1st frogs on my return from St Charles after haveing arrested the progress of a Kickapoo war party [20 Mar 04 WC 2.185]

8 Indians Kick: Came to Camp with meat we recved their pesents of 3 Deer & gave them Whisky [23 May 04 WC 2.246]

passed 12 canoes of Kickapoos assending on a hunting expedition. [21 Sep 06 WC 8.369]

KILN, COAL- A covered pit in which wood was charred into COAL.

Some men employed Gitting hay from the prarie for to cover the Coal kill. [27 Jan 05 JO 9.111]

KILN, TAR- A pile of resinous wood covered with earth and set smoldering in order to extract tar (for caulking the IRON BOAT). *See* COAL, PAY.

2 men burning a tar kill [3 Jul 05 JW 11.217]

our tar-kiln which ought to have began to run this morning has yealded no tar as yet and I am much affraid will not yeald any, if so I fear the whole opperation of my boat will be useless. [3 July 05 ML 4.354]

KINNIKINNICK {kə-NICK-ə-nick} A mixture of bark (e.g., red-osier dogwood) and leaves (e.g., bearberry, sumac, or tobacco) smoked in a pipe. *See* REDWOOD, SACKACOMMIS. Originally an Algonquian word meaning 'ingredient for mixing in.'

we found Some little notions which Some Indian had hung up. Viz. a Scraper a paint bag...kinikaneck bags, flints &c. [20 Apr 05 JO 9.134]

KNEE An angular piece of timber serving as a reinforcement in boat-construction.

the canoes were finished except the putting in some knees. [13 Jul 05 PG 10.111]

we directed Sergt. Pryor to prepare the two Canoes...they wanted some knees to strengthen them and several cracks corked and payed. [18 Mar 06 ML 6.429]

KNIFE, DRAWING- A draw-knife, a two-handled blade used to shave wood by being drawn toward the user.

4 Drawing-knives...[$]1.20 [18 May 03 in Jackson Letters (ed. 2) 1.098]

an Indian Stole a drawing nife. took it again [29 Dec 04 JO 9.106]

KNOB The quintessentially Kentuckian word for a rounded hill. The hills bounding the Kentucky Bluegrass country on the west, south, and east are called *the Knobs. See* GALLED, SUGARLOAF, WASH. (**Appalachians**)

we passd...Round Knob Creek. [28 Jul 04 JW 11.046]

those Mountains...appeared to be Several detached Knobs...riseing from a leven open Countrey [26 May 05 WC 4.203]

L

LAGOON A small, shallow lake or pond, often connecting with a larger body of water.

the small frogs which are common to the lagoons and swam[p]s of the U States. [15 Apr 05 ML 4.041]

LANCE To launch (a boat). An obsolete variant recorded by *OED* only once, from the year 1515.

Lanced the Leather boat, and found that it leaked a little [9 Jul 05 WC 4.371]

Lanced 2 canoes to day [5 Oct 05 WC 5.246]

LANGUID Slow-moving from fatigue or illness.

the men had become very languid from working in the water and many of their feet swolen and so painfull that they could scarcely walk. [5 Aug 05 ML 5.046]

he is nearly free from pain tho' a gooddeel reduced and very languid. [15 Feb 06 ML 6.312]

LARBOARD {LAH-bəd} An obsolete term for the port side (a vessel's left side when looking toward the bow). Abbreviated also *l., lar., lard., lbd., ld. See* STARBOARD.

oposite our landing is the lower pt. of an Island on the Larbd. [20 Nov 03 ML 2.097]

the Barge Struck a Sandbar She Keeld On her labord [13 Jun 04 JW 11.023]

LATITUDE In the northern hemisphere, the angular distance north of the Equator, which was relatively easily measured for determining one's relative north-south position. *See* ALTITUDE, LONGITUDE.

The Latitude is deduced from a number of Meridian altitudes of the ⊙, taken with the sextant and artificial horizon [c. 14 May 04 ML 2.228]

LATTERLY {LÆ-tə-lee} Recently.

at the lower point is a Settlement on land which does not appear to have been over flown latterly [12 Dec 03 WC 2.131]

this village contained verry large houses built in a different form...and laterly abandoned [30 Oct 05 WC 5.357]

LAUDANUM {LAWD-nəm} A pain-killing, sleep-inducing, cough-suppressing medication consisting of opium in alcohol. *See* COLIC.

4 oz. Laudanum [$].50 [26 May 03 in Jackson Letters (ed. 2) 1.080]

I now gave her [Sacagawea]*...30 drops of laudnum which gave her a tolerable nights rest.* [19 Jun 05 ML 4.309]

LAX Diarrhea, also called RELAX, and related to the word *laxative. See* GRIPING.

the party much incomoded frequently with a Lax, (owing to the minerals) [winter 04–05 WC 3.481]

The men are generally Complaining of a lax and gripeing [2 Dec 05 WC 6.105]

LAY (Of wind) subside. *See* LIE. (**South, South Midland**) *the wind has layed and the Swells are fallen.* [10 Nov 05 WC 6.038]

LAY BY = LIE BY.

blew So hard a head that we were obledged to lay by. [17 Oct 04 JO 9.086]

deturmined to lay by and hunt to day [13 Feb 05 WC 3.294]

LAY DOWN To plot on a map.

this mountain and the knife river have...been laid down too far S. W. [12 Apr 05 ML 4.026]

LEAD Bullets were cast as needed from lead transported in the form of bars. A portion of lead was melted down and cast in *bullet-molds* issued to each man. *See* CANISTER, POWDER.

15 Pairs of Bullet Moulds...400 lbs. Lead [26 May 03 ML in Jackson Letters (ed. 2) 1.070]

we burryed on the high land 1 keg of powder 1 bar led [et al.] [11 Jun 05 JO 9.166]

LEAD, SUGAR OF Lead acetate.

See VITRIOL for example.

LEADER {LEE-də} A tendon.

the twitching of the fingers and leaders of the arm [16 Jun 05 ML 4.300]

LEAGUE A measure of distance, approximately two to three miles, used by the captains for the French term *lieue* of the engagés. For another French linear measure, *see* BRACE[1].

he wintered last winter 300 Leagues up the Chien River [1 Oct 04 WC 3.135]

LEARN {lən} To teach. (**South, Midland**)

the white people would learn them how to take the beaver. [22 Aug 06 WC 8.319]

LEEWARD {LOO-wəd} The side opposite that from which the wind is blowing (opposite of *windward*).

the Small brown Martin of which we saw a vast number hovering on the Leward Side of the hill [25 Aug 04 WC 3.010]

LEGGING {LEH-gin} A sleeve-like covering of the leg, extending from the ankle to the knee or above, like gaiters or chaps.

The Dress of the Ricara men is...a pr. of Mockersons & Legins, a flap, and a Buffalow Robe [12 Oct 04 WC 3.161]

1 p[ai]r Scarlet Leggins for the Maha Chief [winter 04–05? 3.494]

I...trod on a verry large rattle Snake. it bit my leggin...I Shot it. [11 Jul 05 JW 11.223]

Some of the men...gave an ordinary check Shirt a pair of old red leggins and a knife only for a tollarable good pack horse. [18 Aug 05 JO 9.206]

LEVEL, SPIRIT An instrument containing one or more elongate vials nearly filled with alcohol—whence the term *spirit*—in which the position of a bubble indicates how nearly horizontal or vertical an object is. A topographic feature's height can be measured by making repeated horizontal sightings during one's ascent or descent, and tallying the number of increments of the height of the observer's eye above the ground.

I in assendending the Clifts to take the hith of the fall was near Slipping into the water... I assended again, and deceded the Clift lower down...and took the hight...with a Spirit Leavels [17 Jun 05 WC 4.304]

LICK A mineral-rich mudhole frequented by animals. See BUSHEL, SALINE. (**Midland**)

the hunters and Capt. Lewis went out to a buffaloe lick two miles. Saw this Salt Spring, but no buffaloe. [7 Jun 04 JW 11.019]

a deer Came in to lick at the Springs and one of our hunters killed it [30 Jun 06 WC 8.068]

LICORICE The licorice-flavored root of the seashore lupine (*Lupinus littoralis*), which, roasted and ground, was eaten by the Lower Chinook Indians and their American visitors.

3 Indians came with Lickorish Sackacomie berries & mats to Sell, for which they asked Such high prices that we did not purchase any [20 Dec 05 WC 6.133]

LIE (Of wind) to diminish. See LAY. (**South**)

if the wind Should lie...I should proceed on down to their Camp [19 Aug 06 WC 8.309]

we had a Small Shower of rain after which the wind lay, and we proceeded on. [23 Aug 06 WC 8.320]

LIE BY To take time off; said especially of the men when vessels remained tied up to the river bank, as when detained by adverse weather. See COME TO, LAY BY, TAKE UP.

our officers lay by this day for observations. [2 Jun 04 JW 11.017]

the wind blew hard all last night, and continued to blow pretty hard all day, but not so much, as to compell us to ly by. [30 Apr 05 ML 4.088]

the day has proved excessively warm and we lay by four hours during the heat of it [20 Jul 06 ML 8.119]

LIE OUT To spend the night away from the party's main camp. (**South, South Midland**)

the 2 men who lay out on that Side we found here. [14 Jun 05 JO 9.167]

LIGHT, AT At first light, just before dawn.

Clear and pleasant. we Set off at light. [11 Apr 05 JO 9.129]

LIGHTS Lungs. See PLUCK. (**South, South Midland**)

after Shooting eight balls in his body Some of them through the lites, he [grizzly] *took the River and was near catching the Man he chased in* [14 May 05 JO 9.148]

LIGHTWOOD   Resinous wood, usually pine, serving as kindling for lighting fires. Here, for making tar. (**South, esp. South Atlantic**)

I set...Shields and J. Fields to collect and split light wood and prepare a pit to make tar. [1 Jul 05 ML 4.349]

LIKE TO   {LIKE-tə} (To be) likely, probable, or near happening. (**South, South Midland**)

a man had like to have Starved to death in a land of Plenty for the want of Bulletes or Something to kill his meat [11 Sep 04 WC 3.066]

The Ossiniboins is at the Big bellie Camp, Some trouble like to take place between them from the loss of horses [16 Nov 04 WC 3.237]

a Bank fell in near one of the Canoes which like to have filled her with water [20 Apr 05 WC 4.056]

our Tar kill like to turn out nothing [4 Jul 05 WC 4.362]

as it was like to rain we accepted of a bed in one of their tents. [20 Sep 06 WC 8.367]

LIKELY   Promising, handsome, vigorous. *See* STOUT.

they [Flathead] are the likelyest and honestest [people] we have seen and are verry friendly to us. [5 Sep 05 JO 9.219]

LIKEWAY(S)   Likewise.

the deer was plentifull...likeway the woolves and Bears [30 Jun 04 JW 11.033]

a party of Each Nation With a Detachment from the Watesoons Nation like-ways [3 Nov 04 JW 11.108]

LIMB   The edge (upper or lower, eastern or western) of the sun or moon's disk.

I took the meridian altd of Sun's L. L. [25 Nov 03 ML 2.112]

observed meridian Altd. of ☉'s Lower Limb, with my Octant & artificial horizan [3 Dec 03 ML 2.121]

I brought the Moons Western limb in contact [with alpha Aquilæ] in stead of her Eastern limb she having passed into her third quarter and of course her Western limb somewhat imperfect. [9 Sep 05 ML 5.193]

LINE   A unit of length, equal to $1/12$ of an inch.

The Buzzard which Ruben Fields killed diameter of one feather is...1 Line [19 Nov 05 WC 6.069]

LINE, TOWING-   = (TOW-)ROPE.

proceeded on with the towing lines. [22 Apr 05 JO 9.135]

we...have a hard time of it oblidged to walk on Shore & haul the towing line and 9/10 of the time barefooted. [3 Jun 05 JW 11.184]

LINEN Underwear.

her linin...seemed to be drawn beneath her girdle of her stroud as also a short Jacket with long sleeves over her linin [23 Nov 03 ML 2.107]

LINIMENT, VOLATILE A medicinal concoction of sweet oil and ammonia, called *volatile* from the speed with which the ammonia evaporated.

Bratton is much wose today, he complains of a violent pain in the small of his back... we...applyed a bandage of flannel to the part and bathed and rubed it well with some vollatile linniment which I prepared with sperits of wine, camphor, castile soap and a little laudinum. [7 Mar 06 ML 6.388]

Capt. C. gave an indian man some volitile linniment to rub his k[n]ee and thye for a pain [5 May 06 ML 7.209]

> William Buchan's *Domestic Medicine* (1785) provides a formulation: "Take of florence oil, an ounce; spirit of hartshorn, half an ounce. Shake them together. This liniment, made with equal parts of the spirit and oil, will be more efficacious, where the patient's skin is able to bear it." *Florence oil* is a high-grade olive oil. *Spirit of hartshorn* is ammonia-water (with deer-antler being the main source of ammonia in earlier times). Lewis & Clark's mixture was improvised.

LINN A basswood or linden tree, *Tilia americana*, known for light, white wood.

each point Covered with Tall timber, Such as...Lynn & ash [30 Jul 04 WC 2.430]

LINT The fuzzy material obtained by raveling or scraping linen fabric, or from other fibers.

2. oz Patent Lint [$].25 [26 May 03 in Jackson Letters (ed. 2) 1.080]

I dressed the arm which was broken Short above the wrist & Supported it with broad Sticks to keep it in place, put in a Sling and furnished him with Some lint bandages &c. [28 Apr 06 WC 7.180]

I took off my cloaths and dressed my wounds myself as well as I could, introducing tents of patent lint into the ball holes [11 Aug 06 ML 8.156]

> Using lint in wound-care dates from at least the third millennium BC in Egypt. During the American Civil War, women still volunteered for the tedious work of producing lint for dressing battlefield wounds, despite the wide availability of cotton-wool and patent dressings. **Patent lint** used by Lewis (*see* TENT) probably was a sort of manufactured cotton gauze. Ironically, after thousands of years of applying loose lint in treating wounds, modern dressings are advertised as "low-lint" or "lint-free."

LIZARD, HORNED {hɔn'd LIH-zəd} = (PRAIRIE) BUFFALO.

LOADING Cargo.

we dryed and aired Some of the loading which had got wet [24 Apr 05 JO 9.136]

We...hung up our loading on poles...extended between trees...and turned back melancholy and disappointed. [17 Jun 06 PG 10.241]

LOCK The firing mechanism of a gun. In a flintlock, the FLINT, actuated by the COCK, strikes a piece of steel (the FRIZZEN) a glancing blow and emits sparks that ignite the PRIMING powder in the PAN. The exploding priming in turn sets off the main charge in the gun's chamber.

Locks to be mended [14 Apr 04 WC 2.201]

Baling Invoice of Sundries, being necessary Stores...3 Setts Rifle Locks...1 Sett of Gunlocks [winter 04–05 3.502-3]

one...returned having broke the lock of his gun [14 Nov 05 PG 10.170]

The guns of Drewyer and Sergt. Pryor were both out of order. the first was repared with a new lock [20 Mar 06 ML 6.441]

LODGE An Indian dwelling. The English word in this sense probably is borrowed directly from Canadian French *loge*.

the Sceouex Camps are...of a Conic form Covered with Buffalow Roabs Painted different Colours and all Compact & hand Somly arranged...each Lodg has a place for Cooking detached, the lodges contain 10 to 15 persons [29 Aug 04 WC 3.022]

found their lodges in this [Arikara] *village...verry close compact. in a round form large & warm covered first after the wood is willows and Grass. Then a thick coat of Earth... except the chimney hole which Goes out at center* [10 Oct 04 JO 9.078]

there was indian camp of eleven leather lodges...the poles only of the lodges remained. [23 Jul 06 ML 8.125]

Lewis & Clark adapted the Plains tepee for their own use.

we were roused late at night by the Sergt. of the guard, and warned of the danger we were in from a large tree that had taken fire and which leant immediately over our lodge. [17 May 05 ML 4.160]

LOG A device for measuring the speed of a watercraft or a stream's current. The procedure is conducted by running out a piece of wood called the SHIP[3] (or *chip*) on a line from a reel on a vessel's stern; or, from a fixed point on shore. In a measured interval of time, 50 FATHOMS played out in 40 seconds, for example, would indicate about 5 miles per hour.

The Common Current taken with a Log runs 50 fathen in 40" [seconds] [17 Jul 04 WC 2.389]

In 1803, Lewis listed a *patent log*, invented in the late 18th century, as being necessary equipment for the upcoming expedition [Jackson Letters (ed. 2) 1.069]. The log consisted of a reel, line, and chip—a built-in counter tallied the number of rotations. The line would be hauled in periodically to read the number of spins, and thus determine the distance (and speed) traveled by water. Given the $1.95 paid for a log, it seems likely that Lewis settled for an old-fashioned design [31 May 03 in Jackson Letters (ed. 2) 1.082].

LOINS The lower abdomen, upper legs, and pubic region. *See* SADDLE.

most Common [are] *Rhumatic disorders & weaknesses in the back and loins* [12 May 06 WC 7.249]

he…is so weak in the loins that he is scarcely able to walk [24 May 06 ML 7.283]

LONGITUDE In North America, the angular distance west of GREENWICH, England. The principle of its determination, based on the difference between Greenwich time and local time, had long been known. Its practical measurement in this era, however, was difficult because observers had to determine the exact time in Greenwich, depending on complex astronomical observations and unreliable clocks. *See* CHRONOMETER, LATITUDE, (LUNAR) OBSERVATION.

The Longitude of the mouth of the River Dubois was calculated from four sets of observations [May 04 ML 2.228]

LOOK OUT Look for, seek out.

we scelected six men, and ordered them to look out some timber [16 Jun 05 ML 4.300]

Capt. Lewis…looked out a place undiscovered from the natives for a carsh [20 Aug 05 JO 9.207]

Capt. Clark and 5 men went…to…look out a place to make Salt [8 Dec 05 JO 9.259]

LOUP[1] {loo} Wolf, as a fur-bearer. This is one of the words that illustrates the pervasive influence of French-Canadians in the fur-trade. (*See* CARCAJOU, LOUP CERVIER, and PEKAN for analogous terms.) *Loup* also made its way from French into Chinook Jargon as *le loo*.

they [Sioux] *furnish Beaver Martain Loues, orter, Pekon Bear and Deer* [31 Aug 04 WC 3.027]

LOUP[2] {loo} A band of the PAWNEE; a French translation of the Pawnee name of the group, variously rendered *Skiri* and *Skidi* and meaning 'wolf' or 'coyote.'

Up this river [Platte] *live three nations of Indians, the Otos, Panis, and Loos, or Wolf Indians.* [21 Jul 04 PG 10.022]

two ¼ Days from the Loups Village [to Council Bluff] [3 Aug 04 WC 2.441]

we met…Alexander La fass and three french men from St. Louis in a Small perogue on his way to trade with the Pania Luup or Wolf Indians. [10 Sep 06 WC 8.355]

lynx

LOUP CERVIER {loo-sai(r)-VYAY} The lynx (*Lynx canadensis*), a species of wildcat trapped for its fur. Literally 'deer-hunting wolf' in French. (**North**)

the Thormometer at Sun rise Stood at 38° below 0…I line my Gloves and have a cap made of the Skin of the Louservia [12 Dec 04 WC 3.256]

LUES VENEREA {LOO-eez və-NEER-ee-ə} Syphilis. Latin for 'venereal plague.' *See* POX, VENEREAL.

bothe gonaroehah and Louis venerae are native disorders of America [19 Aug 05 ML 5.122]

Goodrich has recovered from the Louis veneri which he contracted from an amorous contact with a Chinnook damsel. I cured him...by the uce of murcury. [27 Jan 06 ML 6.239]

They [western Indians] *can cure...not lues which is excessively bad on the Sea Coast* [c. Apr 10 NB in Jackson Letters (ed. 2) 2.506]

LUFF To steer a sailing vessel so near the direction of the wind that the SAIL shakes.

the steersman allarmed, in stead of puting her before the wind, lufted her up into it, the wind was so violent that it drew the brace of the squarsail out of the hand of the man who was attending it, and instantly upset the perogue [14 May 05 ML 4.152]

LULL (Of wind) to go down, or abate. (**Midland, South Atlantic, northern New England**)

at Sun Set the wind luled and Cleared up Cold [2 Sep 04 WC 3.042]

LUMBER {LUM-bə} Unneeded articles taking up space. (**Virginia**)

see that no cooking utensels or loos lumber of any kind is left on the deck [26 May 04 ML 2.256]

LUMBERSOME Unwieldy, awkward to store or transport.

I assort our articles for to be left at this place buried...a few Small lumbersom articles [26 Jun 05 WC 4.335]

M

MACE A small gold coin, and a small unit of weight originally used in the East Indian trade for valuable items such as jewels. The word is of Malay origin.

Baling Invoice of Sundries for Indian Presents...10 maces White Rd. Beads [winter 04–05 3.495]

MAHAHA {mah-HAH-hah} A Mandan name for the AHWAHAWAY, meaning literally 'spread out place.' To be distinguished from the *Mahas: see* OMAHA.

formed a Camp...above the 2d Mandan village & opsd. the Mah-har-ha village [27 Oct 04 WC 3.203]

MAKE[1] To have (someone) do something, without the implication of compulsion present in modern use.

I made McNeal cook the remainder of our meat which afforded a slight breakfast for ourselves and the Cheif. [17 Aug 05 ML 5.109]

MAKE[2] (Of Lewis & Clark) to appoint as chief a man thought likely to advance U.S. interests and useful for molding tribal peoples to that end. By no means did their own people always consider these men leaders. *See* MEDAL, PAROLE.

we...made three Chiefs, one for each Village [10 Oct 04 WC 3.156]

MAKE[3] (Of a topographic feature) to trend, or to extend. Compare with the modern expressions *make one's way*, and *make for*, as in "I made for shelter when it started to rain."

A ridge of Hills...make across the river [26 Nov 03 ML 2.115]

we Campd...above some rocks makeing out in the river in a butifull ellivated plain. [9 Apr 05 WC 4.017]

I passed a small rivulet of clear water making down from the hills [15 Apr 05 ML 4.041]

the mountains make close on each Side of the creek [2 Sep 05 JO 9.216]

MANDAN {MAN-dan} A SIOUAN people of North Dakota living in circular, earth-covered lodges in stockaded agricultural villages along the Missouri River. The Mandan were situated just downstream from the HIDATSA. The Mandan grew maize, bean, squash, pumpkin, sunflower, and tobacco, and also subsisted by hunting, especially of buffalo. The expedition spent the winter of 1804–5 at Fort Mandan, erected near the Mandan villages. The tribe was devastated by smallpox in 1837.

This place we have named Fort Mandan in honour of our Neighbours. [2 Nov 04 ML 3.226]

the Mandan nation...Came out of a Small lake where they had Gardins...the mandans Specke a language peculial to themselves [12 Nov 04 WC 3.233]

> The Mandan were first mentioned by French explorer de la Vérendrye in 1738, who approached the upper Missouri from the north through ASSINIBOINE lands, as did later Canadian traders. Vérendrye adopted in the French form, *Mantannes*, the Assiniboine name for the tribe ♦perhaps ultimately from *Māta*, the Mandan term for the Missouri River. ♦ Transmission of the name by yet another Siouan group is suggested by spelling variants where the final *-n* is replaced by Lakota (TETON) *-l*.

the blacksmith [probably Patrick Heneberry] has traveled far to the north, & Visited the Mandols [Mandans] [1 Jan 04 WC 1.144]

MARROW-BONES Cooked animal bones, cracked open to extract the nutritious inner part (marrow). *See* SHANK-BONE.

I was taken with such violent pain in the intestens that I was unable to partake of the feast of marrowbones. [11 Jun 05 ML 4.278]

my fare is really sumptuous this evening; buffaloe's humps, tongues and marrowbones, fine trout parched meal pepper and salt [13 Jun 05 ML 4.287]

MAST An upright wooden pole, on which the SAILS of a BOAT or PIROGUE were set. (*See* SPRIT.) The Corps' keelboat apparently had two masts when sailing down the Ohio and one when proceeding up the Missouri. (The single mast seems to have pivoted near the lower end.) Masts could be broken by overhanging trees and strong gusts, and so needed frequent repair or replacement.

at 12 oClock the wind was So violent as to take off one of the Mast's [7 Dec 03 WC 2.127]

a Jointed Mast to let down of 32 feet long [Jan 04 WC 2.163]

the Sergt. at the helm run under a bending Tree & broke the mast [4 Jun 04 WC 2.275]

Mended our mast this morning [6 Jun 04 WC 2.281]

MATCH A piece of treated cord used to fire guns that burns at a constant rate (*slow match* or *quick match*) and is difficult to extinguish. The matchlock musket, a predecessor to the *flintlock,* was fired with a match, rather than with a FLINT. *See* PORTFIRE.

1 [Packg. Box for] Slow Match [$]1.25 [30 Jun 03 in Jackson Letters (ed. 2) 1.092]

I had a Small pece of port fire match in my pocket, off of which I cut a pece…& put it into the fire…the port fire cought and burned vehemently…which astonished and alarmed these nativs [2 Apr 06 WC 7.058]

MATCH, SHOOTING- A marksmanship contest often attracting a crowd, whence the expression *the whole shootin'-match.*

the Party made up a Shooting match, with the Country people for a pr. Leagens, Reuben Fields made the best Shot [16 Jan 04 WC 2.156]

MATTER Pus. *See* MATURE.

t[h]e tumor on Capt. Clarks ankle has discharged a considerable quantity of matter but is still much swolen and inflamed [8 Aug 05 ML 5.059]

MATURE {mə-CHə} (Of a boil or abscess) to come to a head and discharge MATTER, usually to a patient's relief.

Capt. Clarks ankle is extreemly painfull to him…the tumor has not yet mature[d]*, he has a slight fever.* [5 Aug 05 ML 5.046]

MEAGER (MEE-gə) (Of malnourished game animals) thin, emaciated. *See* POOR.

I walked on Shore in the evening & killed a Deer which was So meager as to be unfit for use [29 Apr 05 WC 4.087]

MEAL, INDIAN Corn-meal. *See* (LYED) CORN.

should any of the messes prefer indian meal to flour they may recieve it [26 May 04 ML 2.258]

MEAL, PARCH- {pahtch} Parched (dry-roasted) corn-meal. Each of the expedition's bags weighed about 86 pounds, thus a BUSHEL of parch-meal weighed 2½ pounds less than a bushel of HULLED corn.

Articles in readiness for the Voyage...14 Bags of Parchmeal of 2 bus: each about 1200 W [May 04 WC 2.217]

MEALY (Of an animal) speckled or mottled.

the fishing hawk with the crown of the head White and back of a mealy white [7 Mar 06 ML 6.388]

MEDAL Lewis & Clark presented designated chiefs with various-sized medals bearing the image of Thomas Jefferson (and on the reverse side: a hatchet, smoking pipe, and clasped hands), or of George Washington (on reverse: seasonal activities and domesticated animals). *See* MAKE².

after Prepareing Some presents for the Cheifs which we intended [to] make by giving Meadals...we Sent Mr. Dorion in a Perogue for the Cheifs & warreirs [30 Aug 04 WC 3.024]

[the Cheyenne chief] *gave me... the meadal back and informed me that he knew that the white people were all medecine and that he was afraid of the midal or any thing that white people gave to them.* [21 Aug 06 WC 8.314]

MEDICINE A magical power, believed by many American tribal peoples to dwell in certain objects and beings.

every thing which is incomprehensible to the indians they call big medicine, and is the opperation of the presnts and power of the great sperit. [2 May 05 ML 4.101]

all party Paraded, gave a Medal to...the 3d [chief] *Tar-ton-gar-wa-ker, Buffalow medison* [25 Sep 04 WC 3.111]

> The word in this sense probably was borrowed from Canadian French *médecine*. The French word, in turn, renders a native term, such as the Sioux *wakhã*. The latter occurs in the name, *tatãka wakhã*, Buffalo Medicine, one of the Teton chiefs with whom the captains treated in central South Dakota. Though the essence of such power was incomprehensible to humans and held holy, it was not supernatural. Medicine was inherent *in* nature, not superior *to* it. Medicine, though not clearly understood, could be put to use by certain people, among them JUGGLERS. When the term appears in the expedition journals, it is in regard to the natives' customs and beliefs, and their reaction to new or strange phenomena or objects, such as Lewis's air-gun and Clark's Black servant York.

Some of our men go to See a [Mandan] *war medison* [dance] *made at the village on the opposit Side of the river* [11 Jan 05 WC 3.271]

Captaine Clarke...told them his soldiers were good, and that he had more medicine... than would kill twenty such nations in one day. [25 Sep 04 PG 10.045]

the Indians much asstonished at my Black Servent and Call him the big medison [9 Oct 04 WC 3.155]

I also shot my air-gun which was so perfectly incomprehensible that they immediately denominated it the great medicine. [17 Aug 05 ML 5.112] *the Savages did not Trouble us as we had requested them not to come as it was a Great medician day with us. we enjoyed a merry cristmas* [25 Dec 04 JO 9.106]

MEND To repair.

we delayed Some time to mend the rudder of the red perogue which got broke last evening. [4 May 05 JO 9.142]

To recuperate from illness or injury. (**South, South Midland**)

The Sick Chief is much mended [8 Jun 06 WC 7.347]

Capt. Lewis is mending Slowly. [30 Aug 06 WC 8.329]

To tend a fire. (**South, South Midland**)

the fire…was blaizing and appeared to have been mended up afresh [7 Aug 06 ML 8.151]

MENDING HAND, ON THE Recovering; on the mend. Here, of Lewis recuperating after being shot in the backside by CRUZATTE, who mistook the captain for an elk while hunting in thick brush along the Missouri. (**New England**)

Capt. L. is Still on the mending hand he walks a little. I have discontinued the tent in the hole where the ball entered [26 Aug 06 WC 8.324]

MERCURY {Mə-kə-ree} The most widely used anti-venereal drug before antibiotics, usually applied as a salve (Latin *ung[uentum]*), but also administered orally or injected with a *penis syringe*. Patients watched for (or were observed for) excessive salivation, the first symptom of mercury poisoning. *See* POX. Mercury also was the main ingredient of VERMILION, and a PURGATIVE component of RUSH'S PILLS.

1 [lb. Ung.] Mercuriale [$]1.25 [26 May 03 in Jackson Letters (ed. 2) 1.080]

Goodrich has recovered from the Louis veneri…I cured him…by the uce of murcury. [27 Jan 06 ML 6.239]

The Corps' thermometers could measure temperature no lower than mercury's freezing point, -40° Fahrenheit. *See* SATURN.

The Murcery Stood at 72° below the freesing point [10 Jan 05 WC 3.271]

the murcury stood at 80 a. o [above zero] *this is the warmest day except one which we have experienced this summer.* [22 Jul 05 ML 4.416]

MERE {MEE-ə} Absolute, downright, simple. Lewis used the word in the sense of 'nothing less than' or as 'nothing more than,' of which only the latter is used today. In 1768, George Washington wrote in his diary, "it blew a mere Hurricane."

a mear repremand for any improper act [19 Jan 06 ML 6.222]

our Stock of provisions…is now reduced to a mear minnamum. [26 Feb 06 WC 6.353]

the river…runs a mear torrant tearing up the trees by the roots [8 Jul 06 ML 8.097]

MERIDIAN Noon. Ultimately from Latin *meridianus* 'of midday'; from *meri-*, a reshaping of *medi-* 'middle,' and *dies* 'day.' The modern sense as a line of longitude arises from the sun being due south precisely at solar noon.

I...observed the Meridian Altd. of the ☉ *Upper Limb* [20 Nov 03 ML 2.097]

it began to rain and continued untill meridian [31 May 05 ML 4.224]

MESS A serving or dish of prepared food.

Gave them a mess of boiled corn [22 Aug 05 JW 11.280]

Also, a squad of men eating together, forming the expedition's basic organizational unit. In May 1804, the Corps was divided into five messes—three with a sergeant and eight privates each, one of 7 engagés under a PATROON, and one of five men and a corporal. *See* KETTLE.

should any of the messes prefer indian meal to flour they may recieve it [26 May 04 ML 2.258]

Robert Frazer...will be anexed to Sergeant Gass's mess. [8 Oct 04 WC 3.153]

We have heretofore devided the meat when first killed among the four messes, into which we have divided our party [12 Jan 06 WC 6.200]

METTLE, PUT ONE ON ONE'S To test or to challenge someone. *Mettle* means 'courage, strength of character;' originally a variant spelling of *metal.*

to doubt the bravery of a savage is at once to put him on his metal. [15 Aug 05 ML 5.096]

MIAMI A native people speaking a dialect of the Algonquian Miami-ILLINOIS language and inhabiting parts of Wisconsin, Illinois, and Indiana. In the Miami-Illinois language, the name means 'downstream person.' The Miami were part of the Indian confederation defeated by the U.S. Army in the Battle of Fallen TIMBERS (1794).

The Creek...rasin fast, Swept off a Canoo belonging to a Maumies Indian [7 Feb 04 WC 2.174]

MICROMETER {my-KRAH-mə-tə} A device with a finely threaded screw used for careful adjustment of the expedition's SEXTANT and OCTANT, whose angular measurements were read from the NONIUS. Also called TANGENT-SCREW.

A common Octant of 14 Inches radius, graduated to 20', which by means of the nonius was devisbile to 1', half of this sum, or 30" was perceptible by means of the micrometer. [22 Jul 04 ML 2.411]

MIDDLE-DEEP Up to one's waist. *See* HALF-LEG, MIDRIB-DEEP.

We Crossed a Creek, which took us middle deep, which benumbed & Chilled the party very much. [19 Feb 06 JW 11.422]

MIDRIB-DEEP Up to one's chest.

a north branch of the Co-qual-la-isquet is 40 yards wide and was mid-rib deep to our horses, with a rapid current. [6 Jul 06 PG 10.249]

MIFF Offense, annoyance. *See* PET[1], PIQUE.

The 2d Chief of the 2d Mandan Village took a miff at our not attending to him perticelarely...and moved back to his village [2 Apr 05 WC 3.328]

Also, to take offense.

if miffed with any man he [Charbonneau] *wishes to return when he pleases* [12 Mar 05 WC 3.313]

MIGHTY   Very. (**South, South Midland**)

the day Got mighty hot [26 Jun 04 JW 11.031]

the Boat Swong...Exerted them selves mighty well [2 Jul 04 JW 11.033]

MILK   Whiskey in Indian usage; in earlier times, *lait des François*, 'Frenchmen's milk.'

my father as you gave us a fine flag we wish you would give a little powder and a little of our Great fathers milk [31 Aug 04 JO 9.050]

MILT   The spleen. (**South, South Midland**)

I...amused myself catching those white fish...they bit most freely at the melt of a deer [12 Jun 05 ML 4.280]

some were eating the kidnies the melt and liver and the blood runing from the corners of their mouths [16 Aug 05 ML 5.103]

MINITARI   = HIDATSA. Upper Missouri villagers living in earth lodges near the Mandan. In Hidatsa, the name means 'crosses the water.' The Minitari also were known as BIG BELLY and *Gros Ventres of the Missouri.*

after Brackfast we were Visited by the Old Chief of the Big Bellies or menetarres [29 Oct 04 WC 3.208]

Winataree shows the alternation of *m* and *w* characteristic of Hidatsa (*see* SACAGAWEA).

[the Mandan] *moved up near the watersoons & winataree where they now live in peace with those nations* [12 Nov 04 WC 3.233]

Minitari also refers to another people, the GROS VENTRE *of the Prairie*, or ATSINA, who often were mentioned with the qualifier *of Fort des Prairies*, from the tribe's trading relationship with either of two North West Company posts on the south fork of the Saskatchewan River. They were at the time associated with the BLACKFOOT people of the western Plains.

son of a conspicuous [Nez Perce] *chief...was killed not long since by the Minnetares of Fort de Prarie* [11 May 06 ML 7.242]

Lewis apparently considered the two peoples—the *Gros Ventres of the Missouri* (Hidatsa) and the *Gros Ventres of the Prairie* (or *Fort des Prairies*)—as closely related, although they are not.

the football is such as I have seen among the Minetaries [i.e., Hidatsa] *and therefore think it most probable that they are a band of the Minetaries of Fort de Prarie.* [28 May 05 ML 4.211]

MISFIRE OR MISS FIRE   {MIS-fī-ə} (Of a firearm) to SNAP, often due to damp priming powder in the PAN, a loose FLINT, or a plugged touch-hole.

Jos. Fields was attacted by an old hea bear & his gun missed fire [6 Jun 05 JO 9.163]

we Saw two white Bear, one of them was nearly catching Joseph Fields who could not fire, as his gun was wet [4 Jun 05 WC 4.256]

MISSISSIPPI   The Mississippi River was the effective western boundary of American settlement at the time of the expedition (*see* SPANISH). Along with its major tributaries, the Ohio and Missouri, the Mississippi has long served as the preeminent route for commerce in North America. The name is recorded in French as *Riuiere de Missisipi* (in Jacques Marquette's 1674 journal), from an Ojibway or other Algonquian name meaning 'big river.'

this evening landed on the point at which the Ohio and Mississippi form there junchon [14 Nov 04 ML 2.086]

MISSOURI   {evidence in the journals, and the French spelling *Missouri,* usually suggest the pronunciation mih-SOOR-ee or mih-ZOOR-ee, rather than mih-ZOOR-ə, though Clark did write *Missourus* in a letter [WC Letters 61]} A people of the lower Missouri River speaking a now extinct SIOUAN Chiwere dialect related to IOWAY and OTOE.

G Drewyer brought in a Missourie Indian which he met with hunting in the Prarie This Indian is one of the fiew remaining of that nation, & lives with the Otteauz [28 Jul 04 WC 2.424]

two of the Missouries Tribe…went to the Mahars to Steel horses, they Killed them both [18 Aug 04 WC 2.489]

> The name comes from French, first recorded by Marquette in 1673 as *Ouemessourit,* then in 1678 as *Missouri.* The French learned it from the Illinois, whose name for the Missouri in the long form meant 'people who have dugout canoes,' and in the short, simply 'dugout canoe.' The tribal name was only later applied to the Missouri River. The frequent spellings with a final –*s* were probably taken as the possessive form, i.e., '(the river) of the Missouri Indians.'

measured the Missouries at this place and made it 720 yards wide [17 May 04 WC 2.235]

MISTRUST   To suspect.

the Indians need not discover us, or mistrust that we are going to berry any thing at this place [21 Aug 05 JW 11.279]

MOCCASIN   A soft-soled shoe made of animal hide, requiring frequent repair and replacement. During the Great Falls portage, moccasins lasted about two days. Originally an Algonquian word for 'shoe.'

moccasin

a hard white frost last night. our mocassons froze near the fire. [14 May 05 JO 9.147] *in the evening the men mended their mockersons and prepared themselves for the portage.* [19 Jun 05 ML 4.309]

We are now waiting for fair weather in Order to make a Start to the United States...The party has now among them 338 pair of good moccosins. The most of them are strong & made out of Elk skins [20 Mar 06 JW 11.430]

Sometimes used in lieu of horseshoes.

Skin to make mockersons for Some of our lame horses. [16 Jul 06 WC 8.190]

Distinctive styles identified different tribes.

The Indian woman with us exmined the mockersons which we found at these encampments and informed us that they were not of her nation the Snake Indians [29 May 05 ML 4.216]

Moccasin manufacture often indicated impending war, or horse-thievery.

two Towns of the Ricares were makeing their Mockersons, and...we had best take care of Our horses [30 Nov 04 WC 3.246]

Removal from the feet meant times were peaceful; *see* HATCHET.

they [the Mandan] *now Could hunt without fear, & ther womin Could work in the fields without looking everry moment for the Enemey, and put off their mockersons at night* [31 Oct 04 WC 3.218]

MONS VENERIS {mahnz-VEN-ə-rəs} The female pubic region. In Latin, literally 'mountain of Venus.' *See* VENEREAL.

the...breach clout...is a much more indesant article...and bearly covers the Mons venus [30 Mar 06 WC 7.035]

MOON (In Indian context) a period of time between recurrences of the same phases of the moon, such as from new moon to new moon, or from full moon to full moon. Specific days were not counted in these intervals. *See* SLEEP.

they expect him back to trade with them in 3 moons [1 Jan 06 WC 6.155]

MOONACK {MOO-nack} A name for the woodchuck (*Marmota monax*), but apparently transferred to the yellow-bellied marmot (*M. flaviventris*). From a Virginian ALGONQUIAN word meaning 'earth-digger.' *See* PET[2]. (**Maryland, Virginia**)

I have...observed some robes among them [Shoshone] *of beaver, moonax, and small wolves.* [20 Aug 05 ML 5.126]

MOSQUITO {mə-SKEE-tə(r)} Blood-sucking insects, often a constant bane unless wind, wood smoke, frost, or cold seasonal weather intervened. Spanish for 'little fly.' *See* BAR[2], MUSKET.

the Musquetoes begin to Suck our blood this afternoon. [9 Apr 05 JO 9.128]

9th Musquetors troublesom...10th Snow was 8 inches deep this morning. [May 06 ML 7.319]

MOST Almost.

he [a white bear] *was verry old   the tushes most wore out as well as his claws.* [5 May 05 JO 9.143]

MOUTH = DISEMBOGUE.

Clarks river which mouthes imedeately opposit to me forks at about 18 or 20 miles [22 Apr 06 WC 7.158]

MRS. Plural of *Mr.*, not the abbreviation of *Mistress*, as in modern use.

Sent by them a letter to Mrs. Tabbo & Gravoline, at the Ricares Village [2 Dec 04 WC 3.252]

Mrs. La Roche & McKinsey Clerk to the N W. Compy. visit us. [3 Apr 05 WC 3.329]

MULATTO A person of mixed race; from Spanish *mulato*, derived from *mulo* MULE, with reference to hybrid ancestry. The form *mallat* came into English through the French *mulâtre* or its variant *mulat(e)*, which in turn was from Spanish. *See* CRUZATTE, DROUILLARD, HALF-BREED.

The names of the french Ingishees...Pieter Crousatt half Indian[,] *William La Beice [Labiche] Mallat* [4 Jul 04 WC 2.347]

they have a good hunter hired...a malattoe [4 Sep 06 JO 9.358]

MULE Offspring of a male donkey and a mare (*Equus asinus* x *caballus*).

The Indians value their mules very highly. a good mule can not be obtained for less than three and sometimes four horses, and the most indifferent are rated at two horses. their mules generally are the finest I ever saw [19 Aug 05 ML 5.123]

Capt. Lewis traded with them and bought three fine horses and 2 half breed mules for a little Marchandize [22 Aug 05 JO 9.208]

Also, = (MULE-)DEER.

Most of the deer were large fat mule bucks. [19 Jul 06 ML 8.116]

R. Fields killed a mule doe. [19 Jul 06 ML 8.117]

MUSKET A long, smooth-bore gun with a flint LOCK firing mechanism. *See* BUCKSHOT, FUSIL, RIFLE.

> Some expedition members probably carried the U.S. Army Model 1795, a .69-caliber musket. This military weapon, as well as the muskets commonly used in the Indian trade, shot a BALL weighing about an ounce (16 to the pound) and also could fire small SHOT. The word comes through French from the Italian *moschetta*, meaning 'little fly' and 'crossbow bolt' (the projectile of a crossbow), which, like a fly, buzzed and stung. (The Italian word is related to the Spanish MOSQUITO.)

with his clubbed musquet he [McNeal] *struck the bear over the head and cut him with the guard of the gun and broke off the breech* [15 Jul 06 ML 8.110]

[Chinook] *guns are usually of an inferior quality being oald refuse American & brittish Musquits...they have no rifles.* [15 Jan 06 ML 6.206]

CHINOOK Jargon borrowed the word in the sense of any sort of long gun. Here, a Clatsop-speaker refers to Clark's fine marksmanship with a RIFLE.

Clouch Musket... wake, com ma-tax Musket ['a good gun; I don't understand this gun'] [10 Dec 05 WC 6.121]

N

NAME, WAR- An Indian personal name used in war, here referring to CAMEAHWAIT.

This nation Call themselves Cho-shon-nê the Chief is name[d] *Too-et-te-con'l Black Gun is his war name* [17 Aug 05 WC 5.115]

NATION A native people considered by Lewis & Clark as a unit, primarily on the basis of a common language. Not to be construed in the modern political sense and best understood simply as '(a) people.'

a great talk had been held and...all the nations were going to war [25 Dec 03 WC 2.141]

NEAR {NEE-ə} A horse's left side, on which a rider approaches and mounts (and dismounts).

this [halter] *when mounted he draws up on the near side of the horse's neck and holds in the left hand* [24 Aug 05 ML 5.161]

we branded them on the near fore Shoulder with a Stirrup Iron [5 Oct 05 JO 9.234]

NEAR-CUT A shortcut.

I took a near cut and at night came out ahead of the party [22 Jul 05 JW 11.236]

NEAT Net, clear, free of any deduction, as in *net weight*. The related sense, 'pure, unmixed,' survives in the modern expression *neat whiskey.*

I counted 107 Stacks of dried pounded fish in different places on those rocks which must have contained 10,000 w. of neet fish [24 Oct 05 WC 5.335]

NEMAHA RIVER Either of two tributaries (*Big* and *Little Nemaha*) to the Missouri in southeast Nebraska. An IOWAY-OTOE name, *nyī-māha* 'water-muddy,' it occurs both with and without *nyī-*. For another *nyī-* name, *see* PLAT.

I joined the Boat on the Sand Island Situated opposit the mouth of the Ne Mar har River [11 Jul 04 WC 2.366]

We...halted at an island, opposite a creek called Moha [11 Jul 04 PG 10.020]

NEZ PERCE* {modern nez-PURSE} A SAHAPTIAN-speaking people of central Idaho, southeast Washington, and northeast Oregon, known to the journalists as the CHOPUNNISH. Their yearly subsistence round typified that of many Plateau peoples who had appropriated the horse and extended their economic activities and warfare into the buffalo country to the east. From French *nez percé* {nay-pair-SAY}, 'PIERCED NOSE,' after a diminishing custom of wearing a white, thin, dentalium shell about 1½ in. long, inserted horizontally through the septum between the nostrils.

their Situation requires the utmost exertion to prcure food...all the Summer & fall fishing for the Salmon, the winter hunting the deer on Snow Shoes in the plains and taking care of ther emence numbers of horses, & in the Spring cross the mountains to the Missouri to get Buffalow robes and meet...at which time they frequent meet with their enemies & lose their horses & maney of ther people [10 Oct 05 WC 5.259]

NITCH   A bay. A variant of *niche.*

we came too at the remains of an old village at the bottom of this nitch and dined [8 Nov 05 WC 6.036]

NITER   {NIGH-tə} Saltpeter (potassium nitrate), used medicinally to induce sweating and urination. *Sal nitri* 'salt of niter' is druggist's Latin for 'saltpeter.' *See* BROKEN.

2 [lb. Sal] Nitri [26 May 03 in Jackson Letters (ed. 2) 1.080]

one man verry Sick, Struck with the Sun, Capt. Lewis bled him & gave Niter which has revived him much [7 Jul 04 WC 2.356]

the nitre has produced a profuse perspiration this evening [16 Feb 06 ML 6.318]

NONE-SO-PRETTY   Decorative tape used for trimming garments.

Baling Invoice of Sundries for Indian Presents...10 pieces nonsoprettys [winter 04–05 3.494]

NONIUS   {modern NO-nee-us} An old name for a *vernier*, a small auxiliary scale that slides next to the main graduated scale of a measuring instrument, and enables an observer to read smaller divisions than what is possible on the main scale. The expedition's SEXTANT and OCTANT were equipped with noniuses. From (*Petrus*) *Nonius*, the Latinized version of the name of Pedro Nuñez (pronounced {NOO-nyace}), a 16th century Portuguese mathematician and inventor of a primitive sort of vernier. *See* MICROMETER.

a brass Sextant of 10 Inches radius, graduated to 15' which by the assistance of the nonius was devisible to 15" [22 Jul 04 ML 2.410]

NOON IT   To stop at noon for food, rest, and observation of the sun's meridian ALTITUDE.

halted to noon it & wate for Capt. Lewis who lost his horse [13 Sep 05 WC 5.202]

NOOTKA*   A native people of the west coast of Vancouver Island, British Columbia, who lived mainly on marine resources. Their language contributed significant vocabulary to the CHINOOK Jargon. *See* TYEE.

NOOTKA SOUND   A prominent inlet on the Pacific Ocean side of Vancouver Island. The Royal Navy's noted explorer, Captain James Cook, anchored here in 1778. Over the next several decades, the inlet became a center of the fur-trade for the native NOOTKA people and American, British, and other European ships. Following tense international negotiations in the 1790s, Spain grudgingly granted equal trading rights to the British in Nootka Sound and the North Pacific, which to Lewis symbolized the growing English threat to American interests on the Pacific coast.

whether these traders are from Nootka sound, from some other late establishment on this coast, or immediately from the U' States or Great Brittain, I am at a loss to determine [9 Jan 06 ML 6.187]

NORTH WEST COMPANY {nɔth} One of two major British companies contending for the western fur trade. Founded in Montreal (1783), the Nor'Westers pursued operations in the Great Lakes region and the Great Plains (and eventually to the Pacific coast), while developing a bitter rivalry with the HUDSON'S BAY COMPANY. For a time the firm split into the New North West Company and the X Y COMPANY, but later recombined. (Eventually in 1821, the Crown ordered the North West Company to merge with its hostile competitor, the Hudson's Bay Company.)

this establishment might be made to hold in check the views of the British N. West Company on the fur-trade of the upper part of the Missouri, which we believe it is their intention to panopolize [winter 04–05 ML 3.364]

The Trade[r]s who frequnt the Mandans & Minetarres are from two British Companie N W. & Hudsons Bay, Those…Companies have carried their jelousy to Such hite, as to give the Indians a bad oppinion of all whites from that quarter [winter 04–05 WC 3.487]

NOTION A small item, especially when exchanged in trade. Perhaps, Lewis learned this *Yanke phrase* from New Hampshire native John Ordway. *See* KINNICKINNICK. (**New England**)

we found Some little notions which Some Indian had hung up. Viz. a Scraper a paint bag…kinikaneck bags, flints &.c. [20 Apr 05 JO 9.134]

The men…obtained a good store of roots and bread in exchange for a number of little notions, using the Yanke phrase [6 Jun 06 ML 7.339]

NUN'S THREAD Fine white cotton or linen thread.

Baling Invoice of Sundries…½ [lb?] *Nuns thread* [probably winter 04–05 3.502]

> Described in *OED* as thread "formerly spun by nuns," but a likelier origin is suggested by an *OED* example from 1844, in which *ounce-thread* is stated as an equivalent to *nun's thread*. Also, a 1625 quotation makes it clear that *nwnes threid* was sold by the *vnce* (ounce). *Nouns, nowns,* and probably *nwnes* and *nuns* are old variants of the word *ounce,* so it seems likely that *nun's thread* refers to the sale of the thread by the ounce, rather than to its manufacture by nuns. *An ounce* became, for a time, *a nounce.* (*See* OTOE for a similar type of evolving spelling.)

O

OAR, STEERING A long oar extending aft from the stern of a KEELBOAT.

2 men Set at making a Stearing oar for the Big Barge [25 Mar 05 JO 9.123]

OBSERVATION, BACK {ahb-sə-VAY-shun} A measurement of the elevation of an astronomical body made by the use of mirrors with the observer's back to the object. The captains took *back* observations (with a specially adapted OCTANT only) of the sun's altitude when it was too high to allow *fore* sightings with either the SEXTANT or octant. *See* ALTITUDE, (ARTIFICIAL) HORIZON.

this instrument [octant] *was prepared for both the fore and back observation* [22 Jul 04 ML 2.411]

OBSERVATION, LUNAR {LOO-nə} A measurement of the angular distance between the moon and a nearby star (the *lunar distance*), which, with reference to tables, (theoretically) provided GREENWICH time for use in calculating LONGITUDE.

we came to on the Stard. Side below with a view to make some luner observations the night proved Cloudy and we were disapointed [10 Oct 05 WC 5.256]

OCEAN The Pacific, 'peaceful.' Battered in the Columbia estuary by high winds, heavy seas, and almost constant rain, the expedition reached its goal, the Pacific Ocean, November 15–24, 1805, at Station Camp (27 months after Lewis had left Pittsburgh).

The Sea...roars like a repeeted roling thunder and have rored in that way ever Since our arrival...which is now 24 Days Since we arrived in Sight of the Great Western Ocian, I cant say Pasific as Since I have Seen it, it has been the reverse. [1 Dec 05 WC 6.103]

OCTANT {OCK-tənt} An instrument incorporating a graduated eighth of a circle (Latin, *octans*) for making angular measurements in astronomy and navigation. *See* MICROMETER, NONIUS, OBSERVATION, QUADRANT, SEXTANT.

the sun's altitude at noon has been too great to be reached with my sextant, for this purpose I have therefore employed the Octant by the back observation. [22 Jul 04 ML 2.411]

OFFHAND (Of a firearm) fired without the use of a rest.

The practicing party will...discharge only one round each per. day...all at the same target and at the distance of fifty yards off hand. The prize of a gill of extra whiskey will be recieved by the person who makes the best show [20 Feb 04 ML 2.175]

OFFICIOUS Eager to be of service, without the modern negative connotation of meddling bossiness.

he became very officious and seemed anxious to reinstate himself in our good opinions. [8 May 06 ML 7.227]

OHIO Formed by the junction of the Allegheny and Monongahela rivers at Pittsburgh, the Ohio River has long been a vital link in U.S. commerce and communication. Lewis and the first contingents of the Corps of Discovery (joined by Clark at the Falls of the Ohio) sailed the KEELBOAT down its waters to the Mississippi River, August 31-November 14, 1803. The Seneca Iroquois name for the combined Allegheny-Ohio system means 'nice river.'

these Foggs are very common on the Ohio at this season [1 Sep 03 ML 2.067]

OIL-CLOTH   Waterproof cloth for packing goods, usually canvas or other heavy fabric impregnated with oil. The main constituent was linseed oil (often with lampblack as a pigment) to which turpentine and a highly toxic, lead-oxide litharge were added for accelerating drying.

had the articles well oiled and put up in oilcloth baggs and returned to the casks [4 Sep 03 ML 2.071]

OMAHA   {MAH-hah in the journals} A Siouan people of eastern Nebraska sharing with the PONCA a Dhegiha language of the SIOUAN family. The name probably is from Dhegiha *omāhā*, meaning 'upstream,' which was borrowed by the Illinois without the *o-* and then by the French (1673). The Omaha, often called the *Maha*, are not to be confused with the MAHAHA of North Dakota.

Mr. Mackey had a Small fort in which he traded withe the Mahars the winter 95 & 96 [13 Aug 04 WC 2.475]

three Maha men fell a sacrefice to their murceyless fury [24 Aug 04 WC 2.504]

Peter Crusat who spoke Mahar…informed me that the mahar Prisoners told him that the Tetons intended to Stop us [27 Sep 04 WC 3.121]

OPEN   (Of the bowels) experiencing an effective PURGATIVE treatment.

I…gave Such medesine as would keep her body open [29 Apr 06 WC 7.186]

OPERATE   (Of a medicine) to produce an intended effect, in the journals usually with reference to the PURGATIVE results of a PHYSIC. *See* WORK. For other examples, *see* CLYSTER, GLAUBER'S SALTS, RUSH'S PILLS, SCOTT'S PILLS.

The Creem of tartar and sulpher operated several times on the child in the course of last night [23 May 06 ML 7.280]

ORDER   {ɔ-də} Condition, CASE[1]. Now used in the expressions *for good order's sake, in order, out of order. See* TOLERABLE.

we proposed exchangeing a good horse in reather low order for a young horse in tolerable order with a view to kill. [10 May 06 ML 7.237]

OSAGE   {OH-sahzh, modern OH-sage} A people of Missouri, Kansas, Oklahoma, and Arkansas, speaking a Dhegiha language of the SIOUAN family and recorded in French as *Ouchage* (1673). *See* FEMME.

the Saukees had lately Crossed to war against the Osage Nation [17 May 04 WC 2.235]

one perogue Loaded with Bare Skins and Beav and Deer Skins from the osoge village [31 May 04 CF 9.376]

the Antient Villages of the little Osarge & Missouries [15 Jun 04 WC 2.302]

OSAGE APPLE   A spiny tree (*Maclura pomifera*) of the mulberry family thought to have been native to an area extending from Oklahoma to the lower Mississippi valley, and later widely cultivated throughout much of the U.S. It is unrelated to the true apple.

no appearance of the buds of the Osage Apple [10 Apr 04 WC 2.208]

> The wood was prized for the making of bows—whence the French name *bois d'arc,* 'bow-wood,' and the derivative English *bodark*—and for making yellow dye. In the early 19th century, the price of a bodark bow at the Arikara villages was a horse and blanket. The tree now usually is called *Osage orange*, from the color of the wood.

OTOE {OH-toh} A SIOUAN people of southeast Nebraska, speaking a Chiwere dialect closely related to those of the IOWAY and MISSOURI.

This horse Probably had been left by Some party of Otteaus hunters who…hunted in this quarter last fall or Wintr. [11 Jul 04 WC 2.367]

The Corps' diarists often transferred the final *z* sound of the French article *les,* 'the,' to the beginning of the name, thus *les Otteaux* became *the Zotteaus.* (Through an opposite process, *a napron* evolved into *an apron.*)

passed an old fort on the north Side, Where Roe Bennet of St. Louis wintered 2 years & traded with the Zotteaus & paunies. [14 Jul 04 JO 9.025]

about 2 days and half up the Plate 2 nations of Indians Lives vic [i.e., viz.] *The Souttoes the Ponney* [21 Jul 04 CF 9.389]

OVEN, DUTCH A cast-iron kettle with a tight-fitting lid.

we burryed on the high land…tin cups dutch ovens, bear Skins…[11 Jun 05 JO 9.166]

OVERALLS Heavy trousers (without the bib of modern overalls), often made of RUSSIA SHEETING. In November 1803, Corporal Warfington was issued 4 pairs of overalls—1 woolen, 2 linen, and 1 COARSE (Moore & Haynes, 78).

Baling Invoice of Sundries, being necessary Stores…3 pr Russia Over Alls [winter 04–05 writer unknown 3.502]

they are also previded with Shirts Overalls Capoes of dressed Elk Skins for the homeward journey. [12 Mar 06 WC 6.407]

OVERFLOWN {oh-və-FLONE} (Of the flood-plain of a river) flooded.

proceeded…thro a wide bottom which appears to be overflown every year [27 Jul 05 WC 4.438]

OVERHAUL[1] To remove items from containers (or cargo from a boat) for reconditioning, especially drying.

we employ'd ourselves in overhawling sundry Articles which we had in the Boat. [24 July 04 JW 11.044]

I overhalled our merchandize and dryed it by the fire [6 Jan 06 ML 6.169]

OVERHAUL[2] To overtake.

he was running of[f] *with R. Fields and his brothers Jo Fields guns. Reuben overhalled him* [28 Jul 06 JO 9.342]

OVERSET (Of a boat) to capsize. *See* JIBE.

one of their canoes had just overset and all the baggage wet [6 Aug 05 ML 5.052]

P

PACE A measurement equal to the length of a man's stride between successive falls of the same foot—approximately 5 feet, with two steps equaling one *pace*. A mile was figured at about 1,000 paces. (English *mile* is from Latin *mille passuum* 'one thousand paces,' the *passus* being reckoned at 5 feet.) *See* STEP OFF.

East to Pompys Tower. 200 feet high. 400 paces around [25 Jul 06 WC 8.227]

PACK To load a horse, or a person, with a burden. (**South Midland, Mississippi Valley**)

One of our hunters...haveing killed an elk packed his horses & could not overtake us [7 Sep 05 WC 5.190]

those Chiefs gave us Some meat which they packed on their wives [25 Feb 05 WC 3.303]

Also, to carry on one's back.

I killed a Deer which york Packed on his back [24 Aug 04 WC 2.504]

we went out and packed in the Elk meat. [19 Mar 06 JO 9.278]

PACKSADDLE A padded frame strapped to the back of a pack-animal (usually a horse or mule), to which a load is secured. Lewis ordered packsaddles to be constructed of rawhide, with the wooden parts coming from oars and packing-crates [5.125].

This morning I sent out the hunters, and set several additional hands about the packsaddles. [17 Apr 06 ML 7.130]

PAINT Pigment adorning the body, especially the face—usually charcoal (black), ocher (*yallow oaker creek* [2.350]), VERMILION, clay, and other minerals or *earths* (yellow, red, white, red, green, blue). Paints were important in native ritual and prized in trade. *See* PALOTPALO, (WAR-)STRIPES.

White Paint River [4 Sep 04 WC 3.047]

they [Arikara] *wanted red paint mostly, but would Give whatever they had to Spare for any kind of Goods* [12 Oct 04 JO 9.083]

Green Earth...the natives procure this earth in the neighberhood of the Rocky mountain...the Indians also paint their Skins with it. [ML? 3.475]

The Ricaras appear fond of Paint Blue Beeds rings the Tale & feathers of the Calumet Eagle and...also horses. [winter 04–05 WC 3.484] *underneath this scaffold a human body was lying...and near it a bag...containg sundry articles belonging to the disceased...a pare of mockersons, some red and blue earth, beaver's nails, instruments for dressing the Buffalo skin, some dryed roots, several platts of the sweet grass, and a small quantity of Mandan tobacco.* [20 Apr 05 ML 4.054]

PALM, BESTOW THE Designate a champion.

nor could I for some time determine on which of those two great cataracts to bestoe the palm [14 Jun 05 ML 4.290]

PALOTPALO {pə-LOTE-pə-lo} A subdivision of the Nez Perce people. The name is Nez Perce for 'green people,' perhaps with reference to facial painting.

Drewyer and Shannon Sent on a head to go to the villages of the pel-oll-pellow nation [18 Jun 05 JO 9.324]

Pel-lote-pal-lah...Band of Chopunnish reside on the Kooskooske [Clearwater River] *above the forks...and Sometimes pass over to the Missouri* [winter 05–06 WC 6.482]

a man of the Pallote pellows arrived from the West side of the Rocky mountains [4 Jul 06 ML 8.087]

Clark includes in a list of Indian tribes [3.435] the *Blue Mud Indians*, who probably were the Nez Perce, perhaps so named for a predilection to using blue earth as face-paint.

the dress of the [Chopunnish] *men* [includes]*...different Coloured Paints which they find in their Countrey Generally white, Green & light Blue* [10 Oct 05 WC 5.259]

> *Palotpalo* occasionally is confused with a somewhat similar name for the neighboring Palouse tribe of southeast Washington, but the two are distinct phonetically. Fur trader Alexander Ross (c. 1820, 1.185) explicitly made a distinction when listing the *Pallet-to Pallas* (Palotpalo) and the *Paw-luch* (Palouse) as being attached to Fort Nez Percés at the Walla Walla-Columbia junction.

PALSY *See* SHAKE HAND.

PAN A part of a flintlock's firing mechanism holding a PRIMING charge of black powder. The combined pan-cover and FRIZZEN protected the primer in the pan. *See* LOCK, MISFIRE.

the fellow finding Drewyer too strong for him and discovering that he must yeald the gun had p[r]esents of mind to open the pan and cast the priming before he let the gun escape from his hands [22 Aug 05 ML 5.142]

> An ignition failure resulting in a gun misfiring (often due to a blocked touch-hole to the main charge in the barrel) was called *a flash in the pan*, hence its figurative sense as something transitory or without substantial effect. Each soldier was issued a brush for cleaning the pan, and a wire for reaming the touch-hole.

Invoice of Articles to be Dld. Cap. Lewis...15 Gun Slings...30 Brushes & Wires...15 Cartouch Box Belts [18 May 03 in Jackson Letters (ed. 2) 1.098]

PANTHER {PAN-thə, colloquial PAIN-tə} Mountain lion, cougar (*Felis concolor*). (**South, South Midland**)

2 miles to River on the South Side Colled painter River [30 May 04 CF 9.376]

The Island...is...Called the Isle of Panters [19 Jun 04 WC 2.308]

two of our men fired on a panther...and wounded it; they informed us it was very large, had just killed a deer partly devoured it [16 May 05 ML 4.157]

I purchased...a Panthor Skin and Some Lickorish roots [23 Dec 05 WC 6.135]

PAPSPALO {PAHPS-pə-lo} The Okanogan Indians, a SALISHAN people of north central Washington. The name is Nez Perce, literally 'Douglas fir people,' which also came to be the Nez Perce designation for 'cannibal.' Clark applied the name to a northern tributary of the Columbia River not visited by the expedition.

Parps-pal-low R[iver] [WC 1 map 96]

PARACHUTE A late 18th century invention for safely descending from a hot-air balloon. Here, the seeds of the cottonwood.

the wind...drives it through the air to a great distance being supported by a parrishoot of this cottonlike substance [winter 04–05 ML 3.452]

PARAKEET The fruit-eating Carolina parakeet (*Conuropsis carolinensis*), which became extinct in the 20th century. The beauty of its yellow head and green body was lost on the settlers whose crops were being devoured by screaming flocks of parakeets.

Carolina parakeet

I observed a great number of Parrot queets this evening [26 Jun 04 WC 2.324]

PARCEL {PAH-səl or PÆ-səl} A quantity or collection; a "bunch." (**South, South Midland**)

I...saw several parsels of buffaloe's hair hanging on the rose bushes [18 Apr 05 ML 4.051]

we scarcely see a gang of buffaloe without observing a parsel of those faithfull shepherds [wolves] *on their skirts in readiness to take care of the mamed & wounded.* [5 May 05 ML 4.113]

others at work to make a parsel of packsaddles. [16 Apr 06 ML 7.126]

Frazier...returned with a pasel of Roots and bread [20 May 06 ML 7.274]

the Minnetares of Fort de prarie...have a large pasel of horses. [6 Jul 06 ML 8.093]

PARK {pahk} An enclosure for trapping and slaying wild game, such as buffalo and pronghorn. The animals were driven between funnel-like fences into a corral. Also called POUND.

a Creek comes in on the North Side called parques or fence Creek [2 Jul 04 JO 9.019] *there was a park which they* [Assiniboine] *had formed of timber and brush, for the purpose of taking the Cabrie or Antelope.* [15 Apr 05 ML 4.042]

PAROLE {pə-ROLL} A certificate presented by the captains to an appointed chief, recognizing the man's "Sincrrity and good Conduct" [3.210]. From the French *parole*, literally 'word,' and, by extension, 'formal promise; password.' *See* MAKE[2].

To the Grand Chief we gave a Flag and the parole [30 Aug 04 WC 3.024]

PARTICOLOR(ED) {PAH-tee KUH-lə(d)} Variegated.

the Chemise is roomy and comes down below the middle of the leg...the breast is usually ornament with various figures of party colours rought with the quills of the Porcupine. [21 Aug 05 ML 5.134]

The Indian dog is usually small...they are party coloured [16 Feb 06 ML 6.318]

the young of the partycoloured corvus [magpie] *begin to fly.* [20 May 06 ML 7.320]

PARTISAN {PAH-tə-zən} A war party leader. Originally a French term for one who takes sides—thus a member and leader of a raiding party.

gave a Medal to the grand Chief...Un-ton gar-Sar bar, or Black Buffalow— 2° Torto-hongar, Partezon (Bad fellow) [25 Sep 04 WC 3.111]

In English, *partisan* came to have the pejorative sense of a 'blind, prejudiced, unreasoning, or fanatical adherent' (*OED*). In the above quotation, Clark perceived the Teton chief, *Torto-hongar*, in that way. *Torto-hongar* is Sioux for 'leader of a war-party,' and the captains considered him an obstructionist. Clark's spelling probably represents a pronunciation like {mdoe-TĀ-hoon-KAH}, with the un-English initial consonant cluster *md-* simplified to *d-*.

PASHECO {pə-SHEE-ko} A Shoshone name for CAMAS, *BAH-see-go*, meaning 'water sego.' (Now widely grown as an ornamental, the sego lily once was important to western Indians for its edible root.) (**Rockies**)

[Nez Perce] *women were busily employed in gathering and drying the Pa-she co root of which they had great quantities dug in piles* [23 Sep 05 WC 5.232]

Collins made Some excellent beer of the Pasheco quar mash bread of roots [22 Oct 05 WC 5.315]

Skil-lute Indians...gave us Wappato and pashaquaw roots to eate [27 Mar 06 WC 7.019]

PASS A river-crossing, such as that referred to on the Missouri (below). In French, **passage**. *See* CALUMET.

those rivers is the place that all nations who meet are at peace with each other, Called the Seaux pass of the 3 rivers. [19 Sep 04 WC 3.090]

passed a Small Island...opposit Passage De Soux [15 May 04 WC 2.230]

PATROON The person in charge of a boat, especially in a French-Canadian context. From French *patron*. *See* GREASE.

Sent a Perogue for them, the Patroon & Bowman of the Perogue French [9 July 04 WC 2.362]

one perogue (Bapteest Le Joness...Patroon) lost her Colours [6 Aug 04 WC 2.452]

PAUNCH   Stomach, entrails, especially as food, or for use as a container. *See* CROW, GUTS. (**South, South Midland**)

the vessels they carry their worter in are Deers ponches [27 Sep 04 JO 9.070]

our Indian guide and the young Indian who accompanied him Eat the paunch and all the Small guts of the Deer. [4 Sep 05 JW 11.299]

PAWNEE   {pɔ-NEE, PƆ-nee-ə} A farming and buffalo-hunting people residing in villages in central Nebraska and north-central Kansas, and speaking a CADDOAN language closely related to ARIKARA. They included the Chaui (Grand Pawnee), Kitkehahki (REPUBLICAN Pawnee), Pitahauerat (Tapage Pawnee), and Skiri (Pawnee LOUP, Pawnee Wolf, Pawnee Maha). The name in English is from French *Pani,* or directly from Illinois *pani(a),* which in turn was borrowed from a Siouan language or languages. *See* OTOE.

a Caussee [CAJEU] *came too from the Pania [Pawnee] nation loaded with furs* [14 Jun 04 WC 2.300]

we passed some Frenchmen from the Poenese or Ponis nation of Indians [14 Jun 04 PG 10.014]

the Ponie [Pawnee] call it Cho car tooch [BRAROW] [30 Jul 04 WC 2.429]

Panani is the Sioux name for the Pawnee.

Parnarne Arparbe (Struck by the Pania) 3d Cheif rose and made a Short Speech [31 Aug 04 WC 3.034]

Lewis & Clark sometimes referred to the Arikara as *Pawnee.*

we [the Mandan] *Sent a Chief and a pipe to the Pania to Smoke and they killed them* [1 Nov 04 WC 3.224]

PAY   To make a boat's hull watertight by sealing seams with tar, pitch, tallow, etc. *See* CAULK, (TAR-)KILN.

we unloaded all the canoes Shaved the bottoms Smooth and pay them over [26 Oct 05 JW 11.372]

it Continued to rain So constantly dureing the day that Sergt. Pryor Could not Pay his Canoes. [19 Mar 06 WC 6.440]

PECK   A volume of measure, equal to ¼ of a BUSHEL.

gave the 2 principal Chiefs a blanket & a peck of Corn each [27 Sep 04 WC 3.121]

PECORA   {PECK-ə-rə} Ungulates, hooved animals. The plural form of Latin *pecus.*

this recepticle [tear-duct] *in the Elk is larger than in any of the pecora order with which I am acquainted.* [10 May 05 ML 4.138]

PEGASUS {PEG-ə-səs, possessive PEG-ə-sigh} The constellation in which bluish-white Markab is the alpha star. Lewis applied the Latin possessive form of the name with the Greek letter *alpha* understood: α *pegasi*.

This...is most probably Pegassi; but the star appeared very small [10 Jul 05 ML 4.373]

PEKAN {PECK-ən} A Canadian French word for the fisher (*Martes pennanti*), borrowed from the Eastern Algonquian Abenaki language. The fur of the fisher (of the weasel family) was prized in the northern fur trade. *See* LOUP.

PELTRY {PEL-tree} (In the fur trade) animal skins retaining the fur. The phrase *furs and peltries* probably is a translation of the French expression *fourrures et pelleteries*. Originally there may have been a distinction between *furs* (dressed) and *peltries* (undressed), but the phrase seems generally used in a formulaic way to include all types of fur-skins. The English word *peltry* was borrowed from the French twice, first in the 15th century, and—having disappeared from the language in the 16th century—again in ca. 1700, this time from French Canadian traders.

4 Cajaux or rafts loaded with furs and peltres came too[,] *one from the Paunees the other from Grand Osage* [27 May 04 WC 2.260]

Presses packed furs into bundles (or BALLOTS), each of about 100 pounds, for transport.

the Tradeing house...divided into four equal apartments....one for peltery &C. 2 peltery presses. [22 Sep 04 JO 9.064]

PEMBINA {modern PEM-bə-nə, pem-BEE-nə} The high-bush cranberry, *Viburnum trilobum*. A word of Cree or Chippewa origin. (**North**)

This Countrey abounds in a variety of wild froot, Such as Plumbs, Cherris, Currents, Rasburies, Sarvis berry, High bush Cram burry (or Pimbanah) [winter 04–05 WC 3.481]

PEMMICAN {PEM-ə-kən} The Cree word for pounded dried meat, usually buffalo, mixed with GREASE and fruit—a high-energy, long-keeping food, useful as travel rations. Also **pemitigon** {pə-MIT-əgən}, from Ojibway. Both words come from the ALGONQUIAN root *pem-* meaning 'grease.' *See* JERK.

I Saw & eat Pemitigon [26 Sep 04 WC 3.119]

The Father of the Mandan who was killed Came and made us a present of Some Dried Simnens & a little pemicon [3 Dec 04 WC 3.252]

some hunters were sent out to kill buffaloe in order to make pemecon to take with us [3 Jul 05 ML 4.354]

PENNYROYAL {pen-ee-RILE, modern pen-ee-ROIL; also with accent on first syllable instead} Various species of the mint family, most of which were considered useful in folk medicine.

found Some penerial the first we Saw on the River. [12 Jun 05 JW 11.194]

Reference here may be to wild mint, *Mentha arvensis*. Ordway and Whitehouse used spellings reflecting a dialect pronunciation, though the latter corrects it to *pennyroyal* in his second draft; *see* BOIL[1], SPOILT. Central Kentucky's *Pennyrile* region is named for an abundance of eastern North American pennyroyal, *Hedeoma pulegioides*. The *penny-* part of the word has no relation to the coin, but comes from an Old French word for 'thyme,' whereas *-royal* does mean 'royal.'

PENNYWEIGHT A unit of weight used for precious metals and stones, equal to 24 GRAINS[1].

The natives are extravegantly fond of the most common cheap blue and white beads, of moderate size, or such that from 50 to 70 will weigh one penneyweight. [9 Jan 06 ML 6.187]

PERCH {pəch} A measure of length in surveying, of about 16½ feet. A name derived from the *perch* (or ROD) used in taking the measurement. *See* POLE[1].

Some of the men went about 40 perches up the river and caught 15 fine large fish. [11 Nov 05 PG 10.170]

PERSPICUITY {pəs-pih-KUE-ə-tee} Insight.

this man possesses more integrety, firmness, inteligence and perspicuety of mind than any indian I have met with in this quarter [8 Feb 05 ML 3.289]

PET[1] A peevish taking of offence. *See* MIFF, PIQUE.

Several of those from below returned down the river in a bad humer, haveing got into this pet by being prevented doeing as they wished with our articles [27 Oct 05 WC 5.345]

PET[2] To tame (an animal).

saw...a Moonax which the natives had petted. [24 Apr 06 ML 7.163]

PETTIAUGER {PEH-tee-ah-gə} A variant of PIROGUE. Reshaped as though to include *petty* 'small,' it is a later and more bookish form. Where Whitehouse's daily journal has two versions, the rough draft has a variant of *pirogue*, while the edited version uses *pettiauger*, which appears to be a "correcting" of colloquial *pirogue* to the more formal *pettiauger*. (**lower Mississippi Valley**)

the white pierogue had hard Crossing the River to bring the Meat from the hunters [8 Jun 04 JW 11.020]

we sent a Pettiauger to bring the bear meat to the boat, but the hands had very great difficulty in crossing the River [8 Jun 04 JW 11.020]

PEWTER {PYOO-tə} An alloy of tin with lead and other metals, commonly used in tableware.

4 Pewter Penis Syringes [Jun 03 ML in Jackson Letters (ed. 2) 1.074]

purchased Some wood & 3 dogs for which we gave pewter buttons [21 Apr 06 WC 7.153]

PHILANTHROPY In the original sense, 'love of mankind,' without allusion to charitable giving. Lewis & Clark named western Montana's Ruby River the *Philanthropy River*. Here, referring ironically to a farmer charging $1 to haul the expedition boat over the Ohio River's Logtown riffle with a horse and ox.

the inhabitants who live near these riffles live much by the distresed situation of traveller are generally lazy charge extravegantly when they are called for assistance and have no filantrophy or contience [2 Sep 03 ML 2.068]

PHOCA {FO-kə} The harbor seal, *Phoca vitulina.* The English pronunciation of Latin *phocæ* ('seals') is {FO-see}, which partially explains Clark's form in the first quotation.

Those animals which I took to be the Sea Otter from the Great Falls of the Columbia to the mouth, proves to be the Phosia or Seal [23 Feb 06 WC 6.340]

to the Phoca rock in midl. [of Columbia] *Rivr....Saw Seal's* [winter 05–06 WC 6.457]

PHYSIC A medicine; specifically a strong laxative. *See* GLAUBER'S SALTS, PURGATIVE, PURGE, RUSH'S PILLS, SCOTT'S PILLS.

the fessic I took yesterday work to day. [26 Jan 04 WC 2.165]

PICKET Pointed log posts set vertically in the ground, forming a defensive wall; also, to erect pickets.

all our Men, were employ'd in procuring pickets and picketting in our Fort which the Officers were determined to have made Strong. [1 Dec 04 JW 11.110]

Also, a stake (or stakes with a line between) for tying up a horse or horses.

had our horses led out and held to grass untill dusk when they were all brought to Camp, and pickets, drove in the ground and the horses tied up. [22 Apr 06 WC 7.158]

And, to tether a horse to a picket.

we took the precaution of picqueting and Spancelling our horses this evening [21 Apr 06 WC 7.155]

PICKLE DOWN To preserve by salting.

we pickled down our Buffelow meat, & jerked the venison [23 Aug 04 JO 9.043]

PIEBALD (Of horses) of two different colors, especially black and white. *See* PIED.

we found a horse of pybald colour [12 Jul 04 JW 11.039]

PIECE, BOW- A gun mounted on the BOW of a vessel, usually of large caliber. *See* GUN.

fired our bow peace and gave three cheers [21 May 04 JW 11.011]

July 4th...ussered in the day by a discharge of one shot from our Bow piece [4 Jul 04 WC 2.347]

PIED Variegated. *See* PIEBALD.

saw a number of black & white pided ducks [21 Nov 03 ML 2.099]

some of those horses are pided with large spots of white irregularly...intermixed with the black brown bey or some other dark colour [15 Feb 06 ML 6.313]

PIERCED NOSE INDIANS   Also **Pierce Nose**. The NEZ PERCE of central Idaho, northeast Oregon, and southeast Washington, more usually called CHOPUNNISH by the captains. *Pierced Nose* is a translation of the French *Nez Percé*.

the persed nosed Indians...inhabit this river below the rocky mountains [14 Aug 05 ML 5.089]

The captains also applied the name to some SAHAPTIN-speaking groups near the Columbia's great cataracts, just east of the Cascade Range. Clark described these people with "a long taper'd piece of Shell or beed put through the nose" [5.318], a custom presumably imported (along with dentalium shells) from nose-piercing Chinookan peoples on the lower Columbia. (Ironically, among the actual *Nez Perce* themselves, the custom was rare and diminishing.)

Several Canoes loaded with Indians (Pierce noses) came to See us [21 Oct 05 WC 5.315]

PIGEON, WILD   The passenger pigeon (*Ectopistes migratorius*), which became extinct 109 years later.

I saw a number of turtledoves and some pigeons today. of the latter I shot one; they are the same common to the United States, or the wild pigeon as they are called. [13 Jul 05 ML 4.378]

passenger pigeon

PIN   A thole-pin. A pair of vertical wood pins (forming an oarlock) on a boat's GUNWALE, between which an oar was placed, thus providing a fulcrum for rowing.

pins to row by [c. 21 Jan 04 WC 2.163]

PINE   Broadly, any tree of the pine family, including the spruces (genus *Picea*) and firs (*Abies*), as well as true pines (*Pinus*).

the pine...in maney places verry thick So covered with Snow, as in passing I became wet discover 8 distinct kinds of pine on those mountains [16 Sep 05 WC 5.207]

PIPESTONE   A fine-grained, reddish rock, also called *catlinite*, highly valued by Indians for fashioning into tobacco pipes and other items. Pipestone is found in southwest Minnesota not far from the Big Sioux River, which flows southward to the Missouri. The Big Sioux River and its tributary, Pipestone Creek, provided access to the quarries. *See* CALUMET.

a Creek coms in on which the red pipe Stone is percured, & in the praries about, a place of Peace with all nations. [21 Aug 04 WC 2.497]

PIQUE   {peek} Irritate, offend. *See* MIFF, PET.

I began to fear he was ~~miffed~~ piqued with the sharp reprimand I gave him [10 Sep 03 ML 2.076]

PIROGUE   {pə-ROGUE or peh-ROGUE in the journals} A wooden boat, smaller than a KEELBOAT, but usually larger than a canoe. (The word sometimes was used interchangeably with *canoe*.) *See* PETTIAUGER, RUDDER-IRONS, SAIL. (**lower Mississippi Valley**)

When leaving Camp Wood and starting up the Missouri on May 14, 1804, the expedition's flotilla included two pirogues, each with a crew of six or seven men—one called the *red pirogue* or *French pirogue* (for its French crew), and the other the *white pirogue* or *soldiers' pirogue*. (In addition, the bulk of the Corps' members manned the keelboat.) The pirogues hauled about 8 tons [2.196], and probably measured between 30 and 40 feet long. The red pirogue was cached near the Missouri-Marias junction in 1805. However, when retrieved during the 1806 return journey, it was rotted beyond use. The white pirogue, left below the Great Falls in 1805, proved serviceable again in 1806. *Pirogue* is of Caribbean Indian origin, having been borrowed into Spanish as *piragua*, then into French as *pirogue*.

7 french in a large Perogue, a Corp[oral] *and 6 Soldiers in a large Perogue.* [14 May 04 WC 2.227]

this River is…navagable for Purogues [13 Jun 04 WC 2.296]

the white pearogue could hardly Sail for want of Ballass, we put in Several kegs of pork [21 Aug 04 JO 9.042]

by bad Stearing the parogu Struck the Cable with Such force as to brake it near the anchor [27 Sep 04 WC 3.121]

we…hoisted both the sails in the White Perogue [13 Apr 05 ML 4.029]

We were detained this morning…in order to repare the rudder irons of the red perogue which were broken last evening in landing [4 May 05 ML 4.108]

"Pirogues" on the Columbia were dugouts.

we determined to make the portage to the head of the long narrows with…five small canoes. the 2 perogues we could take no further and therefore cut them up for fuel. [18 Apr 06 ML 7.137]

PISS-ANT An ant named for excreting urinous-smelling formic acid. Also **pismire**.

we Saw Several holes in the ground. Some Stone piss ants &.C. [25 Aug 04 JO 9.044]

the air temperate, birds singing, the pizmire…in motion. [7 Apr 06 ML 7.192]

PITCH Any slope or slanting area, but especially a waterfall or rapids.

this pitch which I called the crooked falls occupys about three fourths of the width of the river [14 Jun 05 ML 4.289]

the towing line of the Captains canoe broke in the pitch of the rapid [1 Aug 05 JO 9.193]

we…proceeded on up a high mountain at the first pich one of the horses fell backward and roled over [1 Sep 05 JO 9.215]

PITCH ON To settle on, to decide on.

we Set out at 8 oClock down to the place Capt Lewis pitched on for winter quarters [7 Dec 05 WC 6.109]

I...told them to pitch on Some Man on which they could rely on and Send him to See their Great father [15 Aug 06 WC 8.301]

PLAIN A relatively level and treeless (or nearly so) tract of land, usually grass-covered.

Originally, meaning any flat piece of terrain, even if covered with trees. As westward-trekking English-speakers encountered extensive grasslands in cultivable river BOTTOMS, especially west of the Mississippi, the definition was expanded to include vast size and treelessness, as well as relative flatness. The captains' use of the word *plain* similarly expanded—as did *prairie*—to include not just river *flood plains*, but also the seemingly limitless, dry grasslands now known as *the (Great) Plains*. In the journals, *plain* is nearly synonymous with PRAIRIE. Clark, for example, translates the French *Prairie du Chien* as *the Dog Plains* [2.458], and virtually equates *plain* and *prairie* in the entries below. A plain can be large or small, low land or high.

the plains and woodlands are here [near St. Louis] *indiscriminately interspersed* [20 May 04 ML 2.240]

the plain on which it [St. Charles] *stands—is narrow* [20 May 04 ML 2.241]

on the L. S. is a butifull bottom Plain of about 2000 acres [10 Jul 04 WC 2.365]

Came Suddenly into an open and bound less Prarie, I Say bound less because I could not See the extent of the plain in any Derection...this Prarie was Covered with grass about 18 Inches or 2 feat high [19 Jul 04 WC 2.394]

PLAIT {PLATT} A braid; also, to braid. *See* QUEUE, SWEET-GRASS. (**South, South Midland**)

the Clatsop...brought with them Split & Straw or Grass hatts for sale. they make those kind of hatts by platting them very ingeniously [22 Feb 06 JW 11.422]

[Shoshone] *ornements are...beeds of Shells platted grass, and Small Strings of Otter Skin dressed...* [21 Aug 05 WC 5.139]

PLANTER {PLAN-tə} = SAWYER[2]. A tree snag so called for being *planted* firmly in the bottom or bank of a river. (**Mississippi and Missouri Valleys**)

The difficulties which oppose themselves to the navigation of this immence [Missouri] *river, arise from the rapidity of it's current, it's falling banks, sandbars, and timber that remains...concealed in it's bed, usually called...Sawyers or planters.* [31 Mar 05 ML in Jackson Letters (ed. 2) 1.222]

PLASTER {PLAS-tə} A dressing for applying medicine (as a *salve*) or to close a wound. *See* BASILICON.

I applied a plaster of Sarve made of the Rozen of the long leafed pine, Beas wax and Beare oil mixed, which has Subsided the inflomation [5 Jun 06 WC 7.336]

PLAT(E) (Of topographic features) flat (in French).

Passed a Place Lbord Called the Plattes, a flat rock projecting from the foot of a hill [15 May 04 WC 2.231]

Specifically, the Platte River, a broad, shallow river flowing eastward from Colorado and Wyoming headwaters across Nebraska to the Missouri River. From French *rivière plate*, 'shallow river,' which in turn comes from Ioway-Otoe *nyĩ braske* or Omaha *nĩ bdhaska* (Nebraska), meaning 'flat water.' (For another name with the same Siouan prefix, *see* NEMAHA RIVER.)

arrived at the lower Mouth of the Great River Platt at 10 oClock [21 Jul 04 WC 2.402]

Also, the Little Platte River (of Iowa and Missouri).

passd the mouth of a Small river...called by the french Petite River Platte (or Shoal river) [30 Jun 04 WC 2.334]

PLATOON A volley of gunshots, as to mark a holiday.

I was awakened...by a discharge of 3 platoons [25 Dec 04 WC 3.261]

PLEURISY {PLUR-iss-ee} A painful inflammation of the pleura (a membrane surrounding the lungs), resulting from an infection such as pneumonia.

one man taken violently Bad with the Plurisee [26 Jan 05 WC 3.278]

I Bleed the man with the Plurisy to day & Swet him [27 Jan 05 WC 3.279]

The Diseases Commons to our party was Tumers in Summer & Plouresis in Winter [winter 04-05 WC 3.481]

PLOVER {Clark's PLEE-və, modern PLUH-vər} A shore-bird of the family Charadriidæ, with a rounded body, and short tail and bill. Clark's spellings depict an archaic pronunciation arising from the variant French form *pleuvier*, rather than from *plouvier*; both of which mean 'rainy (bird).'

I observe but fiew Gulls or Pleaver in this part of the river [6 Oct 04 WC 3.147]

here we made a fire and dined on 4 brant and 48 Pliver [18 Nov 05 WC 6.066]

two Species of Plevers. [5 Mar 06 WC 6.383]

saw some...woodpeckers plover robins [et al.] [6 Jul 06 ML 8.093]

PLUCK An animal's internal organs, especially the heart, liver, and lungs. The sense was extended to exhibiting courage and fortitude by *having guts* or *pluck. See* LIGHTS. (**Northeast, central Atlantic**)

they returned...with...the flesh of three Elk, that of one of them having become putrid from the liver and pluck having been carelessly left in the animal all night. [15 Mar 06 ML 6.416]

PLUNDER {PLUN-də} Baggage, gear. Lewis's use of the word in this sense is the earliest on record. (**South, South Midland**)

we now took dinner and embarcked with our plunder [6 Jun 05 ML 4.260]

I dispatched Sergt. Ordway with 4 Canoes and 8 men to take up a load of baggage as far as Capt. Clark's camp return for the remainder of our plunder. [10 Jul 05 ML 4.371]

POGAMOGGAN {pə-GAH-mə-gahn} A war-club; from a Chippewa word meaning 'hitting instrument.' **(North)**

pogamoggan

a weapon called by the Cippeways...the pog-gar´-mag-gon´. [19 Aug 05 ML 5.122]

The Poggamoggon is an instrument with a handle of wood covered with dressed leather about the size of a whip handle and 22 inches long; a round stone of 2 pounds weight is also covered with leather and...united to the...handle by a throng of 2 inches long [23 Aug 05 ML 5.151]

POILE {standard French pwahl, Canadian French pwell} Fine-textured animal hair.

the Buffaloe I killed yesterday had cast his long hare, and the poil which remained was very thick, fine, and about 2 inches in length. [18 Apr 05 ML 4.051]

the poil of these bear were infinitely longer finer and thicker than the black bear [15 May 06 ML 7.260]

POINT[1] Usually a point of land projecting into a river, but sometimes other prominent natural features along the shore, such as an island, bluff, or woodland edge. The captains' bearings and distances along a river usually were measured from point to point. Rivermen noted a day's progress by keeping track of the number of points passed. *See* COURSE, TRAVERSE.

on the 4th point of to day is a Small Island & a Sand bar 2 miles out in the river [6 Jul 04 WC 2.352]

N. 45 W. to a point of Woodland on Lard. side 4 [miles]
N. 28 W. to a point of Woodland Stard. side 3
S. 35 W. to a point of Woodland on Std. side...4
[13 Apr 05 ML 4.032]

POINT[2] Short, narrow, black bars woven into the edges of woolen blankets made for the Indian trade, especially those sold by the Hudson's Bay and North West companies.

Each point originally represented one high-quality beaver-pelt in trade value for a blanket—the higher the number of points, the wider and heavier the blanket. The blankets usually were a natural off-white, with indigo-blue or black stripes near the ends. They were made of two pieces—width was limited by loom size—sewn together along their length. Sizes and markings were not standardized until later in the 19th century. In one particular shipment to the upper Mississippi country in 1818, a 2½-point blanket (the most common size) measured 54 by 72 inches and weighed 5 pounds; a 3-point blanket was 63 by 72 inches, and 6¾ pounds (*ASPIA* II. 336).

the robe woarn by the Shoshonees...are generally about the size of a 2½ point blanket [20 Aug 05 ML 5.126]

This traffic on the part of the whites consists in vending... blankets from two to three point [9 Jan 06 ML 6.187]

POLE[1] A measure of length in surveying, usually 16½ feet, normally marked off with a standardized *chain*. Originally, a pole represented the width of a strip of field allotted to one man to plow. *See* PERCH, ROD.

1 Mariner's Compas & 2 pole chain [Jun 03 ML in Jackson Letters (ed. 2) 1.069]

48 poles to a pile of Stones on a Dividing ridge [17–19 Jun 05 WC 4.311]

POLE[2] Also (SETTING) POLE, SOCKET(-pole). A long pole that was used to propel a boat (especially upstream) by pushing against the river-bottom. An iron socket protected its lower end. Poling was unfeasible when the water was too deep, or the river bottom too soft.

the 20 Oars & Poals could with much dificuelty Stem the Current [2 Jul 04 WC 2.340]

we employed the chord generally to which we also gave the assistance of the pole at the riffles and rocky points [28 May 05 ML 4.210]

I occasionly encourage them by assisting in the labour of navigating the canoes, and have learned to push a tolerable good pole in their fraize. [24 July 05 ML 4.423]

POLE, DOG One of a pair of poles harnessed to an Indian dog and on which belongings were secured for transport (travois).

we found Some of their ceeder dog poles, they answer us for Setting poles. [22 Sep 04 JO 9.064]

POLE, LODGE One of the long, thin poles comprising the frame of a tepee or lodge. When traveling, lodge poles were lashed to a horse's back and dragged behind on the ground, forming a travois frame for hauling baggage. *Lodgepole pine* (*Pinus contorta*) is so named because young pines made good lodge poles.

found a new indian lodge pole today...it was woarn at one end as if draged by dogs or horses [28 May 05 ML 4.211]

POLE, SCALP A pole fixed in the ground at an Indian camp, for displaying enemy scalps as trophies of war.

a band of Indians had went before them. Saw one of their Sculp poles [19 Jul 06 JO 9.338]

POLE, SETTING = POLE[2]. *See* (DOG-)POLE.

Sergt. at the bow... will...be provided with a seting pole and assist the bowsman in poling [26 May 04 ML 2.257]

willow... is white light and tough, and is generally used by the watermen for setting poles [winter 04–05 ML 3.455]

the Water froze to our Setting poles, as we worked the Pettyaugers along [3 May 05 JW 11.144] *killed one Beaver with a Setting pole.* [11 Aug 05 WC 5.072]

POLECAT   Skunks (genus *Mephitis*) were attracted to salmon being processed by Indians along the Columbia. *See* BOIS ROULÉ, SMOKABLE. (**South, Midland**)

I returned through a rockey open countrey infested with pole-cats [24 Oct 05 WC 5.335]

skunk

> The designation *polecat* for New World skunks is borrowed from the Old World where, similarly to skunks, various other members of the weasel family spray a noxious fluid. Eurasian and American polecats also share a predilection for barnyard fowl; ◆*pole-* may descend from the Old French word *po(u)le* 'hen,' whence comes also English *pullet.*◆

POLICE   Maintenance of order, especially in a military setting.

to promote a regular Police in Camp, The Commanding officers, have thought to devide the detachment into three Squads [1 Apr 04 WC 2.188]

POMP   Clark's nickname for Jean Baptiste (born February 11, 1805, at Fort Mandan), the son of SACAGAWEA and Toussaint CHARBONNEAU.

> It has been suggested that the name reflects the Shoshone word *bambi* (sometimes written *pampi*) 'head.' This hypothesis is weakened, however, by the fact that though modern Shoshone has *-mb-* in *bambi*, the dialect encountered by Lewis & Clark had only *-b-* (written *-p-*): Clark's record of the Shoshone name for BEAVERHAD ROCK, for instance, has *pap,* not *pamp,* and he writes *Year-pah* for YAMPA. (Given that he writes *pap* for the head of a beaver, it seems unlikely that Clark would write *Pomp* for 'head' as a personal name in another situation.) It seems more likely that Clark's feelings for Jean Baptiste found expression in a paternalistic naming tradition of the Eastern elit. *Pompey,* the name of a famous Roman general, was used as a pet name in the Virginian English of the period: George Washington refers in his diary to "the little Spaniel dog Pompey" (1768) and to a dark bay horse with the same name (1787). *Pompey, Pompy,* and *Pomp* were common names for slaves and ex-slaves (usually blacks, but in one case at least, an Indian) in the 18th and 19th centuries, from Georgia to New Hampshire. (There were other slave-names of Roman origin, such as *Cato* and *Scipio.*) In the vernacular usage of Clark's time, the name *Pompey* no longer denoted the Roman military hero, but was merely a patronizing (if in this case affectionate) nickname given to one's social inferior.

In a letter to Charbonneau, in which he also refers to Jean Baptiste as "my boy Pomp" and "my little danceing boy Baptiest," Clark stated:

if you wish to return to trade with the indians and will leave your little Son Pomp with me, I will assist you [20 Aug 06 WC in Jackson Letters (ed. 2) 1.315]

Continuing *in loco parentis* in 1820, Clark charged the government $16.37½ "for two quarters' tuition of J. B. Charboneau, a half Indian boy, and firewood and ink" and $1.50 for "one Roman history for the boy," besides other educational and maintenance expenses (*ASPIA* II. 291).

Clark may have named the prominent sandstone butte in central Montana after *Pompey's Pillar*, an 88-ft.-high granite column in Alexandria, Egypt (actually dedicated in the 3rd century AD to the Roman emperor Diocletian, and not to Pompey). It seems reasonable to assume, in any case, that Clark had Jean Baptiste in mind when he named the prominent feature.

This rock which I shall Call Pompy's Tower is 200 feet high and 400 paces in secumphrance [25 Jul 06 WC 8.225]

PONASHITA The Shoshone name for the Bannock, a Northern Paiute horse people living among the Shoshone, especially in southern Idaho and western Wyoming. Clark here applies the name to a tributary of the Snake River. (The English name, *Bannock,* is derived from the related Northern Paiute name for these people.)

Kimooenem has two forks on the South Side, & Camps of Inds. all the way up 2d fork called Pâr-nâsh-te about 50 ms. [10 Oct 05 WC 5.255]

PONCA {PɔN-kə, PUN-kə} A Siouan people of northern Nebraska and southern South Dakota. The Ponca and OMAHA share a Dhegiha language of the SIOUAN family.

I Saw the grave...where the Grand chief of the Punckhas was buried [13 Aug 04 JO 9.038]

PONDY Swampy, marshy. (**South, South Midland**)

the high lands...does not touch the Sea Coast again below point Lewis leaveing a low pondey countrey [19 Nov 05 WC 6.070]

POOR {poə} (Of animals) = MEAGER. (**South, South Midland**)

Two men Sent out to hunt this evening. brought in a Buck & a pore Turkey. [21 Jun 04 WC 2.313]

(Of land) not fertile.

the Land is High Cliefts and...pore [19 Jul 04 CF 9.388]

PORTAGE {Pɔ-dij} The carrying of cargo and, where necessary, boats around an obstruction.

a portage on this side of the river will be attended by much difficulty in consequence of several deep ravines [15 Jun 05 ML 4.297]

Also, the CARRYING PLACE itself, such as that around the GREAT FALLS[1] of the Missouri, the GREAT FALLS[2] of the Columbia, and over the Rockies between Missouri and Columbia headwaters.

we dry meat for the men to eat on their return from the upper part of the portage [21 Jun 05 WC 4.324]

PORTER {PƆ-tə} A bitter, dark-brown beer, brewed from malt processed at high temperature, and originally favored by *porters* (carriers) and other laborers in Britain. Porter freezes at about 29° Fahrenheit.

at 6 oClock 14° abov o, Porter all frosed and several bottles broke [28 Jan 04 WC 2.166]

PORTFIRE {PƆT-fī-ə} Flammable material; probably a cord impregnated with gunpowder, saltpeter, and sulfur, serving as a handheld fuse (or MATCH) for firing a SWIVEL gun. Here, in a tense standoff with the Teton, Clark seeks to avert a potentially lethal situation.

I threw a Carot of Tobacco to 1s[t] Chief...took the port fire from the gunner [28 Sep 04 WC 3.124]

PORTLY Handsome, having a distinguished bearing. The usual modern meaning 'corpulent' is a later development.

The Minetarras Maharhas & Crow Indians are large portley men, Tall women well proportioned. [winter 04–05 WC 3.487]

PORTMANTEAU {pɔt-man-TOE} A suitcase.

one horse Strayed from us...with a pair of port Mantaus with Some Marchandize and Capt. Lewises winter cloths [20 Sept 05 JO 9.227]

POTATO The edible tuber of the Indian potato or ground-nut, *Apios americana*, a perennial vine of the pea family. For another root-plant of the pea family, *see* (WHITE) APPLE. (**Plains**)

The common wild pittatoe...form another article of food in savage life[.] this they boil untill the skin leaves the pulp easily...the pettatoe...is exposed on a scaffold to the sun or a slow fire untill it is thoroughly dryed [winter 03–04 ML 2.223]

I saw Homney [hominy] of ground Potatos [26 Sep 04 WC 3.117]

Also (abbreviated in the plural as **potas.**) = WAPATO.

Janey in favour of a place where there is plenty of Potas. [24 Nov 05 WC 6.084]

POTAWATOMI {pah-tə-WAH-tə-mee} A people whose home-territory included the southern Lake Michigan region and extended southward between the Illinois and Mississippi rivers. Their ALGONQUIAN language is closely related to CHIPPEWA. The name appears in French, as *Pouteoutami*, on Marquette's 1673 Mississippi map.

two Canoos of Potowautomi Indians Came up...and landed [12 Dec 03 WC 2.131]

POT-METAL The cast iron in cooking pots.

when they happen to have no ball or shot, they substitute gravel or peices of potmettal, and are insensible of the damage done thereby to their guns. [15 Jan 06 ML 6.206]

POUCH, (BULLET-, SHOT-) A leather pouch containing lead balls and shot.

To 15 rifle pouches...$26.25 The...fifteen Pouches were attached to a like number of Powder Horns and delivered to Capt. M. Lewis [16 Jun 03 in Jackson Letters (ed. 2) 1.090]

one of the hunters took his rifle & bullitt pouch on Shore [23 May 05 JW 11.165]

I took my gun & Shot pouch in my left hand, and with the right Scrambled up the hill pushing the Interpreters wife (who had her Child in her arms) [29 Jun 05 WC 4.343]

POULTICE {POHL-tiss} A warm, soft, moist dressing applied to ease pain or heal an injured or diseased part of the body. *See* CATAPLASM.

Shabonoes Son a Small child is, dangerously ill...we apply a poltice of Onions. [22 May 06 WC 7.280]

I derected Shields to...hunt for Some Wild Ginger for a Poltice for Gibsons wound. [19 Jul 06 WC 8.205]

POUND = PARK.

we had a Strong pound formed to day in order to take them [horses] *at pleasure* [29 May 06 WC 7.307]

POVERTY {PAH-və-tee} (Of an animal) poor condition. *See* POOR.

Colter joined us...haveing killed a Bear, which from his discription of it's poverty and distance we did not think proper to send after. [24 Jun 06 WC 8.050]

POWDER {POW-də} Gunpowder. *See* BALL, CANISTER.

Ammunition 200 lbs. Best rifle powder 400 lbs. lead [Jun 03 ML in Jackson Letters (ed. 2) 1.070]

today we opened and examined all our ammunition, which had been secured in leaden canesters. we found twenty seven of the best rifle powder, 4 of common rifle, three of glaized and one of the musqut powder in good order...these cannesters contain four lbs. of powder each and 8 of lead. [1 Feb 06 ML 6.265]

we now gave the Twisted hair one gun and a hundred balls and 2 lbs. of powder [12 May 06 ML 7.248]

Gunpowder was graded as to quality and grain-size, with RIFLE powder being finer grained than MUSKET powder. (*Glazed powder* was tumbled in wooden drums with a small amount of powdered graphite to achieve a more uniform grain-size and shape, to improve moisture resistance, and for better flow.) The preferred weight ratio of LEAD to powder in ammunition supplies was, as it had been for some time, 2 to 1. In 1673, the governing council of (South) Carolina advised that there be provided "1^{lb} of powder & 2^{lbs} of shott for every man" (*Shaftesbury Papers*, 1897, 428). In 1790, the U.S. Secretary of War ordered "two tons of best rifle and musket powder, four tons leaden bullets" for Federal troops on the Ohio frontier (*ASPIA* I. 99). In Missouri in 1820, powder cost 40 to 50¢ per pound, and lead 6 to 10¢ (*ASPIA* II. 291, 300).

POX Syphilis, a bacterial disease usually contracted during sexual intercourse. *See* also LUES VENEREA, VENEREAL.

Pocks & Venerial is Common amongst them I Saw one man & one woman who appeared to be all in Scabs [21 Nov 05 WC 6.074]

chastity is not very highly esteemed by these people, and...the severe and loathsome effects of certain French principles are not uncommon among them. [5 Apr 05 PG 10.076]

> Syphilis initially leads to genital sores, followed by skin ulcerations causing large pockmarks, and finally (sometimes years later) to a tertiary stage resulting in neurological damage, including dementia. The disease probably was common among the expedition's men, and was treated primarily with MERCURY, both in salve and pill forms. (Mercury remained the treatment of choice until the development of antibiotics.) Pox, called *French, Neapolitan, Spanish,* or *Indian* depending on the party blamed for its transmission, may have originated in the Americas, and after Columbus's voyages spread rapidly through the Old World. It sometimes was called the *great pox* to distinguish it from SMALL POX.

PRAIRIE {PREH-ree, pə-REH-ree} A treeless, grassy area, ranging in size from a few acres, to thousands of square miles—from a meadow, to a great PLAIN. Originally, a French word for 'meadow.' *See* GLADE.

a Small Preree on the Larbd. Side [12 Dec 03 WC 2.130]

the first 5 miles of our rout laid through a beatifull high leavel and fertile prarie which incircles the town of St. Louis [20 May 04 ML 2.240]

Camped in a Prarie on the L. S....composed of good Land and plenty of water roleing & interspursed with points of timbered land, Those Praries are not like those...E. of the Mississippi Void of every thing except grass, they abound with Hasel Grapes & a wild plumb...I Saw great numbers of Deer in the Praries [10 Jun 04 WC 2.292]

Got on our way at hard Scrable Perarie [25 Jun 04 JW 11.030]

In those Small Praries or glades I saw wild Timothey [14 Jul 04 WC 2.378]

crossed thro: the plains...with the view of finding Elk, we walked all day through those praries without Seeing any [20 Jul 04 WC 2.397]

those Indians are now out in the praries...Hunting the buffalow [20 Jul 04 WC 2.399]

The Prairie are not as one would suppose from the name, meadows or bottoms but a sort of high plain...without timber...This Prairie ground extends from the Wabash to the Mountains [c. Apr 10 NB in Jackson Letters (ed. 2) 2.507]

PRETTY MUCH An expression still current today in colloquial English, though quite new at the time of the expedition.

dry wood pretty much doated [16 Mar 05 ML 3.315]

PRIMING A small amount of fine-grained gunpowder in the pan of a flintLOCK firing mechanism. Here, a Shoshone knocked back the FRIZZEN of Drouillard's gun, thus opening the PAN-cover and causing the priming to spill out, which would prevent Drouillard from firing the weapon.

blunderbuss with flintlock firing mechanism

he then jurked...his gun & jurked the pan open lost the primeing [22 Aug 05 JO 9.208]

A **priming wire** cleared the vent (or touch-hole), through which burning priming-powder ignited the main charge. A *brush* removed residue from the pan.

Bailing Invoice of Sundries...Primg. wires & Brushes [probably winter 04–05 3.504]

PRIZE A pry-bar, lever. (**South, South Midland**)

we Commenced...the Cutting loose the boat...with the assistance of Great prises we lousened her [24 Feb 05 WC 3.302]

all hands employed cutting the Ice from round the Barge. Got large prizes & attempted to Shake hir loose [28 Jan 05 JO 9.111]

PROCEED ON A hallmark phrase repeated throughout the Lewis & Clark journals. *We Proceeded On* is the quarterly publication of today's Lewis and Clark Trail Heritage Foundation.

at 11 oClock I proceeded on [11 Dec 03 WC 2.129]

PROMISCUOUSLY At random, in a disorderly manner.

Those people [Flathead] *wore their hair (as follows)...the women loose promisquisly over ther Sholdrs & face* [5 Sep 05 WC 5.188]

found...a few children Setting permiscuesly in the Lodg, in the greatest agutation, Some crying and ringing theer hands [19 Oct 05 WC 5.305]

passed Several places where the rocks...have the appearance of haveing...fallen promiscuisly into the river [30 Oct 05 WC 5.355]

PRONGHORN* A ruminant of the West. The scientific name, *Antilocapra americana* 'American antelope-goat,' echoes the captains' indecision whether to designate the unfamiliar creature as ANTELOPE or GOAT.

PROPORTION {pə-PO-shən} Quantity, amount, number (of).

River...with a great perpotion of timber on its borders. [16 Jul 06 WC 8.191]

PUBLIC[1] Belonging to or under contract with the government, and administered by the COMMISSARY; here, Major Nathan Rumsey. (Note the difference from the usual modern sense, 'open, available, or pertaining to all; not private.')

Mr. Rumsey ride a public horse to St Louis [7 May 04 WC 2.212]

La Liberty...was lost as we expect with a publick horse. [7 Aug 04 JO 9.035]

Reed...Confessed that he "Deserted & Stold a public Rifle Shot-pouch Powder & Bals" [18 Aug 04 WC 2.489]

PUBLIC[2] Pertaining to a *public house*, or tavern (whence the modern word *pub*).

Majr. W. Christy...had Settled in this town in a public line as a Tavern Keeper. [23 Sep 06 WC 8.371]

PUDDING, HASTY {pood'n} A batter of corn-meal and water. (**New England**)

they also prepare an agreeable dish with them [bread-root] *by boiling and mashing them...until the whole be of the consistency of a haisty pudding.* [8 May 05 ML 4.126]

PUDDING, WHITE A mixture of suet, meat, flour or oatmeal, and other ingredients, packed into animal entrails. The original meaning of *pudding*, from the Old French *boudin*, is 'sausage,' which originally was made in a casing of stomach or intestine. *See* FILLET, SUET.

from the cow I killed we saved the necessary materials for making what our wrighthand cook Charbono calls the boudin blanc...this white pudding we all esteem one of the greatest delacies of the forrest...About 6 feet of the lower extremity of the large gut of the Buffaloe is the first mosel that the cook makes love to...he gently compresses it, and discharges what he says is not good to eat...the mustle lying underneath the shoulder blade next to the back, and fillets are next saught, these are needed up very fine with a good portion of kidney suit [suet]; to this...is then added...pepper and salt and a small quantity of flour...by stuffing and compressing he soon distends the recepticle to the utmost limmits [9 May 05 ML 4.131]

PUKE An emetic, to induce vomiting. Pukes and PURGES were believed to rid the body of harmful substances.

Several men bad, Capt Lewis Sick I gave Pukes Salts &c. to Several [26 Sep 05 WC 5.234]

PUMICE {PUH-mee, modern PUH-miss} In the journals, reddish clinkers formed by the sintering action of burning coal beds on the contiguous rock layers. The color, like that of rust, is due to the presence of oxidized iron. Also *pummy. See* BURNT HILLS.

the mineral appearances of salts, coal and sulpher, together with birnt hills & pumicestone still continue.— while we remained at the entrance of the little Missouri, we saw several pieces of pumice stone floating down [14 Apr 05 ML 4.034]

PUNCHEON {PUN-chən} A log having one side roughly dressed flat, usually with an axe. *See* GUTTER.

a floor of puncheons or split plank were laid, and covered with grass and clay [3 Nov 04 PG 10.062]

we continue to Cover our Huts with hewed punchens [24 Nov 04 WC 3.240]

PUNK A prostitute.

An old bawd with her punks, may also be found in some of the villages on the Missouri, as well as in the large cities of polished nations. [5 Apr 05 PG 10.076]

PURGATIVE {Pə-gə-tiv} Having a laxative effect; of the nature of a PURGE.

the water is extreemly unpleasant to the taste and has a purgative effect. [11 Apr 05 ML 4.022]

PURGE {pəj} Treatment with a laxative. *See* PHYSIC, PUKE.

I gave this man a jentle pirge cleaned & dressed his Sore [5 May 06 WC 7.212]

PUT INTO   (Of a vessel) to enter (a harbor, inlet, etc.)

the wind...blew So hard...that we were obliged to put into a Small Creek [6 Jan 06 WC 6.171]

Q

QUADRANT   {KWƆD-rənt} A common synonym for OCTANT. *See* TANGENT-SCREW.

Mathematical Instruments...1 Hadleys Quadrant with Tangt Screw [$]4 [May 03 in Jackson Letters (ed. 2) 1.096]

Missed the altidude at 12 oClock with the quadrent [17 Dec 03 WC 2.134]

QUAKER COLOR   Grey, the subdued color of Quaker clothing.

the upper part of the neck, back, and wings are of a fine, quaker colour, or bright dove colour with reather more of a bluish tint [5 Aug 04 ML 2.451]

QUARTER[1]   {KWƆ-tə} The after (sternmost) half of a boat.

The Storm...Struck the...boat on the Starbd. quarter [14 Jul 04 WC 2.377]

QUARTER[2]   To proceed at an angle to a river's current, to 'crab.'

a Violent Storm...Struck the boat nearly Starboard, quatering, & blowing down the Current [14 Jul 04 WC 2.377]

I derected all to follow Shannon and pass quartering up the river which they done and passed over tolerably well the water running over the back of the 2 Smaller horses only. [5 Jul 06 WC 8.164]

QUEUE   {kyoo} A braid of hair; a pigtail (*see* PLAIT).

they [Walla Walla] *all cut their hair in their forehead and most of the men wear the two cews over each sholder in front of the body* [29 Apr 06 ML 7.183]

Also, to braid one's hair in a pigtail.

in one of those Canoes a Indian wore his hair cued, and had on a round hat. [28 Oct 05 WC 5.346]

QUIETING   Gelding (castration) of a horse, usually resulting in quieter behavior. *See* CUT.

An Indian performed the quieting operation on two more of our horses. [16 May 06 PG 10.229]

QUINNAT   {KWIN-nət} A Lower Chinook word for a large Pacific salmon (*Oncorhynchus tshawytscha*), now called *king* or *chinook* salmon. (**Pacific Northwest**)

salmon

we arrived at the entrance of Quinnette creek [15 Apr 06 ML 7.123]

QUOITS {quīts} A game in which small rope rings are pitched at a stake.

they...have been amusing themselves very merrily today in runing footraces pitching quites, prison basse &c. [9 Jun 06 ML 7.349]

R

RABBIT-BERRY A shrub (*Shepherdia argentea*) common along Great Plains water-courses. Also known as *buffalo-berry*, its brilliant red berries have long been an important food for native peoples. *See* GRAISSE DE BUFFLE. (**Plains**)

the bottoms are...covered with rose bushes & Rabbit berry bushes [18 May 05 JO 9.150]

RADICLE A rootlet.

the roots...have been...devested of the black or outer coat and radicles [11 Jun 06 ML 8.016]

RAGGED Rugged.

passed verry high ragid clifts, and a bad rapid [1 Aug 05 JW 11.250]

RAIN-CROW Not a crow, but a cuckoo, either yellow-billed (*Coccyzus americanus*) or black-billed (*C. erythrophthalmus*). (**South, Midland**)

I saw...the Cookkoo or as it is sometimes called the rain craw. [16 Jul 06 ML 8.112]

RAISE To reach the top of.

we raised a Steep bank back of this bottom which brot us on the level prarie [30 Nov 04 JO 9.099]

RASCALITY Delinquent, meddlesome conduct.

Sent Jessomme to the Main Chief of the mandans to know the Cause of his detaining...a horse of Chabonoe our big belly interpreter, which we found was thro: the rascallity of one Lafrance a trader from the N W. Company [18 Dec 04 WC 3.259]

RAT A pack-rat, or wood-rat, genus *Neotoma*.

Several rats of Considerable Size was Cought in the woods [31 May 04 WC 2.266]

RATE OF GOING The rate at which a CHRONOMETER clock is running. Even if the time being kept is inaccurate, the rate should be constant and thus its error predictable.

when she was again set in motion, and her rate of going determined by a series of equal altitudes of the ☉ taken for that purpose, it was found to be the same precisely [15 Jul 04 ML 2.382]

RAVEN INDIANS = CROW.

The Ravin Indians have 400 Lodges & about 1200 men, & follow the Buffalow [12 Nov 04 WC 3.234]

RAVINE {rə-VEEN} A narrow, steep-sided gully or valley, subject to flash-flooding. *See* DRAFT, GULLEY, HOLLOW.

This Countrey has a romantick appearance river inclosed between high and Steep hills Cut to pieces by revines [25 Jun 05 WC 4.332]

they found that part of rivene in…which Capt. C. had been seting yesterday, filled with huge rocks. [30 Jun 05 ML 4.345]

RAZOR-BLADE {RAY-zə} Whitehouse apparently is the earliest on record to use the term in the English language.

They sold one of these Hatts to one of our party for an old Razor blade. [19 Nov 05 JW 11.396]

REACH[1] To extend.

this Lake is Large and was once the Bead of the River[.] it reaches Parrelel for Several miles [4 Jul 04 CF 9.385]

REACH[2] A straight stretch of river between two bends.

entered the long reach, so called from the Ohio runing in strait direction for 18 miles [11 Sep 03 ML 2.079]

RECRUIT To recuperate, or allow to recuperate.

Delayed 3 hours on this Island to recruit the men [10 Jul 04 WC 2.365]

the men recruiting a little, all at work which are able. [30 Sep 05 WC 5.237]

REDWOOD Red-osier dogwood, *Cornus sericea. See* SMOKABLE.

the undergrowth consists of rosebushes, goosberry and current bushes, honeysuckle small, and the red wood, the inner bark of which the engages are fond of smoking mixed with tobacco. [21 Jun 05 ML 4.324]

REE = ARIKARA. An English spelling of a French variant, *Ris*, or perhaps the last syllable of a variant English pronunciation {ə-RICK-ə-ree}.

we passed a handsome bottom, where a band of Rees lived last winter. [6 Oct 04 PG 10.051]

REED Tall (up to 10 feet or so), hollow-stemmed grass, *Phragmites communis*, growing in wetlands throughout much of the central and eastern U.S. Early growth provided good grazing for horses and cattle. *See* CANE, (SAND) RUSH.

we have not Seen one Stalk of reed or cane on the Missouries [5 Jul 04 WC 2.351]

REEF To reduce the amount of exposed sail in a strong wind—by folding a SAIL up from the bottom, and then securing it with short ropes worked through the sail in one or more horizontal bands.

proceeded on under a Double reafed Sale [30 Sep 04 WC 3.128]

Also, such a fold in the sail.

the wind blew so hard that we were obldged to take a reefe in our Sail [21 Aug 04 JO 9.041]

REGULATE {REH-gə-late} To sight in; to adjust gun SIGHTS³.

my air gun was out of order and her sights had been removed...I put her in order and regulated her. [7 Aug 05 ML 5.055]

we made our men exersise themselves in Shooting and regulateing their guns, found Several of them that had their Sights moved by accident [7 Apr 06 WC 7.092]

REGULUS {REG-yə-ləs} The bluish-white alpha star of the constellation Leo. *See* ALDEBARAN.

observed time and distance of ☽*'s Eastern Limb from regulus with Sextant* ★ *West* [4 Apr 06 WC 7.074]

RELAX Diarrhea, LAX.

Several of the party Sick with a relax by a Sudden change of diet and water [26 Sep 05 JO 9.230]

REPINE To feel or express dissatisfaction; to complain.

we are about to enter on the most perilous and dificuelt part of our Voyage, yet I See no one repineing [20 Jun 05 WC 4.319]

REPUBLICAN A PAWNEE band. The Republican River, flowing through parts of Nebraska and Kansas, is named for these people.

The Pania, Loups, Republican, Pania Pickey and Ricaras Speake the Same Language [winter 04–05 WC 3.490]

Mr. Chouteau...met a Deputation from the Republican Panis [22 Sep 03 in Jackson Letters (ed. 2) 1.260]

RETURN {rə-TƏN} A profit.

Colter and Bratten were permitted to visit the Indian Village to day for the purpose of tradeing for roots and bread, they were fortunate and made a good return. [5 Jun 06 WC 7.336]

RHEUMATISM {ROO-mə-tiz'm} A generic term for any disorder causing pain, stiffness, and disability in the muscles and joints of the extremities, neck, and back.

I was...Suddinly attacked with the Rhumitism in the neck which was So violent I could not move [22 Oct 04 WC 3.191]

Girtey has the Rhumertism verry bad [26 Mar 04 WC 2.181]

RIC = ARIKARA.

Severl large parties of Seauex Set out from the rics [1 Oct 04 WC 3.135]

RIFFLE A shoal or rapids. *See* RIPPLE.

I have passed as many as five of those bars [on the Ohio River], *(or as they are here called riffles) in a day* [8 Sep 03 ML in Jackson Letters (ed. 2) 1.122] *passed a verry bad riffle of rocks* [25 Oct 04 WC 3.197]

in the rapid we saw a Dow Elk & her faun, which gave rise to the name of Elk & faun Riffle [26 May 05 WC 4.205]

they were obliged to drag the canoes over many riffles [10 Aug 05 ML 5.066]

(Of a stream) to run with rapids.

we came...in View of a Sand bar...over which the water riffleed and roered like a great fall [20 Jun 04 WC 2.310]

the North fork more White and riffling than it was [8 Jun 05 JW 11.190]

RIFLE A long gun with spiral grooves cut on the inside of the barrel, giving the bullet a spin, which greatly increases accuracy and range over that of a smooth-bore weapon like the MUSKET. *See* BALL, BREECH.

Arms & Accoutrements 15 Rifles...15 Gun Slings [Jun 03 ML in Jackson Letters (ed. 2) 1.070]

we caused all the men who had short rifles to carry them, in order to be prepared for the natives [12 Apr 06 ML 7.111]

Drewyer and Shannon Sent on a head to go to the villages of the pel-oll-pellow nation they took one of the Short rifles in order to git a pilot [18 Jun 06 JO 9.324]

the ball had lodged in my breeches which I knew to be the ball of the short rifles such as that he had [11 Aug 06 ML 8.156]

The expedition's Army-issue rifles, which a number of the men carried, were either the .45-.47 caliber U.S. Model 1792 (about 50 bullets per pound of lead), or (perhaps less likely) a shorter (33-inch) U.S. Model 1803 prototype of .54 caliber (about 30 bullets per pound)—*caliber* indicates the inside diameter of the barrel measured in hundredths of an inch. Military rifles were fitted with bayonets [9.325] and slings. The *short rifles* mentioned in the journals might be either these Army weapons, or personal guns carried by the men; in either case they had shorter barrels than the (*Kentucky*) *long rifle*. Some of the men apparently carried personally owned, or Army-issued, *long rifles*. Most *long rifles* were about .45 to .50 caliber (50 to 37 per pound). Developed by Pennsylvania gunsmiths based on German immigrant gun technology, they were renowned for accuracy. In addition to the men with rifles, a few other Corps' soldiers apparently were armed with the U.S. MUSKET.

Clark's *small* (or *little*) *gun*, probably a personal Kentucky rifle, was so-called because of its small bore—SMALL refers to the barrel's inside diameter, not its length. Clark's reference to shooting 100 balls per pound of lead equates roughly to a gun with a .36 caliber bore, often called a *squirrel rifle*. *See* CUT OUT.

Little gun all my hunting [21 Oct 04 WC 3.189]

one of the Indians pointed to a flock of Brant Sitting in the creek...and requested me to Shute one, I walked down with my Small rifle and killed two at about 40 yds distance... the Size of the ball...was 100 to the pound [10 Dec 05 WC 6.121]

RILEY (Of a stream) muddy, turbid, riled. (**North, North Midland**)

the South fork of the Missourie is high & of a yellow coulour to day, & the North fork more white & rile [8 Jun 05 JW 11.190]

this run... verry riley and bad tasted. [30 Jun 05 JO 9.177]

RIPPLE = RIFFLE. Sometimes crews had to lighten boat loads to pass these water obstructions.

called the hands aboard and proceeded to a ripple of McKee's rock where we were obleged to get out all hands and lift the boat [30 Aug 03 ML 2.065]

I have been enabled to get on without the necessity [of] *employing oxen or horses to drag my boat over the ripples* [13 Sep 03 ML in Jackson Letters (ed. 2) 1.124]

our boat turned in a ripple, and nearly upset. [24 May 04 PG 10.009]

RISING = BOIL[1], abscess. Infections were common for boatmen constantly working in the water. (**South, South Midland**)

one man a bad riseing on his left breast. [23 Jul 04 WC 2.415]

RIVE To split.

we found that the C. W. [cottonwood] will rive well [8 Nov 04 JO 9.095]

this timber [Sitka spruce] is white and soft...and rives better than any other species which we have tryed. [4 Feb 06 ML 6.277]

ROAD A trail or track; and sometimes scarcely that.

I fel into a Buffalow road [4 Sep 04 WC 3.046]

road emencely bad as usial [17 Sep 05 WC 5.210]

the road was excessively dangerous along this creek being a narrow rockey path generally on the side of steep precipice, from which in many places if ether man or horse were precipitated they would inevitably be dashed in pieces. [19 Sep 05 ML 5.215]

ROCHE JAUNE RIVER {rɔsh-ZHƆN, rə-ZHƆN} = YELLOWSTONE RIVER. French for 'yellow rock.'

the river rejone recves 6 Small rivers on the S. Side [7 Jan 05 WC 3.269]

The Clifts on the South Side of the Rochejhone are Generally compd. of a yellowish Gritty Soft rock [28 Jul 06 WC 8.243]

ROCKY MOUNTAIN INDIANS = CROW.

a party of the Assinniboins...had been to war against the rocky mountain Indians [17 Apr 05 ML 4.048]

The metal...they obtained in exchange for horses from the Crow or Rocky Mountain Indians on the yellowstone River. [23 Aug 05 ML 5.149] *the great Chief of the Menetaras Spoke...he Said that he had opened his ears and followed our Councils, he had made peace with the Chyennes and rocky mountain indians* [15 Aug 06 WC 8.301]

ROCKY MOUNTAINS Before Lewis & Clark's exploration, many in the East presumed that a narrow mountain chain or height of land, easily passable, divided the continent between the Missouri and Columbia watersheds. At Fort Mandan in the winter of 1804–5, the Corps learned otherwise from the Indians. The Rockies, also called the *Shining* or *Stoney (Stony)* mountains, loomed as the most formidable obstacle to the expedition's progress. *See* SNOWY MOUNTAINS.

from this point I beheld the Rocky Mountains for the first time with Certainty...I felt a Secret pleasure in finding myself So near the head of the heretofore Conceived boundless Missouri [26 May 05 WC 4.204]

ROD = PERCH or POLE[1], a measure of 16½ feet.

it is not uncommon for the Magpie to build [with]*in a few rods of the eagle* [26 Apr 05 WC 4.075]

ROD, RAM- A rod for ramming a charge (powder, wad, and ball) down the barrel of a muzzle-loading firearm. *See* WAD.

we Substitute the Cherry in place of Hickory for ax hilthes ram rods, &c. [10 Jul 05 WC 4.374]

ROD, WIPING- A gun rod tipped with a WIPER.

Sarbono lost his gun shot pouch, horn, tomahawk, and my wiping rod [29 Jun 05 ML 4.341]

ROLLING (Of a landscape) undulating, perhaps the earliest use of the word in English as applied to terrain.

found the Country roleing open & rich, with plenty of water [10 Jun 04 WC 2.291]

(Of river-bottom sand and mud) shifting, moving by the action of waves and current.

batteaux...are wide and flat not Subject to the dangers of the roleing Sands [20 Sep 06 WC 8.367]

The Missouri River's course, sandbars, and shorelines were in constant flux, some-times even from hour to hour. During the expedition's 1806 descent, some of the river's route had changed drastically since the 1804 ascent. On August 20, 1806, Clark noted, "I observe a great alteration in the Corrent course and appearance of this pt. of the Missouri. in places where there was Sand bars in the fall 1804 at this time the main Current passes, and where the current then passed is now a Sand bar—Sand bars which were then naked are now covered with willow Several feet high. the enteranc of Some of the Rivers & Creeks Changed owing to the mud thrown into them, and a layor of mud over Some of the bottoms of 8 inches thick" [8.310]. A good pilot was a necessity.

ROPE, TOW- A heavy rope for pulling a vessel, hauled on by men walking along the shoreline. On the upper Missouri, the white pirogue's tow-rope was hemp, but the expedition's other tow-ropes usually consisted of twisted animal skins. *See* CORD, (TOWING-)LINE.

we had some difficulty in passing a sandbar, the tow-rope having broke [26 Jun 04 PG 10.017]

currant strong, we therefore employ the toe rope when ever the banks permit the use of it; the water is reather deep for the seting pole [20 Jul 05 ML 4.406]

ROPE-WALK A long rectangular area where the men made rope.

Made 20 Oars & 600 feet of Roap at the Roap Walk Camp [17 Jun 04 JW 11.025]

ROSIN {RƆ-zin} Pitch from pine, fir, or other conifers for waterproofing and preparing medical dressings. *See* BEAR-GRASS, PLASTER. (**South**)

we directed that...Gibson and his crew should...employ themselves in collectng rozin which our canoes are now in want of. [9 Apr 06 ML 7.098]

RUDDER-IRONS {RUH-də} The hinges suspending a rudder from a boat's stern.

the rudder irons of the white perogue were broken by her runing fowl on a sawyer, she was however refitted in a few minutes with some tugs of raw hide and nales. [5 May 05 ML 4.111]

RUN[1] A small stream. *See* CREEK. (**Midland**)

the run began to rise and rose 6 feet in a few minits [29 Jun 05 WC 4.343]

on arrival at the Camp on the willow run—met the party who had returned in great Confusion [29 Jun 05 WC 4.343]

A *spring run* is fed by a spring or springs, and usually colder than streams flowing with surface runoff.

Several Spring runs falling from the mountains on the left [25 Aug 05 WC 5.169]

RUN[2] (Of fish) migrating to spawn, usually up a stream or river, or onto a beach. Here, at the Columbia's mouth, the EULACHON.

these women informed us that the small fish began to run which we suppose to be herring [22 Feb 06 ML 6.336]

RUN[3] To take (a vessel) down rapids.

there were five shoals neither of which could be passed with loaded canoes nor even run with empty ones. [23 Aug 05 ML 5.153]

RUN[4] = RUT.

the Elk beginning to run. the Buffalow are done running & the bulls are pore. [19 Aug 06 WC 8.310]

RUSH, SAND- or SCRUBBING-   Horsetail (genus *Equisetum*), a primitive plant with jointed round stems. The surface tissues contain silica particles, an abrasive useful for scouring pots and pans. Horsetail retained its deep-green color in winter, and thus was considered good forage. (Today, however, it is known that horses consuming excessive amounts can acquire a serious thiamine-deficiency disease, *equisetosis*.) *See* CANE, REED.

the [Mississippi's] *banks appear every where to abound with the sand or scrubing Rush, it grows much thicker, and arrises to a much greater hight in the bottoms of this river than I ever observed it elsewhere, I measured a stalk of it which was 8 feet 2 inches in length & 3¹/₈ inches in circumpherence...the favorite soil for this plant is a rich loam intermixed with a considerable portion of sand.* [22 Nov 03 ML 2.102]

I observe large quantities of the sand rush in these [Three Forks] *bottoms which grow... as high as a man's breast and stand as thick as the stalks of wheat...this affords one of the best winter pastures on earth for horses or cows* [28 Jul 05 ML 5.008]

RUSH'S PILLS   A powerful PHYSIC compound, developed by Dr. Benjamin Rush of Philadelphia. The main ingredients were JALAP and calomel (mercury chloride). Before the expedition, Dr. Rush served as Lewis's primary source for professional medical advice. *See* BILE, BILIOUS.

I took a doze of Rush's pills which operated extremly well and I found myself...intirely clear of fever by the evening. [14 Nov 03 ML 2.086]

all Complain of a Lax & heaviness at the Stomack, I gave rushes Pills to Several [24 Sep 05 WC 5.232]

I gave him a doze of Dr. Rush's which...I have found extreemly efficatious in fevers which are in any measure caused by the presence of boil [bile?]. [16 Feb 06 ML 6.318]

RUSSIA SHEETING   A heavy, canvas-like linen fabric, for OVERALLS, shirts, tents, containers, etc., and originally, at least, imported from Russia. At between 50¢ and $1 a yard, Russia sheeting cost about the same as white linen.

To making the Russia Sheeting into 45 bags...[$]9. [15 Jun 03 in Jackson Letters (ed. 2) 1.090]

Bailing Invoice of Sundries, being necessary Stores...3 pr Russia Over Alls [winter 04–05 3.502]

RUT   (Of hooved animals) ready for, or engaged in, autumn mating. *See* RUN⁴.

September 21st Antilopes ruting, as are the Elk, the Buffaloe is nearly ceased [21 Sep 04 ML 3.131]

S

SACAGAWEA   {sə-CAH-gah-WEE-ə} A teenaged SHOSHONE woman (sister of CAMEAHWAIT) captured by raiding HIDATSA in the Rocky Mountains (ca. 1799–1800), and taken to the upper Missouri villages in North Dakota. When the Corps of Discovery

fur-trade era family

arrived among the Mandan in 1804, she was a young wife to Toussaint CHARBONNEAU. In addition to speaking Shoshone, she knew the Hidatsa tongue (via which she communicated with Charbonneau). Caring for her infant son (POMP), she accompanied the Corps to the Pacific and back, serving as an INTERPRETER with Shoshone (SNAKE) speakers, an informant regarding the terrain in her original Missouri headwaters homeland, and a gatherer of wild plants. *See* MINITARI, POTATO, WAPATO.

Sâh-câh-gâh, we â, our Indian woman is very sick this evening; Capt. C. blead her. [10 Jun 05 ML 4.276]

Sah-cah-gar-we-ah...was one of the female prisoners taken...tho' I cannot discover that she shews any immotion of sorrow in recollecting this event, or of joy in being again restored to her native country [28 Jul 05 ML 5.009]

In the journals, Sacagawea often is simply called *the Indian woman, the squaw,* or *Charbonneau's wife.* The captains gave her the nickname *Janey.*

The wife of Shabono our interpetr we find reconsiles all the Indians, as to our friendly intentions a woman with a party of men is a token of peace [13 Oct 05 WC 5.268]

The indian woman...has been of great Service to me as a pilot through this Country [13 Jul 06 WC 8.180]

The form of her name in the following quotation is an example of the use of *m* for *w* in careful speech in the Hidatsa language. (This variation also occurs in AHWAHAWAY and in Hidatsa *a-WAH-tee* 'river, or Missouri River,' which Lewis [4.246] records as *Amahte.*) This characteristic alternation, along with Lewis's translation and his division of the name into two words, as well as the close similarity to the Hidatsa words for 'bird' (*tsah-KAH-kah*) and 'woman' (*WEE-ah / MEE-ah*), support the traditional interpretation of Sacagawea's name as *Bird Woman* in Hidatsa, the language of her captor-adopters, and its pronunciation with a hard *g* rather than the *j* sound that later became popular.

this stream we called Sâh-câ-gar me-âh or bird woman's River, after our interpreter the Snake woman. [20 May 05 ML 4.171]

Ordway writes her name as though knowing *wea* meant simply 'woman' and so omitted it.

Sahcahgah our Indian woman verry Sick & was bled. [10 Jun 05 JO 9.165]

Sacagawea's fate after the expedition is uncertain, but she appears to have died at a young age. In the late 1820s, Clark—when recounting for the latter fate of all the expedition's members—noted that Sacagawea had died. Years earlier, Missouri fur-trader John Luttig at Fort Manuel noted, December 20, 1812, "this Evening the Wife of Charbonneau a Snake Squaw, died of a putrid fever she was a good and the best Women in the fort, aged abt 25 years she left a fine infant girl." The death by what was perhaps typhus or typhoid of this unnamed "Wife of Charbonneau a Snake" occurred in northern South Dakota.

SACCHARUM Druggist's Latin for 'sugar.'

See SATURN for an example.

SACKACOMMIS {SACK-ə-KO-mee, SACK-ee-KO-mee} Bearberry leaves (*Arctostaphylos uva-ursi*), especially when dried as a SMOKABLE. The Chippewa word for bearberry, *suh-GAH-koh-min*, often was interpreted by French-Canadians as *sac à commis*, because trading-company clerks (*commis* 'one who is commissioned') carried bearberry leaves in their smoking bags. *See* KINNIKINNICK.

our Sackey Commy out...dispatched two men to the open lands near the Ocian for Sackacome, which we make use of to mix with our tobacco to Smoke which has an agreeable flavour. [21 Dec 05 WC 6.134]

Edible red berries grow on this low, spreading plant of the heather family.

This chief gave us to eate Sackacommis burries Hasel nuts fish Pounded, and a kind of Bread made of roots [29 Oct 05 WC 5.348]

SADDLE A cut of meat consisting of a section of the backbone and both LOINS.

halted early and partook of a Sumptious Dinner of a fat Saddle of Venison and Mush of Cows (roots) [4 Jul 06 WC 8.163]

SAGE[1] An aromatic herb, *Salvia officinalis*, with grayish-green leaves, formerly much used in medicine, and still today as a kitchen spice. Lewis also called it *common sage*; *see* SAGE[2].

George Drewyer taken with the Ploursey last evening[.] *Bled & gave him Some Sage tea* [31 Jan 05 WC 3.281]

SAGE[2] Shrubs of the genus *Artemisia*, including sagebrush (with silvery-green leaves), common in the arid American West. Lewis was the first to apply its English name. Also called HYSSOP, SOUTHERN WOOD. (**West**)

the leaves are white...this is common to all the praries above the Kancez river; from it's resemblance in taste smell &c to the common Sage I have called it the wild Sage. [winter 04–05 ML 3.459]

a kind of wild sage or hyssop, as high as a man's head...grows in these bottoms [27 Aug 05 PG 10.133]

the sage bushes...grow in great abundance on some part of these plains [27 Apr 06 PG 10.217]

SAHAPTIAN* {sə-HAP-tee-ən} A language family comprising SAHAPTIN and NEZ PERCE.

SAHAPTIN* {sə-HAP-tən} A language spoken by peoples located west of the Nez Perce in eastern Washington and Oregon; also its speakers, including the WALLA WALLA. *See* CHOPUNNISH for etymology.

SAIL, SPRIT- A quadrangular sail with the forward edge secured to a mast. Extending back from the mast, it is stretched out and up by a SPRIT. Compare with (SQUARE) SAIL, and *see* JIBE.

sprit-sail

we...hoisted both the sails in the White Perogue, consisting of a small squar sail, and spritsail [13 Apr 05 ML 4.029]

SAIL, SQUARE A rectangular sail suspended from a yard (a wooden spar extending more or less across a boat's width). On the Missouri in 1804, the expedition's KEELBOAT used one square sail. Compare with (SPRIT-)SAIL, and *see* LUFF.

we fortunately escaped and pursued our journey under the [pirogue's] *square sail, which shortly after the* [sprit-sail's] *accident I directed to be again hoisted.* [13 Apr 05 ML 4.030]

The party on Starting from Wood river had one large Keel boat...with one square sail—rowing 22 oars [c. Apr 1810 NB in Jackson Letters (ed. 2) 2.534]

SALAL An evergreen shrub (*Gaultheria shallon*) of the Pacific coast belonging to the heather family, and growing large, edible, dark-purple berries. (Lewis delivered *Shallan* seeds to horticulturist Thomas Jefferson.) Natives pounded and formed the berries into 10-pound cakes for preservation. Elk favored the foliage. *Salal* is a Lower Chinookan name, which also entered the CHINOOK Jargon. (**Pacific Northwest**)

in the eveng an old woman presented a bowl made of a light Coloured horn a kind of Surup made of Dried berries...which the natives Call Shele wele...they Gave me Cockle Shells to eate a kind of Seuip made of bread of the Shele well berries mixed with roots...which they presented in neet trenchers made of wood. [9 Dec 05 WC 6.119]

The Shallon is the production of a shrub which I have heretofore taken to be a speceis of loral...and that the Elk fed much on it's leaves. [8 Feb 06 ML 6.287]

pocket gopher

SALAMANDER {SAL-ə-MAN-də} Here, meaning the pocket gopher (family Geomidæ), not an amphibian. (**South, South Midland**)

their work resembles that of the salamander common to the sand hills of the States of South Carolina and Georgia [9 Apr 05 ML 4.015]

SALINE {SAY-leen} A salt spring, or a surface salt deposit, often marshy. *See* LICK.

There are three principal salines on this stream [Salt River] [winter 04–05 ML 3.349]

passed Saleen Creek...Salt has been made their [6 Jun 04 JO 9.011]

SALISH, SALISHAN* {modern SAY-lish} A widespread language family of the Pacific Northwest and British Columbia. Salishan speakers included inland tribes such as the FLATHEAD (*Salish* or *Shalee*) of Montana, coast peoples like the TILLAMOOK in Oregon, and various Puget Sound and Strait of Georgia groups. As with most Pacific

Northwest languages, Salishan has a complex inventory of consonants that test the phonetic abilities of even well skilled linguists.

the two young men...are going on a party of pleasure mearly to the...Sha-lees a band of the Tush-she-pah nation [26 Jun 06 ML 8.053]

We saw the fresh track of a horse...which the indians supposed to be a Shale spye. [3 Jul 06 ML 8.086]

SALT-WORKS {SƆ(L)T-wəks} From January 2 until February 21, 1806, a small detachment (usually 3 men) from Fort Clatsop maintained a *salt makers* camp on the coastline near Seaside, Oregon. Kettles of sea-water were constantly kept on a fire, producing as much as a gallon of salt a day (about 16 pounds), which required boiling nearly 100 gallons of salt-water. About 20 gallons of salt (over 300 pounds) was produced for the Corps' homeward journey.

Willard arrived late in the evening from the Saltworks, had cut his knee very badly with his tommahawk. [10 Feb 06 ML 6.293]

the Salt makers had made a neet Close Camp, Convenient to wood Salt water and the fresh water of the Clat sop river which at this place was within 100 paces of the Ocian [7 Jan 06 WC 6.177]

SAME...OF Same as.

proceeded on the Same Course of last night [24 Aug 04 WC 2.503]

[Shoshone] *tobacco is of the same kind of that used by the Minnetares Mandans and Ricares* [13 Aug 05 ML 5.081]

the baskets were the same in form of the others. [21 Aug 05 ML 5.137]

SAND Sandbars were a shifting menace to navigation, particularly on the Missouri, and windblown sand a nuisance. *See* ROLLING.

as we approach this Great River Platt the Sand bars are much more noumerous...and the quick & roleing Sands much more danjerous [19 Jul 04 WC 2.395]

The Wind blew hard West and raised the Sands off the bar in Such Clouds that we Could Scercely See [23 Aug 04 WC 2.503]

SAPOLIL {SHAP-ə-lel in the journals} On the lower Columbia, the Indian name for cakes made from COUS roots. In the following examples, *Shapelell* is the biscuit, not the cous root from which it is made. (**Pacific Northwest**)

those beeds the[y] *trafick with Indians Still higher up this river for roabs, Skins, cha-pel-el bread, beargrass &c.* [1 Nov 05 WC 5.371]

for these [European trade goods] *they receive...from the natives...a kind of buisquit, which the natives make of roots called by them shapelell.* [9 Jan 06 ML 6.187]

Here we got some Shap-e-leel, a kind of bread the natives make of roots, and bake in the sun; and which is strong and palatable. [15 May 06 PG 10.211] *bought 2 dogs Several cakes of chappalell* [18 Apr 06 JO 9.294]

purchased Some wood and 4 dogs & Shapillele...the party purchased a great quantity of Chapellell and Some berries [22 Apr 06 WC 7.158]

most of our men went to the village...and bought considerable of couse & Shappallel [23 May 06 JO 9.314]

> The term *sapolil* became a part of the CHINOOK Jargon in the sense of 'bread, wheat, grain, flour.' A similar word, *sapíl* 'root cakes' occurs in Sahaptin. The Puget Sound Salish language Lushootseed also borrowed its word *siplǝl* from the Chinook Jargon term, as did English.

SASKATCHEWAN RIVER {sǝ-SKÆ-chǝ-wǝn} An extensive river, which rises in the Canadian Rockies and flows east across the Great Plains to Lake Winnipeg, and which facilitated water transportation for Canada's western fur-trade. From Cree, literally 'fast-flowing river.'

Perhaps...[Milk] river also might furnish a practicable... communication with the Saskashiwan river [8 May 05 ML 4.124]

SATURN {SÆ-tǝn} The Roman god of agriculture, identified in Greek tradition with Kronos, who ruled the universe until deposed by his son Zeus and driven into Italy. This deity came to represent the large, slow-moving ringed planet of the outer solar system. People born under this astrological sign were *saturnine*, 'sluggish, gloomy, taciturn.' The *Imps of Saturn* are the god's offspring, whom Lewis compares to the temporarily surly Shoshone. (An *imp* originally was a shoot or scion of a plant.)

they were now very cheerfull and gay, and two hours ago they looked as sirly as so many imps of satturn. [15 Aug 05 ML 5.097]

> *Saturn* also was the alchemist's name for lead, a heavy dull metal thought to be the antithesis of liquid mercury. In the 19th century, *saturnine* also came to mean 'suffering from lead poisoning.' The old name for lead acetate, an ingredient in EYE-WATER, was (*ophthalmic*) *sugar of lead*; in druggist's Latin *saccharum Saturni* (*ophthalmicum*). An alternate name was *lacteum Saturni* 'tear(s) of Saturn.' (*Ela v V.* is presumably white VITRIOL, the other main active ingredient in eye-water.)

6 oz. Sacchar. Saturn. opt. [$].37 [26 May 03 in Jackson Letters (ed. 2) 1.080]

4 oz Lacteaum Saturni [Jun 03 ML in Jackson Letters (ed. 2) 1.074]

we also gave Some Eye water 1 G. of Ela v V. & 2 grs. of Sacchm. Stry. to an ounce of water [29 Apr 06 WC 7.186]

SAUK {sɔk} The Sauk (or Sakis), an ALGONQUIAN-speaking people inhabiting parts of a the wide region between Lake Michigan and Oklahoma.

a Prarie in which the Missouries Indians once lived and the Spot where 300 of them fell a Sacrifise to the fury of the Saukees [13 Jun 04 WC 2.296]

SAULTEAUX = CHIPPEWA. Originally the name of a Chippewa band residing part of the year at Sault Ste. Marie, 'St. Mary's Rapids,' the eastern outlet of Lake Superior. French, for 'those of the rapids.'

The Chipiways or sateaus call this plant Wab-bis-sa-pin or Swan-root [Nelumbo lutea] [spring 04 ML 2.223]

SAVAGE A Native American; applied in the journals in mostly a neutral way, with little of the modern negative connotation. (Ultimately from Latin *silva,* 'forest.') A savage might best be defined as an Indian living in the wilderness beyond the limits of Euro-American civilization. In this sense, also *Indian* and *native. See* SQUAW.

the 2 Indians at our Camp behave verry well and their Squaws mend our mockisons... and are as friendly as any Savages we have yet Seen. [20 Aug 05 JO 9.207]

SAWYER[1] {sɔ-yə} A workman employed in sawing lumber. Whipsawing boards, with one man below in a pit and the other above, required teamwork.

the Sawyears, come on to day better than usial, Whitehouse & Reed, agree better than they did last week—or in other Words Re[ed] Saws better from practice. [6 Jan 04 WC 2.152]

SAWYER[2] A SNAG imbedded in a river, with an end floating high enough to endanger a boat. Probably so named from the similar bobbing action of the top man on a whipsaw (SAWYER[1]). *See* PLANTER, RUDDER-IRONS. (**Mississippi and Ohio Valleys**)

the Sturn of the Boat Struck a moveing Sand & turned within 6 Inches of a large Sawyer, if the Boat had Struck the Sawyer, her Bow must have been Knocked off [29 Jun 04 WC 2.328]

in passing a bend...they were drawn by the currant in among a parsel of sawyers, under one of which the canoe was driven and throwed Willard who was steering overboard; he caught the sawyer and held by it [4 Aug 06 ML 8.147]

SAWYER[3] = CHITTEDIDDLE. A katydid, perhaps thought to make a sound like a SAWYER[1] at work. (**Virginia**)

SCAFFOLD A wooden rack for meat and fish, raised off the ground to facilitate drying or smoking and for protection from animals. Also, for the funereal laying-out of human bodies. (**South Midland**)

katydid

he had a scaffal of jurk [7 Sep 04 JO 9.055]

we...determined to encamp...in order to dry meat, in surch of which we sent a party...and employed others in preparing scaffoalds and collecting firewood [6 Apr 06 ML 7.079]

Also, to place on a scaffold for such purposes.

I Scaffeled up the Deer [17 Oct 04 WC 3.180]

the Mandans and the nations about them Scaffold their dead and pay great Devotion to them after Death [winter 04–05 WC 3.488]

SCANTLING {SKANT-lin} Lumber ranging in size between about 2x2 and 4x4 inches, and thicker in relation to the breadth than a *plank*.

Cotton-wood...is a soft white wood, by no means dureable, and of which it is extreemly difficult to make plank or scantling. [winter 04–05 ML 3.354]

SCARCE OF {SKEH-əs, skase} Short of.

we have been confined for 6 days...Scerce of Provisions, and torents of rain poreing on us [15 Nov 05 WC 6.049]

Also **scarce off for.**

our Interpeter & wife came over with them & all were Scarse off for provissions [22 Aug 05 JW 11.280]

SCARLET {SKAH-lət} Cloth dyed a bright red.

three of our party found in the back of a bottom 3 pieces of Scarlet one brace in each, which had been left as a Sacrifice near one of their Swet houses [3 May 05 WC 4.105]

SCATTERING Scattered, occasional. (**South, South Midland**)

Some Scattering Timber on the Bottoms about the mouth of [Cheyenne River] [1 Oct 04 JO 9.074]

I saw Great numbers of Antelopes, also Scattering Buffalow [30 Apr 05 WC 4.090]

SCHOONER {SKOO-nə} A sailing vessel with at least two masts carrying gaff-rigged sails—i.e., quadrangular sails extending aft from the masts (rather than slung across them), with spars at both the top and bottom of each sail. *See* BRIG, SHIP, SLOOP.

[Captain] *Washilton In a Skooner, they expect him in 3 months* [1 Jan 06 WC 6.155]

SCOTT'S PILLS A patent PHYSIC.

I gave Bratten 6 of Scotts pills which did not work him. [19 Feb 06 WC 6.329]

Gave Willard a dose of Scots pills; they opperated very well. [21 Feb 06 WC 6.335]

Lapage is taken sick, gave him a doze of Scots pills which did not operate. [3 Mar 06 ML 6.374]

> *The Household Cyclopedia of General Information* (1881) listed aloe as a main ingredient in Scott's Pills and cautioned against pregnant women taking the pills as a laxative, since aloe was believed to cause hemorrhoids. (Today, however, aloe is an ingredient in over-the-counter hemorrhoid remedies.) William Byrd, an archetypal Virginia aristocrat, noted in 1739: "My head was much out of order, for which I took two Scott's pills" (Woodfin 26); and, a 1794 London directory lists a James Inglish as *Proprietor of the Scott's Pills*, 165, Strand.

SCROFULA {SCRɔ-fə-lə} A form of tuberculosis affecting the skeletal system and lymph-glands, especially of the neck, and causing skin inflammations resulting in scarring. Here, in reference to the Nez Perce, the term probably applied to skin disorders in general.

Ther disorders are but fiew and those fiew of a scofelous nature. [10 Oct 05 WC 5.259]

schrofela, ulsers, rheumatism, soar eyes, and the loss of the uce of their limbs are the most common cases [11 May 06 ML 7.243]

SEAMAN Lewis's Newfoundland dog, purchased for $20 (apparently in summer 1803), and prized "for his docility and qualifications generally for my journey" [2.089], which eventually included BEAVER hunting. Until 1985, the dog's name was thought to be *Scannon* due to a misreading of the journals,

we came to for Dinner at a Beever house, Cap Lewis's Dog Seamon went in & drove them out. [5 Jul 04 WC 2.350]

SEINE A relatively long, narrow net, usually with floats along the upper edge and weights on the lower. A seine hangs vertically in the water and is used to surround fish. *See* DRAG.

they take their fish...with Small Seines of 15 or 18 feet long drawn by two persons [29 Apr 06 WC 7.184]

SERVICE-BERRY {sĂ-vus} Juneberry or shadbush, a shrub of the genus *Amelanchier* (in the apple subfamily of the rose family) with showy white flowers and edible, dark-purple fruit. *Service* is not derived from *serve*, but ultimately from Latin *sorbus*, the name of a Mediterranean tree resembling the mountain ash. (**South Midland**)

This Countrey abounds in a variety of wild froot, Such as...Sarvis berry, High bush Cram burry... [winter 04–05 WC 3.481]

Capt. Clark our Intrepter & wife walked on Shore and found a great number of fine berrys which is called Servis berrys. our Ints. wife gethered a pale full & gave them to the party at noon [16 Aug 05 JW 11.270]

SEVERAL Different, separate.

the barge run foul three several times—on logs [15 May 04 ML 2.229]

SEWELLEL {sə-WELL-lel} A primitive Pacific Northwest rodent (*Aplodontia rufa*), also called *mountain beaver*. Lewis applied the Chinookan name for a robe made of its skins to the animal itself. (**Pacific Northwest**)

Sewelel is the Chinnook and Clatsop name for a small animal found in the timbered country on this coast...the natives make great use of the skins of this animal in forming their robes [26 Feb 06 ML 6.351]

Capt. Lewis bought...Some other Small Skins which the Indians Call Shugolell which they make robes of. [13 Dec 05 JO 9.260]

SEXTANT {SEKS-tunt} An instrument similar in use to the OCTANT from which it was developed, but employing a graduated *sixth* of a circle. It included several other improvements as well, and was accurate enough for measuring moon-star distances for determining longitude. *See* MICROMETER, NONIUS.

Mathematical Instruments...1 Metal Sextant [$]*90* [May 03 in Jackson Letters (ed. 2) 1.096] *at the time of our departure from the River Dubois untill the present moment, the sun's altitude at noon has been too great to be reached with my sextant, for this purpose I have therefore employed the Octant by the back observation.* [22 Jul 04 ML 2.411]

Observed Meridian altitude of ⊙ *U. L. with Sextant and glass artifical Horizon.* [13 Jan 05 ML 3.273]

SHAHA {shaw-HAY} = CHEYENNE. A variant borrowed from the Arikara language.

The mandans apprehended danger from the Shar has as they were at peace with the Seaux [1 Dec 04 WC 3.251]

SHAKE A FOOT   To dance; a surprising form of recreation for men traversing the grueling, cactus-infested PORTAGE around the GREAT FALLS[1].

such as were able to shake a foot amused themselves in dancing on the green to the music of the violin which Cruzatte plays extreemly well. [25 Jun 05 ML 4.332]

SHAKE HAND   A SIOUX chief met in council near the Nebraska-South Dakota line and probably so named for a hand tremor (or *palsy*).

1st: Polsey 2 White Crain 3 Little Bowl 4 red hand [28 Aug 04 WC 3.019]

The Shake hand 1st Chief Spoke [31 Aug 04 WC 3.028]

SHANK-BONE   Thigh-bone. *See* MARROW-BONE.

after eateing the marrow out of two Shank bones of an Elk, the Squar choped the bones fine boiled them and extracted a pint of Grease [3 Dec 05 WC 6.107]

SHARER   {SHEHR-ə} One sharing in business expenses and profits; a shareholder.

Colter...expressed a desire to join Some trappers who offered to become Shearers with and furnish traps &c. [15 Aug 06 WC 8.302]

SHAVE   To remove hair from an animal hide. *See* GRAIN[2].

Several men employed in Shaveing & Graneing Elk hides...for the Iron boat. [21 Jun 05 WC 4.324]

we had it [dried elk meat] *Secured in dried Shaved Elk Skins* [7 Apr 06 WC 7.092]

SHAWNATAHQUE   {perhaps shaw-nə-TAH-kwee} The sweet black root of an edible thistle (*Cirsium edule*), baked or pounded into mush. (**Pacific Northwest**.) *See* SWEAT[2].

those people brought...Some Wappato roots, mats made of flags and rushes dried fish, and a fiew Shaw-na tâh-que and Dressed Elk Skins [31 Dec 05 WC 6.147]

SHAWNEE   {modern shə-NEE; journals SHAW(-wə)-no, SHAW(-wə)-nee, SHƆ-nee?} An ALGONQUIAN-speaking people, who in the 18th and 19th centuries were dispersed over large areas of the eastern U.S., though the focus of their territory seems to have been southern Ohio. By 1800, a large portion of the tribe, the so-called Absentee Shawnee, had moved west of the Mississippi, particularly to southeast Missouri, where they maintained close relations with the DELAWARE. By 1815, the Shawnee population around Cape Girardeau was estimated at 1,200 (*ASPIA* II. 76). In 1825, the Shawnee ceded rights to Cape Girardeau in return for land in Kansas; they now live primarily in Oklahoma. The name *Shawnee* ultimately comes from an Algonquian term for 'southerner,' and was recorded in French as *Chaouanon* on Marquette's 1673 map.

found six Shawano hunting camps [18 Nov 03 ML 2.093]

his wife is a Shawnee woman...she dresses after the Shawnee manner with a stroud leggings and mockinsons [23 Nov 03 ML 2.107]

Shawonies...near Cape Gerardeau [winter 03–04 WC 3.446]

SHE A female mammal. *See* HE. (**South Midland**)

The She Goats have verry little horns but are a handsome animal [20 Sep 04 JO 9.062]

when the bear was in a fiew paces of the Shore I Shot it in the head. the mean hauled her on Shore and proved to be an old Shee [2 Aug 06 WC 8.272]

Also, a gun.

The guns...were both out of order...the second had the cock screw broken which was replaced by a duplicate which had been prepared for the lock at Harpers ferry where she was manufactured. [20 Mar 06 ML 6.441]

SHEEP, (ROCKY) MOUNTAIN = BIGHORN.

we precured two horns of the animale the french Call the rock mountain Sheep [22 Dec 04 WC 3.260]

I saw one of the mountain Sheep, th[e] wool thick and long [29 Oct 05 WC 5.350]

SHEER OFF {SHEE-ə} To veer away, a nautical term.

three men...Sheared off as I aproached the Shore [19 Oct 05 WC 5.305]

SHELVING Overhanging, projecting.

this is one of the grandest views in nature...the Missouri falling over a Shelveing rock for 47 feet 8 Inches. [18 Jun 05 WC 4.307]

he discovered a deep rivene where there were some shelving rocks under which he took shelter [29 Jun 05 ML 4.341]

SHIELDS, JOHN The expedition's blacksmith, gunsmith, and indispensable handyman. When the North West Company's Charles Mackenzie encountered the Corps at the Hidatsa villages, he quoted chief Le Borgne as saying, "there are only two sensible men among them, the worker of iron and the mender of guns," presumably referring to Alexander Willard and John Shields (Masson 1.330).

John Shields Cut out my Small rifle & brought hir to Shoot very well. the party ows much to the injenuity of this man, by whome their guns are repared when they get out of order which is very often. [8 Apr 06 WC 7.095]

SHIP[1] A large sailing vessel, technically having (SQUARE) SAILS on three masts and a bowsprit. *See* BRIG, SCHOONER, SLOOP.

Mr. Haley Visits them in a Ship & they expect him back to trade with them in 3 moons
[1 Jan 06 WC 6.155]

SHIP[2] (Of a boat) to take on (water), especially over a GUNWALE when listing or in rough seas.

She Shipt about 2 Barrels of water [14 Jul 04 CF 9.387]

SHIP[3] A flat piece of wood in the form of a quarter-circle, with lead weights inserted in the circular edge to keep the piece upright in water; also called *log-chip*. Together with the *log line* and *log reel*, comprising the LOG.

log line, reel & log ship [$]*1.95* [31 May 03 in Jackson Letters (ed. 2) 1.082]

SHISHIQUAW {SHIH-shih-kwah} A rattle of native design. The word, also spelled *shishiquoi*, was borrowed into Canadian French from Ojibway *zheesheegwun*. The name was applied to Haystack Butte in western Montana, perhaps for a resemblance to the shape of a rattle. (**North**)

the Shishiquaw mountain is a high insulated conic mountain [8 Jul 06 ML 8.097]

SHOAL, SHOALED, SHOALY Shallow. *See* BATTURE, ROLLING.

we haule the Boat over a Sand bar, River wide & Shoal [1 Oct 04 WC 3.133]

passed a rapid and sholde place in the river were obliged to get out and drag the boat
[25 Oct 04 ML 3.222]

The river is verry Shoaley and the bad places are verry numerous [27 May 05 WC 4.209]

SHOE = AHWAHAWAY. Translated from French *soulier,* 'shoe, moccasin.'

a large party...of Gross Ventres...were on their way down from their Camps...to revenge on the Shoe tribe an injurey which they had received by a Shoe man Steeling a Gross Venters Girl [1 Jan 05 WC 3.267]

SHOE-PACK A high-topped, moccasin-like boot. From the DELAWARE word for 'shoe.'

one of our party...had previously made him a present of a pair of Cannadian shoes or shoe-packs. [7 Jul 06 ML 7.344]

SHOOT[1] A gun-shot. (**South Midland**)

the little game...was so extremly shy that the hunters could not get in shoot of them.
[12 Apr 05 ML 4.026]

They saw a large brown bear feeding on currants but could not get a shoot at him. [1 Aug 05 ML 5.028]

SHOOT[2] A narrow, fast-flowing stretch of river; a rapid. From French *chute*.

the toe line of our canoe broke in the shoot of the rapids and swung on the rocks and had very nearly overset. [1 Aug 05 ML 5.028]

The *great* or *grand shoot* of the Cascades of the Columbia.

The Indians...took their Canoes on ther Sholders and Carried them below the Great Shute [1 Nov 05 WC 5.369]

SHOSHONE {shoh-SHOH-nee; in early records, with emphasis sometimes on the first syllable, sometimes on the last.} The expedition obtained horses from the Shoshone along the Idaho-Montana continental divide. *See* SACAGAWEA, SNAKE.

we were anxious now to meet with the Sosonees or snake Indians as soon as possible in order to obtain information relative to the geography of the country and also if necessary, some horses [18 Jul 05 ML 4.398]

the Shoshonees do not cultivate this plant [tobacco], *but obtain it from the Rocky mountain Indians* [13 Aug 05 ML 5.081]

This nation Call themselves Cho-shon-nê [17 Aug 05 WC 5.115]

SHOT Lead pellets, of smaller diameter than BALLS. Several were loaded at a time into a smoothbore weapon for firing. *See* BUCKSHOT, POT-METAL, POUCH.

This traffic on the part of the whites Consist in vending...guns, principally old British or American Musquets, powder, balls and Shote... [14 Jan 06 WC 6.205]

white circular spots, about the size of a brister blue shot. [8 Jul 05 ML 4.367]

Brister blue shot, of bird shot size, was named after Bristol, England, where shot was first made in quantity (and more cheaply than by laborious casting methods) by dropping small spheres of molten lead into a water tank at the bottom of a tall *shot tower*. *Bristol* also was called *Bristow*, which the *r*-dropping Lewis writes as *brister* with a silent *r*, just as Clark spells *window* as *winder*. In *Observations on Hudsons Bay* (1743), James Isham referred to "Bristow Shott or Grey goose shott." (Some writers have suggested that today's *BB* shot is named after *Bristol blue*. It is more likely, however, that *BB* is simply one of a series of shot sizes designated by numbers and letters—*A*, *AA*, *B*, *BB*, and *BBB* among them.)

SHUT OF Rid of, or free of; usually appearing in dialect use as *shet of* or *shed of*. (**South, South Midland, Northeast**)

finding that we could not get Shut of those people for one night, we landed and Encamped [4 Nov 05 WC 6.018]

SHY (Of a horse) skittish, unmanageable; the opposite of GENTLE.

There are no horses in this quarter which can...be termed wild. there are some few which have been left by the indians at large for so great a length of time that they have become shye [24 Aug 05 ML 5.162]

SICK (Of a woman) menstruating. *See* COVENTRY, SITUATION.

the Second lodge is Small & appears to be intended for the Sick women who always retire to a Seperate lodge when they have the [blank] [9 May 06 WC 7.235]

SIDELING {SĪD-lin} Sloping. (**Midland**)

we Suped on a little portable Soup and lay down on this Sideling mount. [18 Sep 05 JW 11.321]

Also, sideways or oblique; extending across a hillside.

the Small Indian parth...led up this mountain and appeared to assend in a Sideling direction [7 Jan 06 WC 6.178]

SIGHT[1] A large quantity or number, surviving today in such an expression as *a damn sight better*. (**South, South Midland, New England**)

they...had an amence Side of Bufloe Green Skins &C [12 Jun 04 JO 9.013]

we Saw an emence Site of fowls on the plain [17 Oct 05 JW 11.356]

they have a vast Site of horses. [29 Apr 06 JO 9.300]

SIGHT[2] The pupil of the eye.

the [jackrabbit's] *sight is circular, deep sea green* [14 Sep 04 ML 3.072]

SIGHT[3] Either of two small metal indicators at the front and back of a gun-barrel. A shooter aimed a weapon (rifle, musket, or pistol) by aligning the two sights on the target. *See* REGULATE.

Labuish...having by some accedent lost the fore sight of his gun shot a great number of times [15 Mar 06 ML 6.416]

we made our men exersise themselves in Shooting and regulateing their guns, found Several of them that had their Sights moved by accident [7 Apr 06 WC 7.092]

SIGN[1] Evidence of an animal's (or person's) presence, especially tracks, droppings, or foraging activity, such as beaver-gnawed trees and limbs. Also, in the case of humans, dead campfires, tepee rings, travois marks, etc.

I observe great quantities of Bear Sign, they are after Mulbiries [24 Jun 04 WC 2.319]

the Elke Sine is [v]erry plenty [18 Jul 04 CF 9.388]

we saw great signs of beaver [9 May 05 JW 11.151]

finding no fresh Indian Sign returned down the river four miles and Camped [21 Jul 05 WC 4.414]

SIGN[2] A hand gesture used in communication between speakers of different languages. On the southern Plains, sign language (eventually with a thousand or more standardized gestures) probably developed before the arrival of Europeans, and spread to the northern Plains and adjacent areas before Lewis & Clark's time.

The means I had of communicating with these people [Shoshone] *was by way of Drewyer who understood perfectly the common language of jesticulation or signs which seems to be universally understood by all the Nations we have yet seen...this language is imperfect and liable to error but is much less so than would be expected. the strong parts of the ideas are seldom mistaken.* [14 Aug 05 ML 5.088]

We could not understand what they [a Chopunnish war party] *had done, as we could only converse by signs.* [27 Sep 05 PG 10.149]

those [Clatsop] *indians made Signs that they had a town on the Seacoast* [9 Dec 05 WC 6.118]

I now asked them by sighns if they were the Minnetares of the North which they answered in the affermative [26 Jul 06 ML 8.130]

Also, to communicate by sign language.

these Savages [an Upper Chinook group] *were Surprized to See us*[.] *they Signed to us that they thought that we had rained down out of the clouds.* [30 Oct 05 JW 11.377]

SILK-GRASS In the eastern United States, usually referred to Adam's needle (*Yucca filamentosa*), with leaves that can be used for string-like fiber. (**South, South Midland**) The Corps extended the term to other fiber-producing plants in the West. In describing how the Shoshone assembled a handsome scarf-like TIPPET, for example, Lewis probably was referring to soapweed, another yucca species (*Y. glauca*).

[Otter skin] *is sewed arround a small cord of the silk-grass twisted for the purpose* [20 Aug 05 ML 5.127]

On November 19, 1805, Gass described a Chinook hat, "made of white cedar and bear-grass" [10.175], but later (below), ◆he apparently substituted *silk grass* as a synonym for bear-grass (*Xerophyllum tenax*).◆

A number of Chinook Indians came to the fort with hats to trade. They are made of cedar bark and silk grass, look handsome and keep out the rain. [20 Feb 06 PG 10.194]

> ◆In the vicinity of The Dalles on the Columbia, *silk-grass* may refer to Indian hemp (or dogbane), *Apocynum cannabinum*, a common plant with 2- to 4-ft.-long stalks yielding useable fiber. Yucca and Indian hemp plants look very different. Lewis (below) would not have confused the two, but probably simply was likening the Indian hemp fiber that he observed to the yucca he was familiar with.◆

they use the silk grass in manufacturing their fishing nets and bags, the bear grass and cedar bark are employed in forming a variety of articles. [20 Apr 06 ML 7.146]

SIMLIN A kind of summer squash (*Cucurbita pepo*), also called *cymling* and *pattypan*, a close relative of the pumpkin. *Simlin* is a variant of an old English name for a kind of bread or fruit-cake (*simnel*), and is related to *semolina*, a wheat product used in making pasta. The simlin squash is flat and round with ribbed sides and a knobby top. It resembles the Lenten cake for which it was named. (**South, South Midland**)

they had raised Corn, Beans, pease & Simblins at that place [29 Sep 04 JW 11.092]

those Indians [Arikara] *Cultivate on the Island Corn Beens Simmins, Tobacco &c.* [8 Oct 04 WC 3.151]

I walked up to the Black Cats village & eate some Simnins with him, and Smoked a pipe [14 Aug 06 WC 8.298] *they brought us a breakfast of boild siniblins & beans* [15 Aug 06 JO 9.350]

SIMPLE A medicine with a single active ingredient. *See* SOVEREIGN, SPECIFIC.

left Some Simple Medesene to be taken. [29 Apr 06 WC 7.186]

Used here in reference to the treatment of syphilis.

I cannot learn that the Indians have any simples which are sovereign specifics in the cure of this disease [27 Jan 06 ML 6.239]

SINGE Clark here uses an old dialect variant.

the flesh of this animal [seal] *is highly prised by the nativs who Swinge the hair off and then roste the flesh on Sticks before the fire.* [23 Feb 06 WC 6.342]

SINK A natural or manmade depression.

Camped at a Small branch on the mountain near a round deep Sinque hole full of water. [17 Sep 05 JW 11.319]

the remains of a…Village…I could plainly trace by the Sinks in which they formed their houses [31 Oct 05 WC 5.362]

a country almost inaccessible from the fallen timber, brush and sink-holes [27 Jan 06 ML 6.239]

Also, a latrine. *See* VAULT.

I derected Sinks to be dug [31 Dec 05 WC 6.146]

dug 2 Sinques [31 Dec 05 JO 9.263]

SIOUAN* {S(Y)OO-un} A widespread language family, primarily comprising Plains groups, SIOUX among them. The *Chiwere* language includes the IOWAY, MISSOURI, and OTOE dialects. *Dhegiha* languages include KANSA-OSAGE, Omaha-PONCA (*see* MAHA), and Quapaw. The MANDAN and CROW-HIDATSA languages (though these tribes were neighbors) are not closely related to each other, or to the other Siouan languages.

SIOUX {soo} A numerous people of the northern Plains (speaking the Sioux language), comprising the Santee and SISSETON on the east, the TETON (or Lakota) to the west, and the YANKTON-YANKTONAI in between. The English name *Sioux* comes through French, from a Chippewa name that probably stems from a word for rattlesnake. Lewis & Clark had the most contact with the Teton, mostly in tense confrontation.

Several Frenchmen…came from the Shew nation. [12 Jun 04 JO 9.013]

those Soues…follow the Buffalow, & Kill them on foot, they pack their Dogs [c. 24 Aug 04 WC 2.507]

SISSETON {SISS-ə-tən} A subdivision of the SIOUX, residing primarily in western Minnesota.

See YANKTON for an example.

SITUATION {sih-tee-AY-shun} A euphemism for 'menstrual period.' *See* COVENTRY, SICK. During such occurrences, female isolation was the rule in many traditional societies.

this man has a daughter new arrived at the age of puberty, who being in a certain situation is not permitted to ascociate with the family but sleeps at a distance from her father's camp and when traveling follows at some distance behind. in this state...the female is not permitted to eat, nor to touch any article of a culinary nature or manly occupation. [30 Apr 06 ML 7.187]

SKATE A ray, a flat fish of the genus *Raja*, with broad, wing-like pectoral fins.

on the bank found a Skeet fish which had been lef by the tide [7 Jan 06 WC 6.175]

SKELETONIZE To strip flesh and clean bones when preparing a scientific specimen.

the 2 Fields killed two large Rams which had large horns. Capt. Lewis had them Scallintinized...to take to the Seat of government. [29 Jul 06 JO 9.343]

SKILLOOT A CHINOOKAN people residing on the Oregon side of the Columbia River. The name probably stems from Clark's misinterpretation of the Chinook word for 'look at him!'

This village contains about 200 men of the Skil-loot nation I counted 52 canoes on the bank in front of this village [4 Nov 05 WC 6.017]

the intermediate merchants and carryers, the Skillutes, may possibly consume a part of this fish themselves [14 Jan 06 ML 6.203]

SKIRT {skət} Margin, border.

we scarcely see a gang of buffaloe without observing a parsel of those faithfull shepherds [wolves] on their skirts [5 May 05 ML 4.113]

The Skirt of timber in the bend above the Chyenne is not very Considerable [25 Aug 06 WC 8.322]

SLAKY (Of land) muddy, the earliest known record of the word in English.

Slaik'y and bad on the N. Side [30 Jun 04 WC 2.333]

SLASH A swamp. **(South)**

I landed and formed a camp on the highest Spot I could find between the hight of the tides, and the Slashers in a Small bottom [15 Nov 05 WC 6.050]

I am...verry Sick, and wet to my Skins waiding the Slashes and marshes. [21 Feb 06 JO 9.273]

I observed Small Canoes which the women make use of to gather Wappato & roots in the Slashes. [2 Apr 06 WC 7.057]

Hence **slashy**.

the Slashey parts have Bull rushes & flags [6 Nov 05 WC 6.027] *we Encamped 10 days in a narrow bottom Slashey in full view of the Ocian* [16 Nov 05 WC 6.059]

SLEEP A night, as a measure of travel. *See* MOON.

from the mouth of that river to the falls is 5 Sleeps [22 Sep 05 WC 5.230]

SLEIGH A sled.

dog Slays [20 Apr 05 WC 4.056]

SLIDE A sled.

Some of the men went down for the meat with a Slide [12 Jan 05 JW 11.119]

SLOOP A sailing vessel with a single mast carrying triangular fore-and-aft sails; more generally, a small ship. *See* BRIG, SCHOONER, SHIP.

[Captain] *Lemon In a Slupe, and they expect him in 3 moons to trade with them.* [1 Jan 06 WC 6.156]

SLOUGH {sloo} A swampy area, or BAYOU. (**South, South Midland**)

I counted 14 large houses in front next the slew [5 Nov 05 WC 6.022]

SLUICE {sloos} A small stream of natural origin, not manmade as in the usual modern sense. *See* BEAVER.

into the Sluce of a large high Island seperated from the S. E Side by a narrow chanel [9 Apr 06 WC 7.100]

SMALL Narrow (the original meaning in Old English).

they ware a kind of leather breech clout…the width of a Common pocket Handerkerchief or Something Smaller and longer. [30 Mar 06 WC 7.035]

Also, regarding a small caliber RIFLE bullet.

I fired 4 times at one [elk] *& did not Kill him, my ball being Small* [.36 caliber] *I think was the reason* [8 Aug 04 WC 2.459]

SMALLPOX An acutely dangerous and infectious viral disease, characterized by high fever and the eruption of small pustules, leaving survivors with pock-marked skin, especially on the face. *See* POX.

the ravages of the Small Pox…swept off 400 [Omaha] *men & women & Children…whin this fatal malady was among them they Carried ther franzey to verry extroadinary length, not only of burning their Village, but they put their wives & Children to D[e]ath with a view of their all going together to Some better Countrey* [14 Aug 04 WC 2.479]

the small pox…is known to be imported [19 Aug 05 ML 5.122]

[On the lower Columbia] *an old man…brought foward a woman who was badly marked with the Small Pox and made Signs that they all died with the disorder which marked her face* [3 Apr 06 WC 7.065]

An Old World disease, smallpox wreaked havoc when introduced among American natives, often causing catastrophic population declines. (In an 1855 Pacific railroad survey report, scientist George Gibbs reported to Congress that few lower Columbia Chinook remained: "the smallpox having nearly finished its work...Some lodges upon the southern peninsula of Shoalwater bay were left without a survivor, and the dead were found by the whites lying wrapped in their blankets as if asleep.") In the expedition's era, inoculation with cowpox, a related but benign disease, recently had been developed as a smallpox preventative. Though Jefferson hoped the Corps might introduce vaccination to the western tribes, logistical and other difficulties apparently prevented Lewis & Clark from doing so.

SMOKABLE Plant material smoked in a pipe, especially in lieu of tobacco (the last of the Corps' tobacco was distributed Christmas Day, 1805). *See* BOIS ROULÉ, REDWOOD, SACKACOMMIS.

a polecat Skin to hold their Smokeables [26 Sep 04 WC 3.115]

SMOKE[1] Tobacco, for smoking.

after brackfast we gave all the Indian men Smoke [20 Oct 05 WC 5.311]

SMOKE[2] (Of cold air over a warm body of water) to produce rising wisps of fog. When the air temperature is very low, as in the following instance, a fog of ice crystals, known as *frost smoke,* arises.

The branch of Trees and the Small groth ar gilded with Ice from the frost of last night... the river began to Smoke at 8 oClock and the Thermometer Stood at 2° below 0 [25 Jan 04 WC 2.165]

SMOKEY Foggy, misty.

a Dark Smokey morning Some rain [28 Jul 04 WC 2.424]

SNAG[1] A tree or large branch embedded in the bottom of a river, posing a risk to passing watercraft. Riverboats were customarily loaded heavy at the bow, to lessen the chance of the hull running up on a snag and hanging up or being overturned. *See* BOW, PLANTER, SAWYER[2].

She Swung round on the Snag, with her broad Side to the Current...by the active exertions of our party we got her off in a fiew Mints. without engerey [9 Jun 04 WC 2.290]

one of the Perogues run a Snag thro her and was near Sinking [28 Aug 04 WC 3.020]

Hence **snaggy**, obstructed by snags.

the Sand bars which Choked up the Missouri and Confined the [river?] to a narrow Snagey Chanel [9 Sep 06 WC 8.354]

SNAG[2] To impale, as on a broken tree limb or branch.

an excellent horse of Cruzatte's snagged himself so badly in the groin in jumping over a parsel of fallen timber that he will...be of no further service [21 Jun 06 ML 8.043]

Also, the impaling object.

Gibson...fell...on a Snag and sent it nearly two inches into the Muskeler part of his thy.
[18 Jul 06 WC 8.202]

SNAKE   Any of various North American peoples speaking Uto-Aztecan languages,
especially the SHOSHONE. *See* (SPANISH MILLED) DOLLAR.

> The Uto-Aztecan family is widespread in the western United States and Mexico,
> and includes Comanche and Nahuatl, the preeminent language of the Aztec
> empire. The captains probably extended the name *Snake* to the Uto-Aztecan
> Northern Paiute, and perhaps also to peoples of other linguistic affliations in the
> region south of the Columbia River. The sign for the Snake Indians in the Plains
> sign language was the same as that for a snake (reptile).

The woman that is with us is a squaw of the Snake nation [8 Apr 05 PG 10.077]

*Our present Camp is the prosise Spot the Snake Indians were Camped at the time the
Minetarries came in Sight, attacked & killed 4 men 4 women & a number of boys* [28
Jul 05 WC 5.009]

*The Indians are afraid to hunt or be on th Lard Side of this Columbia river for fear of
the Snake Ind.* [29 Oct 05 WC 5.349]

*a Canoe arrived...with...a woman whome had been taken prisoner from the Snake Inds.
on Clarks River* [the Deschutes.] *I Sent the Interpreters wife who is a So So ne or Snake
Indian of the Missouri, to Speake to this Squar, they Could not understand each other
Sufficiently to Converse.* [3 Nov 05 WC 6.013]

SNAKE, BLOWING   Clark would have known the eastern hog-nosed snake and here
probably is referring to the western species, *Heterodon nasicus.* A small, non-poisonous
snake, when threatened it bluffs by flattening its head and neck, and striking with a loud
hiss.

Saw a blowing Snake. [7 Jul 06 WC 8.264]

SNAP   (Of a gun) to MISFIRE by failure of the powder charge to ignite. (Of the shooter)
to pull the trigger, without result. The reference is to the sound made by the COCK
snapping forward and the FLINT striking the FRIZZEN. *See* PAN.

*Snaped 7 tims at a large buck. it is Singular as my gun has a Steel frisen and never
Snaped 7 times before in examining her found the flint loose* [16 Sep 05 WC 5.209]

SNIP   A light-colored mark on a horse, especially on the nose or lip.

much the larger portion [of Indian horses] *are of a uniform Colour with Stars, snips,
and white feet* [15 Feb 06 WC 6.315]

SNOWY MOUNTAINS   The Rockies. More specifically here, probably Montana's
Lewis Range.

the wind all this day blew violently hard from the S W. off the Snowey mountains, Cool
[19 Jun 05 WC 4.310]

SOAP, CASTILE A fine white soap consisting of olive oil and lye (sodium hydroxide), named after a region in northern Spain, and still used today for wound care. For another use of olive oil, *see* (VOLATILE) LINIMENT, and of lye, (LYED) CORN.

Pkg 12 lbs Castile Soap [May 03 in Jackson Letters (ed. 2) 1.095]

I gave this man a jentle pirge cleaned & dressed his Sore and left him Some Casteel Soap to wash the Sore [5 May 06 WC 7.212]

SOCKET An iron shoe fitted to the end of a POLE² as protection from rock damage.

most of our small sockets were lost, and the stones were so smooth that the points of their poles sliped [23 Jul 05 ML 4.420]

one of the men killed an otter with a Socket pole [19 Jul 05 JO 9.186]

I detected a fellow in stealing an iron socket of a canoe pole and gave him several severe blows [21 Apr 06 ML 7.152]

SOIL, RIGHT OF Ownership of land.

the bear are...tenatious of their right of soil in this neighbourhood. [17 Jun 05 ML 4.304]

SOLDIER {SOHL-jə} A Plains Indian warrior with policing powers. Warrior societies provided social control during significant diplomatic, ceremonial, and other tribal gatherings, and for large buffalo hunts.

when we were about Setting out... the Soldiars took possession of the Cable [28 Sep 04 WC 3.123]

SOLUS {SOHL-us} Alone (a bookish use of a Latin word).

we nooned it as usual at Collins's Creek where we found Frazier, solus [24 Jun 06 ML 8.048]

SOME Somewhat.

a heavy Deaw last night. Some foggy this morning. [20 Jul 04 JO 9.028]

Also, an indefinite amount, here regarding time.

thoug Some of the pieces appear to be excellent Coal it resists the fire for Some, and consumes without emiting much flaim. [11 Apr 05 WC 4.023]

SOMETHING {SUM-thən} Somewhat.

the Bull Snake, his Colour Some thing like a rattle Snake [5 Aug 04 WC 2.447]

I am Something better of the Rhumutim in my neck [24 Oct 04 WC 3.195]

weather something Colder than yesterday [27 Dec 04 WC 3.262]

SON OF A BITCH Linguistic evidence of CHINOOKAN contact with English-speaking seaborne traders.

the Indians inform us that they speak the same language with ourselves, and give us proofs of their varacity by repeating many words of English, as musquit, powder, shot, nife, file, damned rascal, sun of a bitch &c. [9 Jan 06 ML 6.187]

SORE-EYES   An eye irritation or infection. *See* EYE-WATER, VITRIOL.

a very singular disorder is takeing place amongst our party that of the Sore eyes. three of the party have their eyes inflamed and Sweled in Such a manner as to render them extreamly painfull [19 Sep 06 WC 8.366]

> Such infections probably were various types of conjunctivitis (including the mild form, *pink eye*), caused by bacteria and viruses affecting the eyelid's inner surface. More serious forms of *sore-eyes,* including trachoma and gonorrhea-caused infections, can lead to permanent cornea damage and even blindness.

the Soar eyes...is a violent inflamation of the eyes attended with high fevers and headach, and is extreemly distressing, and frequently attended with the loss of sight [winter 04–05 ML 3.453]

Along the Columbia River, native people suffered greatly from eye problems exacerbated by sand, wind, sun, and other environmental factors.

they have almost invariably soar eyes at all stages of life. the loss of an eye is very common among them; blindness in perdsons of middle age is by no means uncommon, and it is almost invariably a concommitant of old age. [6 Apr 06 ML 7.085]

SORREL   A horse of a reddish-brown color.

the sorrel I obtained is an eligant strong active well broke horse [6 May 06 ML 7.215]

SOUND   The swim-bladder of a fish, by the varying inflation of which a fish controls its vertical position in the water.

the flesh of the beaver is esteemed a delecacy...I think the tale a most delicious morsal, when boiled it resembles in flavor the fresh tongues and sounds of the codfish [2 May 05 ML 4.100]

SOUND-BACK   (Of a horse) not injured by overuse or a poorly fitted saddle.

we...exchanged 2 of our indeferent horses for Sound back horses. [8 Jun 06 WC 7.347]

SOUP, PORTABLE   Dried meat broth, originally developed as a non-perishable food for naval use. The expedition's supply was carried in 32 canisters.

193 lbs. of Portable Soup at 150 Cents $289.50 [30 May 03 in Jackson Letters (ed. 2) 1.081]

we dined & suped on a skant proportion of portable soupe, a few canesters of which, a little bears oil and about 20 lbs. of candles form our stock of provision [18 Sep 05 ML 5.211]

we melted Snow to drink & make some portable Soup [15 Sep 05 JW 11.317]

SOUTHERN WOOD   = SAGE². Originally the name of an aromatic southern European shrub, *Artemisia abrotanum*. (**West**) *the narrow bottoms of the Missouri producing little else but Hysop or southern wood and the pulpy leafed thorn.* [24 May 05 ML 4.189]

SOVEREIGN   (Of a medicine) most efficacious for a specific ailment. *See* GRAIN[1], SIMPLE.

yellow root...is a sovereighn remidy for a disorder common in this quarter called the Soar eyes [winter 04–05 ML 3.453]

I prevailed on him to take a doze of Rushes pills, which I have always found sovereign in such cases [27 Jul 05 ML 4.436]

SPANCEL   {SPAN-səl} To fetter, or HOBBLE, a horse.

Notwithstanding all the precautions I had taken with rispect to the horses one of them had broken his cord of 5 strands of Elkskin and had gone off spanseled. [21 Apr 06 ML 7.151]

SPANISH   (Of the lands west of the Mississippi) under nominal Spanish governance. *See* AMERICAN BOTTOM, CHEYENNE, ILLINOIS.

> The Mississippi country originally was claimed by France in the 17th century, but later ceded to Spain in 1762 following the French and Indian War. For several decades, Spanish galleys and gunboats patrolled the Mississippi from New Orleans to the Illinois country, as the English acquired the east bank (1763), followed by the Americans after the Revolutionary War (1783). In 1800, Napoleon Bonaparte diplomatically wrested Upper Louisiana back into French ownership from the Spanish crown, but French officialdom was slow in coming. Consequently, when Lewis & Clark arrived on the Mississippi in late 1803, Spanish administrators still controlled the Mississippi's west or *Spanish side*, though the non-native immigrant population was mostly French-Canadian and American. Following the Louisiana Purchase (1803), ownership of Upper Louisiana was ceremonially transferred at St. Louis, March 9–10, 1804, from Spain, to France, and then the United States, with Lewis & Clark in attendance.

on our return landed on the spanish side [18 Nov 03 ML 2.093]

arrived oposite three new habitation of some Americans who had settled under the spanish government [22 Nov 03 ML 2.101]

they are bound for the Spanish Country by way of River platte to the panies Indians & purchase horses and cross the Mountains...and git the Spaniards to come and bring their silver & gold and trade it for goods [17 Sep 06 JO 9.364]

Plains horses originally were descended from stock brought to North America by the Spanish beginning in the 16th century. In Lewis & Clark's time, Southern Plains and Southwest tribes continued to trade (and steal) horses from the northern Mexican frontier settlements. *See* (SPANISH MILLED) DOLLAR.

Among the Sosones...we saw several horses with spanish brands on them [15 Feb 06 ML 6.314]

SPECIE {SPEE-shee} Coin, hard cash.

these people have some specia among them, but their circulating medium is principally Horses, Cattle, Cotton & lead [23 Nov 03 ML 2.106]

SPECIFIC A medicine intended to treat a particular illness.

See SIMPLE for an example.

SPICA {SPIKE-ə} The brilliant, bluish alpha star of the constellation Virgo, visible in the summer evening sky, and used by Lewis & Clark for lunar OBSERVATIONS.

Observed the moon ☽ *& Spica* ★ *Star West* [17 Jul 04 WC 2.388]

SPIRE {SPY-ə} The slender stem or stalk of a plant.

every Spire of Grass was covered with the Sand or Dust [23 Aug 04 WC 2.503]

every spire of grass was eaten up by their horses [15 Jul 06 ML 8.109]

SPIRITS Distilled alcoholic beverages, such as brandy, rum, and whiskey. *See* GILL, KEG.

Captain Lewis gave each of the party a Glass of spirit [1 Jan 05 JW 11.115]

we drank the last of our spirits celebrating the day [4 Jul 05 PG 10.109]

Ardent originally meant 'inflammable,' because of spirits containing sufficient alcohol to burn.

they were tradors from St. Louis...they gave us ardent Spirits buiscuits and cheese [14 Sep 06 JO 9.362]

Hence **spirituous**.

We had no spirituous liquors to elevate our spirits this Christmas [25 Dec 05 PG 10.184]

Proof is a measure of alcohol content in beverages—e.g., "100 proof" in modern American terms indicates 50–58% alcohol by volume, the exact ratio depending on the measurement system used. Regarding Gass's entry (below), Clark recorded -10° Fahrenheit at sunrise that day; real proof spirits should not have frozen until the temperature fell to about -40°; thus Gass's spirits must have been watered down.

proof spirits...in fifteen minutes froze into hard ice. [10 Dec 04 PG 10.065]

Spirits were also used in thermometers and (SPIRIT) LEVELS.

Observed Equal altitudes with Sextant and artificial Horizon...in which sperits were substituted for water, it being to could [15° Fahrenheit] *to use the latter.* [28 Jan 05 ML 3.279]

SPLINTER {SPLIN-tə} To immobilize (a broken bone) with a splint.

Cap C Splintered the arm of the man which was broke. [28 Apr 06 WC? 7.178]

SPLIT[1] A splint; a thin, narrow, flexible piece of fiber or wood used in making baskets, hats, or garments.

the head chief had on a jacket that was made of Some kind of worked Splits which would defend off the arrows. [25 Oct 05 JW 11.370]

I purchased...Small baskets to hold Water made of Split and Straw [21 Nov 05 WC 6.076]

Several of the natives...sold our Men several Hatts, which were made out of splits. They were very handsome & curiously worked [19 Jan 06 JW 11.414]

SPLIT² To cut open a fish from head to tail, usually along the back-bone, and gut in preparation for cooking or drying.

I saw maney Squars engaged Splitting and drying Salmon. [17 Oct 05 WC 5.288]

SPOILT {spīlt} Spoiled.

Our Diner to day Consisted of pore Elk boiled, Spilt fish & Some roots, a bad Christmass diner [25 Dec 05 WC 6.137]

SPONGING Wiping the inside of a gun barrel with a rod and patch to remove fouling (powder residue, dirt, and dust).

See FILLET for an example.

SPRIT {spreet, modern spritt} A spar running diagonally up and back from low on the MAST, serving to extend the upper after (rear) corner of a (SPRIT-)SAIL.

> ♦It has been assumed that Lewis's *sprits* in the following passage are simply the yards, or horizontal spars from which the (SQUARE) SAILS of the BOAT were suspended, but it would be uncharacteristic of Lewis to use a technical nautical term so loosely. Both of his phonetic spellings of *sprit* reflect the prevailing nautical pronunciation, and he was familiar with a spritsail rig and distinguished it from a square rig, as is obvious from his reference to the use of both rigs in the white pirogue; *see* (SPRIT-)SAIL. Also, the fact that the sail could still be furled after its spar broke implies that it was a spritsail, since a spritsail would be furled to the mast, which remained standing, whereas a square sail is furled to the yard (which was broken). A square sail with a broken yard certainly would have been lowered immediately, and thus could not have helped carry the boat at "pretty good speed." Though square rigging predominated on western rivers, there are examples of keelboats with gaff rigs, another type of fore-and-aft rig. It thus seems possible that on the Ohio River, Lewis's keelboat carried a spritsail on each of its two masts.♦

hoisted our fore sale...a sudan squal broke the sprete and had very nearly carried away the mast, after which we firled an[d] secured it tho' the wind was so strong as to carry us pretty good speed by means of the arning and firled sails.— struck on a riffle...hoisted our mainsail to assist in driving us over the riffle the wind blew so heard as to break the spreat [6 Sep 03 ML 2.073]

SPRUCE-PINE A name for the genus *Picea*, usually today simply called *spruce*. *Spruce* originally meant a species of fir from *Prussia*.

the timber on the edge of the Prarie is white oke, back is Spruce pine [4 Nov 05 WC 6.015]

SPUCK An immature sea otter (*Enhydra lutris*), from the Lower Chinookan word for 'gray.' (**Pacific Northwest**)

female sea otter with spuck

the spear or gig is used to take the sea otter, the common otter, spuck, and beaver. [15 Jan 05 ML 6.208]

SPUN (Of tobacco) in a TWIST.

50 lbs. Spun Tobacco. [Jun 03 ML in Jackson Letters (ed. 2) 1.072]

SPY A scout.

our...Spis discovered the sign of a war party [5 Jun 04 WC 2.278]

SQUAW An Indian woman. *Squaw* appears in the journals without the derogatory connotation in current use. In early 17th-century New England, the word was adopted into English from an Algonquian language, in which it meant simply 'woman.' *See* SAVAGE.

In one Camp found 3 Squars & 3 young ones [26 Mar 04 WC 2.181]

prairie dog

as Soon as they saw the Squar wife of the interperters they pointed to her...the sight of This Indian woman...confirmed those people of our friendly intentions [19 Oct 05 WC 5.306]

SQUIRREL, BARKING The prairie dog, which French Canadians called *petit chien*, 'little dog.'

I Saw a village of Barking Squriel 970 yds. long, and 800 yds. wide [11 Sep 04 WC 3.065]

> Lewis is credited for recording the first zoological description of the prairie dog, whence its Linnean name *Cynomys ludovicianus*, meaning 'Lewis's dog-mouse.' *Lewis* is an English spelling of French *Louis*, derived from an early Germanic name rendered in Latin as *Ludovicus* (consequently, the Latin source for the prairie dog's scientific name). German *Ludwig*, Italian *Luigi*, and Spanish *Luis* are also descended from *Ludovicus*.

STALKING-HEAD A decoy used in hunting.

I observed in all the Lodges...decoys, or Stocking heads as they are Sometimes called. these decoys are for the deer and is formed of the Skin of the head and upper portion of the neck of that animale extended in the nateral Shape by means of a fiew little Sticks placed within. the hunter when he Sees a deer conseals himself and with his hand givs to the decoy the action of a deer at feed [7 May 06 WC 7.224]

STALLED, STALL-FED (Of an animal) kept and fed in a stall for fattening.

the Men eat the flesh of it [a horse] *with as good a relish as they would have done had it been a Stalled fed beef.* [2 Oct 05 JW 11.337]

STANCHION {STƆN-shən, modern STAN-shən} (In a boat) a fixed upright support.

This Iron boat, or rather frame was made out of wrought Iron…and had ribbs, Stauncheons & beams of the same [21 Jun 05 JW 11.207]

STAND When a body of water is neither rising nor falling.

the right hand fork falling[,] the other at a Stand [3 Jun 05 WC 4.251]

STAR, MORNING {MOH-nən STAH} The planet Venus, visible in the eastern sky on the morning of August 27, 1804.

the Morning Star was observed to be very large [27 Aug 04 WC 3.016]

STAR, POLE The North Star, or Polaris, the last star in the Little Dipper's handle. For an observer on earth, it is positioned very close to true north. Determining the North Star's AZIMUTH with a compass gives magnetic VARIATION, and measuring its elevation yields LATITUDE.

Observed Altitude of pole Star with Sextant [17 Jul 04 ML 2.390]

STARBOARD {STAH-bəd} (When in a vessel and looking forward) the right side of the hull. Abbreviated also *s.*, *sd.*, *stard*. *See* LARBOARD.

we came too on the Starbd side and stayed all night [20 Nov 03 ML 2.097]

START {staht} To break loose. *See* CLEVERLY.

they got out on the rock and attempted to Shove the canoe off the rock, but could not Start hir [14 Oct 05 JW 11.352]

STAVE To make a hole (in a boat's hull), usually accidentally. Originally, to break a BARREL into its component *staves*.

I had my canoe stove, and she sunk. [8 Oct 05 PG 10.151]

STAY To reside for a considerable time (in a place), a common expression in the **South**. *See* STOUT.

Two men belonging to the N. W. Company, who stay at the Grossventers village, came to the fort. [18 Jan 05 PG 10.070]

STEEL = FIRE-STEEL.

30 Steels for striking or making fire [Jun 03 ML in Jackson Letters (ed. 2) 1.071]

STEM Making headway, or at least holding one's own, against current or wind. *See* POLE^2.

water verry Strong So Hard that we Could Hardley Stem it [3 Jul 04 CF 9.385]

the Boat was in danger of being thrown up of the Sand but the men were all out in an Instant holding hir out Stemming the wind [14 Jul 04 JO 9.025]

STEP OFF To pace off; to measure distance by counting one's steps. *See* PACE.

Sent one man…to Step off the Distance across Isthmus [12 Aug 04 WC 2.471]

STERLING {STə-lin} English currency, which for some time after the Revolution continued as legal tender in the new United States.

[Indian trade] *merchandise is estimated at an advance of 125 per cent. on the sterling cost.* [1806 WC 3.390]

STERN {stən} The after (back) end of a boat. *Astern* means toward, or at, the stern. *See* BOW.

the Boat run on Logs three times to day, owing her being too heavyly loaded a Sturn [15 May 04 WC 2.231]

I had the loading in the Boat & perogue examined and changed So as the Bow of each may be heavyer laded than the Stern [18 May 04 WC 2.237]

STERN-MAN The crewman stationed at the stern of a canoe or pirogue. *See* BOW-MAN.

the bowsman Cruzatte by repeated threats so far brought Charbono the Sternman to his recollection that he did his duty while two hands bailed the perogue [14 May 05 WC 4.154]

STICKLE To haggle in trading. *See* HIGGLER, TIGHT.

they are Close deelers, & Stickle for a verry little, never close a bargin except they think they have the advantage [12 Dec 05 WC 6.123]

STOCK The wooden piece on which a gun's barrel and LOCK are mounted, whence the expression *lock, stock, and barrel* for 'the whole works.'

the fire broke out into the woods, and burned up his shot pouch powder horn & the stalk of his rifle. [23 May 05 JW 11.165]

the stock of one of the bluntderbushes on board [29 May 05 ML 4.215]

STOMACHIC {modern stə-MACK-ik} (Of a medicine) good for the stomach, aiding digestion.

wild ginger…is a strong stomatic stimelent, and frequently used in sperits with bitter herbs [winter 04–05 ML 3.453]

STONE A male animal's testicle or other gland. *See* (STONE-)HORSE.

The male beaver has six stones [7 Jan 06 ML 6.175]

he cut them [horses] *without tying the string of the stone* [14 May 06 ML 7.257]

STOUT (Of a person or animal) strong. Here, referring to members of a Sioux warrior society. (**South, South Midland**)

those are Stout likely men who Stay by them Selves, fond of mirth and assume a degree of Superiority [30 Aug 04 WC 3.024]

(Of a stream) substantial. *See* BOLD, HARD², STRONG.

we followed the creek downwards about two miles, passing a stout branch...which flowed in on the wright. [13 May 06 ML 7.252]

STRAITEN To suffer from a shortage.

their relations...were much streightened at that place for the want of food [1 Apr 06 ML 7.049]

STRATUM A rock layer. The captains often used the plural *strata* as singular, and sometimes *stratums* as plural. *See* BITUMINOUS.

a High bluff...containing many horizontal narrow Stratas of Carbonated wood [8 Apr 05 WC 4.014]

In the face of this tremendeous precipic...there is a Strater of white earth [7 Jan 06 WC 6.178]

STRING The *vas deferens*, a thin muscular tube carrying semen from the testicle (STONE) to the ejaculatory duct. Cutting of the string is part of the QUIETING procedure on a (STONE-)HORSE.

he cut them [horses] without tying the string of the stone as is usual...he takes care to scrape the string very clean and to seperate it from all the adhereing veigns before he cuts it. [14 May 06 ML 7.257]

STRIP, WAY- ♦Perhaps one of the thin strips of wood or bark for *lining* the (IRON) BOAT.♦

I set [Patrick Gass] at work to make the way strips out of some willow limbs which tho' indifferent were the best which could be obtained. [1 Jul 05 ML 4.349]

some were making tar or attempting to make it, others were attatching the skins on the boat, other cuting and fiting the bark for lining puting in the woodworke &c [3 Jul 05 ML 4.354]

STRIPE To whip, a meaning not recorded since the 16th century in *OED*.

we hurried down from the bluff on which we were and...striped our horses [28 Jul 06 ML 8.138]

STRIPES, WAR- War PAINT on the face.

they wished to live in peace and bury their war Stripes in the ground. [1 Jul 06 JO 9.329]

STRONG (Of a stream) hard flowing. *See* BOLD, HARD[2], STOUT.

had strong Watter to Goe throug [8 Jun 04 JW 11.020]

day Clear water Strong [14 Jun 04 CF 9.380]

(Of water) containing large amounts of dissolved minerals. *See* FREESTONE.

Sergt. Pryor and Drewyer discovered a bold salt spring of strong water [10 Sep 04 ML 3.063]

(Of diet) nourishing.

as our fatigues hard we find that poor meat alone is not Strong diet [10 Aug 05 JW 11.263]

STROUD A type of heavy woolen cloth manufactured for the Indian trade.

she dresses after the Shawnee manner with stroud leggings and mockinsons [23 Nov 03 ML 2.107]

we [Arikara] are pore our women have no Strouds & Knives to Cut their meat [12 Oct 04 WC 3.165]

STUD A stallion, not yet subjected to QUIETING. *See* (STONE-)HORSE.

our horses are troublesome as the most of them are Studs. [23 Apr 06 JO 9.296]

we eat Several of our Stud horses [14 May 06 JO 9.310]

SUBLUNARY {SUB-lə-nerry} Material, ephemeral, mundane, earthly (literally, 'under the moon').

This day I completed my thirty first year, and conceived that I had in all human probability now existed about half the period which I am to remain in this Sublunary world. [18 Aug 05 ML 5.118]

> Lewis overestimated the time remaining to him. Long plagued by depression, in 1809 he died at age 35 of two pistol-shot wounds to the head and chest, apparently self-inflicted.

SUBTRACTIVE (Of an error in an instrument's observation) low. *See* ADDITIVE.

Error of Sextant Subtractive…8' 45" [12 Apr 05 ML 4.025]

The Standing error of the Sextant is 8' 45" – or Subs. [9 Jun 05 ML 4.273]

SUCK A whirlpool. *See* BOIL².

an Indian…Swam to the Goose and brought in on Shore, at the head of the Suck [31 Oct WC 5.363]

SUET {SYOO-it} Solid fat around the kidneys and either side of the lower backbone, used in cooking. *See* (WHITE) PUDDING.

a bear…eat up about thirty weight of buffaloe suit which was hanging on a pole. [27 Jun 05 ML 4.336]

we had a very comfortable dinner, of bacon, beans, suit dumplings & buffaloe beaf [4 Jul 05 ML 4.362]

SUGAR-TREE {SHə-gə} The sugar maple, *Acer saccharum*, the sap of which yields good syrup in spring when thawing days alternate with freezing nights.

sugar maple

a Butifull a peas of Land as ever I saw walnut shoger tree ash and mulber trees [4 Jun 04 CF 9.377]

the fist appearance of the blue crain, sugar trees run [13 Feb 04 WC 2.177]

SUGARLOAF Sugar in a molded, hardened cone.

A high Mound which rises to a point like a Sugar lofe [c25 Nov 03 WC 1 map 3b]

those lodges are about 15 to 20 feet Diametr Stetched on Poles like a Sugar Loaf, made of Buffalow Skins Dressed [26 Sep 04 WC 3.115]

Also, a conical hill or mountain. *See* KNOB.

The sugarloaf point or nobb [26 Nov 03 ML 2.114]

SUIT Someone, or something, provided (attached).

met with Colo. Rodney...in his suit was Majr Claiborne [7 Sep 03 ML 2.074]

he is remarkable for having once had a remarkable suit of hair [23 Nov 03 ML 2.107]

the boat...is strong and will carry at least 8,000 lbs. with her suit of hands [5 Jul 05 ML 4.363]

SULFUR, FLOWER OF {SUL-fə} Powdered sulfur, usually applied as a fungicide or insecticide, or for intestinal worms. Clark's intention (below) in giving it to a quadriplegic Nez Perce (perhaps paralyzed by a stroke) is a mystery; *see* SWEAT.

this man I had given a fiew doses of Flower of Sulpher & Creme of Tarter and derected he Should take the Cold bath every morning. [24 May 06 WC 7.285]

SULTRY {probably Sɔ-tree or Sɔ-təree in the journals} Humid, muggy. (**South, South Midland**)

dark Sultrey weather...Some Thunder [20 Apr 04 WC 2.205]

the Climate is every day perceptably wormer and air more Sultery than I have experienced for a long time. [9 Sep 06 WC 8.354]

SUMAC {SHOO-make, SHOO-mate; modern SOO-mack, SHOO-mack} Any of various shrubs of the genus *Rhus*. See BEAR-GRASS.

I saw near the creek...the shumate of the small species [13 Aug 05 ML 5.077]

mountain ash

Here, probably referring to mountain ash (genus *Sorbus*). Both mountain ash and sumac have compound leaves and red or orange fruit.

[*A thrush*] *was feeding on the buries of a species of shoemake or ash* [20 Sep 05 ML 5.217]

SUN, REFLECTING Bright images seen on opposite sides of the sun, caused by reflection from ice particles in the atmosphere. Also called *sun dog, mock sun, parhelion.*

The Indians kill great numbers of Buffalow to day— 2 reflecting...Suns to day [8 Dec 04 WC 3.255]

SUNFLOWER A tall plant (*Helianthus annuus*) common along the Missouri. In some areas, the oil-rich seeds served as an important food.

The sunflower is in bloom and abundant in the river bottoms. The Indians of the Missouri particularly those who do not cultivate maze make great uce of the seed of this plant for bread, or use it in thickening their soope. [17 Jul 05 ML 4.391]

On the Columbia, Clark probably meant a sunflower relative—the springtime-blooming arrowleaf balsamroot, *Balsamorhiza sagittata*. The latter's stem is edible; the Missouri sunflower's is not.

met Several parties of women and boys in Serch of herbs & roots..maney of them had parcels of the Stems of the Sun flower [14 Apr 06 WC 7.121]

SWATH {swɔth} A strip of crop cut down with a scythe; also, the grass or grain so harvested.

the grass is also luxouriant and would afford a fine swarth of hay [28 Jul 05 ML 5.008]

SWEAT[1] A steam-bath. See HOT-HOUSE.

3 pieces of Scarlet...had been left as a Sacrifice near one of their Swet houses [3 May 05 WC 4.105]

I saw a curious Swet house under ground, with a Small whole at top to pass in...the hot Stones, which those in threw on as much water as to create the temperature of heat they wished [11 Oct 05 WC 5.262]

Here, treatment for paralysis (*see* SULFUR).

we gave the sick [Nez Perce] *Cheif a severe sweat today, shortly after which he could... work his toes pretty well* [30 May 06 ML 7.308]

SWEAT[2] To steam roots such as CAMAS in a pit in the ground, rendering them palatable by converting complex carbohydrates into sugars.

The Chief Set before me a large platter of Onions which had been Sweeted. [16 Apr 06 WC 7.128]

gave us Some commass roots which had been Swetted last fall. [10 May 06 JO 9.308]

SWEET-GRASS A fragrant grass (*Hierochloe odorata*) prized by native people for religious ceremonies and in basket-making. See PAINT.

Sweet grass which the Indian plat and ware around their necks for its cent which is of a Strong sent like that of the Vinella [24 Jul 06 WC 8.218]

SWELL As in the modern sense, a large, wind-driven wave. (*See* LAY for an example.)

Also, a large standing wave in a rapids.

The Swells were So high and the Canoes roled in Such a manner as to cause Several to be verry Sick [8 Nov 05 WC 6.035]

SWIM To set afloat.

several of the creeks would yet swim our horses [3 Jun 06 ML 7.331]

SWIM, HORSE- To cross a body of water on, or with, a swimming horse.

in passing the 6th and last Chanel Colter horse Swam and with Some dificuelty he made the Opposite Shore [5 Jul 06 WC 8.164]

SWIVEL A large-bore gun mounted on a pivoting rest. The powerful recoil allowed its use only on the keelboat. *See* BLUNDERBUSS.

we heard Several guns fire down the river, we answered them by a Discharge of a Swivile on the Bow [29 May 04 WC 2.263]

the large Swivel loaded...with 16 Musquet Ball...the 2 other Swivels loaded well with Buck Shot [25 Sep 04 JO 9.068]

our Swivel Could no longer be Serveceable to us as it could not be fireed on board the largest Perogue [16 Aug 06 WC 8.303]

T

TABLE A mesa, or flat-topped hill. (*Mesa* means 'table' in Spanish.)

some remakable tables in the Lard. plains [28 Jul 06 WC 8.242]

TACK (Of a sailing vessel or, figuratively, of anything waterborne) to change course.

[A bear] Came within about 40 yards of us, and tacked about. [6 Aug 06 WC 8.282]

TACKLE To harness (a draft animal). *See* GEAR.

we got up our 4 horses tackled them in the truck waggons [20 Jul 06 JO 9.339]

TAFIA {TAFF-ee-yə} A low-grade rum distilled from molasses or brown sugar. In 1791, soldiers on the Ohio frontier received "one gill of whiskey, or half a gill of taffia, per day" (*ASPIA* I. 166).

the men merrily Disposed, I give them all a little Taffia and permitted 3 Cannon fired [25 Dec 04 WC 3.261]

our officers Gave each man a drink of Taffe, which we Stood in need off [30 Nov 04 JO 9.100]

TAIL, MILL- A channel carrying fast-flowing water downstream from a mill-wheel.

the River all confined in a narrow channel...ran as [s]wift as a mill tale [13 Oct 05 JW 11.351]

TAKE Enter; take to (the water, etc.)

they found it to be 17 miles...to where we can take water again. [20 Jun 05 JW 11.204]

a deer...took the river tho the Inds had wounded it [22 May 06 JO 9.314]

we...took the hills on to a ridge of falling timber [16 Jun 06 JO 9.323]

To go; "take off."

[Mountain sheep] *took down the bluffs* [29 Apr 05 JO 9.139]

TAKE UP To stop (as for the night). *See* COME TO, LIE BY.

took up at the head of Brown's Island [5 Sep 03 ML 2.072]

TALK A speech delivered to Indians. *See* (RED) FLAG.

by him we Sent a talk to the nation, explanitory of our hoisting the red flag under the white [28 Sep 04 WC 3.124]

TAMARACK {TAM-ə-rack} Western larch, *Larix occidentalis.* Of ALGONQUIAN origin, the name originally applied to *Larix laricina* of northeast North America. Larches are unusual among conifers for shedding needles in the fall. *See* HACKMATACK. (**North**)

this Mountain is covered with Spruce & Pitch pine fir, & what is called to the Northard Hackmatack & Tamerack [14 Sep 05 WC 5.204]

TANGENT-SCREW = MICROMETER. *See* QUADRANT.

Tangent screw Quadrant [$]22. [31 May 03 in Jackson Letters (ed. 2) 1.082]

TANNER'S OOZE {TÆ-nəz OOZ} Liquid in a tanner's vat. Its color is due to the infusion of tannin-rich materials such as oak-bark and sumac, and the strong odor comes from hides soaking in it during tanning (*see* CASTOR).

[Red squirrel] *bellies are of a redish yellow, or tanners ooze colour* [1 Dec 05 ML 6.102]

TARTAR {TAH-tə} A potassium salt taken to induce vomiting.

1 [oz.] Tartar Emetic [$].10 [26 May 03 in Jackson Letters (ed. 2) 1.080]

Capt. Clarks black man York is very unwell today and he gave him a doze of tartar emettic which operated very well [7 July 05 ML 4.365]

my man York Sick, I give him a dosh of Tarter. [7 Jul 05 WC 4.366]

we gave [Sacagawea's son]...a doze of creem of tartar and applyed a fresh poltice of onions. [24 May 06 ML 7.282]

TELL OFF To count off and detach men for duty.

the Captn. formd. his men...and told them off in Sections [3 Nov 04 JW 11.108]

TENT A piece of gauze or other fabric placed in a wound to keep it open and promote healing from the inside out. A tent perhaps prevented Lewis's gunshot wound from becoming dangerously abscessed. *See* LINT, MENDING HAND.

Capt. C. opened the absess introduced a tent and dressed it with basilicon [5 May 06 ML 7.210]

TENT, COMMON An A-frame canvas tent, 6 or 7 feet square and about 6 feet high, designed to accommodate five or six soldiers.

I had [trade goods]*...secured with my oilcloths and a common-tent* [17 Sep 03 ML 2.083]

TERRAPIN {TERR-ə-pən} Any of several salt-marsh turtles of the east coast, where English colonists adopted the Virginia ALGONQUIAN name *torope*. Here, probably referring to the painted turtle, *Chrysemys picta*.

see a number of water tarripens. [25 Jun 05 ML 4.331]

TETON {TEE-tɔn} A division of the Sioux people, also known as the Lakota. The name is Sioux, probably meaning 'prairie-dwellers.'

a Band of Sieux called the Tetons of 80 Lodges wer Camped near the mouth of the next River [23 Sep 04 WC 3.104]

THAWY {THɔ-wee} (Of weather) thawing.

the weather is thoughy So that the Snow melts off the huts [15 Jan 05 JO 9.110]

THONG *Throng* is a rare variant of *thong*, perhaps influenced by *throng* 'crowd.' The phrase, "2 longest coach whip Throngs," appears in a Virginia business letter written to London in 1773. *See* POGGAMAGON, WATAP.

[Wild] pettatoe...is...strung upon throngs of leather or bark and hung in the roofs of their lodges [winter 03–04 ML 2.223]

The dogs at the Cathlahmahs had bitten the trong assunder which confined his canoe and she had gone a drift. [11 Mar 06 ML 6.401]

THORN, FLESHY-LEAFED Also **pulpy-leaved thorn**. Greasewood (*Sarcobatus vermiculatus*) is a shrub that characteristically grows in dry, alkaline soils of the West.

the wild hysop sage, fleshey leaf thorn, and some other herbs also grow in the plains and hills [12 May 05 ML 4.146]

THRING To throw or dash violently.

~~thrung~~ throwed the Stearsman over board [8 Oct 05 JW 11.341]

THUNDER-GUST {THUN-də} A strong wind (squall) accompanying a thunderstorm.

in the evining a thunder gust passed from the S W, without rain [17 Apr 05 WC 4.049]

TIDE The twice-daily falling (or low) tide is an *ebb* tide; whereas a rising (or high) tide is the *flood*.

we are compelled to form our Camp between the hite of the Ebb and flood tides, and rase our baggage on logs [8 Nov 05 WC 6.036]

We loaded our Canoes and went with the ebb tide down the River about 4 Miles [15 Nov 05 JW 11.393]

the Wind high from the So West, This caused the Tide of flood to rise much higher, than it commonly did [22 Nov 05 JW 11.397]

A spring tide, occurring twice a month at the new and full moons, has a greater rise and fall than normal.

a Spring tide...rose 2 feet higher than Common flud tides [4 Dec 05 WC 6.107]

Here, a river's seasonal water-level.

the yellowstone river...was falling at this time & appeard to be nearly at it's summer tide. [26 Apr 05 ML 4.071]

TIDEWATER {TĪD-wah-tə} The coastal zone, extending inland as far as ocean tides affect the lower reaches of rivers and streams. *See* WATERMARK.

we first met with this brant on tide water. [15 Mar 06 WC 6.420]

beacon rock...may be esteemed the head of [Columbia] *tide water* [6 Apr 06 ML 7.078]

TIDEWAY The lower portion of a river subject to tidal fluctuations. Here, regarding the Columbia.

We are now [in] *tide way* [4 Nov 05 JW 11.385]

TIGHT Compact, neatly constructed.

The fusies are Short and tight. [winter 04–05 WC 3.484]

Also, hard-bargaining. *See* HIGGLER, STICKLE.

they [Clatsop] *are tite Deelers, value Blu & white beeds verry highly* [12 Dec 05 WC 6.123]

TILLAMOOK {TILL-ə-mook} A Salishan-speaking people of the Oregon coast, south of the CLATSOP. A Chinookan name meaning 'those of Nehalem Bay.'

this blubber...they [Clatsop] *had obtained from their neighbours the Callamucks...near whose vilage a whale had recently perished.* [3 Jan 06 ML 6.162]

they wer...Situated near 4 houses of Clatsops & Killamox, who they informed me had been verry kind and attentive to them. [7 Jan 06 WC 6.177]

TIMBER, FALLEN {TIM-bə} Blown-down trees, sometimes in impenetrable tangles.

the fallen timber in addition to the slippry roads made our march slow and extreemly laborious on our horses. [15 Jun 06 ML 8.025]

In the 1900 U.S. census, a West Virginia stream was consecutively referred to as *Fallen Timber Run* and *Falling Timber Run*: <http://www.us-census.org/states/ westvirginia/teams/Wetzel1900.htm> (2004). *Falling* here, as in Clark's quotation below, may be a reverse spelling of *fallen*, with *-n* hypercorrected to *-ng*.

Killed nothing in those emence mountains of stones falling timber & brush [18 Sep 05 WC 5.213]

At the Battle of Fallen Timbers (August 1794), General "Mad Anthony" Wayne defeated an Indian confederation that for two decades forestalled white settlement of the Old Northwest's trans-Ohio frontier. Lt. William Clark, 24 years old at the time, participated in the Ohio campaign. Fought in a blowdown close to the Maumee River (today's Toledo, Ohio, vicinity), the clash sometimes is called the Battle of *Falling* Timbers.

TIME, MEAN   The time kept by a CHRONOMETER for the purpose of determining LONGITUDE, based on the constant motion of an imaginary *mean sun* returning to the MERIDIAN exactly at noon each day in all seasons of the year. Abbreviated M.T.

Chronometer's daily rate of going...is too slow on mean time [15 Jan 05 ML 3.275]

TIPPET   A scarf-like garment.

The tippet of the Snake Indians is the most eligant peice of Indian dress I ever saw, the neck or collar...formed of a strip of dressed Otter skin with the fur...they attach one to two hundred and fifty little roles of Ermin skin [20 Aug 05 ML 5.127]

I observed a tippit woarn by Hohâstillpilp, which was formed of human scalps and ornamented with the thumbs and fingers of several men which he had slain in battle. [13 May 06 ML 7.253]

TIRESOME   {TY-ə-sum} Tiring.

Th party much fatigued in crossing 1 mountain & 4 high Points Steep & Slipery, also Stony Beach Slippery and tiresom [8 Jan 06 WC 6.181]

TO   Compared with.

warm to what it has been. [15 Jan 05 JW 11.120]

TOLERABLE   Fair, passable; moderately.

I walked on the bank, &...Shot a beaver & 2 Deer, one of the Deer in tolerable order [26 Apr 05 WC 4.073]

they Shot a Bull buffaloe which was Tollorable fat. [21 Oct 04 JO 9.088]

this evening...would have been verry agreeable, had the Misquiters been tolerably Pacifick [27 Jul 04 WC 2.421]

TOMAHAWK, PIPE-   A tomahawk with a hollow handle and a pipe-bowl affixed to the back of the blade head. Lewis requested two dozen, apparently for issuing to the expedition's men.

Arms & Accoutrements...24 Pipe Tomahawks [Jun 03 ML in Jackson Letters (ed. 2) 1.070]

I left my Tommahawk on the Small Island...which makes me verry Sorry...as I had used it common to Smoak in. [1 Aug 05 JW 11.250]

two canoe loads of Savages followed us and Stole Capt. Clarks pipe tommahawk which he had been Smoaking with them. [4 Nov 05 JO 9.250]

this Chief had a large fine pipe tomahawk which...he got from a Trader [11 Apr 06 WC 7.109]

TONGUE, COUPLING-   A wooden pole connecting the front set of TRUCK wheels to the rear wheels.

we had great dificuelty in getting on as the axeltree broke Several times, and the Cuppling tongus of the wheels which was of Cotton & willow [22 Jun 05 WC 4.326]

TOTE To carry. Originally a southern word, probably introduced into English by Bantu-speaking African slaves, and now common in modern American speech. (**South**)

we Saw a great nomber of Squaws employed in toteing wood across the River in their Buffalow hide cannoes [12 Oct 04 JO 9.083]

TOUCH ON THE RIGHT STRING A musical metaphor; to strike the right chord (with someone).

I soon found that I had touched him on the right string [15 Aug 05 ML 5.096]

TOW A mass of cleaned, but unspun, flax or hemp fibers, useful for medical purposes, wiping gun barrels, and as packing material.

I found much difficulty in stoping the blood which I could not effect untill I applyed a tight bandage with a little cushon of wood and tow on the veign below the wound. [18 Jun 06 ML 8.035]

TRADE American and European traders were included in the highly developed economic inter-relationships of the lower Columbia's native peoples when sailing vessels began frequenting the North Pacific in the 1790s. Such indigenous trade networks existed, to varying degrees, throughout all of North America. On the Great Plains, a primary node for native trade centered on the MANDAN villages. *See* CATHLAMET, CHINOOK, (SPANISH MILLED) DOLLAR, GROS VENTRE, SPANISH.

the articles which they [Chinookan tribes] *appear to trade mostly i e' Pounded fish, Beargrass, and roots; cannot be an object of comerce with furin merchants— however they git in return...Blue and white beeds copper Tea Kittles, brass arm bands, some Scarlet and blue robes...those beeds the*[y] *trafick with Indians Still higher up this river for roabs, Skins, cha-pel-el bread, beargrass &c. who in their turn trafick with those under the rockey mountains for Beargrass, Pashico roots & robes &c.* [1 Nov 05 WC 5.371]

TRADING-HOUSE Trading post.

Camped on a Sand bar, opposit a Tradeing house, where a Mr. Valles & 2 men had Some fiew goods to trade with the Sioux [1 Oct 04 WC 3.133]

TRAIL = DRAG.

What we caught were taken with trails or brush nets. [15 Aug 04 PG 10.028]

TRAIN-OIL Whale oil. Of Dutch origin, the word has nothing to do with railroads.

we also purchased a small quantity of train oil for a pair of Brass armbands and a hat for some fishinghooks. [19 Jan 06 ML 6.221]

TRAVERSE {noun TRÆ-vus, verb trə-VƏS} To determine the locations of survey-points by measuring bearings and distances between successive points. *See* COURSE, POINT[1].

they traversed & measured the River and [Great] *falls* [20 Jun 05 JO 9.170]

Also, the survey thus made.

A Circumferentor...has also been employed in taking the traverse of the river [22 Jul 04 ML 2.413]

we...take it's general course and lay down the small bends by the eye on our daily traverse or chart. [15 Jul 05 ML 4.383]

TREAT To negotiate diplomatically.

10 of their nation [Arikara] *had come up to the Mandanes villages to treat & Smoak a peace pipe with them* [7 Apr 05 JO 9.126]

TREATY A council.

Captn. Lewis Brought them [Otoe and Missouri] *to a treaty* [3 Aug 04 JW 11.050]

TREMENDOUS {trə-MEN-juss} Astonishingly terrible. The word usually has negative connotations in the journals.

this fire passed us...and lookd truly tremendious. [29 Oct 04 WC 3.209]

Those Squals were Suckceeded by rain, ! O how Tremendious is the day. [28 Nov 05 WC 6.092]

TRENCHER {TREN-chə} A wooden platter or shallow dish. See SALAL.

we observed...Baskets of different Sizes, wooden boles, robes Skins, trenchers, and various Kind of trinkets [20 Oct 05 WC 5.311]

TRUCK One of the low wagons built to portage boats and baggage around the GREAT FALLS[1]. The wheels (22 inches in diameter) were sections cut from a cottonwood tree. *See* AXLETREE, HOUNDS, (COUPLING-)TONGUE.

I with the party the truck wheels & poles to Stick up in the prarie as a guide, Set out on our return [23 Jun 05 WC 4.328]

the Sales were hoised in the Canoes...and the wind was great relief to them being Sufficently Strong to move the Canoes on the Trucks [25 Jun 05 WC 4.333]

Also **truckle**.

We continued here to repair our waggons or truckles [16 Jul 06 PG 10.254]

TRY To extract oil or grease from flesh by heating. *Try* originally meant 'to separate the valuable from the worthless.'

I had three Kegs of Buffalow Grease tried up. [26 Jun 05 WC 4.335]

we tryed out 5 gallons of bears oil and put it in a keg for the mountains [15 May 06 JO 9.310]

TUCK A blow or stroke (originally of a drumstick on a drum).

we have latterly so frequently had our Stock of provisions reduced to a minimum and Sometimes taken a Small tuck of fasting that 3 days full allowance exites no concern. [20 Jan 06 WC 6.224]

TUG A strap or rope.

See RUDDER-IRONS for quotation.

TUM Celilo Falls on the Columbia River.

the nativs who live near the falls below which place they all discribe by the term Timm [21 Oct 05 WC 5.317]

> *Tum* is CHINOOK Jargon for 'make a sound,' and is found also in *tumtum* 'heart (-beat), mind, will, thought, plan,' and *tumwata* (*tum* + English *water*) 'waterfall.' This is the first (and most upstream) Chinook Jargon word recorded in the journals. In Nez Perce, *tim* means 'thud,' the sound of something falling or dropping. These words are onomatopoetic, however, making it difficult to establish the exact source-language for *Timm*. Clark called Mt. Hood *Timm or falls mountain* [5.318].

TUMOR {TYOO-mə} Any sort of tissue-swelling, especially (as here) a BOIL[1]. In the early 19th century, the word gradually began to be used in the modern way, indicating a cancerous malignancy. *See* FELON, WHITLOW.

three men with Tumers went on shore [14 Jun 05 WC 4.295]

we have two men with toumers and unable to work. [31 July 05 WC 5.020]

TURN {tən} A walk.

Shields took a small tern and killed a deer. [30 Jun 06 ML 8.065]

TUSH Canine tooth, fang; a variant of *tusk*. *See* MOST. (**South, South Midland**)

one of the hunters... killed a panther...the turshes long the tallants large [3 Aug 05 JW 11.253]

TUSHAPAW The SALISHAN-speaking FLATHEAD tribe of western Montana. ♦This name perhaps is from Shoshone *tatasiba* 'people with shaved heads.' ♦

Flat Head Inds...Tut-see-was [winter 04–05 WC 3.444]

my [Shoshone] *guide Shewed me a road from the N Which Came into the one I was in which he Said went to a large river which run to the north on which was a Nation he called Tushapass* [23 Aug 05 WC 5.157]

met with 3 Tushapaw Indians who were in pursuit of 2 Snake Indians that hade taken from ther Camps...21 horses [10 Sep 05 WC 5.197]

we came to the Smooth plains where we Saw the 1st flat heads or Tusepaw last year [5 Jul 06 JO 9.331]

Tush-She-pah's Nation reside on a N. fork of Clarks river and rove on Clarks river in Spring and Summer and the fall and winter on the Missouri. [c. Jun 06 WC 6.488]

TWIST A twisted tobacco roll, usually consisting of one leaf; also called SPUN tobacco. Smaller than a CARROT.

we gave those [Teton] *boys two twists of Tobacco to carry to their Chiefs & Warriors to Smoke* [23 Sep 04 WC 3.104]

they Got 3 feet of twist tobacco for each [wolf] Skin. [21 Jan 05 JO 9.111]

TYEE {TIE-ee} CHINOOK Jargon for 'chief,' from a word meaning 'elder brother' in the NOOTKA language of Vancouver Island. Lewis's spelling suggests that the Chinook Jargon speakers he met pronounced the word {TIE-ay}. *See* KAMOSUK. (**Pacific Northwest**)

we were visited by our near neighbours, Chief or Tiá, Co-mo-wool...and six Clatsops. [3 Jan 06 ML 6.162]

I was visited by Tia Shâh-hâr-wâr-cap and eleven of his [Cathlamet] *nation in one large canoe* [10 Jan 06 ML 6.192]

U

ULTIMO Of the previous calendar month. *See* INSTANT.

here they remained and dryed their articles the evening of the 30th ulto: [1 Jun 06 WC 7.324]

UNBROKEN (Of a horse) not tamed for riding. *See* BROKEN.

I directed the horse...to be led as it was yet unbroke [6 May 06 ML 7.216]

UNDERWOOD {UN-də-wood} Underbrush.

the under wood consists of the narrow leafed or small willow [3 Aug 05 ML 5.036]

UPPAH Nez Perce word for COUS root cakes. *See* SAPOLIL (**Northwest**)

bought considerable uppah and couse from the natives [1 Jun 06 JO 9.318]

USELESS Not presently in use.

under those beads was Stored their bags baskets and useless mats [9 Dec 05 WC 6.119]

V

VACANCY Opening, hole.

one Cow was killed on the ice after drawing her out of a vacancey in the ice in which She had fallen, and Butchered her at the fort [7 Dec 04 WC 3.254]

there appears to have been a Covered way out of the Main work into the Vacan[c]ey between those two walls [c. 1 Sep 06 WC 8.342]

VARIATION The angular difference between true north and magnetic north (now also called *declination*), a quantity important in navigating by compass. *See* (POLE) STAR.

I determined to come too...and determine the variation of the nedle [15 Jul 04 ML 2.382]

VAULT A latrine. *See* SINK.

we dug a vault 100 yds abo. the huts to make...the place healthy. [5 Nov 04 JO 9.094]

VEAL The meat of buffalo calves.

I walked on shore this evening and killed a buffaloe cow and calf, we found the calf most excellent veal. [16 May 05 ML 4.157]

VENEREAL Syphilis and/or gonorrhea. *See* LUES VENEREA, POX. From *Venus*; *see* BATTERY.

Several men with the Venereal cought from the Mandan women [14 Jan 05 WC 3.273]

All the party in high Spirits, but fiew nights pass without a Dance[.] they are helth. except the—vn.—which is common with the Indians and have been communicated to many of our party...those favores bieng easy acquired. [30 Mar 05 WC 3.322]

Pocks & Venerial is Common amongst them [21 Nov 05 WC 6.074]

VENERY Indulgence in sexual activities. *See* VENUS.

The [Chinookan] *women are much inclined to venery, and like those on the Missouri are sold to prostitution at an easy rate.* [21 Mar 06 PG 10.200]

VENT {vend, **South**} (Of a stream) to discharge.

it...vends very little water at this moment [25 Nov 03 ML 2.112]

VERGE {vəj} An edge, a somewhat archaic sense of a word now mostly applied figuratively as *on the verge of collapse.*

ice...appears along the verge of the river. [24 May 05 ML 4.188]

VERMILION A pigment produced from red sulfide of mercury (*cinnabar*), introduced into the Indian trade by Europeans. Vermilion's intense crimson color—applied in very small amounts—made it useful as a PAINT, and thus an attractive trade item.

2 lbs. Vermillion...[$]3 34 [Jun 03 in Jackson Letters (ed. 2) 1.094]

I now painted their tawny cheeks with some vermillion which with this nation [Shoshone] *is emblematic of peace...I distributed some trifles among them, with which they seemed much pleased particularly with the blue beads and vermillion.* [13 Aug 05 ML 5.078]

each man's stock in trade amounts to no more than one awl, one Knitting pin, a half an ounce of vermillion, two nedles, a few scanes of thead and about a yard of ribbon [21 May 06 ML 7.275]

Natives early came to prefer vermilion over traditional red pigments such as clay and ocher (both colored by oxidized iron), but they reverted to these local materials when vermilion was unavailable or too expensive. Alexander Henry (*Travels* 325) noted that Canada's Chipewyans used "red ochre, in defect of vermilion." Riggs's *Dakota-English Dictionary* defined Sioux *makawashesha* as "red earth, used by the Dakota as a paint instead of vermilion." Indian words for local pigments generally seemed to have been extended to the imported pigment. (*Vermilion* placenames usually refer to a naturally occurring source of red pigment, often clay.) Lewis obtained the Corps' vermilion (an initial supply, at least) from the War Office in Washington. In 1820–22, vermilion for the Indian trade was imported from England, China, and Italy (*ASPIA* II. *passim*).

VERSATILE {Və-sə-tile} Subject to change; (of a stream) variable in course.

so capricious, and versatile are these rivers [27 Apr 05 ML 4.077]

VICE {VY-see, vīs} In place of someone; in another's stead. The word continues today as a prefix, as in *vice-admiral.*

apt. Pat Gass a Sergt. Vice Floyd Deceased [26 Aug 04 WC 3.014]

VIOLIN Against all odds, Cruzatte's *fiddle* survived the crossing of the continent (*see* DESK). Cruzatte's fiddling (and perhaps occasionally Gibson's) served well to advance intercultural relations.

Peter Crusat played on the violin and the men danced which delighted the nativs, who Shew every civility towards us. [24 Oct 05 WC 5.336]

VITRIOL {VIH-tree-əl} Sulfuric acid, used medicinally as a tonic and astringent.

¼ [lb.] Elix. Vitriol [$].25 [26 May 03 in Jackson Letters (ed. 2) 1.080]

The Indian woman is recovering fast…I continue same course of medecine and regimen except that I added one doze of 15 drops of the oil of vitriol today [18 Jun 05 ML 4.306]

4 [oz.] Vitriol Alb. [$].12 [26 May 03 in Jackson Letters (ed. 2) 1.080]

for soar eyes a solution of white vitriol and the sugar of lead in the proportion of 2 grs. of the former and one of the latter to each ounce of water. [10 May 05 ML 4.138]

Blue vitriol—copper sulfate, the original source of sulfuric acid.

Green vitriol—iron sulfate, also known as COPPERAS.

Elixir of vitriol—aromatic sulfuric acid, a 10% (more or less) solution of sulfuric acid in alcohol, with small added amounts of aromatic substances such as tincture of ginger, or oil of cinnamon. Prescribed in the 18th and 19th centuries for a variety of ailments, including scurvy and diarrhea, and used as a vehicle for quinine (BARKS).

Oil of vitriol—concentrated sulfuric acid, though Lewis (above) perhaps meant *elixir* of vitriol.

White vitriol (Latin *vitriolum album*)—zinc sulfate.

VULTURE {VUL-chə} The California condor (*Gymnogyps californianus*), now extinct in the Pacific Northwest. *See* BUZZARD.

Reuben Fields killed a Vulter [18 Nov 05 WC 6.063]

W

WAD A patch of leather or cloth (or even wood) rammed into the barrel of a muzzle-loading weapon; *see* (RAM-)ROD. A wad normally sat between the powder and bullet, properly securing the charge in place. Sometimes a wad was rammed down on top of a bullet.

The tetons...wounded this Dixon in the leg with a hard wad. [11 Aug 06 WC 8.288]

> The Teton who shot Dixon perhaps had rammed home the powder with hard or heavy wadding because he did not have a bullet to load. When fired at close quarters, such a charge can wound or even be lethal. To *shoot one's wad* meant to fire only a wad when lead ammunition was exhausted, hence figuratively to make one's final effort.

WAKIACUM {wə-KYE-ə-cum} A CATHLAMET people residing on the lower Columbia's north side just upstream from the CHINOOK proper. The name means 'downstream region' in Chinookan.

the wind had prevented his [Pryor] *going to the fisery...above the Wackiacums* [11 Mar 06 ML 6.401]

WALLA WALLA {WAH-lə WAH-lə} Sometimes *Walula*, a SAHAPTIN people of the Walla Walla drainage, adjacent to the Columbia-Snake junction. Sahaptin for 'little rivers.'

we took leave of these friendly honest people the Wollahwollahs [30 Apr 06 ML 7.187]

WALNUT {Wɔ-nit} Bark of the butternut or white walnut tree (*Juglans cinerea*) served as a PURGE.

Shields to get walnut Bark for pills [5 Feb 04 WC 2.173]

WAMPUM {WAHM-pum} Small sea-shell beads. (*See* KAMOSUK.) A word of Eastern ALGONQUIAN (Massachusett) origin, wampum was worked into special belts having great symbolic significance in treaty negotiations in eastern North America. Though Lewis & Clark used wampum in this way, on the Plains smoking a CALUMET served as the focus of diplomatic ceremonies and agreements.

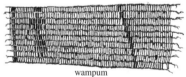

wampum

we gave him a certificate of his good Conduct & a Small Medal, a Carrot of Tobacco and a string of Wompom [7 Apr 05 WC 4.011]

I purchased a canoe from an Indian today for which I gave him six fathoms of wampum beads [1 Apr 06 ML 7.050]

Blue (or *purple* or *black*) *wampum*, consisting only of east coast quahog clam shells, was more highly valued than the white variety (made from various shell species).

we gave also powder & Ball and Some blue wompom & ribin. [12 May 06 WC 7.250]

WAPATO {WAH-pə-too, WAHP-too} The edible root of arrowhead (*Sagittaria latifolia*), an aquatic plant. (**Pacific Northwest**)

they gave us round root near the Size of a hens egg roasted which they call Wap-to to eate [4 Nov 05 WC 6.015]

we purchased a fiew wappato roots…those roots are equal to the Irish potato [22 Nov 05 WC 6.079]

The word was adopted into English from CHINOOK Jargon, which had acquired it from Upper Chinook. ♦Chinookan in turn may have derived the word-stem (*-pdu*) from a neighboring KALAPUYAN language and attached the Chinookan prefix *wa-*.♦ While on the lower Columbia, November 24, 1805, the captains consulted the party for their opinions regarding where to establish winter quarters (eventually, at Fort Clatsop). Clark quoted Sacagawea as wanting to be near root-grounds: "Janey in favour of a place where there is plenty of Potas." (*Potas.* is an abbreviation of *potatoes*, and not a variant of *wapato*.) *See* POTATO.

WARP {wɔp} To move a vessel by hauling on a tow-rope.

we had rapid water, and for about a mile had to warp up our boat by a rope. [21 Jun 04 PG 10.016]

WASH Land or soil eroded by rain and running water.

most of the knobs and river hills wash by rains. [26 May 05 JW 11.169]

WASTE To be diminished through gradual loss.

Many of the creeks which appear to have no water near their mouths have Streams of running water high up which rise & waste in the Sand or gravel [22 May 05 JO 9.153]

WATAP Usually thin, tough conifer roots (such as from spruce or cedar) used for stitching or lashing. The word comes from Cree or Chippewa, probably through Canadian French. (**North**) For other cordage materials, *see* BEAR-GRASS.

these bars…are incerted through holes made in either side of the canoe…and are further secured with strings of waytape [1 Feb 06 ML 6.262]

the peculiar provence of the woman seems to be to collect roots and manufacture various articles…of rushes, flags, cedar bark, bear grass or waytape. [19 Mar 06 ML 6.436]

WATERGATE {WAH-tə-gate} A gate of a town or fort facing a source or body of water.

[Fort Clatsop's] *water-gate may be used freely by the Garrison for the purpose of passing and repassing at all times* [1 Jan 06 ML 6.157]

WATERMAN A boat-man. *See* CRUZATTE.

Charbono cannot swim and is perhaps the most timid waterman in the world [14 May 05 ML 4.152]

Shields...a good hunter and an excellent waterman. [10 Jun 05 ML 4.275]

WATERMARK The trace indicating the highest level reached by a body of water.

from the watermark, it did not appear that it had been more than 2 feet deep [9 May 05 ML 4.130]

Tidewater mark records the height of high tide.

th[e]y have scaffolded their dead in canoes elivating them above tidewater mark. [24 Mar 06 ML 7.009]

WATERMELON {WAH-tə-mill-yun, a typical American pronunciation} It is unknown whether this is an indigenous American species, or today's familiar watermelon (*Citrullus lanata*) that originated in Africa and spread west with (or ahead of) Euro-American expansion.

we Shook hands and gave them [Otoe and Missouri] *Some Tobacco & Provisions, they Sent us Water Millions* [2 Aug 04 WC 2.435]

WATLALA A CHINOOKAN-speaking people of the Columbia River gorge (near present-day Bonneville Dam), relying principally on salmon for subsistence and river craft for transportation. The name is Chinookan for 'small lake (place).' Instead of the prefix *wa-* (marking placenames), some forms use *La-* 'their,' which also appears in names such as CATHLAMET. Though Lewis used the two forms in referring to two different villages and their inhabitants, he probably had heard the simple placename at one point along the river and the possessive group-name while at another location.

we...continued our rout to the Wah-clel-lah Village which is situated on the North side of the river...this village appears to be the winter station of the Wah-clel-lahs and Clahclellars [9 Apr 06 ML 7.096]

we crossed over to the North Side & halted at a village of the wa-cla-lah nation where we bought 5 or 6 fat dogs. [9 Apr 06 JO 9.288]

a few men were absolutely necessary...to guard our baggage from the War-clel-lars who crouded about our camp [11 Apr 06 ML 7.104]

Capt. C. joined me from the lower camp with the Clahclellah cheif. [12 Apr 06 ML 7.111]

WATTLE To interlace thin, flexible branches or twigs. *See* WITHE.

this weare Consists of two Curtains of Small willows wattled together with four lines of withes of the Same Materials extending quite across the river [29 Apr 06 WC 7.183]

WAVERING (Of land) rolling.

The Country...is wavering lands with Scattering pine. [26 Jul 06 WC 8.231]

WAVY = WAVERING.

a valley of wavey country...extends itself for a great distance [21 May 05 ML 4.176]

WEAK (Of various bodily organs or functions, not simply of muscles) debilitated.

William Bratton...is so weak in the loins that he is scarcely able to walk, nor can he set upwright but with the greatest pain. [24 May 06 ML 7.283]

Hence **weakness**.

a weakness and pain in the loins is a common complaint with their women [19 May 06 ML 7.272]

WEIGHT When directly following a number, means *pounds*. See NEAT.

the meet which he killed and that in the lower Deposit amounting to about 3000 wt was brought up on two Slays [21 Feb 05 WC 3.299]

WEIR {WEH-ə, modern WEER} A dam or structure specially designed for trapping fish. See (FISH-)DAM, WATTLE.

there were two...wears formed of poles and willow sticks, quite across the river...each of these were furnished with two baskets; the one wear to take them ascending and the other in decending. [21 Aug 05 ML 5.137]

WELSH INDIANS The imagined descendants of a band of Welshmen supposedly led to the New World by Prince Madoc in the 12th century. Beginning in the 18th century, various native peoples in western North America were identified as being of Welsh stock. Regarding the Sioux, for instance, a 1759 enumeration of Indian nations (Stevens *et al.*, series 21655, p. 87) noted: "These are the People called Welch Indians [they] are very fair, and Speak quick." Though both the Lewis and Meriwether families were of Welsh extraction, Meriwether Lewis probably was not an adherent of the theory.

the Indians were Aborigines not Welshman. [c. Apr 10 NB in Jackson Letters (ed. 2) 2.515]

we Suppose that they [Flathead] are the welch Indians [4 Sep 05 JO 9.218]

he had seen one of the Indians of the Clark-a-mus Nation &...this Indian was white, &...and they had fire Arms...if any Welch nation of Indians are in existence, it must be those Indians, & not the flatt head Nation [2 Apr 06 JW 11.439]

WETESOON The Arikara name for the AHWAHAWAY. *See* MINITARI.

Camped opsd. the Village of the Weter Soon or ah wah har ways [27 Oct 04 WC 3.204]

The principal Chief of the WauteSoon Came and Spoke a fiew words on Various Subjects [30 Oct 04 WC 3.216]

WHEEL To spin around.

we wheeled on a Sawyer which was near injuring us Verry much [15 Jun 04 WC 2.302]

WHIN Originally a prickly British shrub such as gorse, here extended to SAGE[2].

the countrey...all Coverd. with a...plant about 2 & three feet high and resembles the whins. [17 Oct 05 WC 5.288]

WHIPSAW A narrow-bladed, two-man, crosscut saw.

Corpl White house & York Comce [commenced] sawing with the whip Saws [26 Dec 03 WC 2.141]

[Oregon grape] *leafets …are…like the teeth of a whipsaw* [12 Feb 06 ML 6.299]

WHIRL {whǝl} A whirlpool.

I had men on the Shore with ropes to throw in in Case any acidence happened at the Whirl [25 Oct 05 WC 5.336]

3 miles thro a narrow Swift bad Chanel from 50 to 100 yards wide, of Swels Whorls & bad places [25 Oct 05 WC 5.337]

For **whirly**, *see* BOIL[2].

WHITLOW {WIT-lǝ} = FELON. *See* TUMOR.

this man has been unable to work…in consequence of a whitlow on one of his fingers; a complaint which has been very common among the men. [11 Jul 05 ML 4.375]

WILLOW {WILL-ǝ} A shrub or tree of the genus *Salix.* Lewis recognized the willow's role in the ecological succession of river-bottom plant life.

as the willow increses in size and the land gets higher by the annul inundations of the river, the weeker plants decline dye and give place to the cotton-wood [winter 04-05 ML 3.455]

Sand bars which were then [fall 1804] *naked are now covered with willow Several feet high.* [20 Aug 06 WC 8.310]

WIND-SHAKEN (Of timber, especially COTTONWOOD) cracked and thus less suitable for boat-building.

had all the Canoes…corked pitchd & lined oover the Cotton Wood, which is win Shaken [27 Mar 05 WC 3.320]

Capt. Clark…found 2 trees of Cottonwood and cut them down; one proved to be hollow…and was somewhat windshaken [10 Jul 05 ML 4.372]

WINDLASS {WIND-lǝs} A nautical term for a drum turned on a horizontal axis by means of levers or a crank, and used to haul in or let out a rope, as for a boat's anchor.

we have…prepared a large rope of Elk-skin and a windless by means of which we have no doubt of being able to draw the boat on the bank [3 Feb 05 ML 3.285]

we fixed a Windlass and Drew up the two Perogues on the upper bank [25 Feb 05 WC 3.302]

WINTER {WIN-tǝ} To spend the winter, especially in an encampment.

Mr. Vallie informed us he wintered last winter 300 Legus up the Chyemne River under the Black mountains [1 Oct 04 WC 3.133]

below the mouth of this river, is the remains of a Rickorrie Village or Wintering Camp fortified in a circular form of a bout 60 Lodges [7 Oct 04 WC 3.149]

I did not think that we Could get a good wintering ground there [30 Oct 04 WC 3.215]

WIPER {wī-pə} A small corkscrew-like tool attached to the end of a wiping-ROD for holding a cloth or leather patch for cleaning a gun's bore, or to extract a charge from the barrel.

Arms & Accoutrements…15…Wipers or Gun worms [Jun 03 ML in Jackson Letters (ed. 2) 1.070]

Those Indians Stole out of R. F. Shot pouch his knife wipers Compas & Steel [22 Sep 05 WC 5.230]

WITHE {wĭth} A strong, flexible twig, especially of willow, for tieing. *See* WATTLE.

the upper part of the [lodge] *poles are…secured with large wyths of willow brush.* [13 Jul 05 ML 4.378]

two ranges of horizontal poles were…lashed with willow bark and wythes to the ranging poles [21 Aug 05 ML 5.137]

WOLF, PRAIRIE- The coyote (*Canis latrans*), whose bark resembles that of a dog. To be distinguished from the larger gray wolf that usually howls rather than barks.

we heared the prarie woolves bark on the hills [9 Sep 04 JO 9.056]

coyote

WORK {wək} = OPERATE.

I took Some medison last night which has worked me very much [1 Jul 04 WC 2.336]

WORM {wəm} = WIPER.

WORMWOOD An aromatic southern European shrub of the genus *Artemisia*. *See* SAGE[2].

on these hills [western North Dakota] *many aromatic herbs are seen; resembling in taste, smel and appearance, the sage, hysop, wormwood, southernwood* [14 Apr 05 ML 4.035]

Wormwood's bitter taste made it a metaphor for anything intolerable. The prophet Jeremiah in *Lamentations* (3:19) bewails, "mine affliction and my misery, the wormwood and the gall." The word does not originally stem from the invertebrate animal *worm*, though the name has probably been altered analogically from its use as a worm-medicine. It is derived from the old Germanic, *wermod*, of obscure origin. *Wermod* also is the source of *vermouth*, an aromatic white wine in which wormwood was used as a flavoring.

WORRY To fatigue or distress physically.

he had lived very plentifully this trip but looked a good deel worried with his march. [9 Aug 05 ML 5.061]

my dog much worried. [7 Jul 06 ML 8.095]

Hence **worry down**, to weaken an animal by fatiguing it.

the hunters...pursue on their fresh horses thus worrying the poor animal [pronghorn] *down and finally killing them with their arrows.* [14 Aug 05 ML 5.087]

WORST {wəst} To wear out, exhaust.

they had been absent 7 Days Swam many creeks, much worsted. [2 Jun 04 WC 2.269]

The greater part of the horses were in fine order, tho' five of them had been rode & worsted in Such a manner last fall by the Inds. that they had not recovered [9 May 06 WC 7.236]

WOULD Archaic and rare use as the past tense of *will*.

my skins of the bighorn...had every appearance of spoiling, an event which I would not should happen [1 Aug 06 ML 8.145]

WRACK Driftwood and other floating debris.

the River rose, and the wrack run rapidly. [14 Jun 04 JW 11.024]

X-Y-Z

X Y COMPANY A short-lived (1798–1804) offshoot and competitor of Canada's NORTH WEST COMPANY.

the N, W. & X Y Companies have joined, & the head of the N W. Co. is Dead [2 Mar 05 WC 3.308]

YAMPA {YAH-pə, modern YAM-pə} *Perideridia montana* (also known as *P. gairdneri*) belongs to the carrot family (as does COUS) and is native to the West; also called FENNEL, *wild carrot, squaw-root*. Yampa is harvested in spring for its crisp anise- or caraway-flavored roots. The Shoshone word occurs in some dialects without the *-m-*, as indicated by Clark's spelling. (**Rockies**)

The Squar wife to Shabono busied her Self gathering the roots of the fenel Called by the Snake Indians Year-pah for the purpose of drying to eate on the Rocky mountains. [18 May 06 WC 7.270]

YANKEE A New Englander.

a yankey farmer from whom I perchased some corn and pittatoes [12 Sep 03 ML 2.080]

passed...the settlement of Bellpray—a yanke settlement [15 Sep 03 ML 2.082]

> ◆Perhaps from Hudson River Dutch *jonkie*, 'boy, inexperienced person, green-horn.' ◆ New Englanders had settled in the Old Northwest, and Lewis noted several Yankee settlements along the Ohio River. A substantial minority of the expedition's roster were Yankees. *See* NOTION.

YANKTON and **YANKTONAIS** {modern YANK-tən, yank-tən-NYE} Subdivisions of the Dakota SIOUX, occupying the eastern Dakotas and speaking a Sioux dialect.

Respectively, the names translate as 'village on the end' and 'little village on the end.'

he Said...in the Yanktown Souise language that he wanted us to come to Shore. [2 Oct 04 JO 9.075]

the Yanktons of the North, and the Sissitons, who trade with a Mr. Cammaron on the head of the St. Peter's [Minnesota] *river, bring guns, pouder & balls, Kettles, axes, knives...which they barter to the 4 bands of Tetons and the Yanktons Ahnah, who inhabit the borders of the Missouri* [winter 04-05 ML 3.356]

YAWL {yɔl} A sailing ship's small open boat, used for transporting people, supplies, and baggage to and from shore, or between vessels, and also for towing. Usually rowed with three or four oars to a side and sometimes rigged for sailing; length about 3½ times the breadth. *See* (IRON) BOAT.

This Iron boat...was in shape like a Ships Yawl. [21 Jun 05 JW 11.207]

YELLOW {YĂ-lə} (Of blacks and Indians) non-white, but of a light cast. In 1793, Benjamin Hawkins, a U.S. Indian agent in Georgia, reported the escape of three negros, "one a...yellow girl, about 15 or 16 years old, her colour very like that of an Indian" (*Letters* 270).

I...intend taking a tramp myself in a few days to find these yellow gentlemen [Shoshone] *if possible.* [27 Jul 05 ML 4.437]

YELLOWSTONE RIVER Rising in northwestern Wyoming, the Yellowstone flows across two thirds of Montana to join the Missouri River at the North Dakota border. A translation of the French ROCHE JAUNE.

Capt. Lewis concluded to go by land as far as the Rochejhone or yellow Stone river [25 Apr 05 WC 4.068]

ZOTTEAUS = OTOE.

Drewyer found three of the Zotaus Indians Dressing an Elk. [28 Jul 04 JO 9.30]

SUBJECT INDEX

Lewis and Clark Lexicon of Discovery

Astronomy
See *Navigation,*
   Surveying, & Time

Birds
bat
booted
buzzard
calumet-bird [*Aquila*]
corvus
covert
dominicker [*Gallus*]
drum
dub
duckanmallard [*Anas*]
dunghill-fowl
goatsucker [*Chordeiles*]
parakeet [*Conuropsis*]
pied
pigeon, wild
   [*Ectopistes*]
plover [Charadriidæ]
rain-crow [*Coccyzus*]
vulture [*Gymnogyps*]

Boats, Boating, &
Ships
aback, take
awning
ballast
bar[1]
barge
bateau
bilge
boat
boat, iron
boil[2]
bow
bow-man
brace[2]
brickle
brig
cable
cajeu
careen
caulk
charge
coast
come to
cord

crowd sail
double
double-man
douse
draw
drift
drift ice
embarrassment
fall down
float, on
flood
foul
furl
gun
gunwale
hard[2]
heave in sight
hole
hole, gauge
hook, boat
jibe
jury
keel[1,2]
keelboat
kiln, tar-
knee
lance
larboard
lay by
leeward
lie by
line, towing-
loading
log
luff
mast
noon it
oar, steering
overhaul[1]
overset
pay
piece, bow-
pin
pirogue
pettiauger
pole[2]
pole, setting
portage
put into
quarter[1,2]

reef
riffle
ripple
rope, tow-
rope-walk
rudder-irons
run[3]
sail, sprit-
sail, square
sand
sawyer[2]
schooner
ship[1,2,3]
shoal
shoot[2]
sloop
snag[1]
socket
sprit
stanchion
stand
starboard
stave
stem
stern
stern-man
strip, way-
strong
suck
swell
tack
tide
tug
watap
waterman
windlass
wind-shaken
wrack
yawl

Clothes, Ornaments,
& Gear
bandeau
bar[2]
brains
breeches
cap-a-pie
capot
check[2]
chip

coarse
coat, artillery-
coat, blanket-
desk
ear-bob
flannel
flesh-side
fob
gorget
grain[2]
hair-pipe
hat, cocked
legging
linen
moccasin
nun's thread
overalls
paint
point[2]
queue
razor-blade
Russia sheeting
scarlet
shave
shoe-pack
split[1]
sweet-grass
tippet
vermilion
violin
wampum
watap

Fish & Fishing
anchovy
beard
cat
char [*Oncorhynchus*]
crawfish
dam, fish-
drag
eulachon [*Thaleichthys*]
faggot-bone
fish, pounded
fish, scale-
fish-hook
gig
green
quinnat
   [*Oncorhynchus*]

run[2]
seine
skate [*Raja*]
sound
split[2]
trail
weir

Food, Drink, &
Cooking
apple, white
beef
biscuit
breakfast
brisket
buffalo-grease
butch
camas
colt
corn, lyed
cous
culwhamo
dinner
dog
dram
ear, roasting
fare
fat
fennel
filbert
fillet
fish, pounded
fleece
fletch
gill
graisse de buffle
grease
green
grist-mill
grog
guts
haw
hominy
horse
hulled
hump
jerk
licorice
marrow-bones
meal, Indian
meal, parch-
melt
oven, Dutch
paunch
pasheco
pembina
pemmican

pickle down
porter
potato
pudding, hasty
pudding, white
saddle
salal
salt-works
sapolil
service-berry
shank-bone
shawnatahque
simlin
soup, portable
spirits
strong
sunflower
sweat[2]
tafia
train-oil
try
uppah
veal
wapato
watermelon
yampa

Foreign Relations
calumet
considerate
double-spoken
hatchet, bury the
head-right
hug, national
make[2]
medal
medicine
milk
nation
parole
savage
son of a bitch
talk
treat
treaty

Games
base
button
quoits
shake a foot

Geography &
Topography
alum
American Bottom
argil

arsenic
Athabasca country
back[1]
backwater
bald
bar[1]
batture
bayou
Beaverhead Rock
Big Bend
bituminous
Black Hills
boil[2]
bold
Boone's Settlement
bottom[1]
bowling-green
branch
break up
broken
brook
Burnt Hills
burr[2]
butte
Cahokia
calcareous
carbonated
carrying place
cavern, blowing
cliff
climate
coal, pit
coal, stone
Columbian
copperas
copse
Côte Noire
counter-current
cove
creek
cut-off
detour
disembogue
dividing
draft[1]
drain
fork
fountain
freestone
galled
glade
gorge
Great Falls[1,2]
gut
hollow
Illinois
interstice

isinglass
Kaskaskia
Kentucky
knob
lagoon
lay down
leeward
lick
Mississippi
Missouri
mouth
Nemaha River
nitch
Nootka Sound
ocean
Ohio
overflown
pass
pitch
plain
platte
point[1]
pondy
prairie
pumice
ragged
ravine
reach[1,2]
riffle
riley
ripple
Roche Jaune River
Rocky Mountains
rolling
run[1]
saline
sand
Saskatchewan River
shoal
shoot[2]
sideling
sink
slaky
slash
slough
sluice
Snowy Mountains
Spanish
stand
strong
suck
sugarloaf
table
tide
tidewater
tideway
Tum

underwood
vent
wash
watermark
wavering
wavy
whirl
Yellowstone River

Guns
See *Weapons, Hunting, & Trapping*

Horses
bait
bran
broken
caparison
charge
choke
cotton(-wood)
cut
distemper
fall away
gear
geld
hobble
horse, stone-
jaded
mule
near
pack
packsaddle
picket
piebald
shy
snip
sorrel
sound-back
spancel
stone
string
stripe
stud
swim, horse-
tackle
unbroken

Insects
chittediddle
flea
fly, blowing-
gnat, eye-
mosquito
piss-ant
sawyer[3]

Languages
See *Native Peoples & Languages*

Law
head-right
soil, right of

Mammals
antelope
argali
beam
bear [*Ursus*]
bear, grizzly
beaver [*Castor*]
bighorn [*Ovis*]
bottom[2]
brarow [*Taxidea*]
brindle
buffalo [*Bison*]
cabrie
carcajou [*Gulo*]
cat, tiger-
cur-dog
deer [*Odocoileus*]
dog
dog, Spaniard's
dog, turnspit
elk [*Cervus*]
fist (feist)
gang
gentle
goat
he
hough
ibex
loup cervier [*Lynx*]
moonack [*Marmota*]
mule [*Equus*]
panther [*Felis*]
pecora
pekan [*Martes*]
phoca
poile
polecat [*Mephitis*]
pronghorn
    [*Antilocapra*]
rat
run[4]
rut
salamander [Geomidæ/
    pocket gopher]
Seaman
sewellel [*Aplodontia*]
she
sheep, (Rocky)
    Mountain

skeletonize
spuck [*Enhydra*]
squirrel, barking
    [*Cynomys*]
wolf, prairie [*Canis*]

Measures
brace[1]
bushel
draft[2]
fathom
gill
half-leg deep
league
line
middle-deep
midrib-deep
pace
peck
pennyweight
perch
pole[1]
rod
scantling
step off

Medicine
affection
ague
balsam[2]
barks
basilicon
bile
bilious
bleed
boil[1]
broken
cataplasm
clyster
cold
disordered
doctor
dose of salts
dysentery
electricity
eye-water
felon
fit
frosted
Glauber's salts
gonorrhea
grain[1]
griping
hipped
hot-house
hysterical
impostume

influenza
inward
jalap
laudanum
lax
lead, sugar of
liniment, volatile
lint
loins
lues venerea
matter
mature
mend
mercury
niter
open
operate
physic
plaster
pleurisy
poultice
pox
puke
purgative
purge
relax
rheumatism
rising
Rush's pills
saccharum
sage[1]
Saturn
Scott's pills
scrofula
sick
simple
smallpox
soap, Castile
sore-eyes
sovereign
specific
splinter
stomachic
sulfur, flower of
sweat[1]
tartar
tent
tow
tumor
venereal
vitriol
walnut
weak
whitlow
work

Military
accoutrements

canton
cantonment
commissary
contractor
equipage
fatigue
flag, red
flank
flanker
flanking party
mess
platoon

Native Peoples & Languages

Ahwahaway
Algonquian
Arikara
Assiniboine
Big Belly
Blackfoot
Bois Brulé
brave
Burnt Woods
burr[3]
calumet
Cathlamet
Cheyenne
Chehalis
Chinook
Chinookan
Chippewa
Chopunnish
Clackamas
Clatsop
clucking
coventry
Cree
Crow
Dakota
Delaware
Dog Indian
fire[1]
Flathead
Gros Ventre
guggle
hatchet, bury the
Ioway
Kalapuya
Kansa
Kaw
Kickapoo
Loup[2]
Mandan
Mahaha
Miami
Minitari

Missouri
name, war-
nation
Nez Perce
Nootka
Omaha
Osage
Otoe
Palotpalo
Papspalo
Pawnee
Pierced Nose Indians
pole, scalp
Ponashita
Potawatomi
Raven Indians
Ree
Republican
Ric
Rocky Mountain
    Indians
Sahaptian
Sahaptin
Salish
Salishan
Sauk
Saulteaux
savage
Shaha
Shawnee
shishiquaw
Shoe
Shoshone
sign[2]
Siouan
Sioux
Sisseton
Skilloot
Snake
stripes, war-
Teton
Tushapaw
tyee
Wakiacum
Walla Walla
Watlala
Welsh Indians
Wetesoon
Yankton
Yanktonais
yellow

Navigation, Surveying, & Time

additive
Aldebaran
altitude, meridian

altitudes, equal
Antares
Aquila
azimuth
chord
chronometer
circumferentor
course
departure, point of
distance
Greenwich
horizon, artificial
instant
latitude
level, spirit
limb
longitude
meridian
micrometer
moon
nonius
observation, back
observation, lunar
octant
Pegasus
quadrant
rate of going
Regulus
sextant
sleep
Spica
star, morning
star, pole
subtractive
tangent-screw
time, mean
traverse
variation

Obsolete or Dialect Words; Meanings & Pronunciations

a
after part
agreeable to
allow
altogether
amazing
answer
apartment
apprehend
appropriate
assimilate
atonement
banditti
base
battery

beat up one's quarters
bilge
blackguard
blubber
boot, to
brickbat
broken
brown, Spanish
calculate, on
calculated
case[1]
chance
change
chapter of accidents
check[1]
chilly
choice of
clever
cleverly
cliff
clover, in
collation
complain
conceit
confidential
considerable
considerate
contribute
convenient
country
course, of
croup
cry
danger of
deadly
detain
disagreeable
disordered
doted
durable
eat
esculent
essentially
evening
expect
expose
express
fix
flack
flog
fodder-house
fondly
for to
fore-part
forelock, take time
    by the
foretop

gate
get
give back
grateful
griddle
hard-scrabble
higgler
horn, sounding
illy
indurable
information
insomuch
jockey
keep
kettle
languid
latterly
leader
learn
like to
likely
likeway(s)
look out
lumber
lumbersome
make[1,2,3]
meager
mealy
mend
mending hand, on the
mere
mettle, put one on one's
miff
mighty
mistrust
most
neat
oblige
officious
order
overhaul[2]
palm, bestow the
parcel
particolor(ed)
pet[1,2]
philanthropy
pique
pitch on
plait
plunder
portly
pot-metal
poverty
prize
promiscuously
proportion
public[1,2]

punk
Quaker color
rascality
recruit
repine
return
rive
same of
Saturn
scarce of
scattering
several
shake a foot
sheer off
shelving
shut of
sideling
sight[1,2]
singe
situation
skirt
slaky
slash
small
soil, right of
solus
some
something
spire
spoilt
stalled
start
stay
stout
straiten
sublunary
sugarloaf
suit
sultry
swath
swim
tail, mill-
take
take up
tanner's ooze
thring
tight
tiresome
to
tolerable
tote
touch on the right string
tremendous
trencher
tuck
turn
tush

ultimo
useless
vacancy
verge
versatile
vice
waste
watergate
wheel
worry
worst
would

People
blacksmith
Cameahwait
Canadian
Charbonneau
collier
cooper
Cruzatte, Pierre
Drouillard, George
Dutch
engagé
femme
folks
French
gentleman
half-breed
interpreter
jockey
juggler
Mrs.
mulatto
patroon
Pomp
Sacagawea
sawyer[1]
Shake Hand
Shields, John
soldier
squaw
Yankee

Plants & Trees
apple, white
  [*Pediomelum*]
arbor vitæ
arsesmart [*Polygonum*]
artichoke [*Helianthus/
  Cynara*]
balsam[1] [*Abies/
  Pseudotsuga*]
bear-grass
  [*Xerophyllum Yucca*]
blow, in
bois rouge

burr[1]
camas [*Camassia*]
cane [*Amphicarpum/
  Arundinaria*]
cedar, red [*Juniperus*]
cedar, white [*Thuja*]
cotton(-wood)
  [*Populus*]
cous [*Lomatium*]
culwhamo
fennel
filbert [*Corylus*]
flag [*Typha*]
grass, short
hackmatack [*Larix*]
haw [*Cratægus*]
hyssop [*Hyssopus*]
jalap [*Ipomoea*]
licorice [*Lupinus*]
lightwood
linn [*Tilia*]
Osage apple [*Maclura*]
parachute
pasheco
pembina [*Viburnum*]
pennyroyal [*Mentha*]
pine [*Abies/Picea/
  Pinus*]
potato [*Apios*]
rabbit-berry
  [*Shepherdia*]
radicle
redwood [*Cornus*]
reed [*Phragmites*]
rosin
rush, sand- [*Equisetum*]
sackacommis
  [*Arctostaphylos*]
sage[1] [*Salvia*]
sage[2] [*Artemisia*]
salal
service-berry
  [*Amelanchier*]
shawnatahque
  [*Cirsium*]
silk-grass [*Apocynum/
  Yucca*]
simlin [*Cucurbita*]
southern wood
  [*Artemisia*]
spire
spruce-pine [*Picea*]
sugar-tree [*Acer*]
sumac [*Rhus*]
sunflower [*Helianthus/
  Balsamorhiza*]

sweet-grass
  [*Hierochloe*]
tamarack [*Larix*]
thorn, fleshy-leafed
  [*Sarcobatus*]
walnut [*Juglans*]
wapato [*Sagittaria*]
watermelon [*Citrullus*]
whin
willow [*Salix*]
wormwood [*Artemisia*]
yampa [*Perideridia*]

Reptiles
buffalo, prairie
  [*Phrynosoma*]
lizard, horned
  [*Phrynosoma*]
snake, blowing
  [*Heterodon*]
terrapin [*Chrysemys*]

Shelter
back[2]
bower
chink
dob
flea
lodge
pole, lodge
puncheon
scaffold
sink
vault
withe

Smoking
bois roulé
calumet
carrot
kinnikinnick
pipestone
redwood
sackacommis
smokable
smoke[1]
spun
twist

Tools & Tool-Use
adze
awl, moccasin
ax, falling-
bellows
knife, drawing-
fire-steel
gutter

hackle
hew
howel
kiln, coal-
level, spirit
steel
whipsaw

Trade
ax, squaw-
ballot
beads
cost, first
dollar, Spanish milled
dry goods
eye-dag
fish-hook
glass, burning-
glass, sun-
Hudson's Bay
  Company
kamosuk
none-so-pretty
North West Company
notion
peltry
pewter
sharer
specie
sterling
stickle
stroud
tight
tomahawk, pipe-
trade
trading-house
wampum
winter
X Y Company

Travel
axletree
backload
backtrack
barrel
blaze
blind
cache
campment
connect
deposit
fire[2]
gait
head
hobble
hoppus
hounds

keg
league
lie out
light, at
loading
near-cut
oil-cloth
pack
pole, dog
pole, lodge
portmanteau
proceed on
road
sleep
sleigh
slide
snag[2]
spy
tent, common
timber, fallen
tongue, coupling-
truck

Tribes
See *Native Peoples &*
    Languages

Weapons, Hunting, &
Trapping
air-gun
ammunition, fixed
appearance
ax, battle-
ball
bark-stone
battery
beaver
blank
bleat up
blunderbuss
breech
buckshot
canister, powder-
cartridge
case[2]
castor
charge
cock
covert
cut out
deadfall
dirk
espontoon
eye-dag
fillet
fire-steel
flint

fowler
frizzen
fusil
gentle
gun
harangue
horn, powder
japanned
lead
lights
lock
loup[1]
loup cervier
match
match, shooting-
meager
misfire
musket
offhand
pan
park
pekan
piece, bow-
platoon
pluck
pogamoggan
poor
portfire
pouch, shot-
pound
poverty
powder
regulate
rifle
rod, ram-
rod, wiping-
scaffold
she
shoot[1]
shot
sight[3]
sign[1]
snap
spuck
sponging
stock
swivel
wad
wiper
worm
worry

Weather
chop
falling
flawy
flying

APPENDIX 2

SPELLING VARIANTS

Lewis and Clark Lexicon of Discovery

ads adze
Aiawuay Ioway
all awl
all-can eulachon
angegie engagé
antilope antelope
apern, aporn apron
ass smart arsesmart
Athebaskay [Athabasca]
Babruley Bois Brulé
bais roly bois roulé
ball bald
bando bandeau
bar bear
barr bar[1]
base (prisoner's) base
bateu, batteau, batteur batture
bear bar[1]
beare bar[2]
belge bilge
bier bar[2]
bile boil[1]
birnt Burnt Woods
boil bile
brand bran
breechies, brich breech
buffalow grees graisse de buffle
cain cane
cais- cajeu
calk caulk
Callamuck Tillamook
Callahpoewah Kalapuya
callemet calumet
campt campment
cantainment cantonment
cappoe capot
carinated careen
carr char
carsh cache
cas- cajeu
cash cache
Cattarbet Cathlamet
cattrage cartridge
caus- cajeu
Caw Kaw
cew queue
Chabonah Charbonneau
chappalell sapolil
Cheaun, Cheeon Cheyenne
Chiltz Chehalis

Chinnook Chinook
Chipaway Chippewa
Christano Cree
Chyenne Cheyenne
Cippeway Chippewa
Clahclellar Watlala
Clarkamos Clackamas
Claxter [Clatskanie]
coalt colt
Coat Nor Côte Noire
commass camas
contonemt. cantonment
cord chord, cord
contun canton
corse coarse
cork caulk
could cold
Court new/Noir, Cout Noie
    Côte Noire
cows cous
crean careen
croop croup
croud crowd (sail)
cue queue
cutwhamo culwhamo
decissentary dysentery
Dillewar Delaware
disentary dysentery
doated doted
dob daub
drachm dram
drean drain
Drewyer (George) Drouillard
dungal dunghill-fowl
effection affection
enteral entrails
equapage equipage
faim, famn femme
fellet fillet
fessic physic
fest fist (feist)
firl furl
flannin flannel
fletch, flich, flick flitch
flower of sulfur
flowey flawy
fowl foul
fusee, fuzee fusil
frow froe
galip jalap

gait gate
gaulded galled
geling (stone-)horse
girk jerk
gouge gorge
graze, greas graisse de buffle
green swoard greensward
grizzly bear
Grousevaunta Gros Ventre
gunnal gunwale
harrang harangue
higherlin hireling
hist hoist
hubble hobble
ingishee engagé
interal entrails
isoop hyssop
Janey Sacagawea
jirk, jurk jerk
Kilamox Tillamook
kill kiln
Koho, Kohokia Cahokia
laterly latterly
leagens legging
lickorish licorice
lynn linn
luft luff
Mahar Omaha
Maumie Miami
mear mere
melt milt
Menetarre, Minnetare Minitari
Moha [Nemaha]
murcery mercury
musqueto mosquito
Nebraska [Platte]
olthen eulachon
orning awning
Osnaboin, Ossiniboin
    Assiniboine
painter panther
Pallotepellow Palotpalo
Pani Pawnee
Parpspallow Papspalo
parrot queet parakeet
passage pass
pelollpellow, Pellotepallah
    Palotpalo
perogue, pearogue pirogue
philburt filbert

picquet picket
pided pied
pizmire piss-ant
plouresis, plurisee pleurisy
Poenese, Poni, Ponney Pawnee
polsey palsy
poltice poultice
ponch paunch
prarie, preree prairie
prise prize
Punckha Ponca
quamash camas
quates, quites quoits
rejone Roche Jaune River
Ricara, Rick Rea Arikara
sateau Saulteaux
scallintinize skeletonize
schrofela scrofula
sculp scalp
Seaux Sioux

Shalee Salish
shallon salal
shapillele, shappellel sapolil
Sharbono Charbonneau
shear off sheer off
shearer sharer
shelewele salal
Shew Sioux
Shian Cheyenne
shoemake sumac
shoger sugar
shole shoal
shugolell sewellel
shumate sumac
simmin, simnin simlin
skeet skate
skooner schooner
slew slough
slupe sloop
Sosonee Shoshone

Soues Sioux
Souttoe Otoe
spunging sponging
stalk stock
streighten straiten
sturn stern
suit suet
tale [tail]
tern turn
Timm Tum
trong thong
tutseewa Tushapaw
vend vent
Waclalah, Wahclellah,
Warclellar Watlala
Watersoon, Wautesoon
 Wetesoon
wear weir
whorl whirl
yearpah yampa

APPENDIX 3

ABBREVIATIONS AND SYMBOLS

Corps of Discovery *Journals*

2cd second
ad(d)., a(l)td. altitude
Apt. T. apparent time
B. bay
bals. balance
C. creek
c. w(ood). cottonwood
chrotr. chronometer
Co. company
comd. commenced
com(s)y commissary
cromtr. chronometer
d. degree
difft. different
do. ditto
G., gr. grain
Grent. Greenwich
h. hour
id. island
Ind. Indian
inst. instant
is(l)d. island
Kick. Kickapoo
Koho. Cahokia
L. larboard
L.L. lower limb
L.S. larboard side

lar(d)., lad. larboard
latd. latitude
l(b)d., lbord. larboard
lg(s). league(s)
longtd. longitude
M. mile; mountain(s)
M.T. mean time
mdnl. meridional
m(e)(s). mile(s)
Miss. Missouri
mls. miles
mo. mouth
m(t)(s) minute(s)
N. north
N.N.W. north-northwest
N.S. north side
N.W. northwest
obstn., obsvn. observation
opsd., opst. opposite
pr. pair
p(s)d. passed
pt. point
qu(a)dt., qde. quadrant
q(u)tr. quarter
R. river
s. second
S. starboard; south

S.E. southeast
S.S. starboard side
S.S.E. south-southeast
S.W. southwest
sacch. saccharum
sbd. starboard
sd. starboard; side
Sergt. sergeant
sext., sextn., sextt. sextant
star(d)., std. starboard
subs. subtractive
U.L. upper limb
ult(o). ultimo
vil… village
wt. weight
+ additive
∠ angle
° degree
′ minute
″ second
− subtractive
☽ moon
★ star
☉ sun
♍ Virgo

APPENDIX 4

FEATURES OF THE ENGLISH

Corps of Discovery *Journals*

EXAMPLES OF VOCABULARY

Southern or South Midland words—BALD, BASE, BAYOU, BLUBBER, BOTTOM, BRANCH, BREECHES, BRICKLE, CHANCE, CLEVER, COVE, CRAWFISH, CUT-OFF, DOCTOR, DOMINICKER, DRAIN, DRAM, (ROASTING) EAR, EAR-BOB, EAT, EVENING, FIST, FIX, FLANNEL, FORKS, FREESTONE-WATER, GALLED, GANG, GIG, GLADE, HALF-LEG, HOLLOW, JADED, KNOB, LAY, LEARN, LIE, LIE OUT, LIGHTS, LIGHTWOOD, LIKE (TO), LINN, LUMBER, LUMBERSOME, MELT, MEND, MOONACK, PACK, PARCEL, PAUNCH, PIROGUE, PLAIT (platt), PLANTER, PLUNDER, POLECAT, POOR, PRIZE, RAIN-CROW, RISING, ROSIN, RUN[1], SALAMANDER, SAWYER[3], SCAFFOLD, SCATTERING, SHE, SHOOT[1], SHUT OF, SIMLIN, SLASHY, SLOUGH, SNAG[1], SUCK, SINGE, TERRAPIN, TOTE, TUSH.

Northeastern words—A number of the words classified as northeastern in the *Dictionary of American Regional English,* such as BROOK, BUTTON, CHOICE, FALL AWAY, MENDING HAND, PLUCK, (HASTY) PUDDING, and RILEY, may have been in wider eastern use in the early 19th century (*DARE* is a record primarily of 20th-century dialect forms). Lewis's use of the northeastern words HACKMATACK and TAMARACK is an example of his command of an acquired natural history vocabulary, rather than evidence of these New England words being spoken in Virginian English.

Words of French Canadian origin or transmission—BALLOT, BATEAU, BATTURE, BAYOU, BAR[2], BOIS BRÛLÉ, BOIS ROUGE, BRACE[1], BRAROW, (PRAIRIE) BUFFALO, BUFFALO-GREASE, CABRIE, CACHE, CAJEU, CALUMET-BIRD, CAMPMENT, CAPOT, CARCAJOU, CHARBONNEAU, CORD (?), CÔTE NOIRE, CREE, CRUZATTE, DETOUR, DOG INDIAN, DROUILLARD, ENGAGÉ, FEMME, GRAISSE DE BUFFLE, GROS VENTRE, ILLINOIS, JUGGLER, KAW, LEAGUE, LOUP[1], LOUP[2], LOUP CERVIER, MANDAN, MEDICINE, MULATTO, NEZ PERCE, PATROON, PEKAN, PETTIAUGER, PIROGUE, PLAT, (WHITE) PUDDING, ROCHE JAUNE, SHISHIQUAW.

Words of American Indian origin († denotes old loans, borrowed into English in the colonial period)—

Names of places and tribes: (many) such as CATHLAMET, NEMAHA RIVER, SHAWNEE†.

Plants and animals: CAMAS, COUS, CULWHAMO, EULACHON, HACKMATACK†, KAMOSUK, KINNICKINNICK, MOONACK, PASHECO, PEMBINA, QUINNAT, SACKACOMMIS, SALAL, SEWELLEL, SPUCK, TAMARACK†, WAPATO, YAMPA.

Foods: PEMMICAN, SAPOLIL, UPPAH.

People: SQUAW†, TYEE.

Weapons: POGAMOGGAN, TOMAHAWK†.

Other: MOCCASIN†, SHISHIQUAW, WATAP.

Corps of Discovery *Journals* and Peter Pond *Narrative*

SOUNDS AND NONSTANDARD SPELLINGS

In the following catalog of nonstandard spellings from the expedition journals, the sound preceding the arrow symbol →· is the "standard American" pronunciation (with this lexicographer's Midwestern dialect bias), while that following the arrow is the pronunciation inferred from the journals. In cases where there are pairs of reciprocal substitutions, look for both sets under the alphabetically earlier listing of the two sounds (e.g., ɛ —→ ɪ and ɪ—→ ɛ will both be found under ɛ ~ ɪ). Letters enclosed in < > represent spellings only, without phonetic interpretation. Examples from the A to Z entries in the *Lexicon* are in SMALL CAPITALS and listed in the first part of each section. The nonstandard spelling forms from the journals are in parentheses following the standard spellings—e.g., *oblige* (*oblege*).

The symbol + after the bibliographical citation for a word (e.g., [WC 6.217+]), indicates that there is at least one additional example of a nonstandard spelling equivalence for the journalist being cited. The volume/page citation following a spelling variant indicates that it comes from either Gary E. Moulton's *The Journals of the Lewis and Clark Expedition,* 13 volumes (e.g., [WC 3.072]), or James J. Holmberg's *Dear Brother: Letters of William Clark to Jonathan Clark* (for William Clark only; e.g., [WC Letters 204]). The nonstandard spellings are from WC (William Clark), CF (Charles Floyd), ML (Meriwether Lewis), JO (John Ordway), and JW (Joseph Whitehouse). Patrick Gass is excluded from this listing because his *Journal* (released in 1807) was heavily edited by the publisher into formal English. Gass's "original" diary, which no doubt contained numerous spelling variants, has never been found.

By way of comparison with those of the L&C journalists, the nonstandard spellings of Connecticut trader Peter Pond (1740–1807) are also listed here, preceded by the symbol •. A French and Indian War veteran, Pond played a prominent role in Indian affairs and exploration in the Old Northwest, Great Plains, and northwestern Canada during the latter part of the 18th century. The written account of his frontier experiences is included as "The Narrative of Peter Pond" in *Five Fur Traders of the Northwest,* Charles M. Gates, ed. (St. Paul: Minnesota Historical Society, 1965), pages 11–59. Pond's words in Appendix 4 are followed by page number references from this source. Because it is a relatively short manuscript, Pond's "Narrative" provides a smaller sample of words than the Corps of Discovery journals. (For that reason, and because of the idiosyncratic differences among the various journalists, the reader is cautioned when drawing conclusions on the basis of apparent differences in the frequency of particular sound changes.) As with the Moulton and Holmberg citations, the symbol + following Pond's page references indicates there is at least one additional example of an equivalence—e.g., Pond: *gather* (*Geather*) 33+.

Also for Appendix 4, please note—(1) some classes of nonstandard spellings are *reverse spellings* (such as those with added *r*'s) and do not represent real pronunciations; (2) a pronunciation attested for a particular journalist may be peculiar only to him and not characteristic of his dialect as a whole; (3) in some cases it is difficult or impossible to determine the precise pronunciation represented by a spelling; (4) some spellings may simply be mistakes by the writer and have no phonetic significance; (5) diphthongization and monophthongization are especially difficult to identify; and (6), *ea* in nonstandard spellings can represent several sounds, but the most common is probably eh, followed closely by *ee*.

In using this catalog to recreate the speech sounds represented by the journalists' written words, the most conservative and safest policy is—(1) rule out as far as possible all likely sources of error, thus insuring that a spelling being considered *does* indeed indicate the pronunciation inferred; and (2), be cautious in extrapolating a relationship between spelling and pronunciation in one word to another word, even if it is very similar (e.g., *mountain* is sometimes written and pronounced *mounting*, but do not assume that this would be true for fountain).

THE INTERNATIONAL PHONETIC ALPHABET

aɪ	rye		ɔ	caught
aʊ	out		ɔɪ	oil
ɑ	bah		ʃ	ship
æ(Æ)	cat		θ	think
e	late		ð	that
ɛ	let		u	boot
ə	sofa		ʊ	put
i	beet		ʌ	but
ɪ	bit		3	pleasure
j	yet		:	(length)
ŋ	sing		'	(stress)
o	wrote			

aɪ→iː: *dilate* (*delate*) [WC 3.072], *oblige* (*oblege*) [WC 6.183, JO 9.016, 9.052, JW 11.223] (Isolated cases of an archaic form in "long *i*" that survived the reorganization of the English vowel system in the 15th and 16th centuries. The *i* kept the pronunciation it had in Old French.)

aɪ ~ ɔɪ (both probably approximating ʌɪ in the journals):

> aɪ → ɔɪ: BILE (*boil*); also *kind* (*Coind*) [CF 9.390, 9.395+], *line* (*loin*) [WC 6.354 (twice)], *pint* (*point*) [ML 4.278]. *Suployed* (for *supplied*) appears in a 1775 travel journal from Virginia to Kentucky [Speed *Wilderness Road* 35]. Note *joil* for *jail* [WC *Letters* 204].

> ɔɪ → aɪ: BOIL[1] (*bile*), HOIST (*hist*), PENNYROYAL (*penerial*), QUOITS (*quites*), SPOILT (*spilt*); also *point* (*pint*) [WC 3.152, CF 9.377+], *poison* (*pison*) [ML 2.449]

> • Pond: *boiling* (*Bileing*) 37, *hoisted* (*Histed*) 49+, *join* (*gine*) 20+, *point* (*Pint*) 27+, *poisonous* (*Pisenes*) 56, *spoiled* (*spild*) 33

aʊ → o or ɔ: *about* (*abot*) [ML 5.070, 5.143, JO 9.035] (and see *abut* [ML 4.262+]), *amount* (*amoent*) [WC *Letters* 168], *around* (*arond* [ML 2.089], *arrond* [ML 7.107], *arron* [WC 3.315]), *brown* (*bron*) [ML 3.338, 4.367+], *down* (*don*) [ML 2.102, 4.416], *ground* (*grond*) [ML 2.107], *house* (*hose*) [ML 7.082, 7.084], *however* (*hoever*) [ML 4.351, 5.052], *mouth* (*moth*) [ML 3.338], *our* (*or*) [ML 5.009], *powder* (*poder*) [ML 5.053], *without* (*withot*) [JO 9.266]

> • Pond: *about* (*abot*) 23, *down* (*Doan*) 22+, *drowned* (*Droanded*) 22, *ground* (*Groand*) 35, *mouth* (*Moath*) 37, *out* (*Ot*) 47

ɑ ~ ɔ:

> ɑ → ɔ: AWNING (*orning*; also *oarning* [ML 4.152]), DAUB (*dob*), FLAWY (*flowey*), HAW (*how*), PAWNEE (*Ponie*), *palsy* (*polsey* in SHAKE HAND), THAWY (*thoughy*); also *ball* (*Bawl*)

[JW 11.036], *caught* (*Coet* [WC 8.266], *cought* [WC 2.377, 4.415+, JO 9.018]), *cloth* (*Cloath*) [WC 3.310], *cause* (*couse* [CF 9.385], *Cose* [CF 9.387]), *copse* (Coaps) [WC 3.105], *daughter* (*Doughter*) [WC 3.310], *exalt* (*exolt*) [WC 7.349], *exhaust* (*exost* [WC 2.492] and *exorst* [WC 3.285]), *froth* (*froath*) [ML 4.284], *mockingbird* (*Morking bird*) [WC 4.162], *piebald* (*pybold*) [JW 11.038], *tarpaulin* (*tarpoling*) [WC 2.377], *thaw* (*thow* [WC 2.153], *though* [JO 9.217]), *water* (*worter*) [JO 9.070]

ɔ → ɑ: *laurel* (*laral*) [ML 5.160], *portage* (*partage*) [JW 11.207]

ɑ → ʌ: HOBBLE (*hubble*); also *cocklebur* (*Kuckould burr* [WC 2.220], *Cuckle bur* [WC 2.377]), *comrade* (*cumerade* [WC 7.197])

• Pond: *Abercrombie* (*Abeacrumbea*) 23

ɑr → ɛ, æ or ə (or some intermediate vowel): *hard* (*heard* in SPRIT); also *bark* (*beark*) [JW 11.310], *barking* (*bearking*) [JW 11.222], *far* (*fur*) [WC 4.062], *parched* (*perched* [JW 11.209], *pearched* [JO 9.174, 9.187, JW 11.212]), *part* (*Purt*) [WC Letters 269], *particle* (*perticle*) [JW 11.257], *partisan* (*pertison*) [JO 9.049], *quarries* (*queries*) [WC 2.498], *start* (*steart*) [JO 9.175, JW 11.211], *starve* (*sterve*) [JO 9.210]

æ (ɛ) ~ eː:

æ (ɛ) → eː: PANTHER (*painter*); also *cash* (*caish*) [WC Letters 168, 280+], *neck* (*nake*) [WC 3.083]

eː → æ (ɛ): PLAITING (*platting*); also *acre* (*acker*) [JO 9.321], *breaking* (*Bracking*) [WC 2.313], *maintain* (*mentain*) [ML 7.160], *naked* (*nacked* [WC 4.209, 5.057], *neckid* [WC 5.343], *necked* [WC 3.268, 8.219+]), *they* (*the*) [ML 5.149+]

æ ~ ɛ, perhaps actually a vowel intermediate between æ and ɛ or varying between them.

æ → ɛ (ɪ): *accident* (*excident* [JO 9.071, JW 11.360], *exidant* [JO 9.348]), *accidentally* (*exedantly*) [JO 9.112], *attached* (*utechd*) [WC Letters 279], *axletree* (*extletree*) [JO 9.176], *catch* (*Ceatch*) [WC Letters 168], *craggy* (*craiggey*) [ML 5.016], *gather* (*geather* [WC 2.317], *gether* [JO 9.176, 9.188+, JW 11.270, 11.286+], *gither* [JO 9.212]), *last* (*laist* [WC Letters 210], *lest* [JW 11.042]), *Mandan* (*Mandain* [WC 2.438], *Mandin* [WC 3.031]), *rather* (*reather* [ML 2.412, 7.289+, WC Letters 234], *rether* [WC 2.445, ML 3.290, 6.391]), *salary* (*Sellery*) [WC Letters 182], *sand* (*Sind*) [CF 9.384], *shallow* (*shellow*) [CF 9.393]

• Pond: *gather* (*Geather*) 33+, *Mackinack* (*Mecanac*) 49, *manitou* (*Minneto*) 51

ɛ (ɪ) → æ (a): BEAR (*bar*; also *bair* [JO 9.132+, JW 11.146]; note also the reverse spelling of *bear* for (*sand-*)*bar* [WC 8.354]), BEAR-GRASS (*bargrass*) [WC 6.217+], BREAKFAST (*brackfast*; also in SMOKE+; but *brekfast* [ML 5.162, WC 7.148]), SKELETONIZE (*Scallintinize*), TERRAPIN (*tarripen*), *yellow* (*yallow* in RILEY; also [JO 9.021 (and always so?); JW 11.183, 11.194+]); also *beheld* (*behald*) [ML 4.291], *death* (*dath*) [WC 2.479], *elevated* (*allivated*) [WC 2.348], *fearing* (*faring*) [ML 8.115], *feather* (*fathe, father* [ML 2.461], (*un*)*fathered* [ML 2.462]), *frenzy* (*franzey*) [WC 2.479], *ginseng* (*gensang*) [ML 7.234], *guess* (*gass*) [JO 9.295], *hedge* (*hadge*) [JO 9.017], *irreparable* (*irraparable*) [ML 4.369], *sweating* (*swating*) [ML 6.238], *together* (*to Gather*) [CF 9.378], *wear* (*war*) [JO 9.048]

• Pond: *against* (*a Ganst*) 20+, *better* (*Bater*) 31, *business* (*basnes*) 32, *credit* (*Cradeat*) 42+, *death* (*Dath*) 25, *descent* (*Desant*) 19, *endeavor* (*Indaver*) 47+, *escaped* (*Ascaped*) 18, *escort* (*aScort*) 24+, *general* (*Ganeral*) 26, *keg* (*Cag*) 35+, *meadows* (*Madoes*) 37, *measure* (*masher*) 57, *Nipissing* (*Nipasank*) 30, *second* (*sacond*) 21+, *send* (*sand*) 35, *several (Saverl* 40+, *Saveral* 45), *spent (Spant)* 38, *surrendered (Seranderd)* 27, *their (thare)* 34+, *them (tham)* 23+, *themselves (them Salves)* 32, *there (thare)* 18+, *together (to Gather)* 19+, *vessel (Vasel)* 19, *weather (wather)* 38+, *where (whare)* 18+

æ ~ ɔ:

æ —➤ ɔ: STANCHION (*Stauncheon*); also *lance (launce)* [ML 7.211], *sassafras (sausafras)* [ML 2.069, 6.174], *tassel (tossle* and *tosel* [WC 6.030]; *tausel* [WC 2.185])

• Pond: *Mandans (Mondans)* 38

ɔ —➤ æ: *moderate (madderate)* [WC 2.151]

• Pond: *beyond (beand)* 50, *cold (Cald)* 48, *sauce (sas)* 43

æ ~ ʌ

æ —➤ ʌ: *scalp (sculp)* [JO 9.069, JW 11.088, 11.289]

ʌ —➤ æ or a: *puppies (papppies)* [JO 9.136]

• Pond: *blood (Blad)* 48, *country (Cantrey)* 33, *drums (Drams)* 18, *hunt (hant)* 42+, *industriously (Indastresley)* 26, *run (ran)* 58, *summer (samer)* 24, *trouble (trabel)* 22, *vulgar (valgear)* 47

b ~ p:

b —➤ p: HALF-BREED (*half pread*); also *bead (pead)* [ML 6.314], *bitch (pitch)* [WC 6.205], *board (poad)* [WC 5.311], *brarow (prarrow)* [ML 6.382]

• Pond: *number (Numper)* 50

p —➤ b: POOR (~~bore~~ *pore*) [CF 9.388]; also *depth (deabth* [WC 8.284] and *debth* [ML 8.031]), *plum (blumb)* [WC 2.008, 3.045, 8.326], *point (boint)* [WC 4.178], *pond (bond)* [ML 2.153, 2.222], *probable (brobable)* [ML 4.270], *pubescence (bubersense)* [ML 6.303]

• Pond: *Baptiste (Babtest)* 31, *principal (Prinsabel)* 19

b ~ v:

b —➤v: *deliberation (deliveration)* [WC 2.329], *probably (provably)* [WC 2.426], *labor (Lavour)* [WC 3.489]

v —➤ b: *devouring (debowering)* [WC 7.288], *unfavorable (unfabourable)* [WC 8.361]

d —➤ l: *Goodrich (Gulrich)* [WC 2.377]

d ~ ð:

d —➤ ð: *Goodrich (Gutherich)* [WC 6.137]

ð —➤ d: *farther (farder)* [JW 11.032]

d ~ t:

d —➤ t: *Mohammedan (Mahometant* in GNAT); also *assiduity (ascituity)* [WC 7.294], *dirty (tirty)* [WC 5.373], *drove (trove)* [WC 3.089], *flood (floot)* [WC 6.045], *Goodrich (Guterge)* [WC 2.181], *increditable (incretiatable)* [WC 4.297], *merchandise (Merchantise)* [JO 9.064], *method (methot)* [WC 5.311], *perpendicular (perpinticular)* [JO 9.160+, JW 11.367], *quadrant (quaterent)* [WC 2.139], *sandstone (Sant Stone)* [WC 2.465], *standard (standart)* [ML 6.344], *trade (trate)* [WC 3.102], *understood (understoot)* [WC 6.050], *wind (wint)* [WC 2.376]

• Pond: *abundance (a Bantans)* 44, *disposed (Dispost)* 40, *errand (Arrant)* 41, *hogshead (Hogseat)* 45, *road (Roat)* 52, *second (secant)* 20 t —➤ d: (MERIDIAN) ALTITUDE (*altidude*), FILBERT (*filberd*; also *filbird* [ML 6.348]), SIGHT[1] (*Side*), VENT (*vend*); also *diffident* (*deffidend*) [WC 6.142], *distinct* (*Distinkd*) [WC 2.434], *great* (*gread* [WC 2.364], *Greid* [WC 3.055], *gred* [WC 2.429]), *hat* (*had*) [WC 6.346], *hunt* (*hund*) [WC 3.104], *hunter* (*hunder*) [WC 2.277], *hurt* (*hurd*) [WC 3.239], *inhabit* (*inhabid*) [WC 6.061], *instantly* (*instandly*) [ML 2.115], *latitude* (*Latidude*) [JO 9.222], *melt* (*meld*) [WC 7.337], *opposite* (*oppsid*) [WC 2.392], *patrol* (*padrol*) [ML 4.338], *picketed* (*pickeded*) [JW 11.080], *president* (*presidend*) [WC 8.371], *socket* (*Shocked*) [JW 11.232], *street* (*streed*) [ML 3.337], *sunset* (*Sunsed*) [JO 9.130], *texture* (*dexture*) [ML 7.344], *thicket* (*thicked*) [JW 11.202], *went* (*wend*) [WC 3.074]

• Pond: *excellent* (*Exsaland*) 56

d added or deleted:

d added: *an* (*and*) [ML 4.226, 6.095], *bowl* (*bold*) [WC 5.347], *dollar* (*dollard*) [ML 2.085], *knoll* (*nold*) [WC 3.040], *Mandan* (*Mandand*) [ML 5.121], *only* (*ondley*) [CF 9.392], *person* (*perdson*) [ML 7.085], *ribbon* (*ribbond*) [WC 5.288], *runs* (*runds*) [ML 4.248], *sinkhole* (*sinkhold*) [ML 8.092]

• Pond: *down* (*Dound*) 50, *drown* (*Dround*) 36, *Indian* (*Indand*) 38, *line* (*lind*) 32, *only* (*Ondley*) 24+

d deleted: *powder* (*Power*) [WC 2.166]. (See also Reduction of consonant clusters)

• Pond: *indeed* (*indea*) 36, *obliged* (*ablige*) 27+

-diə —➤ -dʒə: *tedious* (*tegious*) [WC 6.276]

eː ~ iː:

eː —➤ iː: DRAIN (*drean, dreen*), SKATE (*skeet* (fish) [WC 6.175]; also *skeet* (on ice) [WC Letters 280]); also *spacious* (*specious* [WC 3.146], *Spicious* [WC 3.147])

iː —➤ eː: BLEAT (*blait*), *increase* (*incrase* in WILLOW); also *bead* (*bad*) [ML 5.069, 5.070], *beak* (*bak* [ML 6.369], but *Becke* [WC 3.083]), *beeswax* (*base wax*) [JO 9.181], *breeze* (*Braise*) [WC 2.281], *fatigue* (*fataigue*) [JW 11.028, 11.029+], *heath* (*heth* [ML 2.101], *haith* [JW 11.357]), *meager* (*magre*) [WC Letters 105], *mosquito* (*Muscator*) [ML 2.216], *pecan* (*paecaun*) [WC 2.339], *repeating* (*repating*) [ML 6.378], *weaken* (*waken*) [ML 4.277]

• Pond: *eastward* (*astward*) 34, *feeble* (*fab[le]*) 55, *Mississippi* (*Masseppay*, cf. *Misseppey* 28)

ɛ —➤ ɛjə: *dead* (*Deed*) [WC 2.383], *fell* (*feell*) [ML 7.3.22], *French* (*freench*) [WC 3.043], *net* (*neitt*) [ML 7.320], *steady* (*Steedy*) [WC 2.434], *stem* (*steem*) [ML 2.102], *theft* (*theift* [WC 2.173], *Thieft* [WC 5.323]). (These constitute very uncertain evidence of the diphthongization of ɛ.)

• Pond: *bell* (*beel*) 57

ɛ ~ ɪ: there is apparently a loss of distinction between these sounds, as evidenced by the interchange of written *e* <e> and *i* <i>. The vowel may have varied between ɛ and ɪ, it might have tended toward one or the other, or it may have been intermediate between them. Note especially *medal* spelled as *midal*, and *middle* as *meadal*; also *deshivled* for *disheveled*, and *errigular* for *irregular*.

<e> (<ai>) —➤ <i>: *ended* (*inded* in GUN), DELAWARE (*Dillewar*), ENGAGÉ (*Ingishee*), ENTRAILS (*interals, intrals*), FRENCH (*frinch* and in [WC 2.232]), GENTLE (*jintle*), GET (*git*),

KETTLE (*kittle*), MEDAL (*midal*), WATERMELON (*Water Million*); also *again* (*agin*) [ML 4.280, 4.285], *bend* (*Bind*) [WC 2.472, 3.205+], *chemical* (*chimical*) [ML 3.283], *commence* (*commince*) [WC 2.289, 4.313], *crevice* (*crivice*) [WC 6.041, ML 4.217, 4.257], *deference* (*difference*) [ML 6.169], *depend* (*depind*) [WC *Letters* 190], *disheveled* (*deshivled*) [ML 5.104], *destitute* (*distitute*) [WC 6.202, 6.253], *ever* (*iver*) [JW 11.337], *extend* (*extind*) [WC 3.096], *extensive* (*estincive* [WC 4.428, 6.457], *extinsive* [WC 3.481, 5.194]), *geld* (*guild*) [WC 7.330], *gelding* (*gilding*) [JO 9.115], *Helen* (*Hilian*) [WC 6.087], *hemmed* (*himed*) [WC 4.256], *hesitate* (*hisitate*) [WC 7.057], *immense* (*eminc* [WC 5.376], *emince* [WC 6.457]), *intelligence* (*intillegence*) [WC 7.325], *intention* (*intintion*) [WC 3.304, 7.333], *irregular* (*errigular*) [WC 4.203], *kegs* (*Kigz*) [WC 3.030], *left* (*lift*) [WC 7.109, JO 9.300], *leggings* (*ligins*) [WC 6.251], *level* (*livel*) [JW 11.201, 11.237,+], *loup cervier* (*Loucirvea*) [WC 3.330], *Mackenzie* (*Mackinzie* [JO 9.115], *McKinsey* [WC 3.318+], *McKinzey* [WC 3.277+]), *mentioned* (*mintioned*) [WC 3.484], *nettle* (*nittle*) [ML 4.380], *next* (*nixt*) [JW 11.031, 11.056], *pelican* (*pilicin* [WC 8.194], *Pillacon* [ML 8.148], *pillecan* [ML 4.094], *pillican* [JO 9.036]), *petrified* (*pitrefied*) [ML 3.062], *precipice* (*pricipice*) [JO 9.185, JW 11.229], *projected* (*projicted*) [WC 6.460], *red* (*Rid*) [WC 3.482], *reddish* (*ridish*) [JW 11.269], *request* (*requist*) [WC *Letters* 148], *restless* (*wristless*) [ML 5.074], *seldom* (*Sildom* [WC 3.272, 6.223], *sildome* [ML 4.400]), *sell* (*sill*) [WC 6.090, 7.103], *semi-* (*simi-*) [ML 2.068, 3.283, 5.081+], *send* (*sind*) [WC *Letters* 84], *Seneca* (*Sinnecca*) [ML 7.283], *sessile* (*sissile*) [ML 7.323], *shell* (*Shill*) [WC 7.010], *them* (*thim*) [WC 3.237, 3.268+], *treble* (*tribble*) [WC 6.134], *vegetation* (*vigitation*) [WC 8.029, JO 9.152], *waistcoat* ['wɛskət] (*wist[c]oat*) [ML 5.124], *webbed* (*wibbed*) [WC 7.168], *well* (*will*) [WC 3.487, JO 9.264], *went* (*wint*) [WC 3.058], *when* (*whin*) [WC 2.392, 2.479+, ML 4.283], *whether* (*whither*) [WC 4.319]

• Pond: *destined* (*Distanade*) 24, *friend* (*frind*) 36+, *friendly* (*frindley*) 36, *general* (*Ginaral*) 21+, *generation* (*Gineration*) 18, *get* (*git*) 19+, *kettle* (*Cittel*) 37, *melons* (*Millans*) 40, *opposite* (*Opaseat*) 24, *regiment* (*Rigment*) 26, *regimental* (*Rigmintal*) 19+, *seldom* (*Sild[om]*) 57, *them* (*thim*) 20, *very* (*Virey*) 36, *when* (*whin*) 35

<i> (<ea, ei, ie>) ➝ <e>: BILGE (*belge*), BILIOUS (*Beliose*), CLIFF (*Cleft*) [WC 2.355], *inside* (*enside* in BACK[2], and [JO 9.222, JW 11.310]), FILLET (*fellet*), FIST (*fest*), FLITCH (*fletch*), ILLINOIS (*Ellynoise*), *hireling* (*hirelen* in ENGAGÉ), *indifferent* (*indeferent* in SOUND-BACK+), INFLUENZA (*Enfluenzey*), LINIMENT (*leniment*), MILT (*melt*), PHYSIC (*fessic*), SPIRITS (*sperits*; also *sperit* [ML 4.101, 6.388], WEIR (*wear*; also *wair* [ML 5.122]); also *been* (*ben*) [JO 9.111], *clear* (*Clare*) [WC 3.038, 5.202, 5.265], *cylindric* (*Celendric*) [WC 6.301], *did* (*ded*) [WC *Letters* 181], *different* (*defferent*) [WC 2.447, 3.389, 7.140+], *diffident* (*deffidend*) [WC 6.142], *disappointed* (*Desapointd*) [WC *Letters* 273], *discharge* (*descharge*) [WC 5.317], *disposition* (*Desposition*) [WC 3.199], *dissipate* (*dessipate*) [ML 2.067], *dissolute* (*dessolute*) [ML 2.106], *distance* (*destance*) [WC 2.363, 8.217, ML 4.121], *distant* (*destant*) [WC 5.304], *dreary* (*drairy*) [ML 4.211], *dysentery* (*desentary*) [ML 5.025], *exigency* (*exegency*) [ML 5.125], *extinguish* (*extenguish*) [ML 7.080], *fierce* (*ferce*) [ML 5.091], *ginseng* (*gensang*) [ML 7.234], *image* (*emige*) [WC 5.359], *imitation* (*emitation*) [WC 5.351], *implement* (*emplement* [WC 5.351], *empliment* [WC 3.122]), *increase* (*encrease*) [ML 4.176], *indifferent* (*endefferent* [WC 4.017], *indefferent* [WC 7.274]), *indiscriminately* (*indiscreminately*) [WC 6.214], *ingenuity* (*engenuity*) [ML 7.283], *inform* (*enform*) [ML 8.154], *injury* (*engerey* [WC 2.290], *enjorie* [WC 5.277]), *instrument* (*Enstrument* [WC 2.155+], *Entrement* [WC 2.167]), *intend* (*entend*) [JO

9.366], *interval (enterval)* [WC 7.274], *invite (envite)* [WC 8.300], *irregular (errigular)* [WC 4.203], *knit (net)* [ML 6.434], *middle (Meadle)* [WC 2.248], *nearly (narely)* [JO 9.177], *origin (Oregean)* [WC 3.027], *petition (petetion)* [WC 4.298], *pigeon (Pegion)* [WC 6.385], *pinnacle (Penical)* [WC 2.467], *risk (resque)* [WC 8.033], *since (Sence)* [WC 3.246, 5.100, *Letters* 81, CF 9.394], *sit (Set)* [ML 6.388+, WC 6.119+], *sufficient (Suffecent)* [WC 2.173], *sycamore (Seckamore)* [JO 9.361], *sympathy (Cempothy)* [WC *Letters* 210], *unprincipled (unprencipaled)* [WC 3.483], *vanilla (Vinella)* [WC 8.218], *weary (wary)* [ML 4.280], *wearied (waryed* [ML 4.263], *waried* [ML 7.325]), *width (wedth* [WC 4.368+, JW 11.043], *weth* [CF 9.376]), *will (well)* [WC *Letters* 201], *wind (wend)* [WC 7.013], *Windsor (Wenser)* [WC 2.195], *withers (wethers* [WC 3.072], *weathers* [WC 7.250])

- Pond: *brings (Brengs)* 42, *civil (Sevel)* 50, *Illinois (Elenoas* 38; *cf. Ilenoa* 46), *influence (Enfluans)* 47, *intelligent (Entelaget)* 34, *interfere (Interfare)* 47, *inter (Entair* 35, *Entare* 58), *intervale (Entervale)* 56, *invite (Envite)* 54, *little (Lattle* 55, *Lettle* 22+, *Leattle* 46+), *minute (mennet)* 23, *sit (Seat)* 41+, *spirit (sperit)* 18+, *Wisconsin (Oesconstan* 45; *cf. Ouisconstan* 35)

ɛ (ɪ) ~ ʌ:

ɛ (ɪ) ⟶ ʌ (ə): *accept (except* [WC *Letters* 197], *acupt* [WC *Letters* 204]), *attention (atuntion)* [WC *Letters* 156], *berry (bury* [ML 3.456], *burry* [ML 7.112]), *bury (burry)* [JO 9.166, 9.181], *except (excupt)* [WC *Letters* 189, 197+], *gesture (justure)* [WC 3.113], *instead (in Stud)* [WC *Letters* 45], *jest (just)* [WC 3.267, 5.256], *jesture (justure)* [WC 3.196], *jet black (jut black)* [WC 6.329, ML 6.406+], *pretty (prutty)* [WC 6.183], *request (requst)* [WC 3.128, 3.244], *steady (Study,* adjective) [WC 8.217], *terrible (turrible* [WC 4.114], *turrouble* [WC 4.343], *turble* [WC *Letters* 226]), *terror (turrow)* [WC 3.119, 4.343], *which (whuch)* [WC 3.046, WC *Letters* 77, 251]

ʌ ⟶ ɛ (ɪ): *buffalo (beffalow)* [WC Osgood facsim. 51], *but (bet)* [ML 5.074], *hunter (henter)* [WC Osgood facsim. 51], *just (jest* [CF 9.375, 9.377+, JO 9.008+], *jist* [JO 9.238]), *Luttig (Lettig)* [WC *Letters* 291], *mulberry (melberry)* [WC Osgood facsim. 60], *nothing (neathing)* [JO 9.104], *onion (Inion)* [JO 9.020, JW 11.238]), *rugged (reged)* [WC Osgood facsim. 52], *Russell (Ressell)* [WC *Letters* 201], *shut (Shet)* [JO 9.100], *suddenly (siddonly)* [ML 6.263], *sundry (Sendry)* [WC *Letters* 168], *touch (tech)* [WC 2.287], *tongue (Teng)* [WC 2.279], *underneath (inderneath)* [ML 5.161], *walnut (walnit)* [WC 2.429]. *Kivered* (for *covered*) appears in a 1775 travel journal from Virginia to Kentucky [Speed *Wilderness Road* 38].

ə ⟶ i: ARIKARA *(rickerries),* INFLUENZA *(Enfluenzey),* KANSA *(Kansies),* SACKACOMMIS *(Sackey Commy);* also *Athabasca (Athabaskey)* [ML 4.035], *ceremony (Serrymony)* [JW 11.058], *complement (complyment)* [ML 2.411], *images (imigies)* [WC 3.256], *implement (implyment)* [ML 6.206], *Martha (Marthey)* [WC 2.087], *peninsula (peninsoley* [WC 6.090, *Peninsuly* [WC 2.447], (plural) *peninsulis* [WC 2.248]), *swallow (Swally)* [WC 2.451], *terrified (terreyfied)* [JO 9.085], *tomahawk (tomehawk* [ML 2.083], *tomy hawk* [writer unknown 3.494])

- Pond: *Canada (Cannaday)* 20+, *Monongahela (Monagahaley)* 18, *Niagara (Niagaray)* 24+

ə ⟶ ijə: TREMENDOUS *(tremendious;* also *tremendeous* [WC 6.040]); also *bituminous (bituminious)* [WC 4.023], *crystal (cristial)* [WC 5.256], *culinary (Culianary)* [WC 6.216],

Helen (Hilian) [WC 6.087], *horizontally (Horizontially)* [WC 6.220], *horrible (horriable)* [WC 5.363, 6.079], *incredible (incrediable)* [WC 5.145, 5.287], *increditable (incretiatable)* [WC 4.297], *mountainous (mountaineous* [JO 9.194] and *mountanious* [WC 4.134]), *numerous (numerious)* [JO 9.017], *perceptible (perceptiable)* [WC 4.209], *reluctance (reluctiance)* [WC 6.145, 6.183], *spiritous (Spiritious)* [WC 4.038], *stratum (Stratium)* [WC 4.087], *stupendous (stupendious)* [ML 7.081], *sulferous (sulphurious)* [ML 4.019+]

ə added or deleted:

> ə added (perhaps as overcorrection for ə-deletion): CABRIE *(Cabberrie)* [JO 9.139], ENTRAILS *(interals;* also *Enterals* [ML 2.089]); also *angry (angerry)* [JO 9.071], *castrate (casterate)* [ML 7.328], *central (Centeral* [WC 3.203], *Senteral* [WC 2.441]), *entrance (enterance)* [WC 8.193, 5.305], *fibrous (fiborus)* [ML 2.223], *gently (jentilley)* [WC 3.297], *hungry (hungary)* [ML 5.095, 5.166], *monstrous (monsterous)* [WC 6.038], *nitrous (niterous)* [WC 3.221], *Ordway (Odderway,* with silent *r)* [WC 2.145, 194], *partridge (pateridge)* [ML 7.275], *prairie (Perarie)* [JW 11.030], *principally (perincipally)* [WC 3.480], *quadrant (quaterent)* [WC 2.139], *sentry (Sentery)* [JO 9.064, JW 11.080], *sultry (Sultery)* [WC 8.354], *sundry (Sundery)* [WC 2.137], *surplus (Surpolous)* [WC 2.427], *truncated (trunnicated)* [ML 3.460]

> ə deleted: CAREEN *(crean),* HOMINY *(homney);* also *azimuth (Azmath* [WC 2.481], *azmoth* [WC 4.174, 5.285]), *below (blow)* [ML 4.255], *blustery (Blustry)* [JO 9.101], *buffalo (Buflow)* [CF 9.394], *carriage (Carrge)* [WC 4.339], *circular (circler)* [WC 7.258], *cranberries (crambries)* [JO 9.244], *different (differnt)* [WC 3.318, CF 9.380], *enough (nough)* [WC 6.042], *mineral (minral)* [JW 11.059], *opposite (opset)* [CF 9.381], *perpendicular (purpendickler)* [CF 9.375], *tolerable (Tolrable)* [JO 9.040], *upon (pon)* [CF 9.393], *watery (watry)* [ML 4.291]

ər → ɛ(r) or æ(r): *merchandise (Marchandize* in MULE; [JW 11.065]), SERVICE-BERRY *(sarvis+; Sarvice* [WC 4.414]); also *clerk (Clark)* [JO 9.364], *curtain (Cartin)* [WC *Letters* 168], *desert (Desarte)* [CF 9.393], *deserter (Desarter)* [CF 9.394], *early (arly* [WC 3.204, *Letters* 76], *Eairly* [JO 9.020, 9.153+]), *hurricane (haricane)* [WC 2.426], *interpreter (entarp.)* [CF 9.389], *learned (larnt)* [ML 5.218], *mercantile (marcantile)* [WC *Letters* 291], *were (ware)* [JW 11.146, 11.156, WC 4.332]

> • Pond: *advert (avart)* 48, *birch (Barch)* 46, *circumstances (Sarkamstanis)* 42, *clergy (Clarge)* 42, *clerk (Clark)* 33+, *concern (Concarn* 39, *Consarn* 47), *converse (Convars)* 34+, *desertion (Desarson)* 39, *determined (Detarmend)* 18+, *dirtily (darteyaly)* 28, *dispersed (Disparst)* 22+, *disturbance (Distarbans)* 50, *early (Eairley)* 28, *eternal (Etarnal)* 34, *furs (fars)* 54+, *girl (Garle)* 41+, *heard (Hard* 24+, *Haird* 39), *her (Hair)* 41, *inter (Entair* 35, *Entare* 58), *interpreter (Intarpreter* 35, *Intarpiter* 48), *Jersey (Garsea)* 24, *learnt (larnt)* 34+, *mirth (Marth)* 18, *observe (Obsarve)* 36+, *perfectly (Parfectly)* 37, *person (parson)* 27, *personally (Parseneley)* 34, *purchase (Parchis)* 38, *return (Retarn)* 55, *serpentine (Sarpentine)* 36+, *served (Sarved)* 19+, *service (Sarvis)* 18+, *surface (Sarfes)* 43, *terms (tarmes)* 27, *turn (tarn)* 37, *verdure (Varder)* 38, *vermin (Varment)* 55, *were (ware)* 18+

ər ~ ɔr:

> ər → ɔr: *thermometer (Thormometer* in LOUP CERVIER); also *currency (Cory.)* [ML 7.153], *current (corrent)* [ML 4.070, JO 9.345], *deserted (decorted)* [WC *Letters* 284], *hurry (horry)* [WC *Letters* 276], *journey (Jorney)* [CF 9.379], *purpose (porpos)* [CF 9.377, 9.389]

• Pond: *deserted* (*Desorted*) 38, *internal* (*Intornal*) 56, *permit* (*Pormit*) 22

ɔr → ər: *foreign* (*furin* in TRADE); also *for* (*fer*) [WC *Letters* 183, 280+]

f → b: *Warfington* (*Worbington*) [WC 3.009]

f ~ p:

    f → p: *atmosphere* (*atmespier* [WC 2.313], *atmispeir* [WC 2.376], *atmispeire* [WC 2.486], *atmespear* [WC 3.256]), *Woolford/Woodford* (*Wolpard*) [WC 2.202+]

    p → f: PHILANTHROPY (*filantrophy*)

f ~ θ:

    f → θ: *Warfington* (*Worthington*) [WC 2.189, 2.198+]

    θ → f: *warmth* (*womph*) [WC 6.135]

f ~ v:

    f → v: *disfigured* (*disvigored*) [ML 5.122], *mastiff* (*mastive*) [ML 6.339], *perform* (*provorm*) [WC *Letters* 160], *Warfington* (*Warvington* [WC 2.188], *Worvington* [JO 9.057, WC *Letters* 84])

    v → f: *severe* (*Sefere*) [WC 7.288]

g ~ k:

    g → k: *goats* (*Coats*) [WC 3.055], *growth* (*Croth*) [WC 6.183]

    k → g (ŋ): *moccasin* (*Moggisin*) [JO 9.083], *rank* (*rang*) [ML 4.422]

h added or deleted initially:

    h- added: *umbrella* (*Humbrallo* in FUSIL); also *James Aird* (*Herd*) [JO 9.358], *ermine* (*hurmen*) [WC 7.134], *erect* (*herect*) [ML 6.337]

    h- deleted: HYSSOP (*Isoop*) [WC 4.039]; also *habit* (*abit*) [ML 5.074], *hanging* (*anging*) [WC 7.110]; and *see* hw → w.

    • Pond: *hogshead* (*Hogseat*) 45

hw (spelled <wh>) → w: *wharf* (*worft* [WC 2.124], *warf* [WC 7.245]), *what* (*waat*) [JO 9.020], *whatever* (*watever*) [ML 4.101], *when* (*wen*) [ML 3.460, 4.300], *where* (*weare*) [JW 11.047], *which* (*wich*) [WC 2.385, 3.072, ML 3.338, 4.436+], *while* (*wile*) [ML 7.255], *whither* (*wither*) [ML 5.079]

    • Pond: *when* (*wen*) 36, *which* (*Wich*) 37, *whooping* (*hooping*) 49, and *cf.* the reverse spelling *would* (*whuld*) 47

iː → ijə: *sleep* (*Sleup*) [WC *Letters* 193]

iː → jiː: *ear* (*year* in CAPARISON; and [WC 8.338, ML 3.315, 4.138, 4.367])

ɪ → i: SPRIT (*sprete* and *spreat*) [ML 2.073]; also *invalids* (*invalledes* [ML 4.382], *Invalleeds* [JO 9.330])

ɪ ~ ijə:

    ɪ → ijə: *cliff* (*Clieft*) [CF 9.388], *imagined* (*immageoned*) [ML 7.325]), *limb* (*Leimb*) [WC 3.102]

    ijə → ɪ (ə): FERRIAGE (*ferrage*) [WC 6.181]; also *foliage* (*folage*) [WC 3.069, ML 4.188]

• Pond: *Indian (Indan)* 29+, *industriously (Indastresley)* 26, *materials (Matearls)* 43+, *previous (Preaves)* 34, *proverbial (Proverbel)* 38, *variance (Varans)* 48, *victorious (Victoras)* 27

ju → aʊ: *cucumber (coucumber)* [ML 4.383]

ju (jə) → ə (i): MERCURY *(Murcery;* also *murckerey* [WC 3.257]), *muscular (Muskeler* in SNAG²), PROMISCUOUSLY *(promisquisly),* SCROFULA *(schrofela),* *stimulant (stimelent* in STOMACHIC), *sumptuous (sumptious* in SADDLE, [WC 8.353]), *usual (usial* in ROAD, SAWYER¹+, *yousel* [CF 9.379], *usal* [JO 9.041]), VULTURE *(Vulter);* also *annual (annul)* [ML 3.455], *calumet (Callamet* [ML 6.406], *Callemet* [WC 3.184]), *continual (contineal)* [WC 3.161], *continually (continerly)* [WC 2.249], *copulate (coppolate)* [ML 4.118], *departure (departer)* [ML 6.426], *disfigured (disvigored)* [ML 5.122], *distributed (distribeted)* [WC 6.337], *figure (figer)* [WC 3.488], *globular (globelar* [ML 6.240, 6.426], *gloubelar* [ML 3.456], *Globaler* [ML 6.242]), *manufacture (manufacter)* [WC 3.288], *musician (misition)* [WC 3.119], *naturalist (natirless)* [WC 2.433], *particularly (perticelarly)* [WC 8.280], *picturesque (picteresk)* [ML 3.343], *popularity (popolarity)* [WC 6.223], *porcupine (porkapine)* [JO 9.057, JW 11.072], *punctual (punctial)* [WC 5.139], *pustule (pustle)* [ML 7.309], *pustulous (pustelus)* [WC 6.076], *rivulet (riverlit;* with silent *r)* [WC 5.312], *singular (Singaler)* [WC 3.257], *situated (Siteated)* [WC Letters 173], *stimulant (stimelent)* [ML 3.454], *sumptuous (Sumpcious)* [WC Letters 77], *turbulence (turbelance)* [WC 2.447], *turbulent (turbelant)* [WC 8.354], *value (vale)* [ML 6.426], *venture (venter)* [WC 4.054, WC 5.347+], *vocabulary (vocabelary* [WC 5.287, 5.344], *vocabil(l)ary* [WC 5.292, 5.347])

• Pond: *calumet (Callemeat)* 35+, *capture (Captore* 20, *Capter* 25+), *future (futer)* 31, *misbehavior (Misbehaver)* 34, *misfortune (Misfortin)* 20, *particular (Partickler)* 24, *ridiculous (Ridicklas)* 24, *rivulet (Riveleat)* 59, *unfortunate (unfortennt)* 28, *unfortunately (unfortnatly)* 21, *usual (yousal)* 32+, *venturesome (Ventersum)* 48, *verdure (Varder)* 38

ju → u: *beautiful (boutifull)* [WC 2.154]

k → t: STOMACHIC *(stomatic),* SUMAC *(shumate)*

l added or deleted:

l added: COUS *(halse);* also *tomahawk (tomahalk)* [WC 3.222], *hawk (halk* [ML 3.080], *haulk* [ML 4.276, 5.217])

l deleted: *challenged (Chang'd)* [WC 2.336], *idol (Ido)* [WC 3.168], *peculiarly (pecuarly)* [ML 3.286]; *see* also under *Reduction of consonant clusters.*

m ~ n:

m → n: FATHOM *(fathen;* also in LOG), SIMLIN *(siniblin);* also *become (becon)* [WC 2.500], *bottom (botton)* [JW 11.019], *circumference (Surcunference)* [JO 9.178], *cream (creen)* [ML 4.112], *custom (Custon)* [WC 3.254], *disembogue (disinboge)* [ML 4.189], *extreme (extreen)* [WC 5.043], *handsome (handson)* [WC 2.375, 3.117, 3.204], *lonesome (loneson)* [WC Letters 189], *medium (medein)* [WC Letters 290], *pumpkin (punkin)* [WC 8.350], *Nathan Rumsey (runsey)* [WC 2.205], *sometimes (Sometines)* [WC Letters 172], *stem (Sten)* [WC 3.116], *stream (Streen)* [WC 2.124], *wampum (Wampun)* [writer unknown 3.497]

• Pond: *employed (Inployde)* 21, *empties (Enteys)* 43

n → m: *laudanum (Lodomem)* [WC 7.273]

m added or deleted:

   m added: *tippet* (*timppet*) [ML 5.128]

   m deleted: (*See* under *Reduction of consonant clusters*)

mbl ~ ml:

   mbl —► ml: *assemblage* (*assemleage*) [ML 4.402]

     • Pond: *assembled* (*aSemeld*) 24

   m(l) —► mbl: SIMLIN (*simblin, siniblin*); also *persimmon* (*persimblan*) [JO 9.120]. Compare with the southern dialect pronunciation *chimbley* for *chimney*.

mb —► b: *scramble* (*scrabble* in HARD-SCRABBLE)

mb —► m: *timber* (*timher*, a typical Scotch-Irish pronunciation) [ML 4.167, 4.172], *timbered* (*timered*) [ML 8.102]

n added or deleted:

   n added: COVENTRY (*Conventrey*); also *breadth* (*Brenth* [JW 11.021], *breanth* [JW 11.042]), *climate* (*climent* [WC 6.073, 6.084], *drawing* (*drawning*) [CF 9.387], *moccasin* (*mockinson*) [JO 9.179]

   n deleted: *down* (*dow*) [ML 2.107], *grown* (*grow*) [ML 6.340] (*See* also under *Reduction of consonant clusters*)

     • Pond: *eleven* (*Eleve*) 48, *then* (*the*) 53

n ~ ŋ:

   n —► ŋ (probably as a reverse spelling): (FALLEN) TIMBER (*falling*); also *chicken* (*Chicking*) [WC *Letters* 172], *Franklin* (*Frankling*) [WC *Letters* 209], *given* (*giving*) [WC 3.488], *mountain* (*mounting* [WC 3.053], *mounteing* [WC 8.383]), *tarpaulin* (*tarpoling*) [WC 2.377]

   ŋ —► n: HIRELING (*higherlin*), (SOUNDING-)HORN (*Sounden horn*), LEGGING (*leggin*), (FLANKING) PARTY (*flanken party*), *raising* (*rasin* in MIAMI, *raisin* [ML 3.455]); also *anything* (*any thin*) [WC *Letters* 32], *cunning* (*Cunin*) [WC 3.203], *feeding* (*feedin*) [WC 4.017], *fishing* (*fishen*) [CF 9.395], *gosling* (*gosselin* [WC 2.231], *goslin* [CF 9.385, JO 9.020]), *hearing* (*hearin*) [JW 11.188], *length* (*lenth*) [CF 9.389, ML 6.162], *making* (*maken*) [CF 9.381], *nothing* (*nothin*) [WC 5.232], *rolling* (*rolin*) [WC 4.023], *stinkingest* (*Stinkenest* [JO 9.280]), *towing* (*towen*) [CF 9.381], *traveling* (*travilen*) [CF 9.390], *yearling* (*yearlin*) [WC 8.276, JO 9.101]

     • Pond: *commanding* (*CumMandin*) 47, *herrings* (*Harens*) 33, *mourning* (*Mornein*) 49, *sapling* (*Sapplen*) 40+, *smattering* (*Smattran*) 56, *trading* (*tradein*) 47

ŋ —► g: *shaving* (*Shaveg*) [JW 11.207], *running* (*runnig*) [WC 2.380] (and other examples from Clark), *string* (*strig*) [ML 6.249]. These may be abbreviations rather than an indication of pronunciation: *cf. passi'g* for *passing* [WC 2.448].

ŋ ~ nd

   ŋ —► nd: *hung* (*hund*) [JO 9.222], *young* (*yound*) [WC 3.118, 7.110]

   nd —►ŋ: *wind* (*wing*) [WC 2.127]

o —► ɔ: *choked up* (*Chocked up*) [WC 3.150], *chokecherry* (*Chock Cherry*) [WC 8.417]

-o(w) —► -ə(r) or nothing: BRISTOL (*brister* in SHOT), CHARBONNEAU (*Chabonah*), HOLLOW (*holler, hollar*), MOSQUITO (*musquetors*); also *Arrowsmith* (*Arrasmith*) [ML 4.266], *burrowing* (*burring*) [WC 6.358], *swallow* ('swɑlə inferred from *Swally*) [WC 2.451], *window* (*winder*) [WC 6.137]; and note the reverse spelling of *Farrar* (*Farrow*) [WC *Letters* 160].

• Pond: *narrow* (*nare*) 37, *tallow* (*taller*) 47

or → ɔwə(r): *floor* (*flower*) [JO 9.280]

ɔ → wɔ: *sore* (*Swore*) [WC 5.060]

p deleted: (*See* under *Reduction of consonant clusters*)

r deleted after a vowel (*See* also under *Reduction of consonant clusters*):

> r deleted after a stressed same-syllable vowel and before a consonant (*see* also under *r deleted from prefixes pre-* and *pro-*): ARSENIC (*asney*), CARTRIDGE (*Caterrrage*), CHARBONNEAU (*Chabonah*), FORK (*fok*), GORGE (*gouge*), *heard* (*head* in ALTOGETHER and [ML 5.052, WC 2.364]), LARBOARD (*labord*), PROPORTION (*perpotion* and [WC 8.232]+), PARCEL (*pasel*), QUARTER[2] (*quater* and [WC 2.415]), *worse* (*wose* in LINIMENT and [ML 6.339]); also *are* (*a*) [ML 6.218], *board* (*boad* [WC 5.357, 6.133+], *poad* [WC 5.311], *bod* [WC 6.220]), *Clark* (*Clak*) [JW 3.058], *coarse* (*Cose* [WC 4.415], *coase* [ML 6.304]), *cormorant* (*comerant*) [WC 5.375, 6.013], *corvus* (*covus*) [ML 8.146], *course* (*couse*) [ML 2.097, 4.364+, WC 5.325, 7.344, JO 9.032], *darling* (*daling*) [ML 4.010], *earth* (*eath*) [ML 3.347, 3.354+], *embarked* (*embaked*) [ML 4.009], *enormous* (*innomus*) [WC or ML 4.348], *extraordinary* (*extrodeanary* [WC 6.119], *extraodanary* [WC 4.229], *extrawdinary* [ML 6.230]), *first* (*fist*) [WC 2.177, ML 2.069, 4.179, 6.201+], *fork* (*fok*) [WC 6.016], *forth* (*foth*) [WC 2.208, 7.125+], *forward* (*fowd.* [WC 7.273], *foword* [WC *Letters* 32]), *Girardeau* (*Jeradeau*) [ML 2.110], *guard* (*guad*) [ML 2.258], *gurgling* (*guggling*) [WC 5.188], *hard* (*had*) [ML 4.092], *harvest* (*havest*) [ML 5.160], *horse* (*hose*) [ML 5.071, 5.158+, WC 2.490, 8.200], *impartiality* (*impatiality*) [WC 2.495], *interpreter* (*inteperter* [WC 3.041], *Intepeter* [WC 3.203]), *journey* (*Jouney*) [CF 9.389], *large* (*lage*) [WC 3.099], *larger* (*lager*) [JW 11.356], *largest* (*lagest*) [ML 4.194], *learnt* (*leant*) [ML 6.313], *march* (*mach*) [ML 7.170], *marshy* (*mashey*) [ML 2.224], *martial* (*matial*) [ML 2.370], *morsel* (*mosel*) [ML 4.131, 4.263], *nor* (*no*) [ML 7.205], *north* (*noth*) [ML 4.248], *northerly* (*Notherley*) [WC 4.185], *observe* (*obseve*) [ML 4.426], *Ordway* (*Oddeway* [WC 2.476], *Odway* [WC 2.173]), *our* (*ou*) [WC 3.130], *pairs* (*pais*) [ML 3.084], *part* (*pat*) [ML 5.078], *partridge* (*pateridge* [ML 3.458, 7.275], *pattridge* [ML 5.027]), *party* (*paty*) [ML 4.070, JO 9.365], *poor* (*poo*) [JW 11.276], *pork* (*pok*) [WC 2.165], *portage* (*potage*) [WC 2.218], *portion* (*potion*) [WC 5.253, *Letters* 154], *proportion* (*perpotion* [WC 4.134, 6.373+], *propotion* [WC 4.204, 6.371], *purpotion* [ML 6.394]), *purport* (*purpote*) [WC 3.118, *Letters* 284], *quartz* (*quats*) [WC 4.143], *remorse* (*remose*) [ML 6.169], *reported* (*repoted*) [ML 6.169], *reserve* (*reseve*) [ML 5.074], *returned* (*retuned*) [WC 3.121], *searched* (*suched*) [ML 7.159], *sharp* (*shap*) [ML 4.142], *shirt* (*shit*) [ML 5.112], *short* (*shot*) [ML 4.132, 7.286, WC 8.200], *shortly* (*shotly*) [ML 4.118], *source* (*souce*) [ML 4.118, 426], *stored* (*Stoed*) [WC 2.139], *surface* (*sufice*) [WC 6.408], *swirl* (*Swill*) [WC 5.333], *there* (*the*) [ML 6.297], *thirsty* (*thisty*) [ML 7.205], *towards* (*towads*) [ML 5.104], *traversed* (*travesed*) [WC 6.061], *uniformly* (*unifomly*) [ML 6.392], *warmth* (*womph*) [WC 6.135], *Warfington* (*Wovington*) [WC 3.007], *whorl* (*whol*) [WC 5.337], *worse* (*wose*) [ML 3.349, 6.339+], *worship* (*weship*) [ML 4.101], *worst* (*wost*) [WC 2.302, ML 3.273], *worthy* (*wothey*) [WC 2.399], *yard* (*yad*) [CF 9.378], *your* (*you*) [WC 3.030, *Letters* 255, 279]

• Pond: *burst (Bust)* 37, *extraordinary (Extrodnerey)* 46+, *first (fist)* 47, *forlorn (falon)* 21, *here (hea)* 48, *more (Mo)* 47, *quarters (Qaters)* 24, *rear (Rea* ?) 18, *returns (Retans)* 23, *there (the)* 48

r deleted between vowels: *appearance (appeance)* [ML 7.118], *temporary (temporry)* [WC 3.191]

• Pond: *considerable (Considabel)* 39, *generally (Genaley)* 58

r deleted (from unstressed syllable, usually final), leaving ə: BATTURE (*batue*), *circumference* (*secumphrance* in POMP), GLAUBER'S SALTS (*Globesalts* 'glɑbəsɑlts), *trader* (*trade* in NORTH WEST COMPANY), *verdure* (*virdue* in BOWLING-GREEN, and [WC 7.336]); also *adversary* (*advosary*) [WC 7.140], *advertised* (*advotisud*) [WC *Letters* 259], *another* (*anoothe*) [WC 5.317], *aperture* (*appertue*) [ML 6.357], *beaver (Beave)* [WC 3.039], *better (bette)* [WC 6.195], *buzzard (buzzad)* [JO 9.272], *cedar (Seede* [WC 2.275, 3.046], *comfortable* (*comfotable*) [JO 9.097], *conversation (Convasation)* [WC 2.438], *diameter (Diamute)* [WC 3.161], *discovered (discoved)* [ML 5.026], *disorders (disordes)* [WC 7.245], *error* (*errow*) [ML 7.094], *fathers (fathes)* [WC 3.116], *feather (feathe)* [ML 2.451], *featured* (*fetued*) [WC 5.222], *figure (figue)* [WC 2.279], *formerly (formaley)* [CF 9.385], *gather* (*guathe*) [WC 5.169], *horror (horrow)* [ML 7.054], *hunters (huntes)* [WC 3.089, 3.238, 5.186], *interfere (intefere)* [ML 7.287], *interpreter (interpetes* [WC 3.217], *Intepeter* [WC 3.203]), *irregular (irregula)* [ML 6.277], *lower (Lowe)* [WC 2.476], *lunar (Lune)* [WC 2.476], *mallard (Malade)* [WC 5.309], *numbers (numbes)* [WC 3.000], *observation* (*obsivation*) [WC 3.044, 3.102], *orchard (orchad* [JO 9.053, 9.060], *orched* [JO 9.065, JW 11.062]), *other (othe)* [WC 3.034, ML 3.452, ML 4.226], *partition (petition)* [WC 6.219], *persuade (peswaid)* [ML 4.265], *pleasure (pleasa)* [WC 3.027], *plover (plove)* [WC 3.131], *predominate (pedominate,* via inferred *perdominate)* [ML 3.050], *prepare* (*pepare,* via inferred *perpare)* [ML 4.302], *present* (verb, *pesent,* via inferred *persent)* [ML 4.290], *presume (pesume,* via inferred *persume)* [ML 4.303], *prisoners (prisones)* [WC 3.116], *procure (pocure,* via inferred *porcure)* [ML 3.292], *produce (poduce,* via inferred *porduce)* [ML 6.246], *resource (resoce)* [ML 3.288], *river (rive)* [WC 2.211, ML 5.024], *saltmakers (Saltmakes)* [ML 6.230], *semicircles (simecicles)* [ML 2.068], *shoulders (Sholdes)* [WC 3.115], *stature (statue)* [ML 6.433, WC 7.167], *subscribers* (*Subscribes*) [WC 2.239], *summer (sunme)* [ML 6.336], *supernumerary (supenumery)* [ML 8.044], *surprisingly (Sepriseingly)* [WC 7.267], *terror (turrow)* [WC 3.119, 4.343], *trousers (Trouses)* [WC 6.040, 6.205], *verdure (virdue)* [WC 3.080, 6.298], *Warner* (*Worne*) [WC 2.158], *warriors (warries)* [JO 9.048, JW 11.089], *water (wate)* [WC 5.359], *watercourse (wartercouse)* [ML 7.344], *woodpecker (woodpecke)* [ML 7.293]. (Note Ordway's spellings of the French names *Petit Voleur (petevaliar)* [JO 9.040] and *Gros Ventre (Grovantr)* [JO 9.091]: as we know that these words *did* have a final *r* sound, they show that he sometimes did write final *-r* when he heard it. Compare with Whitehouse's *Pettit Wallow* [JW 11.056], which suggests that Whitehouse pronounced words in *-ow* with at least a partial *r* sound.)

• Pond: *Abercrombie (Abeacrumbea)* 23, *after (afte)* 42+, *another (anothe)* 33, *before (befou)* 40, *Carver (Carve)* 38, *flavor (flave)* 33, *forlorn (falon)* 21, *interpreter* (*Intarpiter*) 48, *northwest (Nowest)* 55, *over (Ove)* 55, *river (rive)* 36+, *soldier (Solge)* 18, *sugar (Suge)* 30, *Superior (Superea)* 48

<r> added after a vowel. This seems generally to be a reverse spelling and not to represent

the actual intrusion of a pronounced *r*, given especially the Indian words (marked by *) that are recorded phonetically by the journalists (with no interference from a standardized spelling) in variants both with and without *r*. (*Exhaust* and *Jacques* provide similar examples from European languages.) There are possible exceptions, as in the final syllables of words like *hollow, mosquito, widow, willow,* and *window*.

<r> added after a (usually) stressed vowel (usually ɑ, occasionally ɔ): AHWAHAWAY (*Ahwahharway*), AWNING (*orning, awning*; also *arning* [ML 2.073]), CACHE (*carsh, cash*), *CAMAS (*quarmash, quawmash*; also *quarmarsh* [WC 7.035]), colic (*Chorlick* in BILIOUS), CAULK (*cork*), *KALAPUYA (*Cal-lar-po-e-wah* [WC 7.066], *Cal-lâh-po-e-wah* [ML 7.086, 7.093]), MAHAHA (*Mahharha*), *NEMAHA RIVER (*Nemarhar, Moha*), *OMAHA (*Mahar, Maha*), *OSAGE (*Osarge, osoge*), otter (*orter* in LOUP[1] and [WC 4.377, 4.433+]), PASHECO (*pashaquar*), *PAWNEE (*Pania*; also *Parnee* [WC 3.395], *Paunee* [WC 2.260]), *POGAMOGGAN (*pog-gar-mag-gon, Poggamoggon*), PONASHITA (*Pâr-nâsh-te*), *SACAGAWEA (*Sâhcâhgâweâ, Sahcahgarweah*), salve (*sarve* in PLASTER), SHAHA (*Sharha*), SQUAW (*squar*), SWATH (*swarth*), TUSH (*tursh*), YAMPA (*yearpah*); also *ash[tree]* (*arsh*) [JW 11.361, JO 9.130, 9.133], aspen (*Arspine*) [WC 7.014], beeswax (*bears wax*) [JO 9.276], *Catholic* (*Carthlick*) [WC 2.243], chukatus [Pawnee 'badger'] (*Chocartooch*) [WC 2.428], exhaust (*exorst*) [WC 3.285, 5.057] (but *cf. exost* [WC 2.492], exhost [WC 7.328]), fast (*farst*) [WC 8.175], father (*forther*) [WC Letters 169], fish (*firsh*) [ML 5.123], gone (*gorn*) [WC 2.208, 2.439, 8.294+], huzzah (*Huzzar*) [JO 9.366], Jacques (*Jarcke* [WC 4.465], Shark [JO 9.045]; *cf. Jacke* [WC 4.466]), mockingbird (*Morking bird*) [WC 4.162], *Multnomah (*Multnomah* and *Multnomar* [WC 7.059], *Multnomah* and *Moltnomar* [WC 7.066]), *Nodaway (*nordaway* [WC 2.424, JW 11.174], Nodaway [WC 2.424], Nardaway [JO 9.035]), nostril (*Norstral*) [WC 2.424], open (*orpen*) [WC 3.022], pasture (*parsture*) [WC 5.178], path (*parth*) [WC 4.432, 5.155+], pembina (*Pembenar*) [ML 2.220], Poncas (*Porncases*) [WC 3.026], pubescence (*pubersence*; does this indicate stress on first syllable?) [ML 5.075, 7.200], race (*rarce*) [ML 7.347], rather (*rearther*) [ML 4.420], reconnoiter (*reconortre*) [JO 9.023], shapat [Arikara 'woman'] (*Char-part*) [WC 3.175], twánhayuksh [Chinookan 'enemies'] (*Towarnehiooks*) [WC 5.323], water (*worter* [JO 9.070] and *warter* [JW 11.269, ML 3.347, 4.293+]), watercourse (*wartercouse*) [ML 7.344].

• Pond: *father* (*farther*) 59, *lodge* (*Large*) 53, *master* (*Marster*) 44, *ought* (*ort*) 33, *uncouth* (*un Corth*) 34

after ə in unstressed syllables: AQUILA (*Arquile*) [WC 5.247], *Bristol/Bristow* (*brister* in SHOT), DAKOTA (*darcotar*), fatigued (*fortiegued* in BLEED,+), HOLLOW (*holler, hollar, hollow*), HOPPUS (*hopperst*), KANSA (*kansar*), MOCCASIN (*mockerson, mocasson*; Ordway and Whitehouse always *r*-less?), MOSQUITO (*musquetoes, musquetors*; Ordway always *r*-less?), RHEUMATISM (*rhumertism, rhumitism*), SLASH (*slashers, slashes*), STRATUM (*strater, strata*; also *Straturs* [WC 4.082]), *WATLALA (*Warclellar;* also *Wahclellar* [ML 7.105], Wahclellah [ML 7.106]), *WETESOON (*WauteSoon, Weter Soon*); also *bough* (*bower*) [WC 3.069], camas (*quarmarsh*) [WC 7.035], cathartic (*carthartic*) [WC 7.273], continually (*continerly*) [WC 2.249], corolla (*corollar*) [ML 3.460, 7.324], countenance (*Counternance*) [WC 2.438], cultivation (*cultervation*) [JO 9.321], earthen (*earthern*) [WC 6.197], edges (*edgers*) [WC 2.309], familiar (*formiliar*) [ML 6.166, 6.168], familiarize (*fermilurize*) [WC 7.263], Heneberry (*Hannerberry*) [WC 2.144], idea (*idear*) [WC 3.043, 3.139], luckily (*luckerly*) [WC Letters 30], morello (*Morillar*) [ML 4.145], *opposition (oppersition)* [WC 3.245], *Ordway (Odderway)* [WC 2.194], *peninsula (Peninsulear)* [WC 6.096], *possess (pursess)* [WC 3.163], *sinews (Sinears* 'sınyəz) [WC 3.485], *slashes (Slashers)* [WC 6.050], *suffice (surfice)* [WC 4.152], *Tacoutche-Tesse (Tarcouche tesse)* [WC 5.286], *tantalized (tanterlised)* [WC 7.137], *thoroughly (thurerly)* [WC 8.324], *tobacco (Tobaccor)* [WC *Letters* 172], *vanilla (vineller)* [ML 6.175], *velocity (verlocity)* [WC 4.039], **Wakiacum (Warkiacum* [WC 7.016], *Wackiacum* [WC 7.015], *warkiacome* [JO 9.280]), *window (winder)* [WC 6.137, *Letters* 187]; *cf.* also *willows (willars)* [Luttig 75])

- Pond: *diameter (Diamerter)* 58, *especially (a Spacherley)* 45, *family (famerley)* 18+, *method (Meathard)* 42, *potatoes (Protaters)* 32, *revolution (Reverlution)* 34, *tallow (taller)* 47, *Van Veghte (Vanvaeter)* 25

s ~ ʃ:

s ⟶ ʃ: SUMAC (*shumate, shoemake*), *dose (dosh* in TARTAR); also *cutlass (cutlash)* [WC 5.347], *fleece (fleeshe)* [WC 6.137], *hiss (hish)* [JW 11.344], *socket (Shocked)* [JW 11.232]

ʃ ⟶ s: SHOSHONE (*Sosonee*), *fishery (fisery* in WAKIACUM); also *ashore (asore)* [ML 4.153], *brackish (brackis)* [ML 3.349], *chagrin (sagreen)* [WC 7.141], *Charbonneau (Sarbono)* [ML 4.341], *finished (finised)* [ML 5.070], *furnished (furnised)* [ML 4.124], *reddish (redis)* [WC 3.072, ML 5.074], *shore (sore)* [ML 2.089], *should (sould)* [ML 4.211], *shower (Souer)* [CF 9.387], *shrill (Srile)* [WC 6.189], *shrimp (Srimp)* [WC 2.483], *shrub (Srub)* [WC 4.074+, ML 3.451], *Spanish (Spanis)* [ML 2.113], *sufficient (Sufficent)* [WC 2.377], *usher (usser)* [WC 2.347], *whitish (whiteis)* [ML 3.050], *yellowish (yellowis)* [ML 6.427]

- Pond: *confusion (Confusan)* 23, *especially (Aspesaley)* 20, *fresh (fres)* 37, *harsh (Hars)* 35, *motion (Mosin)* 22, *provincials (Provensals)* 21, *Spanish (Spanis)* 57, *stationed (stasond)* 38, *sufficient (Suffisant)* 40+

s ~ z:

s ⟶ z: *dose (doze* in TARTAR; [ML 4.300+]), *pismire (pizmire* in PISS-ANT) [ML 7.192]; also *merchandise (merchandize* [ML 7.126], *merchindize* [WC 7.128]). Compare with the Southern shibboleth *greazy* (below).

z ⟶ s: *beeswax (base wax)* [JO 9.181], *breeze (Brees* [JW 11.026], *Breas* [CF 9.385]), *fuzzy (fussey)* [WC 4.396], *gauzy (gossey)* [ML 6.132, 7.293], *muzzle (muscle)* [WC 8.080], *pheasant (fessent)* [JW 11.298, 11.299+]. And note *Greesey* [WC 3.310], rather than the typical southern *greezey.*

s- deleted: (*See* under *Reduction of consonant clusters*)

t ~ θ:

t ⟶ θ: HILT (*hilth*); also *height (hith)* [WC 3.041, 4.304], *trough (through)* [ML 6.215]
- Pond: *height (Hith)* 38

θ ⟶ t: PANTHER (*painter*; also *Panter* [WC 2.308]), PHILANTHROPY (*filantrophy*); also *three (tree)* [ML 6.214], *throng (trong)* [ML 6.401]

t added or deleted:

t added: AXLETREE (*axltree*), CLIFF (*clift*), DOSE (*dost; doste* [WC 4.287])₀ LUFF (*luft*), *Mohammedan (Mahometant* in GNAT), *suddenly (suddently* in KEEL²), *talon (tallant* in

TUSH); also *attack (attackt)* [JW 11.189, WC 3.244, 8.272+], *blunderbuss (blunder bust)* [WC 4.218], *Christmas (Chrismast)* [JO 9.262], *close (Clost)* [ML 5.155], *convolvulus (convolvalist)* [ML 3.458], *encamped (encampted)* [CF 9.380], *fallen (fallent)* [ML 4.345], *isthmus (Istmust)* [WC 2.464], *mussel (mustel* [WC 4.332], *mustle* [WC 5.312]), *once (onced)* [WC 2.470], *repine (repint)* [WC Letters 248], *rough (rought)* [WC 4.056], *trough (trought)* [WC 6.183, ML 6.193], *wharf (worft)* [WC 2.124], *worse (worst)* [WC 2.396, 8.281+]

• Pond: *thence (thenst)* 28, *vermin (Varment)* 55, *Wisconsin (Ouisconstan)* 35+

t deleted: (*See* under *Reduction of consonant clusters*)

u —▶ o: POOR (*pore*+; also *poar* [ML 4.048]); also *lunar (Loner)* [WC 2.310], *moored (mored)* [ML 6.203], *nourishing (norushing)* [WC 2.346], *root (rote)* [WC 5.314, 5.317], *smooth (smoth* [ML 4.392+, JW 11.150, 11.210+], *smothe* [JO 9.104])

• Pond: *ensuing (Insowing)* 30, *raccoons (Rackones)* 32

u —▶ ju: *dew (diew)* [JO 9.033, JW 11.171], *juices (jeucies)* [ML 6.238], *new (niew)* [JO 9.040, 9.054,+, JW 11.226], *soup (Seuip)* [WC 6.119] (but *soope* [ML 4.391]). (Note the spelling *fiew* [JO 9.093, JW 11.186].)

ʊ —▶ u: *butcher (boocher)* [WC 6.124]

ʊ —▶ ɔ: SUGAR-TREE (*shoger*); also *good (god)* [ML 4.300], *hurry (horry)* [WC Letters 276], *wood (wod)* [WC 6.456], *woods (wods)* [JO 9.136], *wooden (woden)* [ML 6.215], *Woolford/ Woodford (Wolpard)* [WC 2.202]

• Pond: *cooked (Coked)* 50

ʊ —▶ ʌ: *Goodrich (Gulrich* [WC 2.377], *Gutherich* [WC 6.137]), *roof (roughf* [WC 5.290], *rough* [ML 6.219, WC 3.174], *ruff* [WC 5.256, 7.064])

• Pond: *roof (Ruf)* 40+

ʌ —▶ ɔ: *stunned (Stonded* in BREECH); also *blunt (blont)* [ML 2.077, 4.113, 7.302,+], *just (jost)* [WC Letters 204], *lungs (longues)* [WC Letters 193], *number (nomber)* [CF 9.384, JO 9.020, 9.078+, JW 11.077], *swung (swong)* [JO 9.017, WC 2.312, JW 11.033], *unloaded (onloaded)* [WC 2, 261, 3.019, 3.235], *upper (opper)* [CF 9.382]

DELETION OF UNSTRESSED INITIAL SYLLABLES:

descended (scended) [JW 11.299]

METATHESIS (TRANSPOSITION OF SOUNDS, MOST COMMONLY IN WORDS BEGINNING IN PER- AND PRO-):

APRON (*apern*), PROMISCUOUSLY (*permiscuesly*), PROPORTION (*perpotion*); also *circular (circlier)* [WC 6.066], *Goodrich (Guterge)* [WC 2.181], *industrious (industerous)* [WC 3.163], *interpreter* (actual *Intepeter* via inferred *inteperter*) [WC 3.203], *perceivable (proceviable)* [WC 8.264], *perceptible (proceptable)* [WC 4.320], *permission (promission)* [WC 8.189], *perspiration (prespreation* [WC 2.310], *presperation* [WC 4.328]), *persuade (preswade* [ML 8.155], *preswaid* [ML 5.102]), *prevail (pervale)* [WC 4.320], *procure (percure)* [WC 2.497], *pursue (prosue)* [WC 4.150, 8.165]

• Pond: *potatoes* (actual *Protaters* via inferred *portaters*) 32

REDUCTION OF CONSONANT CLUSTERS

d deleted: *dastardly (dasterly* in FLOG), *gelding (geling* in (STONE-)HORSE), HOUNDS (*howns*),

SCAFFOLD (*scaffal*; and *Scaffle* [WC 5.274], *Scaffol* [WC 5.286]), WINDSHAKEN (*win Shaken*); also *and* (*an*) [ML 4.026, 5.018, 6.352, WC 5.190, JW 11.042], *armbands* (*armbans*) [WC 3.311, 7.272], *around* (*arron*) [WC 3.315], *bald* (*ball*) [WC 2.383+], *bend* (*ben*) [WC 8.417], *breadth* (*breth*) [WC 6.205], *cold* (*Col* [WC 5.248], *Cole* [WC 2.227, 3.086]), *cords* (*cores*) [ML7.084], *diamond* (*dimon*) [WC 6.015], *extending* (*extening*) [ML 6.348], *Fields* (*Feels*) [ML 4.283], *funds* (*funs*) [WC Letters 182], *grand* (*Gran*) [CF 9.381], *ground* (*grown* [ML 2.106, 3.250, WC 2.250, 6.186+, CF 9.377], *groun* [WC 5.187]) *hand* (*han*) [WC 3.033], *handsome* (*hansom*) [JW 11.047, ML 4.403], *heard* (*her*) [WC 2.321], *held* (*hel*) [WC 5.271], *hold* (*hole*) [JO 9.015, WC 2.161], *household* (*house hole*) [WC 3.199], *island* (*Islan*) [WC 3.100], *mold* (*mole*) [ML 4.027, 4.383, WC 2.471, 4.027], *mound* (*moun*) [WC 2.269, 2.275+], *pond* (*pon*) [WC 3.038, 5.255+], *pondy* (*ponney*) [WC 6.013], *rind* (*rine* [WC 5.290], *rhine* [WC 6.227, 6.231]), *shoulder* (*Sholr*) [WC 5.188], *strand* (*stran*) [WC 6.032, ML 5.070, 5.127+], *suspended* (*suspen*) [ML 5.134], *told* (*tole*) [WC 6.188], *width* (*weath* [WC 1 map 3b]), *weth* [CF 9.376]), *wild* (*wile*) [WC Letters 172], *woodland* (*wooland*) [ML 4.016], *yielding* (*yealing*) [ML 5.113]

• Pond: *advert* (*avart*) 48, *could* (*Coul*) 53, *grounds* (*grouns*) 47, *hard* (*Har*) 52, *scaffold* (*Scaffel*) 56+

ð deleted: *clothes* (*close*) [JO 9.096]

• Pond: *clothes* (*Close*) 59

k deleted: *junction* (*junchon* in MISSISSIPPI); also *anxious* (*ansioes*) [WC 3.128], *contract* (*contrat*) [WC 3.072], *contractor* (*Contrator*) [WC 2.144]

• Pond: *next* (*nest*) 36, *subject* (*subget*) 20

l deleted (or vocalized after a vowel):

after a vowel: *also* (*aso* [ML 4.435, 6.336], *asso* [WC Letters 197), *axletree* (*axetree*) [ML 4.306], *bushels* (*bushes*) [WC 3.222, 3.226], *children* (*chidren*) [WC Letters 20], *helped* (*heped*) [ML 3.292], *little* (*litte*) [ML 4.227, 4.279], *melting* (*meting*) [ML 7.267], *shelter* (*sheter*) [ML 6.359], *sultry* (*sutery*) [ML 2.216], *vault* (*Vaut*) [WC 5.311]; and compare *hawk* (*halk*) [ML 3.080]

after a consonant: *clouded* (*couded*) [ML 6.364], *cloudy* (*Couday*) [CF 9.382], *flagstaff* (*fags Staff*) [CF 9.390], *fleshy* (*feshey*) [WC 5.131], *remarkably* (*remarkaby*) [ML 6.339]

m deleted: *camp* (*cap*) [ML 6.425], *circumstance* (*cercustance*) [ML 5.055], *competent* (*copetent*) [ML 7.034], *sumptuously* (*suptuously*) [ML 5.031]

n deleted before d, s, t: *antelope* (*Atelope*) [ML 4.035], *cleanse* (*cles*) [ML 3.314], *current* (*curret*) [JO 9.273], *emensity* (*emecity*) [WC 8.359], *found* (*foud*) [ML 6.384, 7.210], *hand* (*had*) [ML 5.058, 5.078+], *handkerchief* (*hadkerchief*) [ML 7.326], *handsome* (*hadsome*) [ML 2.102, 5.064], *hinder* (= rear (adjective), *hiner*) [ML 4.303], *intense* (*intese*) [ML 2.102], *pound* (*poud*) [WC 7.258], *present* (*preset*) [ML 4.412], *succulent* (*succulet*) [ML 6.276], *transport* (*trasport*) [ML 4.370], *wind* (*wid*) [ML 4.378], *wounded* (*wouded*) [ML 4.383, 6.321]

• Pond: *intelligent* (*Entelaget*) 34

p deleted: *accompanying* (*accomnying*) [ML 4.2542], *camp* (*cam*) [JW 11.056, 11.250, ML 7.012], *empty* (*emty*) [ML 2.074, JW 11.093], *encamp* (*Incamd.*) [JW 11.037], *except* (*excet*) [ML 4.194], *jump* (*jum*) [ML 5.103], *swamps* (*swams*) [ML 6.312]

• Pond: *empties* (*Emteys*) 21+

r deleted after θ: *throwed* (*thowed* in THRING); also *three* (*thee*) [ML 4.323, 6.351], *throat* (*thoat*) [ML 7.298], *throw* (*thow*) [ML 4.100, 5.007], *through* (*though*) [ML 4.263]; perhaps an overcorrected form is THONG (*throng*).

• Pond: *through* (*thew*) 38

r deleted from prefixes *pre-* and *pro-* (note that this appears to be a peculiarly Lewisian spelling): *present* (*pesent* in KICKAPOO); also *prepare* (*pepare*) [ML 4.302], *presume* (*pesume*) [ML 4.303, 6.203], *probable* (*pobable*) [ML 4.297], *proceed* (*poceed*) [ML 4.378], *producing* (*poducing*) [ML 5.018], *properly procumbent* (*poperly pocumbent*) [ML 6.245], *proportion* (*poportion*) [ML 4.176], *proved* (*poved*) [ML 5.025], *provided* (*povided*) [ML 5.090]

• Pond: note the reverse spelling *portaters* for *potatoes* (inferred for the actual *Protaters*) 32

r deleted from other clusters: SCROFULA (*scofelous*); also *freezes* (*feizes*) [ML 5.133], *interpreter* (*inturpeter*) [WC 3.253], *scoundrel* (*Scoundal*) [WC 6.018], *sundry* (*Sundy*) [WC 2.211], *surprised* (*Suppised*) [WC 6.181]

s- deleted from initial clusters: *scalded* (*Calded*) [JW 11.034], *scarce* (*Carse*) [CF 9.390], *scooping* (*cooping*) [ML 6.211], *scraped* (*Craped*) [WC 2.318], *smooth* (*mothe*) [ML 6.238], *species* (*pecies*) [ML 6.342], *squashes* (*quashes*) [WC 3.162], *stirrup* (*tirrup*) [ML 5.097, 5.103], *strong* (*trong*) [CF 9.386], *struck* (*truck*) [ML 2.073, WC 2.448], *swift* (*wift*) [JW 11.351]

t deleted: BALLAST (*Ballass*); also *abundantly* (*abundanly*) [ML 4.435], *acceptable* (*excepable*) [ML 4.021], *beautifullest* (*Butifules*) [CF 9.385], *cataract* (*Caterack* [WC 5.349], *chatarac* [ML 6.263]), *delightful* (*delighfull*) [ML 4.297], *draught* (*draugh*) [WC 4.337], *encampment* (*encampmen*) [ML 5.080], *except* (*excep*) [WC Letters 154], *first* (*firs*) [WC 2.285], *gauntlet* (*Ganelet*) [WC 2.488], *greatest* (*greates*) [ML 7.104], *guilty* (*guily*) [ML 4.387], *hoisted* (*hoised*) [WC 4.333], *instantly* (*instanly*) [ML 4.334], *kept* (*kep*) [JO 9.123, JW 11.299], *left* (*lef*) [WC 5.130, 6.175], *locust* (*locas* [JO 9.020], *locus* [WC 8.416]), *longest* (*longes*) [ML 6.322], *might* (*migh*) [ML 5.030], *moist* (*mois*) [ML 2.103], *must* (*mus*) [ML 5.106], *naturalist* (*natirless*) [WC 2.433], *nearest* (*neares*) [WC 3.007], *poultice* (*police*) [ML 7.280], *present* (*preasn*) [WC 2.439], *quadrant* (*quadron*) [JO 9.121], *richest* (*riches*) [ML 6.339], *sent* (*sen*) [ML 4.386], *sextant* (*sexton*) [WC 2.145, 3.100], *smallest* (*Smalles*) [WC Letters 276], *strand* (*Srand*) [WC 6.030], *strangest* (*Stranges*) [JO 9.219], *strong* (*Srong*) [CF 9.381], *vast* (*vas*) [ML 5.018], *went* (*wen*) [W 2.471, JO 9.260]

• Pond: *east* (*Eas*) 59, *first* (*firs*) 55, *inhabitants* (*Inhabatans*) 31+, *least* (*Leas*) 27, *parents* (*Pairans*) 18, *regiment* (*Reagimen*) 20, *twist* (*twish*) 41, *went* (*wen*) 24+, *west* (*wes*) 57

WORD-FORMATION

a- prefixed to present participles in -ing: A (*a comeing, a digging, a fishen, a frolicking, a goeing, a trapping*; note also *a horseback*)

adverbs without -ly: AMAZING, CONSIDERABLE, *frequent* (in NEZ PERCE), TOLERABLE; also *common* [JW 11.250], *constant* [JO 9.220], *exceeding* [WC 9.019], *excessive* [WC 8.281, JW 11.028], *late* [JW 11.357], *particular* [JO 9.171] extra -d- in past tense forms and past participles: GALLED (*galded*), PIED (*pided*), *stole* (*stoled* in PUBLIC[1]), *stunned* (*stonded* in BREECH); also *called* (*Calleded*) [CF 9.381], *drowned* (*drounded* [JW 11.070, WC 8.282] and *drownded* [ML 4.078]), *encamped* (*encampted*) [CF 9.380], *frozen* (*frozend* [WC 8.174] and *frosed* [WC 3.272]), *killed* (*Kilded*) [CF 9.379], *stole* (*Stold*) [WC 6.015], *smelled* (*smelted*) [WC 6.015], *swelled* (*suelded*) [WC 7.095]

• Pond: *drowned* (*Droanded*) 22, *grew* (*growed*) 19

nonstandard past tense forms and past participles: EAT (*eat* for *ate*), *breakfasted* (*Brackfast* in BREAKFAST), *heard* (*heared* in (PRAIRIE) WOLF), *threw* (*thowed* in THRING); also *broke* (*brake*) [ML 6.336], *caught* (*Catchd*) [JW 11.032], *climbed* (*clumb*) [JO 9.130, 9.135+], *did* (*done*) [WC 7.066], *drew* (*drawed*) [WC 6.204], *driven* (*drove*) [WC 6.220], *enlarged* (*enlargened*) [WC 7.294], *froze* (*freized*) [ML 6.261], *ran* (*run*) [ML 4.292], *rised* (*risen*) [WC 2.262], *said* (*Sayed*) [JO 9.071], *seen* (*Sawn*) [JO 9.142], *showed* (*Shew* [WC 5.124]), *shot* (*shotten*) [ML 6.410], *strewed* (*Strowed*) [WC 5.205], *sweated* (*Sweeten*) [WC 7.287], *threw* (*throwed*) [ML 7.143]

• Pond: *ate* (*eat*) 53

SYNTAX

nonstandard agreement in number: *The Ossiniboins is at the Big bellie Camp* [WC 3.237], *the tides was Comeing in* [WC 6.196], *young children was verry good eating* [WC 3.157], *the bottoms is all trod up by the Game* [JW 11.147], *one man have a fellon riseing on his hand* [WC 4.281], *The panias know's we do not begin the war* [WC 3.224], *they tells us* [JO 9.348], *I am verry Sick and Has ben for Sometime* [CF 9.391]

• Pond: *the Ofisers that was Going* 18, *the foxis was Drove* 34, *these Plaseis Produseis the Grateest Qantateys* 37, *We Gits Our Canues over the Caring Plase* 39, *Sum of thare Huts…Contanes Saverl famalyes* 40, *thirty Six men…rose as meney oarse* 45, *the Woods & Meaddoues afords abundans of annamels* 56

double modal: WOULD (*would not should*; rare)

REFERENCES

(The compilation of the *Lewis and Clark Lexicon of Discovery* depended especially on those sources marked with an asterisk *.)

Abel, Annie H. *Chardon's Journal at Fort Clark*. Lincoln: University of Nebraska Press, 1997. [Contains biographical information on CHARBONNEAU.]

Alvord, Clarence W. *The Illinois Country, 1673–1818*. Chicago: A.C. McClurg, 1922; Loyola University Press reprint, 1965.

Ambrose, Stephen E. *Undaunted Courage: Meriwether Lewis, Thomas Jefferson, and the Opening of the American West*. New York: Simon & Schuster, 1996. [An inspiring popular account, but with some factual imperfections.]

American Heritage Dictionary of the English Language, 4th ed. Boston: Houghton-Mifflin, 2000.

Anderson, Irving W. "Sacajawea?—Sakakawea?—Sacagawea? Spelling—Pronunciation—Meaning." *We Proceeded On* Summer 1975: 10–11.

ASPIA: *American State Papers: Indian Affairs*, 2 Vols. Washington D.C.: Gales & Seaton, 1832–34.

Avis, Walter S., *et al.*, eds. *A Dictionary of Canadianisms on Historical Principles*. Toronto: Gage, 1991.

*Bedini, Silvio. "Scientific Instruments of the Lewis and Clark Expedition." *Great Plains Quarterly* 4 (1984): 54–69.

Bennett, J.A. *The Divided Circle: A History of Instruments for Astronomy, Navigation and Surveying*. Oxford: Phaidon–Christie's, 1987.

Benson, Guy, and Heather Moore, curators. "Exploring the West from Monticello: An Exhibition of Maps and Navigational Instruments, on View in the Tracy W. McGregor Room, Alderman Library, University of Virginia July 10 to September 26, 1995." <http://www.lib.virginia.edu/exhibits/lewis_clark/index.html> (2004).

Biddle, Nicholas, ed. *History of the Expedition Under the Command of Captains Lewis and Clark*, 2 Vols. Philadelphia: Bradford and Inskeep, 1814. [Editor Nicholas Biddle's paraphrased edition of the Lewis & Clark journals.]

Boss, Richard C. "Keelboat, Pirogue, and Canoe: Vessels Used by the Lewis and Clark Corps of Discovery." *Nautical Research Journal* June 1993: 68–87.

Bright, William. "A Glossary of Native American Toponyms and Ethnonyms from the Lewis and Clark Journals." *Names* 52, No. 3 (2004): 163–237. [A comprehensive and accurate catalog of place and ethnic names.]

Carver, Craig M. *American Regional Dialects: A Word Geography*. Ann Arbor: University of Michigan Press, 1987. [Identifies vocabulary characteristics of the South and South Midland dialects, among others.]

Catlin, George. *Letters and Notes on the Manners, Customs, and Conditions of the North American Indians*, 2 Vols. London: David Bogue, 1844.

Chuinard, Eldon G. *Only One Man Died: The Medical Aspects of the Lewis and Clark Expedition*. Glendale, California: Arthur H. Clark, 1979.

Clarke, Charles G. *The Men of the Lewis and Clark Expedition: A Biographical Roster of the Fifty-one Members and a Composite Diary of Their Activities from All Known Sources*. Glendale, California: Arthur H. Clark, 1970.

Combs, Josiah. "Language of the Southern Highlanders." *Publications of the Modern Language Association* 46 (1931): 1302–22.

Costa, David J. "Miami-Illinois Tribe Names." *Papers of the 31st Algonquian Conference*, John Nichols, ed. Winnipeg: University of Manitoba Press, 2000.

Coues, Elliott, ed. *The Journal of Jacob Fowler, Narrating an Adventure from Arkansas through the Indian Territory, Oklahoma, Kansas, Colorado, and New Mexico, to the Sources of Rio Grande del Norte, 1821–22*. New York: F.P. Harper, 1898.

Craigie, William A., and James R. Hulbert. *A Dictionary of American English on Historical Principles*, 4 Vols. Chicago: University of Chicago Press, 1938–44.

*Criswell, Elijah H. *Lewis and Clark: Linguistic Pioneers*, University of Missouri Studies, Vol. 15, No. 2. Columbia: University of Missouri Press, 1940.

Cutright, Paul R. *Lewis and Clark: Pioneering Naturalists*. Urbana: University of Illinois Press, 1969.

Davis, Lawrence M., Charles L. Houck, and Clive Upton. "'Sett Out Verry Everly Wensdy': The Spelling and Grammar in the Lewis and Clark Journals." *American Speech* 75, No. 2 (2000): 137–48.

DCHNY. O'Callaghan, Edmund B., ed. *Documents Relative to the Colonial History of the State of New-York*, Vol. 4. Albany: Weed, Parsons, 1854.

*DeMallie, Raymond J., ed. *Handbook of North American Indians*, Vol. 13, *Plains*. Washington D.C.: Smithsonian Institution, 2001.

DeVoto, Bernard, ed. *The Journals of Lewis and Clark*. Boston: Houghton Mifflin, 1953. [An abridgment.]

Dictionary of American Regional English, 4 Vols. Cambridge, Massachusetts: Harvard University Press, 1985–2002.

*Earle, A. Scott, and James. L. Reveal. *Lewis and Clark's Green World: The Expedition and its Plants*. Helena, Montana: Farcountry, 2003. [Gorgeously illustrated and well researched.]

Fenstra, Jaap. "Yankee (Doodle)." *Newsletter, Society for the Study of the Indigenous Languages of the Americas* 22, No. 1 (2003): 7–8. [Etymology of YANKEE.]

Filson, John. *The Discovery, Settlement and Present State of Kentucke*. Wilmington: James Adams, 1784.

Firearms of the Lewis and Clark Expedition. <http://www.lcarchive.org/firearms.html> (2004).

Fischer, David Hackett, and James C. Kelly. *Bound Away: Virginia and the Westward Movement*. Charlottesville: University Press of Virginia, 2000. [A social history of migration to, within, and westward from Virginia.]

Gass, Patrick. *A Journal of the Voyages and Travels of a Corps of Discovery...* Pittsburgh: David McKeehan, 1807. [Extensively edited by the publisher; Gass's original diary has disappeared.]

Gilman, Carolyn, ed. *Lewis and Clark Across the Divide*. Washington D.C.: Smithsonian Books, 2003. [A beautifully illustrated companion volume to *Lewis and Clark: The National Bicentennial Exhibition*, arranged by the Missouri Historical Society. Juxtaposes Indian and Euro-American cultures at time of early contact in the West.]

Goddard, Ives, ed. *Handbook of North American Indians*, Vol. 17, *Languages*. Washington D.C.: Smithsonian Institution, 1996.

Hall, Joseph S. *The Phonetics of Great Smoky Mountain Speech (American Speech Reprints and Monographs, No. 4)*. New York: King's Crown, 1942.

Hartley, Alan H. "Camas." *Newsletter, Society for the Study of the Indigenous Languages of the Americas* 20, No. 3 (2001): 10–11. [Etymology.]

_____. "Sacagawea." *Newsletter, Society for the Study of the Indigenous Languages of the Americas* 20, No. 4 (2002): 12–13. [Etymology.]

Hawkins, Benjamin. *Letters of Benjamin Hawkins, 1796–1806*. Savannah: Georgia Historical Society, 1916.

Henry, Alexander. *Travels and Adventures in Canada and the Indian Territories between the Years 1760 and 1776*. New York: I. Riley, 1809.

*Holmberg, James J., ed. *Dear Brother: Letters of William Clark to Jonathan Clark*. New Haven, Connecticut: Yale University Press, 2002. [A collection of letters shedding light on Clark's life before and after the western journey.]

Hunn, Eugene S. *Nch'i Wána "The Big River": Mid-Columbia Indians and Their Land*. Seattle: University of Washington Press, 1990. [A rich ethnography of SAHAPTIN-speaking people of eastern Washington and Oregon.]

*Jackson, Donald, ed. *Letters of the Lewis and Clark Expedition with Related Documents, 1783–1854*, 2d ed., 2 Vols. Urbana: University of Illinois Press, 1978. [After the journals, the most important document collection relating to the Corps of Discovery.]

_____, ed. *Letters of the Lewis and Clark Expedition with Related Documents, 1783–1854*. Urbana: University of Illinois Press, 1962.

Juneau, Marcel. *Contribution à l'Histoire de la Prononciation Française au Québec*. Quebec, Les Presses de l'Université Laval, 1972. [A study of Canadian French pronunciation as revealed by spellings in archival documents.]

Knuth, Priscilla, ed. *So Far from Home: An Army Bride on the Western Frontier, 1865–1869*. Portland: Oregon Historical Society Press, 1993.

Koontz, John E. *Etymology*. <http://spot.colorado.edu/~koontz/faq/etymology.htm> (2004) [Discussion of CHEYENNE, DAKOTA, Nebraska, POMP, SACAGAWEA, SIOUX, and TETON etymologies.]

*Krapp, George P. *The English Language in America*, 2 Vols. New York: Frederick Ungar, 1960; originally published 1925. [A fine source of information on American English words and sounds; particularly strong regarding northeast U.S. historical records.]

Kurath, Hans. *A Word Geography of the Eastern United States*. Ann Arbor: University of Michigan Press, 1949. [A classic compilation effectively utilizing full-page maps.]

*_____, and Raven I. McDavid, Jr. *The Pronunciation of English in the Atlantic States*. Ann Arbor:

University of Michigan Press, 1961. [A compilation of pronunciations, especially vowels.]

Lawson, John. *A New Voyage to Carolina*. London, 1709.

Luttig, John C. *Journal of a Fur-Trading Expedition on the Upper Missouri, 1812–1813*. New York: Argosy-Antiquarian, 1964. [Contains reference to the death of one of Charbonneau's "Snake" wives, perhaps SACAGAWEA.]

Marquette, Jacques. Untitled autograph journal in *Collections of the State Historical Society of Wisconsin* 16 (1902): facsimile facing p. 96.

_____. Untitled map in *Collections of the State Historical Society of Wisconsin* 16 (1902): facsimile facing p. 88. [A simple but impressive map of the Mississippi basin in 1673.]

Masson, Louis R., *Les Bourgeois de la Compagnie du Nord-ouest*, 2 Vols. Quebec: A. Coté, 1889–90. [French and English documents concerning the Canadian fur-trade.]

Masthay, Carl, ed. *Kaskaskia Illinois-to-French Dictionary*. St. Louis: by author, 2002. [Transcription and analysis of an early 18th-century manuscript dictionary. Masthay provides etymologies for CAHOKIA and KASKASKIA.]

*Mathews, Mitford M. *A Dictionary of Americanisms*, 2 Vols. Chicago: University of Chicago Press, 1951.

McCafferty, Michael. "On the Birthday and Etymology of the Placename Missouri." *Names* 51, No. 2 (2003): 111–25.

McDavid, Raven I., Jr. "The Folk Vocabulary of Eastern Kentucky." In *Varieties of American English*. Stanford, California: Stanford University Press, 1980.

McDermott, John F. *A Glossary of Mississippi Valley French*. St. Louis: Washington University, 1941.

McJimsey, George D. "Topographic Terms in Virginia." *American Speech* 15, No. 1 (1940) 3–38; No. 2 (1940) 149–79; No. 3 (1940) 262–300; and No. 4 (1940) 381–419. [A thorough historical study of the Virginian terminology underpinning the captains' place-naming practices.]

Montgomery, Michael B., and Joseph S. Hall. *Dictionary of Smoky Mountain English*. Knoxville: University of Tennessee Press, 2004.

Moore, Alexander. *Nairne's Muskhogean Journals: The 1708 Expedition to the Mississippi River*. Jackson: University Press of Mississippi, 1988.

Moore, Robert J., Jr., and Michael Haynes. *Lewis & Clark: Tailor Made, Trail Worn*. Helena, Montana: Farcountry, 2003. [A well illustrated study of expedition clothing and accessories.]

*Moulton, Gary E., ed. *The Journals of the Lewis and Clark Expedition*, 13 Vols. Lincoln: University of Nebraska Press, 1983–2001. [The definitive edition of the journals, carefully transcribed and thoroughly annotated.]

Mussulman, Joseph A. "'My Boy Pomp' About That Name." *We Proceeded On* May 1995: 20–23.

Nagle, Stephen J., and Sara L. Sanders, eds. *English in the Southern United States*. Cambridge, U.K.: Cambridge University Press, 2003.

Nasatir, Abraham P. *Spanish War Vessels on the Mississippi*. New Haven, Connecticut: Yale University Press, 1968.

Newsome, A.R. "John Brown's Journal of Travel in Western North Carolina in 1795." *North Carolina Historical Review* 11 (1934): 284–313.

Osgood, Ernest S., ed. *The Field Notes of Captain William Clark, 1803–1805*. New Haven, Connecticut: Yale University Press, 1964. [Notes from the early stages of the Corps' activities; superseded in textual detail by Moulton, but still valuable for large-scale document facsimiles.]

Oxford English Dictionary, 2nd ed., 1989 (ed. J.A. Simpson and E.S.C. Weiner), Additions 1993–7 (ed. John Simpson and Edmund Weiner; Michael Proffitt), and 3rd ed. (in progress) Mar. 2000–(ed. John Simpson). *OED Online*. Oxford University Press. <http://oed.com> (2004)

Paton, Bruce. *Lewis & Clark: Doctors in the Wilderness*. Golden, Colorado: Fulcrum, 2001.

Plamondon, Martin, II. *Lewis and Clark Trail Maps: A Cartographic Reconstruction*, 3 Vols. Pullman: Washington State University Press, 2000, 2001, 2004. [530 carefully researched and highly detailed topographic maps of the expedition's entire western exploration; derived from the captains' extensive TRAVERSE notes.]

*Pond, Peter. "The Narrative of Peter Pond." In *Five Fur Traders of the Northwest*, edited by Charles M. Gates, 11–59. St. Paul: Minnesota Historical Society, 1965.

Random House Dictionary of the English Language. 2d ed. New York: Random House, 1987.

Riggs, Stephen R. *A Dakota-English Dictionary*. Washington D.C.: Government Printing Office, 1890.

Ronda, James P. *Lewis and Clark Among the Indians*. Lincoln: University of Nebraska Press, 1984.

Ross, Alexander. *The Fur Hunters of the Far West; A Narrative of Adventures in the Oregon and Rocky Mountains*, 2 Vols. London: Smith, Elder, 1855.

*Russell, Carl P. "The Guns of the Lewis and Clark Expedition." *North Dakota History* 27 (1960): 25–34.

*_____. *Guns on the Early Frontiers: A History of Firearms from Colonial Times Through the Years of the Western Fur Trade.* Berkeley: University of California Press, 1957.

Schafer, Rollie. "Finding the Way and Fixing the Boundary: The Science and Art of Western Map Making, as Exemplified by William H. Emory and his Colleagues of the U.S. Corps of Topographical Engineers," 1997. <http://www.topogs.org/ Finding.htm> (2004)

Speed, Thomas. *The Wilderness Road.* New York: B. Franklin, 1971. [Includes William Calk's 1775 journal of travel from Virginia to Kentucky.]

Stevens, Sylvester K., Donald H. Kent, and Leo J. Roland, eds. *Papers of Col. Henry Bouquet.* Harrisburg: Department of Public Instruction, Pennsylvania Historical Commission, 1943.

*Suttles, Wayne, ed. *Handbook of North American Indians,* Vol. 7, *Northwest Coast.* Washington D.C.: Smithsonian Institution, 1990.

Tait, Frank A. "The U.S. Contract Rifle Pattern of 1792." *Man At Arms Magazine* 21 (June 1999).

Thwaites, Reuben G., ed. *Original Journals of the Lewis and Clark Expedition, 1804–1806,* 8 Vols. New York: Dodd, Mead, 1904–5.

*USDA, NRCS. *The PLANTS Database,* Version 3.5. National Plant Data Center, Baton Rouge, LA 70874-4490 USA. <http://plants.usda.gov> (2004) [A useful resource for U.S. botany (including plants of the Lewis & Clark expedition), with range maps (down to county level) for species and varieties, up-to-date taxonomic information, and good illustrations.]

Vastag, Brian. "Medicine on the Lewis and Clark Trail." *Journal of the American Medical Association* 289 (2003): 1227–30.

*Walker, Deward E., ed. *Handbook of North American Indians,* Vol. 12, *Plateau.* Washington D.C.: Smithsonian Institution, 1998.

Walker, Douglas C. *The Pronunciation of Canadian French.* Ottawa, University of Ottawa Press, 1984.

Walker, Thomas, (ms. Journal). 1749–50. <http://www.vcdh.virginia.edu/lewisandclark/encounter/projects/adventurers/documents/walkerjournal_titlepage.htm> (no longer available). [Walker led an early exploration of eastern Kentucky.]

Webster's New International Dictionary of the English Language, 2d ed. Springfield, Massachusetts: G. & C. Merriam, 1956.

Woodfin, Maude H., and Marion Tinling, eds. *Another Secret Diary of William Byrd of Westover, 1739–1741.* Richmond, Virginia: Dietz, 1942.

Woodger, Elin, and Brandon Toropov. *Encyclopedia of the Lewis & Clark Expedition.* New York: Facts on File, 2004.